FALSE DAWN

FALSE DAWN

PROTEST, DEMOCRACY, AND VIOLENCE IN THE NEW MIDDLE EAST

STEVEN A. COOK

A Council on Foreign Relations Book

OXFORD
UNIVERSITY PRESS

OXFORD
UNIVERSITY PRESS

Oxford University Press is a department of the University of Oxford. It furthers the University's objective of excellence in research, scholarship, and education by publishing worldwide. Oxford is a registered trade mark of Oxford University Press in the UK and certain other countries.

Published in the United States of America by Oxford University Press
198 Madison Avenue, New York, NY 10016, United States of America.

CIP data is on file at the Library of Congress
ISBN 978-0-19-061141-5

1 3 5 7 9 8 6 4 2

Printed by Edwards Brothers Malloy, United States of America

The Council on Foreign Relations (CFR) is an independent, nonpartisan membership organization, think tank, and publisher dedicated to being a resource for its members, government officials, business executives, journalists, educators and students, civic and religious leaders, and other interested citizens to help them better understand the world and the foreign policy choices facing the United States and other countries. Founded in 1921, CFR carries out its mission by maintaining a diverse membership, with special programs to promote interest and develop expertise in the next generation of foreign policy leaders; convening meetings at its headquarters in New York and in Washington, DC, and other cities where senior government officials, members of Congress, global leaders, and prominent thinkers come together with CFR members to discuss and debate major international issues; supporting a Studies Program that fosters independent research, enabling CFR scholars to produce articles, reports, and books and hold roundtables that analyze foreign policy issues and make concrete policy recommendations; publishing *Foreign Affairs*, the preeminent journal on international affairs and US foreign policy; sponsoring Independent Task Forces that produce reports with both findings and policy prescriptions on the most important foreign policy topics; and providing up-to-date information and analysis about world events and American foreign policy on its website, www.cfr.org.

The Council on Foreign Relations takes no institutional positions on policy issues and has no affiliation with the US government. All views expressed in its publications and on its website are the sole responsibility of the author or authors.

For Lauren, my everything

Egypt is confronting difficult times. . . . The situation ends for Egypt in circumstances in which the youth who called for change and reform will be the first to suffer.

Hosni Mubarak
February 10, 2011

CONTENTS

ACKNOWLEDGMENTS

———⊰◆⊱———

Many thanks to Richard N. Haass, president of the Council on Foreign Relations, and James M. Lindsay, the Council's senior vice president and director of the David Rockefeller Studies Program, for their support, high standards, and interest in my work. At the Council, I am indebted to all my colleagues in the Studies Program for the lively intellectual and collegial environment they have helped create. Robert Danin, Ray Takeyh, Stewart Patrick, Shannon O'Neil, Robert Kahn, Micah Zenko, Michael Levi, Elizabeth Economy, and Adam Segal deserve special mention in this regard. I must also acknowledge Jonathan Tepperman, Gideon Rose, Robert McMahon, Chris Tuttle, and Patrick Costello for their time, attention, and good cheer.

My research associate, Amr Leheta, played an instrumental role making this book possible. He is an indefatigable researcher, terrific source of insight, and good Egyptian nationalist. He also corrects my Arabic. Amr's predecessor, Alexander Brock, helped me conceive this project and I am thrilled he could spare the time to see it through to completion. Special thanks to Elodie Le Fur, Alexander Decina, Karsten Ball, Samia Sekkarie, Abby Kukura, Bradley McCandless, and Samuel Cheam. Laura Puls and the Council on Foreign Relations's library staff proved themselves every day to be invaluable resources.

David McBride at Oxford University Press is a prince. I could not ask for better representation than Alison Fargis and Leila Campoli at Stonesong Press. Many thanks to Chris Robinson for his superior map-making skills and patience.

The New York City trio of Brad Rothschild, Richard Vuernick, and David Efron embody the definition of friendship. Special thanks to Brad for reading parts of the manuscript and offering outstanding advice about it. Adam Kaplan did not help me with this project and admits that he will never read a single word of this book. That is okay. I am just grateful for all the years sitting on the couch watching hockey together. Thank you to the Kass, Myers, and Mattison families. Eric Goldstein, who also read parts of the manuscript, and Bruce Mendelsohn have gone above and beyond.

Thank you to Amy Hawthorne, Eric Trager, Karim Mezran, Brian Katulis, Hisham Melhem, Michele Dunne, Tamara Wittes, Marc Lynch, Julie Taylor, Lindsay Iversen, Yoni Zlotogorski, Yigal Schleiffer, Lauren Bohn, Elmira Bayraslı, Henri J. Barkey, Jon Alterman, the "Cub Scouts"—Michael Koplow, Aaron Stein, Dov Friedman—Maged Atiya, Soli Özel, Joe Glicksberg, Nervana Mahmoud—who also read parts of the manuscript—Michele Commercio, Sanem Güner, Ömer Taşpınar, Okan Altıparmak, Ashraf Swelam, and a long list of other friends and colleagues from whom I have learned so much about the Middle East over many years.

I am grateful to Enzo Viscusi for his friendship and to Eni S.p.A. for their generous support of the Eni Enrico Mattei Chair in Middle East and Africa Studies, which I am privileged to hold. Special thanks to Bart Friedman and Wendy Stein for their unfailing interest in me and my work.

The Schuster and Deich families give me great joy. Many thanks to Nancy and Dick Rossman. Iris Cook has been single-mindedly determined over many years to make anything possible.

I apologize to Madelyn and Mia for missing softball, soccer, ballet, Uno, and "snugging" on the couch. Thank you for always being in my thoughts. There is no way to thank my wife, Lauren. She is simply my everything.

CAST OF CHARACTERS

Egypt

Abdel Fattah al-Sisi: A military general who led the July 2013 coup against President Mohammed Morsi of the Muslim Brotherhood. He was elected president in May 2014.

Abdel Moneim Aboul Fotouh: A doctor and a former member of the Muslim Brotherhood. He ran in the 2012 presidential elections.

Abdul Mawgoud al-Dardery: A member of the Muslim Brotherhood's Freedom and Justice Party. He served on the party's foreign policy committee and represented Luxor in the 2012 parliament.

Adly Mansour: The chief justice of the Supreme Constitutional Court from July 2013 to June 2016. He was Egypt's interim president from July 2013 until May 2014.

Ahmed Maher: A civil engineer who cofounded the April 6th Youth Movement in 2008, which played a prominent role in the 2011 uprising.

Ahmed Shafik: Hosni Mubarak's last prime minister, appointed during the 2011 uprising. He ran in the 2012 presidential elections and lost to Mohammed Morsi.

Amr Moussa: Egypt's minister of foreign affairs from 1991 to 2001 and secretary-general of the Arab League from 2001 to 2011. He ran in the 2012 presidential elections.

Asmaa Mahfouz: A cofounder of the April 6th Youth Movement whose video blog encouraged many to take to the streets on January 25, 2011.

Gamal Mubarak: The younger son of Hosni Mubarak and once-presumed heir to the Egyptian presidency. He led the policies secretariat of the National Democratic Party from 2002 until 2011.

Hosni Mubarak: The former president of Egypt. He held office from October 1981 until he was forced to step down in February 2011 following country-wide protests against his rule.

Khairat al-Shater: An engineer and businessman who was the deputy supreme guide of the Muslim Brotherhood. He was disqualified from running in the 2012 presidential elections.

Khaled Said: A twenty-eight-year-old from Alexandria who was beaten to death by police in June 2010. Images of his corpse and public indignation at the government response prompted the launch of a Facebook page called "We Are All Khaled Said."

Mohammed Hussein al-Tantawi: Egypt's minister of defense from 1991 until Mohammed Morsi sacked him in August 2012. He was head of the Supreme Council of the Armed Forces, which held executive authority between Hosni Mubarak's ouster and when Morsi became president.

Mohammed Morsi: A member of the Muslim Brotherhood, he was president of Egypt from June 2012 until he was overthrown by Abdel Fattah al-Sisi on July 3, 2013, following country-wide protests against his rule.

Omar Suleiman: The director of Egypt's General Intelligence Directorate from 1993 to 2011. He briefly served as Hosni Mubarak's vice president during the 2011 uprising. Suleiman was disqualified from running in the 2012 presidential elections.

Sami Enan: The chief of staff of the Egyptian Armed Forces from 2005 until Mohammed Morsi sacked him in August 2012. He was also deputy chairman of the Supreme Council of the Armed Forces under Mohammed Hussein al-Tantawi.

Wael Ghonim: An Internet activist and Google employee who moderated the Facebook page "We Are All Khaled Said," which proved instrumental in organizing the January 25, 2011, protests. He was arrested during the uprising, but was let go a few days later. A television interview following his release in early February rejuvenated the demonstrations that had begun to lose momentum.

Libya

Abdullah al-Thinni: He led the Tobruk-based House of Representatives—the internationally recognized government of Libya until the establishment of the Government of National Accord in December 2015—as prime minister from March 2014 to March 2016. He presided over Libya's General National Congress before the body split in the summer of 2014.

Abdurrahim al-Keib: The interim prime minister of Libya from November 2011 to November 2012.

Ali Zeidan: A lawyer and human rights activist who was prime minister of Libya from 2012 to 2014.

Fathi Terbil: A lawyer and human rights activist whose arrest in February 2011 sparked a demonstration in Benghazi that quickly erupted into country-wide protests against Muammar al-Qaddafi's rule.

Khalifa Haftar: A Qaddafi-era military officer who leads the Libyan National Army. He is aligned with the Tobruk-based House of Representatives, which was the internationally recognized government of Libya until the establishment of the Government of National Accord in December 2015. Haftar does not recognize the legitimacy of the unity government.

Mahmoud Jibril: A politician who served on the National Transitional Council and was interim prime minister from March to October 2011. He is also the leader of the National Forces Alliance and served under Muammar al-Qaddafi in the 2000s as head of the National Planning Council and the National Economic Development Board.

Mohammed al-Magariaf: The founder of the National Front Party and president of the General National Congress from August 2012 to May 2013. He had been a Libyan diplomat before defecting in 1980. He then led the National Front for the Salvation of Libya, an armed opposition group that tried to topple Muammar al-Qaddafi in 1984 with help from the Central Intelligence Agency.

Muammar al-Qaddafi: The leader of Libya from September 1969 until his death in October 2011. He claimed to have turned the country into a direct democracy through his Jamahiriyya political system.

Mustafa Abdul Jalil: The chairman of the National Transitional Council from March 2011 to August 2012.

Mustafa Abushagur: The deputy prime minister of Libya from November 2011 to November 2012. He was elected by the General National Congress as prime minister in September 2012, but was never sworn in after failing to get approval for his cabinet proposals.

Omar al-Hassi: He led the General National Congress as prime minister from September 2014 to March 2015, elected after the body split in the summer of 2014.

Saif al-Islam al-Qaddafi: The son and once-presumed heir of Muammar al-Qaddafi.

Tunisia

Ali Laarayedh: A former secretary-general of the Ennahda Movement, Tunisia's most prominent Islamist organization. He served as prime minister of Tunisia from March 2013 to January 2014. Laarayedh was the minister of interior from December 2011 to March 2013.

Beji Caid Essebsi: The current president of Tunisia and founder of the secular nationalist party Nidaa Tounes. He was the interim prime minister from February to December 2011. Under Zine al-Abidine Ben Ali, Essebsi was president of the Chamber of Deputies from March 1990 to October 1991. Previously, under Habib Bourguiba, he served as minister of foreign affairs from 1981 to 1986.

Chokri Belaid: A leftist-secularist politician who was assassinated in February 2013 by militant extremists.

Fouad Mebazaa: The acting president of Tunisia after Zine al-Abidine Ben Ali fled the country in January 2011, holding office until December 2011. He had been the president of the Chamber of Deputies under Ben Ali.

Habib Bourguiba: The founder of modern Tunisia, he was a principal figure in the movement for independence from French rule and served as president of Tunisia from 1956 to 1987. Bourguiba was pushed out of power by his last prime minister, Zine al-Abidine Ben Ali.

Habib Essid: The former prime minister of Tunisia, who served as Tunisia's head of government from February 2015 until he lost a vote of confidence in the Tunisian legislature in July 2016. He previously served as minister of interior from March to December 2011.

Hamadi al-Jebali: A member of the Ennahda Movement who was prime minister of Tunisia from December 2011 to March 2013.

Houcine Abassi: The secretary-general of the Tunisian General Labor Union, which was part of the National Dialogue Quartet that won the Nobel Peace Prize in 2015.

Mehdi Jomaa: The prime minister of Tunisia from January 2014 to February 2015. Previously he was the minister of industry from March 2013 to January 2014.

Mohammed al-Bouazizi: The fruit and vegetable vendor whose act of self-immolation in Sidi Bouzid on December 17, 2010, sparked the Arab uprisings of 2010 and 2011.

Mohammed Brahmi: A leftist-secularist politician who was assassinated in July 2013 by militant extremists.

Mohammed al-Ghannouchi: The prime minister of Tunisia from November 1999 to February 2011. He was the country's acting president for one day in the confusion following Zine al-Abidine Ben Ali's flight to Saudi Arabia and before Fouad Mebazaa's appointment.

Mohsen Marzouk: A cofounder of Nidaa Tounes and currently the party's secretary-general.

Moncef al-Marzouki: A doctor, liberal human rights lawyer, and founder of the Congress for the Republic, a centrist and secular political party. He was president of Tunisia from December 2011 to December 2014. He ran in the 2014 presidential elections and lost to Beji Caid Essebsi.

Rachid al-Ghannouchi: The founder and intellectual leader of the Ennahda Movement. After years of self-exile in London, he returned to Tunisia in 2011 following the ouster of Zine al-Abidine Ben Ali.

Youssef Chahed: The prime minister of Tunisia, appointed in August 2016 after Habib Essid lost a vote of confidence in the Tunisian legislature. He is an agricultural engineer, a distant relative of Beji Caid Essebsi, and a member of the Nidaa Tounes party.

Zine al-Abidine Ben Ali: The former president of Tunisia. He led the country from November 1987 until he fled to Saudi Arabia in January 2011 following country-wide protests against his rule.

Turkey

Abdullah Gül: A founder of Turkey's ruling Islamist party, the Justice and Development Party. He was minister of foreign affairs from 2003 to 2007 and president from 2007 to 2014.

Abdullah Öcalan: The founder and leader of the Kurdistan Workers' Party, a terrorist organization that has been at war with the Turkish state since 1984. He has been in prison on İmralı Island in the Sea of Marmara since 1999.

Ahmet Davutoğlu: The prime minister of Turkey from August 2014 to May 2016 and the minister of foreign affairs from 2009 to 2014.

Ali Babacan: A founding member of the Justice and Development Party who was Turkey's deputy prime minister in charge of economic affairs from 2009 to 2015. He was also minister of foreign affairs from 2007 to 2009.

Bülent Arınç: A founding member of the Justice and Development Party, he served as Turkey's deputy prime minister from 2009 to 2015. He was also speaker of the Grand National Assembly from 2002 to 2007.

Bülent Ecevit: The leader of the Democratic Left Party, he was prime minister of Turkey four times, from January to November 1974, from June to July 1977, from January 1978 to November 1979, and finally from January 1999 to November 2002.

Fethullah Gülen: A Turkish cleric who founded the Gülen movement, a transnational religious and social organization. Once an ally of Recep Tayyip Erdoğan, the two are now bitter rivals. Gülen currently lives in self-exile in Pennsylvania. Turkish authorities accused him of masterminding the failed military coup attempt on July 15, 2016.

Mehmet Şimşek: A Kurdish-Turkish economist who is currently a deputy prime minister of Turkey. He was minister of finance from 2009 to 2015.

Recep Tayyip Erdoğan: A founder of the Justice and Development Party who was prime minister from 2003 until 2014 and is currently the president of Turkey.

Others

Abu Bakr al-Baghdadi: The leader and self-declared caliph of the Islamic State group.

Abu Musab al-Zarqawi: The leader of al-Qaeda in Iraq, a precursor to the Islamic State of Iraq and Syria, from 2004 until his death in an American air strike in June 2006.

TIMELINE OF MAJOR EVENTS

—◆—

December 17, 2010

Mohammed al-Bouazizi, a fruit and vegetable vendor from Sidi Bouzid in the Tunisian interior, set himself on fire in an act of protest over his lack of opportunity and poor treatment at the hands of police. His suicide precipitated country-wide anti-government demonstrations.

January 14, 2011

Tunisian President Zine al-Abidine Ben Ali fled the country and headed to Jeddah, Saudi Arabia.

January 25, 2011

Anti-government protests erupted in Cairo, Alexandria, and other major cities across Egypt, demanding an end to President Hosni Mubarak's nearly thirty-year-long rule.

January 28, 2011

"Friday of Rage" protests spread across Egypt. In Cairo, protesters occupied Tahrir Square. The military, recognizing the legitimacy of the protesters' demands, announced that it would not fire on demonstrators and deployed tanks and troops in the streets.

February 2, 2011

The Battle of the Camel took place in Cairo as pro-Mubarak thugs riding camels and horses attacked protesters in Tahrir Square.

February 11, 2011

After eighteen days of protests, Egypt's Supreme Council of the Armed Forces (SCAF) pushed Mubarak from power.

February 17, 2011

Two days after protests in Benghazi over the arrest of Fathi Terbil, a human rights lawyer and activist, a "Day of Revolt" engulfed Libya as protesters demanded the end of Muammar al-Qaddafi's forty-two-year rule.

February 20, 2011

Qaddafi's son and heir apparent, Saif al-Islam al-Qaddafi, appeared on television to warn Libyans of the force and determination with which the government would respond to the uprising.

March 2011

The Libyan uprising descended into civil war.

March 19, 2011

A multi-state coalition began enforcing a no-fly zone over Libya, targeting pro-Qaddafi armed units in an effort to protect civilian-populated areas. NATO Allied Joint Force Command took charge of the operation on March 25.

Libya's newly formed National Transitional Council (NTC) issued its "Vision of a Democratic Libya," outlining a roadmap for Libya's post-Qaddafi future.

A popular referendum in Egypt approved the SCAF's constitutional declaration, designed to guide the country through the transitional period.

August 3, 2011

Mubarak, his sons, and several former government officials appeared in an Egyptian court where they faced various charges including conspiring to kill protesters, selling gas to Israel at below market prices, corruption, embezzlement, and insider trading.

Libya's NTC issued its constitutional declaration, outlining principles for Libya's post-Qaddafi constitution.

August 21, 2011

Rebels captured Tripoli, forcing Qaddafi to flee the Libyan capital.

October 9–10, 2011

Violent clashes between military forces and largely Coptic Christian protesters in front of Cairo's broadcasting and television building, known as Maspero, resulted in twenty-eight deaths.

October 20, 2011

Rebel forces found Qaddafi in a ditch west of the city of Sirte and killed him. Three days later, the NTC declared Libya "liberated."

October 23, 2011

Tunisia held elections for the National Constituent Assembly (NCA), tasked with forming an interim government and writing a new constitution. The Islamist Ennahda Movement won a plurality of votes.

November 19, 2011

Clashes in Cairo between protesters and security forces on Mohammed Mahmoud Street over the military's role in politics and the timing of legislative elections led to a four-day battle that killed between forty and fifty people.

November 28–29, 2011

The first round of Egypt's first post-Mubarak parliamentary elections were held. By the time the third round of voting concluded in January 2012, the Muslim Brotherhood and the Salafi Nour Party had won a majority of the seats.

December 13, 2011

Moncef al-Marzouki, a doctor and liberal human rights activist, elected by members of the NCA a day earlier, was sworn in as Tunisia's interim president.

December 16, 2011

Security forces and protesters clashed in front of the building that houses the Egyptian cabinet.

March 26, 2012

The Egyptian parliament appointed a Constituent Assembly tasked with writing a new constitution. The Muslim Brotherhood and other Islamists dominated this body.

April 9, 2012

Thousands of Tunisians defied a Ministry of Interior ban on demonstrations and celebrated Martyrs' Day, the annual commemoration of those who died protesting French rule in 1938, prompting a violent police response.

May 23–24, 2012

After the first round of Egypt's first post-Mubarak presidential elections, the Muslim Brotherhood's Mohammed Morsi and Mubarak's last prime minister, Ahmed Shafik, headed toward a runoff election.

June 14, 2012

Egypt's Supreme Constitutional Court decreed that the election of one-third of the legislature was unconstitutional, prompting the SCAF to dissolve parliament.

June 16–17, 2012

The second round of voting in the Egyptian presidential elections took place. Late at night on June 17, the SCAF amended the March 2011 constitutional declaration and expanded the military's powers.

June 24, 2012

The Presidential Election Commission declared Morsi the winner of the presidential elections, having garnered just under 52 percent of the vote. Morsi took the oath of office on June 30.

July 7, 2012

Libya held elections for its interim legislative body, the General National Congress (GNC). A moderate, non-Islamist coalition won a plurality of seats. The NTC officially handed power over to the GNC on August 8.

July 8–10, 2012

Egypt's new president, Mohammed Morsi, sought to annul the dissolution of parliament by presidential decree and ordered parliament to reconvene. The Supreme Constitutional Court overruled Morsi's decision, citing that all rulings are final, irreversible, and binding.

August 12, 2012

Morsi sacked the SCAF's leadership, including its chairman, Field Marshal Mohammed Hussein al-Tantawi, and its deputy, Chief of Staff of the Armed Forces Lieutenant General Sami Enan. Morsi promoted Major General Abdel Fattah al-Sisi to be head of the SCAF and minister of defense.

September 11, 2012

As Islamist-led protests erupted at the US Embassy in Cairo and elsewhere around the world in response to an anti-Islam YouTube film, members of Ansar al-Sharia Libya and other jihadi militias attacked the US consulate in Benghazi, killing Ambassador Christopher Stevens and three other Americans.

November 14–21, 2012

The Israel Defense Forces conducted Operation Pillar of Defense in the Gaza Strip.

November 22, 2012

Morsi issued a presidential edict that shielded his decisions, the work of the Constituent Assembly, and the upper house of parliament from judicial review and dissolution. His decree precipitated a full-blown political crisis with angry demonstrations taking place in seventeen governorates across Egypt.

December 4–6, 2012

Protests took place in Cairo outside the Ittihadiyya presidential palace, leading to violent clashes between pro- and anti-Morsi demonstrators as well as security forces.

December 15, 2012

Egypt held a referendum on the new constitution written by the Islamist-dominated Constituent Assembly. After the second round of voting on December 22, the constitution was officially approved.

February 6, 2013

Chokri Belaid, a Tunisian leftist-secularist politician, was assassinated by militant extremists, sparking popular anger against the Ennahda-led government.

May 27, 2013

Demonstrators gathered in Istanbul's Gezi Park to protest the Turkish government's plan to convert the nine acres of trees adjacent to Taksim Square into a shopping mall.

May 30, 2013

Turkish police attacked demonstrators in Gezi Park with tear gas, water cannons, and metal truncheons, galvanizing Turks and bringing thousands more into the streets in Istanbul and across the country.

June 16, 2013

Amid anti-government protests, a massive rally was held in Istanbul in support of Prime Minister Recep Tayyip Erdoğan.

June 26, 2013

As an anti-Morsi movement led by the Egyptian youth organization Tamarrod grew, Morsi addressed the nation during which he emphasized his electoral legitimacy and accused his opponents of engaging in a conspiracy to undermine Egypt's progress.

June 30, 2013

One year after Morsi took office, massive protests erupted across Egypt demanding early elections and the president's removal.

July 3, 2013

Following days of protests and a military ultimatum to meet protesters' demands, Major General Abdel Fattah al-Sisi led a coup d'état that toppled Morsi. The head of the Supreme Constitutional Court, Adly Mansour, was appointed Egypt's interim president.

July 25, 2013

Another Tunisian leftist-secularist politician, Mohammed Brahmi, was assassinated by militant extremists, sparking further outrage against Ennahda and threatening the stability of the government.

August 14, 2013

Egyptian security forces violently and forcibly removed two pro-Morsi sit-ins in Cairo at al-Nahda Square and in front of the Rabaa al-Adawiyya Mosque, killing at least 800 people.

October 5, 2013

In Tunisia, after a group called the National Dialogue Quartet facilitated negotiations, all major parties agreed to a roadmap to de-escalate the political crisis that developed after numerous high-profile assassinations. The agreement stipulated the creation of a new technocratic government to oversee the remainder of the transitional period.

December 17, 2013

Turkish police launch a wide-scale corruption investigation, detaining, among others, forty-three government officials and the children of three cabinet ministers.

December 25, 2013

The Egyptian state declared the Muslim Brotherhood a terrorist organization.

Turkey's minister of economy, minister of interior, and minister of environment and urban planning resigned over the corruption allegations that surfaced eights days earlier. The minister of European Union affairs, who had also come under suspicion, was forced out of office in a cabinet reshuffle.

January 14–15, 2014

Egypt held another referendum to vote on a new draft constitution after the suspended 2012 constitution was amended in the latter half of 2013. The new constitution was easily approved and adopted.

January 26, 2014

Tunisia's Constituent Assembly voted on and adopted a new constitution. Interim President Moncef al-Marzouki signed the constitution into law the following day.

February 14, 2014

General Khalifa Haftar of Libya appeared on television to demand the dissolution of the General National Congress (GNC) and the establishment of a new presidential council.

May 16, 2014

Haftar and his forces launched Operation Dignity, targeting primarily Islamist militias in Benghazi.

May 26–28, 2014

Egypt held its second post-Mubarak presidential elections in which Abdel Fattah al-Sisi, who had been promoted to field marshal before resigning from the military to run for the presidency, won with 97 percent of the vote.

June 10, 2014

The Iraqi city of Mosul fell to insurgents of the Islamic State of Iraq and Syria (ISIS).

June 25, 2014

Following months of political deadlock in Libya's GNC, the legislative body held early elections, handing a victory to liberal and secular political figures.

June 30, 2014

ISIS announced the reestablishment of the caliphate under its leader, Abu Bakr al-Baghdadi, and rebranded itself the "Islamic State."

July 13, 2014

Refusing to recognize the legitimacy of the new elections in Libya, revolutionary and Islamist forces launched Operation Libya Dawn, targeting Tripoli International Airport. As the turmoil increased, the new legislative chamber, known as the House of Representatives, fled Tripoli and convened in Tobruk under the leadership of Prime Minister Abdullah al-Thinni. The losers of the June election reconvened the GNC in Tripoli and elected Omar al-Hassi as their new prime minister.

August 10, 2014

Recep Tayyip Erdoğan was elected president of Turkey.

October 26, 2014

Tunisia held parliamentary elections to elect the first post–Zine al-Abidine Ben Ali legislature. The secular nationalist party Nidaa Tounes, founded by Beji Caid Essebsi, a holdover from the Ben Ali and Habib Bourguiba eras, won the most seats, followed by the Ennahda Movement.

November 23, 2014

After the first round of Tunisia's first post–Ben Ali popular presidential elections, the interim president, Marzouki, and Nidaa Tounes's Essebsi headed toward a runoff election.

December 21, 2014

Essebsi was declared the victor of Tunisia's presidential election, winning around 56 percent of the vote.

January 5, 2015

Turkey's Corruption Investigation Commission, dominated by Justice and Development Party (AKP) members, voted against referring to court those accused of corruption in December 2013 on the grounds that the allegations against the ministers were part of an attempted coup organized by supporters of Erdoğan's rival, the cleric Fethullah Gülen.

February 16, 2015

Egypt conducted a series of air strikes against the Islamic State group in the Libyan city of Derna after a video surfaced of the group beheading twenty-one Egyptian Coptic Christians who had previously been kidnapped in Libya.

March 18, 2015

Two terrorists stormed the Bardo National Museum in Tunis and killed twenty people, including seventeen tourists.

May 16, 2015

An Egyptian court sentenced ousted President Mohammed Morsi to death.

June 7, 2015

In a surprise result, the AKP won only 41 percent of the vote in Turkey's general elections, denying Erdoğan and his party a parliamentary majority for the first time since coming to power in 2002. Erdoğan then directed the leader of the AKP, Prime Minister Ahmet Davutoğlu, to form a coalition government.

June 26, 2015

In Sousse, a Tunisian resort town, a terrorist attack killed thirty-eight tourists, most of them British, and injured another thirty-nine.

July 20, 2015

A suicide bomber killed 32 and injured 104 people in Suruç, a predominantly Kurdish city in southeastern Turkey. The Islamic State claimed responsibility for the attack.

July 23, 2015

Turkey granted the United States and allied forces access to İncirlik airbase, located in Turkey's southeast, for use in the fight against the Islamic State.

October 10, 2015

Tunisia's National Dialogue Quartet was awarded the Nobel Peace Prize in recognition of its efforts in resolving the 2013 political crisis.

October 17, 2015

Legislative elections in Egypt began and lasted several weeks. The final phase of voting took place in December 2015. The new parliament, dominated by pro-Sisi figures, convened for the first time on January 10, 2016.

November 1, 2015

Following the failure to establish a governing coalition, Turkey held a new general election. In this second round the AKP regained its majority in the Turkish legislature, winning over 49 percent of the popular vote.

November 24, 2015

A bomb ripped through a bus in Tunis, killing twelve presidential guards.

December 17, 2015

Libya's House of Representatives and General National Congress signed a political accord agreeing to form a new Government of National Accord.

January 12, 2016

A suicide bomber killed thirteen foreign tourists in one of Istanbul's more popular tourist districts. The perpetrator is believed to have been a Syrian member of the Islamic State.

February 17, 2016

A car bomb in Ankara located near the Grand National Assembly, the prime minister's office, the Ministry of National Defense, and the headquarters of the Turkish General Staff killed at least thirty and injured as many as sixty people. A group called the Kurdistan Freedom Falcons claimed responsibility for the attack.

March 13, 2016

A car bombing in the Kızılay area of Ankara killed at least 34 people and wounded at least 125. The Kurdistan Freedom Falcons also claimed responsibility for this attack.

May 5, 2016

Turkish Prime Minister Ahmet Davutoğlu resigned after falling out with Erdoğan. Binali Yıldırım was named as Davutoğlu's successor and assumed office on May 24.

May 20, 2016

Tunisia's Ennahda Movement announced that it is no longer a political Islamist group, committing itself to promoting the values of "Muslim Democracy."

June 28, 2016

Three suicide attackers opened fire on civilians before blowing themselves up in Istanbul's Atatürk International Airport, killing 47 and injuring more than 200. The Islamic State claimed responsibility for the attack.

July 15, 2016

A faction of the Turkish Armed Forces attempted to carry out a coup d'état. The unsuccessful coup resulted in at least 240 deaths and many more injuries. The government accused the cleric Fethullah Gülen and his supporters within the military and Turkish society of masterminding the attempted putsch. In response, the government launched a widespread crackdown that targeted Gülen's followers and others.

July 30, 2016

Tunisia's parliament voted to dismiss Prime Minister Habib Essid. Youssef Chahed, an agricultural engineer and member of the president's Nidaa Tounes party, was named as Essid's successor and assumed office on August 27.

August 1, 2016

The United States conducted air strikes against the Islamic State's stronghold in the Libyan city of Sirte, which helped ground forces that back Libya's unity government recapture the city.

August 20, 2016

A suicide bomber, reportedly between twelve and fourteen years old, attacked a Kurdish wedding ceremony in Gaziantep in Turkey's southeast, killing over fifty people and injuring more than sixty.

August 24, 2016

The Turkish military crossed the border into Syria to expel Islamic State fighters from the town of Jarabulus and to prevent Syrian Kurdish forces from crossing west of the Euphrates River.

August 30, 2016

Protests partially halted production at Tunisia's state-owned Gafsa Phosphate Company.

October 17, 2016

Iraqi and Kurdish troops launched a joint operation to retake the city of Mosul from the Islamic State.

October 22, 2016

Egypt's Court of Cassation rejected former Mohammed Morsi's bid to overturn his death sentence.

October 31, 2016

Turkish authorities closed fifteen pro-Kurdish media outlets and detained the editor, a cartoonist, and seven board members of the opposition newspaper *Cumhuriyet*.

November 3, 2016

After weeks of speculation, and in the midst of negotiations to secure a $12 billion loan from the International Monetary Fund to alleviate an economic and fiscal crisis, the Central Bank of Egypt floated the Egyptian pound.

November 4, 2016

The Turkish government arrested ten members of the pro-Kurdish Peoples' Democratic Party, including its two leaders, on terrorism-related charges. Shortly after the arrests, a car bomb targeting a police station in the southeastern city of Diyarbakır killed six civilians and two police officers. In response, the government slowed internet access to Twitter and Facebook as well as the phone messaging app WhatsApp.

MAPS

Map of downtown Cairo, Egypt

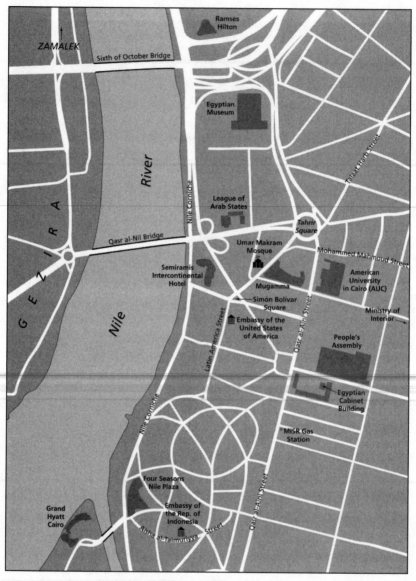

Courtesy of Christopher Robinson.

Map of downtown Tunis, Tunisia

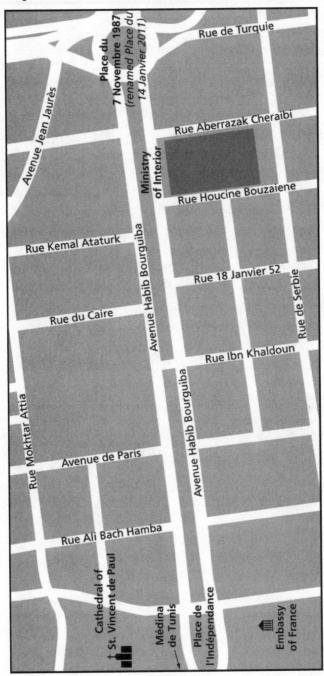

Courtesy of Christopher Robinson.

Map of Gezi Park and Taksim Square, Istanbul, Turkey

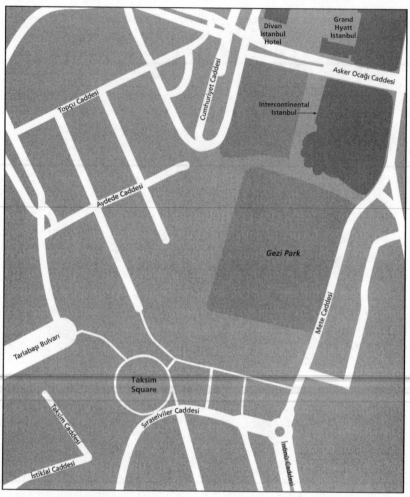

Courtesy of Christopher Robinson.

PROLOGUE: "WE ARE NOW FREE"

———◆———

Cairo, Egypt. January 25, 2011. *About 6:15 P.M. I couldn't concentrate on the meeting at the American University in Cairo. Following my Twitter feed the whole time. This is big. Back at the Grand Hyatt. Ditched my bag and left the group. On foot now. I'll head across the street and past the Four Seasons and wind around on Aisha al-Taimuriyya Street, near the Indonesian embassy. Bad idea: it's next to a police station. Who knows what's up there given everything else going on. Instead, I'll head a little north on the Corniche and duck in along those winding streets whose names I've never bothered to learn. That should take me up to Qasr al-Aini Street. The last email I got from my friend Aaron, who was watching the demonstrations unfold from the other side of the city, was "ISPs are getting shut down . . . protesters made it up the parliament steps . . . I wonder if we'll see actual gunfire?" That was two hours ago.*

Things seem kind of normal. People walking in the streets. Baqqals—the Egyptian version of the bodega—are open. Weird. Koshary! The sight and smell of it makes me hungry. No time now. Okay, I can see Qasr al-Aini. Cars are being turned around by traffic cops. I'll make a left and head toward Tahrir Square. There is a line of riot police. They have pushed the demonstrators back down the street toward the square. What a mess. Chunks of concrete and bricks everywhere. Whoa! A deafening noise . . .

trucks. The ones used to transport Central Security Forces (CSF) soldiers around. One, two, five, seven, ten of them rush by. Something big is about to happen. No Twitter. Damn—battery is dying. I'll call CFR's communications office in New York and have them tweet for me. Call failed. Call failed. Call failed. Call failed. More trucks screaming down Qasr al-Aini. Connected!

"Hi, Nidhi? Are you there?"

Don't disconnect. Don't disconnect.

"Yes I am, hi!"

"Hey, it's Steven. Listen, I'm in Cairo. The demonstrations are big. Something is about to happen. I need you to tweet for me. Twitter is down and my Blackberry is dying."

"Oh my God, Steven. Are you okay?!"

"Yes, I'm fine. Please tweet . . . Can you hear me? . . . Please tweet, 'Something big is happening. Lots of CSF troops are moving into Tahrir.' Yes, that is T-A-H-R-I-R. Just say Liberation Square. Okay, I'll call back."

Going to try to get up closer. I'll just walk up casually and see what I can see. Okay, now all the soldiers are getting off the trucks. Shields, helmets, batons, metal pipes. A motley crew. Maybe they're seventeen or eighteen years of age. They look scared.

"*Ya awlad!*"—"Okay, boys!"—*screams one of the officers.*

They are lining up. Rows of two. Holy moly, they are charging the protesters! Trucks are following fast. Someone is going to die. Cannot believe this. Call CFR. Call failed. Call failed. Call failed. Service! Twitter is back!

"@stevenacook Never seen so many CSF. Holy crap."

"@stevenacook Another ten trucks just pulled up. #Jan25"

"@stevenacook Troops moving. Lots of commotion. 'Mubarak go to Saudi'"

"@stevenacook No more organized chants."

Let me get further up along Qasr al-Aini. How far did they move the protestors? Is anyone hurt? I see one ambulance speed past and another pull up. Can't tell what's happening. Blocked at the Misr gas station. Traffic police and plainclothes guys hanging around. It's the guys not in uniform who scare me the most. Let me try getting around them on a side street and get into Tahrir. All quiet here. Makwagi—*a launderer—working away, seemingly oblivious.*

I am blocked. Police at the end of the street. I'll try another way. What if I just walked past the American embassy? I have my passport—the blue shield!— with me. What would the cops do? I'll go left toward Latin America Street and make a right, heading to the embassy. If they stop me, I'll show them my passport. Say I have business at the embassy. Oh, lots of police. Lost my nerve. I'll walk around back to the Corniche and head toward the Semiramis Hotel. Traffic moving well on the Corniche. Tourists strolling. Don't they have a clue what's happening? I can see the Semiramis. Police all around, but no one is stopping me. Tons of ambulances in Simón Bolívar Square. Lots of CSF trucks lining the street next to the Umar Makram Mosque and the Mugamma. I'll just saunter in between. An opening next to the Mugamma. No one is stopping me. I'm in!

Wow.

Half the square is filled with protesters stretching from the old university campus clear across to Talaat Harb Street. Must be anywhere from 15,000 to 25,000 people! I see what's happening. The police are trying to seal everyone inside the square. Kind of like the student demonstrations of 1968. I speak to the first young guy I see.

"*Izzayyak? Ismee* Steven."—"What's up? My name is Steven."— "What's going on here?"

"Our government is crazy. We want our president to leave." *He pauses.* "Where are you from?"

"I am American. Where do you want him to go? Why?"

"We want him to go to Saudi Arabia with Ben Ali."

"Okay, I can see that, but why?"

"We have no freedom. There is bad corruption. We hate *al-Hizb al-Watany*"—*the ruling National Democratic Party*—"no to Mubarak and no to Gamal. We want a new government."

Time to move on. People rushing in from Qasr al-Nil, the bridge that connects upscale Zamalek and downtown. They must have broken the police cordon. This is serious, but the police haven't lost their swagger.

It's starting to get heated. Protesters are beginning to work themselves into a bit of a frenzy. No telling what the police will do. I am not twenty-five years old anymore. Time to duck into the Semiramis.

A Police Day celebration is going on in the hotel. Bizarre. Officers in full dress uniform; their wives dressed to the nines. Has anyone in here noticed the huge demonstration going on outside? Blackberry completely dead now. Can't believe it lasted that long.

Twenty minutes later. Back out. Things seem to have settled. Not much action. Thousands milling about. The chants have lulled. Police seem to be happy maintaining a cordon. Will find my friend from grad school, Joe. He is staying at the Semiramis. First time in Egypt together in ten years and an uprising happens. Now on the eighteenth floor of the hotel with Joe. Full view of the protests. Joe's been watching all night from this perch. Rumors of a curfew on Twitter. The hotel staff look very anxious. Do I stay? Not sure. We can see ambulances moving toward the square. Not a good sign. I have to get back down the Corniche to my own hotel. No telling how long I'll be here if I don't.

Hustling down the Corniche now. Loudspeaker screaming something indecipherable. What is that muffled pop? Crap, it's tear gas . . . run!

Almost three weeks later, and after I had returned to Washington, DC, my phone rang on a gray February afternoon. The telltale +2–010 told me immediately that it was someone from Egypt. The call was from Ashraf Swelam, an old friend and diplomat who, along with a colleague of his at the Foreign Ministry, had spent many a night in the previous five years introducing me to various aspects of the Cairo nightlife that I never knew existed. In between, we would discuss Egyptian, American, and global politics. Ashraf was a rising star within Egypt's exclusive diplomatic corps, having served stints in Washington and the Foreign Ministry before a sabbatical as a Yale World Fellow and later as the director general of Egypt's International Economic Forum, a business nongovernmental organization. I had seen Ashraf in Cairo on January 24, the day before the uprising began, at a meeting he had graciously agreed to arrange for a visiting delegation from the Council on Foreign Relations and a group of Egyptian officials and opinion leaders. We were in touch on and off throughout the demonstrations, first with my quick email impressions from Tahrir Square, and then, after I left Egypt, Ashraf updated me from time to time with his own thoughts on events as they unfolded. On February 11, after President Hosni Mubarak had taken flight to Sharm el-Sheikh, I made a few phone calls and sent some emails to friends in Cairo wishing them *mabrouk*, my congratulations. To Ashraf, I sent a message via Facebook: "How are you?" He was now calling in response. After enthusiastic greetings he said, "Why did you ask me how I was? What could be wrong? I have never been better. We are now free."

Introduction: Springtime

WEEKS BEFORE EGYPTIANS EXPERIENCED the exhilaration of throwing off their dictator, the Tunisian people had already begun to chart what they hoped would be a free and democratic future. Once a tiny backwater, Tunisia suddenly became the most important country in the Middle East and North Africa after its uprising, which began in mid-December 2010. There had been coups d'état and independence "revolutions" in the 1940s, 1950s, and 1960s, but leaders in the Arab world had never succumbed to popular demonstrations until the plane carrying President Zine al-Abidine Ben Ali hurriedly departed from Tunis on January 14, 2011. Subsequently, millions of consumers of newspapers, magazines, blogs, news radio, and television were informed that Tunisia—birthplace of the "Arab Spring," the site of the "Jasmine Revolution"—was primed for a democratic breakthrough. It was hard not to love the country and its people. Had Henri Matisse visited when he was also painting in Morocco in the early twentieth century he surely would have captured on canvas the royal blue doors and magenta bougainvillea of Sidi Bou Said, a little town outside Tunis. The doors, framed in stone, painted a flat white, and often decorated with crescents and stars, are stunning, blending northern Tunisia's Mediterranean backdrop, Islam, and the Afro-Arab culture of the Maghreb. For all the unique beauty of the country's culture and arts, Tunisia's location in Africa, its dominant Arab ethnicity and language, and its proximity to Europe has made for a polyglot society.

The founder of independent Tunisia, a lawyer named Habib Bourguiba, was a fierce nationalist but also an admirer of Europe and educated in France. The French colonialists built Tunis out from an ancient medina with wide boulevards and squares that evoked Paris. Today Tunis is shabby and ramshackle, suggesting nothing of the French capital, yet Tunisians have embraced a particularly European café culture—different from the coffee shops and tea houses of Cairo and Istanbul, for example—right down to the wicker chairs that line Avenue Habib Bourguiba. Of course, this phenomenon is limited to a coastal population only a two-hour flight from Paris. Life is significantly different for the more than nine million people (out of a population of eleven million) who live outside Tunis and its environs. Many of the people of inland Tunisia live in squalid towns and villages with little in the way of infrastructure, few government services, and too much desperation. It was in this part of the country where the uprising against Ben Ali began.

To virtually everyone in the world who cared, Tunisia was the Arab country with the "best chance" to become a democracy and not necessarily without good reason. The sense of shared responsibility is palpable among Tunisians and underpins a civic culture that provided a strong foundation for a new political system. Only ten months after Ben Ali fell, elections in Tunisia produced a coalition government under the leadership of the Islamist Ennahda (Renaissance) Movement. The group's leader, Rachid al-Ghannouchi, had visited the United States once before the uprising and four times since in an effort to convince skeptical Americans that consensus politics and compromise were integral parts of his Islamism. He had been a Nasserist in the 1950s and 1960s and a Muslim Brotherhood fellow traveler in the 1970s and 1980s, and then embraced democracy and Islamic liberalism while living in exile in London in the 1990s.[1] Ghannouchi did not have official status in the interim government but rather positioned himself as the moral conscience of the nation even if many Tunisians harbored doubts about Ennahda and its commitment to democracy. The country's first post–Ben Ali leader was Moncef al-Marzouki, who served as interim president from December 2011 until December 2014. The modest, even humble, French-educated dissident and human rights activist was a welcome contrast to the self-important Ben Ali, who presided over a fearsome police state that failed him at the very moment for which it was built. Marzouki (and Ghannouchi) seemed more sincere in their desire to build a democratic and just Tunisia.

The story got even better when Tunisians pressed ahead with their transition despite profound mistrust among major political groups. They eschewed divisive politics and rescued themselves and the country from potential instability and violence. In response to the outcry over the assassinations of leftist-secularist politicians Chokri Belaid and Mohammed Brahmi in 2013 and criticism over ineffective administration as well as a faltering economy, the elected government withdrew in favor of nonpolitical technocrats. This was something new in the Arab world and that Ennahda, which initially resisted, was the senior governing partner made it all the more extraordinary for a variety of commentators who harbored low expectations of the Islamists. Having defied the canard that Islamists were interested in elections for "one man, one vote, one time," Ennahda was universally praised as a new leadership under a nonaffiliated prime minister stepped in. Tunisian politicians then produced a new constitution. By early 2014, analysts, journalists, editors, and bloggers had come to the conclusion that Tunisia's transition to democracy was working. Peaceful parliamentary and presidential elections in the fall of 2014, in which the losing Islamists graciously accepted the outcome, and the 2015 Nobel Peace Prize, awarded to a group called the National Dialogue Quartet that had saved Tunisia from violence, sent a wave of optimism through the op-ed pages and editorials of the newspapers of record. In the collective imagination of Middle East analysts, journalists, and government officials in the United States and Europe, Tunisia was shaping up to be the little country that was going to finally break out of the authoritarian trap.

Tunisia was also a place that, despite its rich history and cultural legacies, had long been peripheral in the Arab world. In contrast there was Egypt, which has long stood at the center of the Middle East. As a result, when Egyptians gave voice to their collective frustrations on January 25, 2011, Cairo's Tahrir Square immediately supplanted Tunis's Avenue Habib Bourguiba as the most important place in the world. Egypt had seen uprisings before—in 1919, 1968, 1972, and 1977—so when Egyptians rose up to demand "the end of the regime," it was an extraordinary news story but, unbeknownst to many who covered and commented on it, hardly unprecedented. The uprising also came at a time when street protests had become a common feature of Egypt's political landscape. So much so that the evening before the demonstrations began, at the home of a prominent Egyptian-American businessman, influential members of the ruling National Democratic Party were decidedly nonchalant about what would transpire. "Perhaps fifty [people] will show up," remarked one who was known to be particularly close to President Hosni Mubarak's younger son and presumptive heir, Gamal, defying the tens of thousands who had indicated on Facebook that they planned to attend the protest.

It was no surprise then that Egyptian officials, foreign observers, and the demonstrators themselves were amazed by what happened next. For years, observers of Egypt's politics believed that Mubarak's rule was stable. He had not aroused the emotions of either of his predecessors, Gamal Abdel Nasser or Anwar al-Sadat, but that was probably a good thing. Mubarak was steady, unimaginative, and durable. His opponents were disorganized or subjected to the heavy hand of Egypt's internal security services. The only question was who would follow Mubarak when he died in office. When the Egyptian leader fell after only eighteen days of protest, the collective sense that anything was possible seemed to stretch from Cairo to Tripoli to Damascus to Sanaa to Muscat to other regional capitals. Egypt did not produce a regional "revolutionary bandwagon"—protests were under way in four other Middle Eastern countries before Egyptians took to the streets. Yet because the country has the largest population in the region and has historically had so much political, cultural, and social influence in the Middle East, Egypt's uprising overshadowed the tumult that came before it and colored the way analysts viewed the demonstrations that came after Mubarak departed.

Next door to Egypt sits Libya, where on February 15, 2011, Muammar al-Qaddafi's forty-two-year rule began to crumble. When he came to power in a 1969 coup d'état, he modeled himself after Egypt's Gamal Abdel Nasser. The Egyptian leader, who was the giant of mid-twentieth-century Middle Eastern politics with his uncompromising nationalism and message of Arab empowerment, had built what would become the archetypal Middle Eastern police state. In the ensuing decades, however, Qaddafi charted his own unique path. In March 1977, he declared

Libya to be a Socialist People's Libyan Arab Jamahiriyya, the expression of the direct democracy he claimed to be building. That is why, during the Libyan uprising in 2011, when those in the streets of Tripoli and Benghazi as well as Western capitals demanded that he step down, Qaddafi's retort was essentially "Step down from what?" His position as head of state, he explained, was informal; the very essence of the Jamahiriyya was a collective utopia in which decisions both large and small trickled up and down to those who would execute the will of the people.

When Qaddafi was toppled and murdered after eight months of fighting, optimism about the country's potential was immense. Libya not only possesses what is believed to be forty-seven billion barrels of the highest quality light, sweet crude oil that could be used to develop the country, but it also had genuine hope that a successful transition to democracy was possible. The supposed advantage in Qaddafi's radical approach to governance for Libya's new leaders was not that Libyans had become well practiced in the consensual decision making and compromise allegedly intrinsic to the Jamahiriyya—this was all nonsense—but rather that Libya was left with no formal political institutions to speak of.[2] Unlike activists in Egypt or Tunisia, who had to contend with the rules, laws, decrees, and regulations by which Mubarak and Ben Ali ruled, Libyan revolutionaries were thought to be unencumbered. The country was a blank slate on which to build democracy. The elections for the General National Congress in July 2012 in which a non-Islamist, moderate coalition earned a plurality in the new body was widely regarded in the West and the Arab world as a harbinger of Libya's democratic potential.

The displays of people power in Tunisia, Egypt, and Libya were spellbinding for all those who watched, and in the moment of enthusiasm observers declared that Turkey was an excellent model for these Arab countries. In the eight decades after Turkish nationalists founded the Republic of Turkey following the collapse of the Ottoman Empire, the country's leaders pursued a policy designed to avoid entanglements in foreign conflict, especially the Middle East. Yet after the Justice and Development Party (in Turkish, Adalet ve Kalkınma Partisi, or AKP) came to power in 2002, its expansive view of Turkish foreign policy included a leading role for Ankara in the

Muslim world. The leaders of the AKP, which emerged from a split within Turkey's Islamist movement, venerated the Ottoman era and regarded themselves as the future of the Middle East and beyond. They described themselves purposefully as "Muslim Democrats"— an analogue to Europe's Christian Democrats—and sought to open themselves to the world and return Turkey to its rightful place as a leading country in the Middle East and beyond. For a wide variety of observers, in the early 2000s, Turkey's was a feel-good story about a middle-income country that is 99.8 percent Muslim, is a longtime NATO ally of the United States, aspired to be in Europe, wanted to play a constructive and active role in resolving problems in the Middle East, and is run by Islamists who express fealty to their country's officially secular political system. For Americans, in the emotionally fraught atmosphere of the immediate post–9/11 era, just before the occupation of Iraq went from bad to horribly bad, Turkey and its leaders seemed to be an answer to the dark forces that Americans were battling in Fallujah, Kandahar, and Waziristan.

It was not just Westerners who felt the allure of the so-called Turkish model. For many years prior to the 2000s, Turkey and the Arab countries eyed each other warily across the Mediterranean Sea and mountainous borders. The Turks with their radically secular political system and decidedly Western foreign policy orientation offended Islamists and secular nationalists in the Arab world alike. There were also the hard memories that lingered from the late Ottoman period when much of the Middle East comprised provinces of a once great but failing empire administered from Istanbul. There are Arabs alive today who remember a father or grandfather taken and presumably killed by Ottoman soldiers during World War I. Nevertheless, after the emergence of the AKP, but especially following the uprisings in Tunisia, Egypt, and Libya, Arabs from all over the Middle East made their way to Istanbul and Ankara to learn how they could emulate Turkey's success. The Turks, it seemed, had resolved the related problems of Islamist political power, democracy, and prosperity.

But for all of the genuine enthusiasm that greeted the Arab uprisings and Turkey's role as a model for its neighbors, the much-anticipated transitions to democratic political systems in the Middle East never occurred. A rather different and significantly darker reality—bleaker than most observers have been willing to admit—has emerged in the region. The revolts of 2010 to 2013 were a false dawn. The early predictions of a democratic future were understandable given the romance of the Middle Eastern barricades. Instead, Egypt has lurched from crisis to crisis after Mubarak's fall in February 2011, including a coup d'état that pushed out the country's first democratically elected president in the summer of 2013. Since that time, the officers have overseen the development of a decidedly nondemocratic political order built on violence, repression, and fear. Qaddafi's legacy in Libya is the chaos of a country that was bequeathed no political institutions and no common animating national idea. Tunisia has been spared the calamities of its neighbors and remains a hopeful case, but there are signs—contrary to cheery headlines—that Tunisia's transition could unravel. The country has tremendous advantages over its neighbors, but the resilience of the old order, identity politics, and extremism have at times conspired against Tunisia's transition. The story is not wholly negative, though. Tunisia simply does not fit neatly into any post–Arab Spring category; it is neither a success nor is it a failure. There has been plenty of bloodshed there, but not civil war. Hope exists alongside frustration and cynicism as the government struggles to cope with bleak economic prospects and extremism.

At times, developments in Tunisia seemed so good that it looked like it had overtaken Turkey as a model for the region. This was because after making strides in the early 2000s toward building a more open and just society, Turkey had become a case study in the rollback of democratic reforms. It did not have an uprising like those in neighboring Middle Eastern countries, but it did experience the convulsion of the 2013 Gezi Park protests. And like demonstrators in Tunisia, Egypt, Libya, and elsewhere, Turks demanded an end to the arrogance of power, arbitrary government, crony capitalism, and police brutality. In the aftermath of the Gezi Park protests, it was stretching credulity to refer to Turkey as a democracy, but there was hope among some observers that the country's political institutions nevertheless remained resilient enough to check and balance the ambitions of President Recep Tayyip Erdoğan.[3] This proved unsustainable after Erdoğan forced the country to hold general elections in November 2015 because he did not like how Turks voted in elections held the previous June. It was an argument made even harder after he pushed the prime minister out of office some months later, a power the Turkish president does not formally possess. Yet if there was an indication that Turkey had descended into an elected autocracy, it was the aftermath of a failed coup attempt in July 2016. The putschists and their supporters were hardly democrats and demonstrated a shocking level of ruthlessness in their attempted power grab, killing at least 240 Turks and bombing the Grand National Assembly. Erdoğan prevailed in large part because Turks of many political stripes do not want to live in a society where the military can determine political outcomes, but the widespread crackdown and purge of anyone suspected of association with or supporting the coup plotters fell well outside democratic principles and norms. Not only were military officers cashiered, but so were large numbers of judges, police officers, civil servants, journalists, teachers, and even soccer referees on the flimsiest of accusations. For Erdoğan, the attempted coup was, as he claimed, "a great gift from God," allowing him to clear the field of his opponents—both real and imagined.

What went wrong? That is the question this book seeks to answer. In the years after the uprisings and the Gezi Park protests, a sobering reality has set in. Transitions to democracy, with perhaps the exception of Tunisia, seem to be a distant thwarted dream. Analysts have begun to try to understand how the promise and ideals of Arab revolutionaries and Turkish democrats remain unrealized. In one sense, it is not much of a mystery. The setbacks across the Middle East should have been expected, obscured only by the overwhelmingly optimistic commentary that came when people filled the now-famous squares of the region. Scholars have long understood that democracy is but one possible outcome when dictators fall.

That the direction of political developments in the Middle East is similar to those in other regions may be important (especially against the backdrop of a popular discourse that conveys images of Arabs and Muslims in overwhelmingly negative ways), but it is also an abstraction. The comparison does not offer insight into how and why events conspired against the development of more just, open, and democratic societies in the region. The sweeping narrative that follows does. Within the dizzying complexities and contradictions of the contemporary Middle East are three interrelated factors that have produced significant obstacles to democratic transitions: the continuity of politics, institutions, and identity.

When journalists, editors, policymakers, Middle Easterners, and other observers are not referring to the Arab Spring, they often invoke the "revolutions" of the region to describe the events of late 2010 and 2011. For some this is undoubtedly shorthand, meant merely to convey the idea that people rose up and toppled their leaders, but it is imprecise. Revolutions are far more complex affairs, both in origin and in outcome. For a revolution to be successful, "actual change of state and class structure" are needed.[4] Because the uprisings were not revolutions, what Egyptians, Tunisians, and Libyans found when their leaders fled was critical for the future before them. In Libya, Qaddafi left little in the way of national, political, or social institutions, contributing to the chaos that followed. In Egypt, the continuing coherence of a ruling class along with the battered but nevertheless largely intact authoritarian foundations of the old political system helped make the defeat of the revolutionaries, the Muslim Brothers, liberals, and democrats possible. The emergence of Beji Caid Essebsi, a relic of Tunisia's founding generation, who became president in late 2014, represented a soft restoration that was greatly facilitated by the ability of representatives of the old guard to leverage the remnant of Ben Ali's political order to their advantage. Even in Turkey, where the leadership promised to undo the authoritarian legacies of the past, it nevertheless used nondemocratic institutions to undermine and intimidate its domestic opponents. Only a decade after Turkey was formally invited to begin negotiations to join the European Union—a club of liberal democratic states—it looks more like a Middle Eastern dictatorship than a European democracy.

Related to these unsatisfying outcomes of uprisings and protests that gripped the region are conflicts over nationalism, identity, and citizenship in Egypt, Tunisia, Syria, Libya, Iraq, Yemen, Lebanon, Turkey, and everywhere else in the Middle East. When people in the Middle East began taking to the streets to demand change, it was hard not to share with them an overwhelming sense of joy and hope. Like the episodic demonstrations that dotted the Arab and Turkish histories of the twentieth century, they were sending the message that the fear with which leaders in the region ruled could no longer be counted on to ensure political quiescence. Yet as much as the anger was about brutality, arrogance, and corruption, it also represented profound dismay over the inability of Arabs and Turks—leaders and citizens alike—to answer related questions about who they are, how they wanted to be governed, the role of religion in society, and where they belonged in the global political, economic, and cultural order.[5]

With the exception of Turkey, where the ruling Justice and Development Party has forged a new, though hotly contested, identity, the new crop of Arab leaders has failed, at least thus far, to offer a national vision that is deeply appealing to a majority of their people. Ideological rivalry, ethnic tension, sectarian differences, violence, and authoritarianism have filled this void with devastating results for the region, not only setting back democracy, but also taking the lives of hundreds of thousands. It is from this wreckage that the self-declared Islamic State, with its grotesque beheadings, enslavement of women, massacres of Christian sects, and other outrages, has come to the fore. Although it existed for at least a decade before the Arab uprisings, the Islamic State is a representation of the Arab and Muslim worlds in the failed aftermath of the Middle East's most recent version of people power. That is, whereas the nihilism of the Islamic State captured the attention of the media, its grand religious and political project—re-establishing the caliphate—captured the imagination of a significant number of people in the Middle East (and the West). After all the failures—of the American war in Iraq, Arab nationalism, the Muslim Brotherhood's brand of Islamism, and the push for democracy—some Arabs and Muslims are seeking authenticity and identity in the Islamic State. The group has been so successful where it has failed before precisely because of the present moment of disorientation, when many in the region are engaged in an existential struggle to define their societies and their individual places in them.

The violence and resurgent authoritarianism of the Middle East raises important questions about the responsibility and role of the United States in the region. It goes without saying that the folly that was the invasion of Iraq in 2003 was transformative, though not in the ways that its architects and supporters fervently believed. Rather than democracy as Operation Iraqi Freedom intended, Washington unleashed forces in Iraq that have torn the country asunder. The sectarian tensions that came into play as Iraq became consumed with violence only added urgency to a long-standing struggle between the Arab Gulf states and Iran over who would dominate the Persian Gulf region and beyond. This played out tragically in Syria once the 2011 uprising against Assad evolved into a civil war, as well as in Bahrain, Lebanon, and Yemen. These developments, combined with the collapse of Libya after the NATO intervention in 2011 and the indiscriminate use of violence as a tool of counterterrorism, have all contributed to the profound sense of calamity and failure in the region. The Bush and Obama administrations do not bear all the blame for the instability and repression gripping the Middle East, yet the combination of malice and incompetence has contributed to the violence of a blood-soaked region. It is odd, then, that under these circumstances, the American foreign policy establishment still believes Washington "must get the Middle East right." Perhaps this is a sense of obligation, but more likely it is the erroneous belief that the United States has the resources, diplomatic means, and wisdom to decisively influence the trajectory of politics in Middle Eastern countries.

The bookends of the first fifteen years of the twenty-first century are the big—albeit flawed—ideas that led the United States into Iraq and the reality that developments in the Middle East are less a function of American policy than many officials and observers have come to believe.

The situation in the Middle East is bleak. It is hard to know precisely how events in the region will unfold in the coming years. For most of the period following the decolonization of the 1950s and 1960s, the Middle East was undemocratic and leaders were believed to be politically stable. Until one day they were not. For the moment, it seems clear that instability, violence, and authoritarianism will be critical features of the political landscape. Understanding the underlying political, institutional, structural, and historical forces that have produced volatile, bloody, and repressive politics is the subject of this book. The chapters that follow explore how the quite natural expectations of a better, democratic future for the Middle East became undone, starting with those heady days following the departure of two of the region's long-serving leaders, both believed to be the most secure dictators: Zine al-Abidine Ben Ali and Hosni Mubarak. After critically examining how the uprisings happened and how they unraveled, readers will encounter the heart of this volume, a detailed explanation of why the promise of reform and progressive change never came to pass, the consequences of this failure, and how the false dawn of democratic change in the Middle East will likely shape the patterns of politics in the region and America's role in it.

I

Freedom's Ride

VISITORS TO WASHINGTON, DC, are often taken with the breathtaking beauty of a city frequently caricatured in television and movies as unfailingly provincial, incestuous, and politically bankrupt. The monuments that dot downtown and the National Mall—marble temples to founders, presidents, fallen heroes, and modern day sages—are deeply moving in ways unique to Washington. New York may have the Metropolitan Museum of Art and Paris the Musée d'Orsay, but Washington has the National Gallery of Art, stunning in its own right with permanent collections featuring the works of Joan Miró, Pablo Picasso, Mark Rothko, Georgia O'Keeffe, and Jackson Pollock. The city's long boulevards, designed to converge (more or less) on Capitol Hill, are lined with sturdy, colonnaded government agencies, built during an era when public architecture meant something important. These buildings exude power and purpose. Then, of course, there is the Capitol building itself, that metaphorical beacon of liberty with the nineteen-foot, six-inch bronze Statue of Freedom capping its famous white dome. This is the Washington that anywhere between fifteen and seventeen million tourists visit each year. The city of cherry blossoms and ubiquitous motorcades.

Washington has another face, however. Although more Northern Virginia than actual District of Columbia, it is part of the city's unique professional world—the nondescript suburban office buildings and the equally bland conference rooms nestled within them. These faux marble palaces in hues of pink, tan, and pinkish tan are also monuments of sorts. Rather than memorializing courage, wisdom, and greatness, they are a testament to the ever-growing federal government and its unseen corps of contractors. The tourists along Independence Avenue likely have a rough idea of what goes on inside the Department of Agriculture or the Department of Energy, but few, if any, have a clue as to what happens inside the office parks along Route 123 or Wilson Boulevard. Yet it is within these soulless buildings that a lot of the people's work is done, especially in the areas of defense and intelligence. A cottage industry of firms with alphabet soup–like acronyms has flourished in Washington, providing consulting services for clients within the US government. More often than not, however, these companies do not provide much in the way of actual advising. Rather, recognizing that a direct inquiry from the Central Intelligence Agency (CIA) or the Defense Intelligence Agency is unlikely to be met with enthusiasm from someone within the professoriate, these firms provide cover for both government employees and outside experts. The arrangement works well for all concerned. Intelligence analysts get an interesting and fresh perspective on an important issue of the day and academics get to share their expertise with a new audience.

On December 13, 2010, one of those firms convened a meeting of intelligence analysts and nongovernment experts to explore future political trends in the Middle East. Drawn from the outside were three or four faculty members from universities along the Northeast Corridor and an equal number of "think tankers"—typically people with academic training who have chosen not to enter the ranks of academia as well as former government officials many of whom also have advanced degrees in history, political science, or economics. The American intelligence community is often slandered in the press and among the television punditocracy for missing major events and developments. No doubt it has had its spectacular failures—the attack on Pearl Harbor, the Tet Offensive, and the Soviet invasion of Afghanistan, to name some of the most notorious—but the intelligence community's record is better than many might suggest. Policymakers have a penchant for publicly flogging it to mask their misjudgments. There was the blame shifting after the September 2001 attacks on New York and Washington, DC.

On August 6, 2001, twenty-five days before the World Trade Center fell and parts of the Pentagon's E Ring were destroyed, the CIA included an item in its premiere product, the President's Daily Brief, titled "Bin Ladin Determined to Strike in US." The brief, which was released in 2004 after the conclusion of the 9/11 Commission, was vague in parts and incorrect in others, but warned starkly that "FBI information . . . indicates patterns of suspicious activities in this country consistent with preparations for hijackings or other types of attacks."[1] In the frenzied aftermath of September 11, officials from the George W. Bush administration acknowledged the brief and emphasized how hard they worked to generate more details about the plan in order to stop it. These protestations only reinforced the fact that the intelligence community understood that al-Qaeda was planning something big on American soil. Then during the march to war in Iraq, senior officials placed political pressure on the intelligence analysts to prove the existence of Saddam Hussein's development of weapons of mass destruction and questioned the competence and professional integrity of those analysts who expressed skepticism at the White House's claims about Iraq's alleged possession of a fearsome arsenal of chemical, nuclear, and biological weapons.

The December 2010 meeting was called primarily because intelligence officials had grown concerned about the prospects for instability in the Middle East and were seeking external checks on its thinking. The informal day-long discussion was rich and ranged across the region with sophistication and nuance. By the time everyone headed off to confront the Washington area's bruising late afternoon traffic, the consensus seemed to be that change in the Middle East was actually not at hand. Despite some quibbling on the margins, the nongovernment experts emphasized that the most salient feature of the Middle East's politics of the previous two decades—political stability—was likely to be the most significant characteristic of regional politics "for the foreseeable future." They concluded that the only likely significant changes in the Arab world would be the death of a national leader. Here virtually everyone had Egypt's Hosni Mubarak in mind. The then eighty-one-year-old Mubarak had spent four weeks in Germany in early 2010 recovering from what his office stated was gallbladder trouble, but few believed it. Cairo's robust rumor mill decided instead that Mubarak had undergone surgery for a serious illness—possibly pancreatic cancer—during his stay. Yet even if the Egyptian strongman or any other leader died, the gathered analysts, professors, and think tank fellows believed that successions to new leaders would be smooth and would not alter the authoritarian political direction of the governments of the region.

Less than a week after the meeting, a young man named Mohammed al-Bouazizi set himself aflame in the central Tunisian town of Sidi Bouzid. No one knows why Bouazizi did what he did, though it is universally believed that he was responding to the frustration of his difficult economic circumstances and the humiliation at the hands of a capricious and arbitrary government.[2] The day of his self-immolation, a policewoman had reportedly slapped him and had his fruit and vegetable cart confiscated after he failed to produce the documents permitting him to sell produce. Regardless of what motivated Bouazizi, his gruesome act touched off a month-long uprising that chased Tunisia's longtime dictator, Zine al-Abidine Ben Ali, from power. Less than two weeks after that, on January 25, Egyptians poured into Tahrir Square and other public spaces around the country demanding "bread, freedom, and social justice." By the second week of February, the Egyptian armed forces informed Mubarak that his nearly thirty-year rule was over and bundled him aboard a private jet bound for the resort town of Sharm el-Sheikh in the southern Sinai Peninsula, where the generals hoped he would quietly fade away under virtual house—though it was more like a palace—arrest. Although the Egyptian uprising was the most spectacular and most widely covered in the West, Algeria, Jordan, and Oman experienced protests even before Egypt. Yemenis demanded that their president, Ali Abdullah Saleh, resign at the same time that Egyptians called on Mubarak to leave. Similarly, Sudanese leaders confronted street protests that began on January 30 and lasted on and off through much of 2013. In the roughly four weeks after Mubarak's night flight to Sharm el-Sheikh, Bahrain—a country that had experienced years of sectarian-based protests—erupted, and Libyans in the eastern city of Benghazi began their eight-month effort to bring down Muammar al-Qaddafi, the longest-serving leader in the Middle East. Then came demonstrations in Kuwait, Morocco, Lebanon, and even Saudi Arabia. On March 15, a group of Syrian teenagers scrawled anti–Bashar al-Assad graffiti on walls in the southern town of Deraa. In response, the government's internal security forces tortured the perpetrators, kicking off an uprising that in ensuing years has evolved into a civil war, a proxy war, the center of transnational jihad, and a major humanitarian disaster.

A sense of dumbstruck awe prevailed among those living, witnessing, and reporting on the uprisings. The Arab and Western media covered the so-called revolutions in the Middle East "wall-to-wall," in the parlance of television news producers. Prominent American journalists such as Brian Williams, Katie Couric, Anderson Cooper—with his black T-shirt—and Christiane Amanpour, and well-known print columnists such as Thomas Friedman and Nicholas Kristof, along with an entire team of correspondents from the BBC, descended on Tahrir Square. The French, Germans, and Canadians were also there. The journalists of Al Jazeera, which had raised the ire of Arab leaders since it launched in 1996 with its refreshingly unvarnished coverage of the Middle East—except for Qatar and its ruling family who are the channel's paymasters—were courageous. It was hard not to have a man crush on Ayman Mohyeldin, who worked for the network before joining NBC. He reported fearlessly on events in Tahrir Square as he dodged Egyptian policemen. The uprisings were an exhilarating and inspiring story. The Middle East was, it seemed to many casual observers, politicians, and journalists on the scene, suddenly having its own 1989—the year in which the Berlin Wall and the communist regimes of Eastern and Central Europe fell. Ben Ali was the Arab world's Erich Honeker, Mubarak its General Wojciech Jaruzelski, and in the fall of 2011 Qaddafi would come to an end much like that of Romania's Nicolae Ceaușescu.

The events unfolding across the region during the winter and spring of 2011 were surprising, even if the popular conception of the Middle East was already that of a region of endemic instability. There was reason to believe this narrative given the history of four regional Arab-Israeli wars, two major Israeli invasions of Lebanon (along with countless other incursions), the Lebanese civil war, the Iran-Iraq war, the Iraqi invasion of Kuwait, Operation Desert Storm, Operation Iraqi Freedom, two Palestinian intifadas, and terrorist outrages too numerous to count. Yet, for all of this bloodshed, the political systems within the countries of the region remained remarkably durable. Leaders never fell and regimes remained intact. Save only non-Arab Iran, there were no revolutions. This is why the uprisings of late 2010 and early 2011 were so remarkable. Those countries believed to be stable—where "the barriers to collective action were too high" for weak oppositions to scale, as the participants in the intelligence community–sponsored roundtable concluded in December 2010—proved surprisingly brittle. As protests gained momentum, fear evaporated, and security services lost their grip, leaving veteran Middle East watchers flabbergasted and muttering, "I never thought I would witness this." The wonder of it all and the romance of the barricades produced names like the Jasmine Revolution for Tunisia's uprising, the Lotus Revolution for Egypt's, the Arab Awakening—as if Middle Easterners had been in a collective slumber until Bouazizi's desperate act—and the Arab Spring, a play on the Prague Spring of 1968 when citizens of Czechoslovakia rose up against communist rule.

WASHINGTON'S UPRISINGS

The sudden spate of newly minted former Arab leaders and political tumult also produced some hand-wringing in Washington. Senator Diane Feinstein (D-CA), who at the time was the chairperson of the Senate Select Committee on Intelligence, which is charged with oversight of America's sprawling intelligence community of seventeen agencies, wanted to know why no one saw the uprisings coming. The United States had been through this before. When Iran's shah, Mohammed Reza Pahlavi, fell in February 1979, the Subcommittee on Evaluation of the House Permanent Select Committee on Intelligence investigated why and how the CIA had been caught so off guard. Feinstein's question, like the one posed in the late 1970s, was both a fair and an unfair question at the same time. The analytic and policy communities inside the Beltway and beyond actually understood in detail that all was not well with the Middle East. The region had accumulated problems of political repression, uneven economic development, and a host of social indicators that stubbornly pointed in the wrong direction. Surely the experts should have known that this was a region on the edge of revolutions, shouldn't they?

Senator Feinstein's query aside, analysts had long understood that uprisings and revolutions were beyond prediction. Like Iranian revolutionaries or Poland's Solidarity movement, Egypt's revolutionary youth, for example, were as surprised as anyone that they managed to push their leader from office. For almost a decade before January 25, 2011, street protests had become a part of the Egyptian political landscape. None of them were as large as on that Tuesday, but some were quite large indeed. Between 10,000 and 15,000 people protested in March 2003 against the US invasion of Iraq, an event that evolved into an anti-Mubarak demonstration. In May 2005, large numbers of Egyptians again turned out in the streets across the country to voice their opposition to controversial constitutional amendments. In early April 2008, the industrial center Mahalla al-Kubra was in open revolt against the government. Yet only the January 25 protests drove Mubarak from power. Why? No one knows.

In an influential 1991 essay examining the revolutions in Eastern Europe, Timur Kuran, a professor of economics and political science at Duke University, developed a compelling theory not to predict revolutions but rather to explain their unpredictability.[3] Kuran posited that revolutions, which he defined as the "mass seizure of political power that aims to transform the social order," are based on the interaction of "social and psychological factors [that] make it inherently difficult to predict the outcome of political contestation."[4] In political systems like the communist regimes of Eastern Europe, the Soviet Union, and the authoritarian governments of the Middle East, people often expressed public support for governments that privately they did not like. This willingness to say and do things in public despite holding very different views when the lights are off and the sheets pulled up at night is what Kuran calls preference falsification and was the result of the fear associated with public dissent. In East Germany, as in Ben Ali's Tunisia, people had much to lose if they spoke out against the system. They included both dissidents who paid a heavy price for their opposition and true believers who were rewarded (often handsomely) for their loyalty. To get along in life, the vast majority of people simply mouthed public support for the government. Although these systems seem stable, and were for years, some combination of personal reasons and what social scientists call structural factors—politics, socioeconomic issues, and societal norms, to name a few—can produce a process through which an individual's public and private views align in opposition to the government. If this happens with enough people, the costs of opposing the government decline as do the benefits of remaining loyal to it. The result is what's called a revolutionary bandwagon.

In real-world terms, Bouazizi's self-immolation in Tunisia encouraged some people to shift their public preference and demonstrate against Ben Ali's rule, which in turn emboldened others to do the same. As the protests gained momentum, it became increasingly unacceptable to remain publicly supportive of the regime and increasingly rewarding to oppose it. Under these circumstances, it was only a matter of time before Ben Ali was overwhelmed by the mass opposition to his continued leadership. In Egypt, the November 2010 parliamentary elections, which were rigged to shut the Muslim Brotherhood and Mubarak's other opponents out of the legislature, seemed to be a critical factor that began altering people's public preferences. But maybe it was the Church of the Saints bombing in Alexandria on New Year's Day 2011 that stoked widespread suspicions that the brutal and corrupt agents of the Ministry of Interior— not terrorists—were responsible. It could have been the murder of Khaled Said; the twenty-eight-year-old Alexandrian had become an icon for opponents of the Egyptian regime after policemen killed him the previous June. Then there was the sharp uptick in the price of tomatoes. It might have also been the—more than usual—heavy-handed way in which the government sought to control information during the run-up to the parliamentary vote. The problem for Senator Feinstein and others who wanted to investigate the failure to anticipate the uprisings is the impossibility of knowing precisely what produced the changes in Egyptians' public preferences, resulting in the January 25 uprising and Mubarak's departure. As Kuran notes, "It is always a conjunction of factors, many of them intrinsically unimportant and thus unobserved, if not unobservable, that determines the flow of events. A major global event can produce drastically different outcomes in two settings that differ trivially."[5] The inability to know or predict precisely when they will occur— what Kuran calls the inevitability of surprise—is the essence of revolutions and uprisings.

While members of Congress were erroneously blaming the CIA for missing the uprisings, President Barack Obama and his advisors were busy trying to assess what exactly was happening in the region, and little time was available to ponder why it was all happening. The foreign policy bureaucracy, especially the State Department, was slow to respond to the protests that began in Tunisia on December 17. When asked about it during the department's daily press briefing on January 4, 2011—ten days before Ben Ali's forced departure—Assistant Secretary of State for Public Affairs Philip Crowley stated that he had not been briefed that day on developments in Tunisia. In a follow-up query, the same journalist asked Crowley when he had last been briefed on the topic. The rhetorical question was met with derisive laughter among the correspondents accredited to the State Department, who knew very well that Tunisia was a backwater of American policy and that therefore Crowley had almost certainly not been briefed on it. When Ben Ali fell, Secretary of State Hillary Clinton released a statement that read, in part, "The United States has a long and historic relationship with Tunisia. We are committed to helping the people and government bring peace and stability to their country and we hope that they will work together to build a stronger, more democratic society that respects the rights of all people."[6]

This kind of caution was warranted. Ben Ali, who had ruled Tunisia since 1987 when he ousted the country's founder in a palace coup, was still en route to Saudi Arabia, where he and his family would find safe harbor.[7] The military seemed to be in control of the country, but it was a relatively small and underprivileged force (by Middle Eastern standards) compared with the police and Ministry of Interior that had been the president's bastion of support. Although the Tunisians moved with alacrity to set up an interim government, no one knew what would happen next. The United States had a small diplomatic presence in the country and limited capacity to understand quickly unfolding events. Less than a week later and as the situation in Tunisia became clearer, the State Department issued another statement:

> We hope the interim government takes this opportunity to chart a course for their country that provides for the inclusion of all peaceful and democratic forces in the political process, through open and fair elections, and by investigating the abuses of the past. We see this as a

moment in time and an important opportunity for the government
to meet the aspirations and demands of the Tunisian people.[8]

This guarded encouragement reflected the fact that Tunisia's future
was up for grabs. Still, underlying this caution was the idea that once
Tunisia's authoritarian system came undone, the United States had a
role to play in its democratic development.

When Egypt's uprising began, the Obama administration approached
the demonstrations with utmost care. Mubarak's Egypt had been a critical ally of the United States, playing a central role in a regional political
order that made it relatively easier and less expensive for Washington
to pursue its interests in the region. Under Mubarak, the Egypt–Israel
peace treaty had become institutionalized, even if Israelis and their supporters in the United States complained that Cairo did everything to
keep relations between the two countries "cold." The Egyptians also
played a behind-the-scenes role in providing US military forces in the
region with logistical support, with the exception of Operations Desert
Shield and Desert Storm in 1990 and 1991 when they actually deployed
35,000 soldiers to Saudi Arabia to take part in the liberation of Kuwait.
Although they did little fighting, the presence of Egyptian forces so-
lidified Arab participation in the anti–Saddam Hussein coalition and
greatly enhanced its legitimacy. Two decades later, Cairo became a partner of sorts in the global war on terrorism, accepting battlefield prisoners from Afghanistan and Iraq for interrogation.

Even as the administration was scrambling to understand events
of January 25, Secretary Clinton declared that Egypt was stable.[9] Yet
just twelve days earlier, Clinton had warned a gathering of Arab foreign ministers in the Qatari capital Doha that "Those who cling to the
status quo may be able to hold back the full impact of their countries'
problems for a little while, but not forever." This was certainly prescient given what was to unfold in the coming months. The full quote,
though, indicates why Clinton was so careful when tens of thousands of
Egyptians began demanding that Mubarak leave: "If leaders don't offer
a positive vision and give young people meaningful ways to contribute, others will fill the vacuum. Extremist elements, terrorist groups,
and others who would prey on desperation and poverty are already out
there, appealing for allegiance and competing for influence. So this is

a critical moment, and this is a test of leadership for all of us."[10] This was a concern that had vexed American policymakers, and leaders like Mubarak used it to their advantage, telling the five American presidents with whom he had worked that though they might dislike his methods, what might come after him would be worse.

In five short days, however, the administration came to understand precisely what was clear to most people who were witnessing the uprising firsthand. Mubarak's almost three-decade reign was in trouble. In a January 30 appearance on NBC's *Meet the Press*, the secretary of state told host David Gregory, "any efforts by this [the Egyptian] government to respond to the needs of their people, to take steps that will result in a peaceful, orderly transition to a democratic regime, is what is in the best interests of everyone, including the current government."[11] She made similar statements on *Fox News Sunday*, CNN's *State of the Union*, and CBS's *Face the Nation*. After the Egyptian armed forces maneuvered Mubarak out of power almost two weeks later, Obama appeared in the Grand Foyer of the White House and offered brief remarks reflecting on the historic change that had taken place that day. He sounded notes of caution and offered Washington's assistance, but his words revealed a belief that a path toward democracy was laid before Egyptians: "I'm sure there will be difficult days ahead, and many questions remain unanswered. But I am confident that the people of Egypt can find the answers, and do so peacefully, constructively, and in the spirit of unity that has defined these last few weeks. For Egyptians have made it clear that nothing less than genuine democracy will carry the day."[12]

It was ironic that the uprisings happened during Obama's tenure. He had come to office with a studied indifference to democracy promotion and his advisors seemed intent on repairing relations with allies, especially Egypt and Saudi Arabia, that had been bruised during the Bush years. In the president's famous speech at Cairo University on June 4, 2009, titled "A New Beginning," Obama outlined seven sources of tension between the United States and the Muslim world, one of which was the promotion of democracy. Although he affirmed his commitment to advancing democracy, Obama indicated that Washington would not press the issue, allowing that "Each nation gives life to this principle [democracy] in its own way, grounded in the traditions of its own people. America does not presume to know what is best for everyone, just as we would not presume to pick the outcome of a peaceful election."[13] When Ben Ali and Mubarak were driven from office, Obama seemed to "luck" into what every media outlet in the world had dubbed the Arab Spring.

For Washington's neoconservatives it was unfair that the uprisings were sweeping the Middle East when they did, but they nevertheless sensed vindication that Arabs were throwing off dictatorship. Throughout the post–World War II period, American foreign policy had at times previously promoted democracy—at least rhetorically—but in November 2003 former president George W. Bush announced a "forward strategy of freedom in the Middle East." The Freedom Agenda, as it became known, was based on the belief that democracy was the best form of government, the assertion that "authoritarian stability was no stability at all," and that people wanted freedom. To the deeply cynical, these may have sounded like mere slogans, but they had the benefit of being self-evidently true. The Bush administration's democracy promotion was also based on assumptions that democracies in the Middle East would be better partners for the United States and that whatever political turbulence might occur in the region as a result of transitions from authoritarianism to democracy, American interests would remain secure "over the long run."[14] The Freedom Agenda also took a page from Immanuel Kant's "To Perpetual Peace: A Philosophical Sketch"— or at least a Cliffs Notes version of the eighteenth-century German philosopher's essay—the central insight of which was that democracies do not fight each other. Thus, for the Middle East to be a more pacific region, the countries there needed to become democracies. Academics fought over Kant's original theory with great intensity, refining it in ways that advanced the understanding of democratic states in the international system. When all was said and done, it turns out to be true that advanced democracies tend not to fight each other, but that those undergoing a transition tend to be unstable and warlike.[15] Supporters of democracy promotion emphasized the former conclusion at the expense of the latter qualification.

Bush was not just forceful in his public support for democratic change in the Middle East. Even before he articulated his broad vision for democracy promotion at an address in late 2003 on the twenty-fifth anniversary for the National Endowment of Democracy, he oversaw the development of a new bureaucratic structure, the US-Middle East Partnership Initiative, to advance change. MEPI—as it is known both affectionately and derisively—would do the work that the United States Agency for International Development (USAID) could not do because its programs were subject to the approval of host governments. This did not mean that USAID did not participate in democracy building initiatives. It actually has a history of providing technical assistance in support of reform in a variety of Middle Eastern countries. Yet the foreign service officers, civil servants, and political appointees who ran and administered MEPI were charged with doing something somewhat different from USAID: reaching directly into Arab societies and working with partners there, whether they had approval from governments to do so or not. To that end, the Middle East Partnership Initiative supported democracy, economic reform, educational reform, and women's empowerment.[16] Few in Congress could argue with these laudable goals, especially given that many in Washington believed that democracy made terrorism less likely, giving MEPI broad bipartisan support if not a huge amount in the way of resources.

The Middle East Partnership Initiative and the work that USAID undertook were only part of the Bush administration's push for freedom in the Middle East. The centerpiece, of course, was the US invasion of Iraq on March 20, 2003. Many reasons justified it—the steady erosion of the sanctions imposed on Saddam Hussein after he swallowed Kuwait in August 1990; the drag on the US military from enforcing no-fly zones in northern and southern Iraq for more than a decade; the conviction that the Iraqis were developing nuclear, biological, and chemical weapons; and the belief that Saddam Hussein was a threat to his neighbors even after years of sanctions and continuous American military surveillance. Some, like then secretary of defense Donald Rumsfeld, believed that Washington needed to demonstrate strength after the blow of the September 11 attacks. His deputy, Paul Wolfowitz, argued that regime change in Iraq would usher in an era of democracy in that country, which would in turn transform the Middle East.[17] The last was particularly important to neoconservative thinkers both within and outside the Bush administration. It was not that they gave any less weight to the other reasons offered to justify the war but rather they believed that if Iraq were a democracy, it would minimize the other problems in the region. As the code name for the invasion—Operation Iraqi Freedom—implied, the war was not to restore some status quo as America's previous war with Iraq had done in 1991 but rather to be a thoroughly transformative event.[18]

When Arabs rose up against their leaders, prominent neoconservatives and servants of the Bush administration saw their own hands in the Arab Spring. Widely derided and discredited after Iraq became a bloody quagmire, neoconservatives declared a nonexistent connection between Cairo's Tahrir Square and Baghdad's Firdous Square, where eight years earlier a contingent of American marines helped jubilant Iraqis tear down a towering statue of Saddam Hussein. Peter Wehner, a former Bush speechwriter and director of the White House's Office of Strategic Initiatives, told the readers of *Commentary* magazine's blog *Contentions* that "it appears as if the Egyptian people, and not only the Egyptian people, are longing for what the people of Iraq have embraced: self-government."[19] This was either an analytic sleight of hand or the case of an accomplished wordsmith choosing the wrong words. Wehner was correct that Arabs embraced self-government, something that they all enjoyed since decolonization in the mid-twentieth century and Great Britain's final exit from the Persian Gulf in the autumn of 1971. What they actually wanted was democracy and good governance, though not brought to them at the muzzle end of an American tank. The suggestion that Iraq was somehow an inspiration for Egypt and the rest of the Arab world betrayed just how little Wehner and his colleagues actually knew about the Middle East even after years of war there. As the season of Arab uprisings demonstrated, the desire for freedom is universal, but against the backdrop of the region's tortured history with foreign domination, it is odd, to say the least, to believe that Arab activists sought inspiration from what many regarded as an illegitimate invasion and destructive occupation.

Wehner's fantasy about the connection between Iraq and the uprisings was not isolated to someone who served in the Bush administration and was now in search of redemption. Writing on March 4, 2011, *Washington Post* columnist Charles Krauthammer offered the following perspective:

Now, it can be argued that the price in blood and treasure that America paid to establish Iraq's democracy was too high. But whatever side you take on that question, what's unmistakable is that to the Middle Easterner, Iraq today is the only functioning Arab democracy, with multiparty elections and the freest press. Its democracy is fragile and imperfect ... but were Egypt to be as politically developed in, say, a year as is Iraq today, we would think it is a great success.[20]

Krauthammer's claims do not hold up under scrutiny, however. Public opinion polls conducted since Operation Iraqi Freedom demonstrate that large majorities of Arabs believe that Iraq was better off under Saddam Hussein, that the country will never be a stable democracy, and that it would spawn instability throughout the region.[21] All the people polled may be wrong, but to the extent that these polls are a reflection of what Middle Easterners believe, it is the opposite of Krauthammer's implicit assertion of some sort of Iraq effect that contributed to uprisings in Tunisia, Egypt, Libya, and elsewhere.[22]

How the Arab world viewed the invasion of Iraq mattered little anyway because, as with so much about the neoconservative encounter with the Middle East, it did not fit a specific narrative. Like Wehner and Krauthammer, Christopher Hitchens insisted on the existence of an "Iraq effect" on the politics of the region. Hitchens was not a self-identifying neoconservative, though he traveled a similar ideological path as the founders of the movement, who had at one time been leftists. For Hitchens, it was the shock and horror of the September 11 attacks that drew him to many of the same conclusions as those who were neoconservatives.[23] In a contribution to Slate.com under a blog created for him called *Fighting Words*, Hitchens posed the following question: "Can anyone imagine how the Arab spring would have played out if a keystone Arab state, oil-rich and heavily armed with a track record of intervention in its neighbors' affairs and a history of all-out mass repression against its own civilians, were still the private property of a sadistic crime family?"[24] Actually, one could imagine the Arab uprisings with Saddam Hussein still in power. The Iraqi dictator would have surely enjoyed Mubarak's fall and the efforts to bring Qaddafi and Assad, whose father supported Iran during its war with Iraq that took place over eight bloody years between 1980 and 1988, to an end, all the while minimizing the risk to himself through unimaginable repression. The massive use of force is precisely what the Libyan leadership tried (and failed) and precisely how Assad has sought to prevail.

Hitchens was not playing a thought experiment, however. He answered his own question in the manner expected of someone who believed that Operation Iraqi Freedom was an unambiguous good: "As it is, to have had Iraq on the other scale from the outset has been an unnoticed and unacknowledged benefit whose extent is impossible to compute. And the influence of Iraq on the Libyan equation has also been uniformly positive in ways that are likewise often overlooked." Hitchens allows that Iraq had little do with what brought Tunisians and Egyptians to the streets, but from his perspective they did not have to because "Iraq already has, albeit in tenuous form, the free press, the written constitution, and the parliamentary election system that is the minimum demand of Arab civil society." He was, however, overlooking the fact that written constitutions and regularly scheduled parliamentary elections had become the norm in the Arab world since the 1980s and 1990s. What was even more curious was his invocation of Iraq's media environment as some sort of model given that in 2011 the Committee to Protect Journalists ranked Iraq dead last in its Impunity Index, meaning that journalists were routinely killed in Iraq and the prospect of their murderers ever being brought to justice was minimal at best. Still, Hitchens and others were nevertheless convinced that "these lessons and experiences [from Iraq's postwar reconstruction] . . . are useful not just to Mesopotamia."[25]

FREEDOM'S RIDE

It is easy to pick on the neoconservatives and other supporters of the Iraq war, but the media, the commentariat, Middle East specialists, all types of foreign policy experts, and government officials were alternating between confusion over what was happening in the Middle East and embracing the expected democratic change to come. Despite the oft-repeated admonition that "the hard work is just beginning" and other weak caveats that appeared in so many articles, editorials, and op-eds, the spring of 2011 and most of 2012 was a moment of enthusiasm.

The end of Ben Ali and Mubarak, the sudden groundswell of opposition to Qaddafi, and the outpouring of opposition against other leaders around the region produced a torrent of commentary in newspapers, magazines, and policy journals. The rate of production and publication was astounding. Some of this work was superficial, especially pieces pondering whether Twitter, Facebook, and the Internet more generally had caused the uprisings.[26] It was interesting—for a moment—to understand how activists leveraged these technologies to mobilize large numbers of people, but it was not actually a new story. In the broad historical sweep of people power and revolutions, new or newish technologies often rallied the masses. The audiocassette, for example, was critical in Iran's upheaval three decades earlier.

The broader commentary on the region's cascade of uprisings did not escape a "wonder of the moment" quality. On February 3, 2011—the day after the infamous Battle of the Camel, when paid pro-Mubarak thugs attacked protesters in Tahrir Square—the *New York Times* columnist Nicholas Kristof offered this view from Cairo's streets:

> Whatever Mr. Mubarak is planning, it does feel as if something has changed, as if the Egyptian people have awoken . . . The lion-hearted Egyptians I met on Tahrir Square are risking their lives to stand up for democracy and liberty, and they deserve our strongest support— and, frankly, they should inspire us as well. A quick lesson in colloquial Arabic, *Innarhda, ehna kullina Misryeen*! Today, we are all Egyptians![27]

The *Economist*'s February 19 edition titled "The Awakening" exuded a staid British detachment in contrast to Kristof's out-of-breath, cliché-ridden dispatch from Tahrir Square but was nevertheless as revealing of the emerging zeitgeist as Kristof's paean to brave Egyptians: "Since the millennium, democracy has struggled to dispel the fear that it cannot withstand Islamism or the economic potency of an authoritarian China. Egypt promises to undermine both those propositions. Authoritarianism is not the best answer to Islamism. And it rarely creates prosperity. As the Arab world awakens, a better future beck-ons."[28] What is striking is the authors' implicit assumption that with Ben Ali gone, Mubarak disgraced, and protests flaring throughout the region, democracy would follow.

By late February, Kristof was back in Cairo taking on the question "Are Arabs too politically immature to handle democracy?" Paired with him that day on the back page of the *New York Times* was Fouad Ajami, who had long held the Majid Khadduri chair at the Johns Hopkins School of Advanced International Studies. Over many years of con-tributions to the *Times*, the *Washington Post*, the *Wall Street Journal*, *U.S. News and World Report*, the *New Republic, Foreign Affairs*, and else-where, Ajami had become a leading public intellectual in the United States. For a time, he was the only Arab interpreter of the Middle East to appear on major network television news. This success, combined with unrivaled eloquence and the way he positioned himself as truth teller to the Arab world as well as slayer of the received wisdom that per-meated the halls of university Middle East centers, made him a reviled figure among his colleagues in the field, often in an irrationally obses-sive way. They regarded his work as shoddy political cover for American adventurism in the Middle East.[29] He had his passionate supporters as well, from a polyglot group of Arab students who saw the world in similar ways as their professor to liberal internationalists, members of the foreign policy establishment, and neoconservatives. His associa-tion with the latter during the last decade of his life gave Ajami entrée into the Oval Office during the Bush administration. And though his work was dedicated to explaining the Arab world, it was also simultane-ously a project in self-discovery. Ajami was a Shiite from an Arabized Persian family, came of age in Lebanon in the Arab nationalist heyday of the 1960s, and subsequently became an American citizen with what seemed like distinctive Republican Party leanings. As it did for his less knowledgeable friends and acolytes, the uprisings denoted vindication for Ajami. He had been writing passionately for decades about what he regarded as the lies, cruelty, and self-abnegation that contemporary Arab politics required. The multitudes who came forth to demand change in 2011 had finally realized what he had understood and had been telling them for so long. In "How the Arabs Turned Shame into Liberty," Ajami rejoices that "in those big, public spaces in Tunis, Cairo and Manama, Bahrain, in the Libyan cities of Benghazi and Tobruk, millions of Arabs came together to bid farewell to an age of quiescence. They were done with the politics of fear and silence."[30] As with virtually everyone who commented on the uprisings, Ajami made his readers aware that "errors" were possible, but now that Middle Easterners had discarded the old order they would take "freedom's ride."

After the uprisings, commentators also went full tilt on the role of Islamists in the change taking place around the region. Islamist movements had been a common feature of Middle Eastern political arenas for quite some time. Among the smattering of liberals, leftists, and all kinds of nationalist opponents to various regimes around the region, Islamists had often proven themselves the most effective in drawing the important distinction between what Arab leaders were telling their citizens and how these people experienced objective reality. The Islamist vision of clean governance, independent foreign policies, adherence to the values and ideals of Islam including *shura*, or consultation, were, Western and Middle Eastern observers believed, a deeply appealing alternative to the authoritarian systems around the region, especially the republics—Algeria, Egypt, Iraq, Syria, Tunisia, and Yemen. Some of the same analysts who argued that the Arab uprisings were good for the Islamists (they were), also claimed that these groups would be a constructive force for democratic politics in the region.[31]

This optimistic sentiment was on full display when the Muslim Brotherhood made its inaugural voyage to Washington in April 2012. The delegation included a woman named Sondos Asem, who was often the "tweep" behind the Brotherhood's popular English-language Twitter account @Ikhwanweb, and Abdul Mawgoud al-Dardery, a former Peace Fellow at the University of Pittsburgh and a Brotherhood member from Luxor. Along with them was Khaled al-Qazzaz—a resident of Toronto until shortly after the January 25 uprising—who would go on to be an advisor to Egypt's first post-Mubarak president, Mohammed Morsi. Hussein al-Qazzaz, the final member of the delegation, was involved in writing the Brotherhood's plan for Egypt's economic rebirth. This group was carefully calibrated to push all of Washington's buttons—a twenty-something female expert in social media, a guy educated in the United States thanks to a program the American and Egyptian governments established after the 1979 Egypt-Israel peace treaty, a burly father of three who lived in Canada, and a businessman who sounded like any good capitalist. Their message was all about prosperity, democracy, regional peace, and good relations with the United States. It was hard to argue with the first, but the latter three ran opposite to what the Brotherhood had stood for since its founding in March 1928. Over the three decades before the uprising, the members of the Brotherhood had become adept at using the language of political reform and positioning themselves as a moderate alternative to Egypt's leadership, though their authoritarian worldview belied their alleged democratic credentials. They had also never dropped their hostility to the exercise of American power in the Middle East. Yet in the optimistic afterglow of Tahrir Square, the Brotherhood delegation presented the organization as a partner to the United States. It was not at all credible, but there were few skeptics in Washington at the time. After the meeting in the spring of 2012, one credulous former member of Congress virtually hurdled a table to present Asem with her business card. For those who took a more jaundiced view of the Brotherhood and insisted on asking the delegation pointed questions, Asem, Dardery, Qazzaz, and Qazzaz were evasive at best. They parried questions with questions and slippery non-answers as their Washington well-wishers looked on disdainfully at those who sought to poke holes in the sunny post-uprisings narrative about Islamists and democracy.

Washington's old fears of "one man, one vote, one time" had dissipated in the aftermath of the uprisings as groups such as Egypt's Muslim Brotherhood and Tunisia's Ennahda Movement came to be seen as good stewards of democratic and open political systems even though few analysts argued that Islamists had actually embraced democratic ideals. Rather, these observers often argued that Islamists had embraced the "alternation of power, popular sovereignty, and judicial independence" out of a pragmatism imposed by the incentives and constraints of the political systems in which they operated. This was a riff on the arguments advanced in an influential edited volume published in 1994 titled *Democracy without Democrats? The Renewal of Politics in the Muslim World.* The twelve contributions represented the thinking of an impressive array of Western and Arab scholars addressing a wide range of issues including demographics, the fiscal well-being of oil-producing states, socioeconomic change, political mobilization, and Islamist mobilization from different disciplinary perspectives. The starting point, however, was the idea the book's editor, Ghassan Salamé, articulated: "Democrats may not exist at all, or they may not exist in great numbers. Yet democracy can still be sought as an instrument of civil peace and hopefully, gradually, inadvertently, produce its own defenders."[32] This was a deeply appealing idea because it presented a neat and clean way out of the messy argument about what people believe in their hearts and minds. Islamist leaders, for example, need not be Jeffersonian democrats to govern democratically. After the uprisings, the French scholar Olivier Roy made a similar point, drawing on the experience of the Roman Catholic Church and the emergence of Christian Democrats in Europe, neither of which initially had any particular commitment to democratic institutions but embraced democracy over time.[33] It was a fail-safe argument when all others failed: if the church accepted democracy, Islamists could too. Comparing the two cases did not necessarily mean they were the same, however.

THE MODEL

Analysts did not need to draw analogies to nineteenth-century Europe; instead they turned to twenty-first-century Anatolia. A prominent Muslim Brother named Sobhi Saleh told Marc Champion and Keith Johnson of the *Wall Street Journal* shortly before Mubarak fell that the Brotherhood was "much closer to the Turkish example" than Iran's clerical regime.[34] As the *Economist* magazine noted in March 2011, the Arab "Islamist mainstream looks for its model not to theocracies such as Iran's, but to the democratically elected AK party in Turkey, with its Islamic flavour diluted by tolerance for others and respect for secular institutions."[35] The leader of Tunisia's Ennahda Movement, Rachid al-Ghannouchi, saw things somewhat differently. He regarded his many writings to be "the reference point for the AKP [Justice and Development Party]," but he allowed that Ennahda "admire[d] the Turkish case and those who are in charge of it are our close friends."[36] This was a significant change for Islamists. They had long looked warily across the Mediterranean at Turkey with its radical secularism, NATO membership, and aspirations to join the European Union.

Turkey's mystique in the Arab Middle East began only in November 2002, when the Justice and Development Party came to power. The party, which had been founded only a little more than a year earlier, was the latest iteration in a series of Turkish Islamist parties dating back to the late 1960s and early 1970s. Each time the military stepped into Turkish politics to remove governments that the officers did not like—roughly once every ten years between 1960 and 1997—the Islamists were banned and their parties shuttered. Yet each time these parties were closed, the Islamists returned to the political arena under a new party name and ostensibly new leadership. Thus the National Order Party became the National Salvation Party, which became the Welfare Party, which became the Virtue Party, which in turn split into the Happiness Party and the AKP in August 2001.

The younger and self-declared reformist leadership of the AKP, the most well-known of whom were Recep Tayyip Erdoğan and Abdullah Gül, promised something entirely different from the anti-Western, paranoid, and authoritarian outlook of their predecessors. Beginning in January 2003, the AKP oversaw five constitutional reform packages designed to help Turkey conform to the European Union's Copenhagen Criteria, which were political and economic benchmarks that countries were required to meet just to begin negotiations to join Europe's exclusive club. At the same time, the Turkish economy began a period of significant growth, reversing a sharp downturn that began in 2001 and extended through 2002. Erdoğan, who was prime minister from 2003 until he was elected president in 2014, was not the author of the reforms that made Turkey one of the fastest-growing economies in the world by the middle of the decade—the credit belongs to the previous government—but he and the AKP reaped the political rewards. In 2007, the AKP gained another parliamentary majority carrying a broad coalition of pious Turks, Kurds, liberals, big business, the new middle class, and cosmopolitan elites that represented 47 percent of the popular vote.

In foreign policy, the AKP quickly sought to change the studied disinterest with which Ankara had generally approached the Middle East. Erdoğan, Gül, and Gül's two successors at the foreign ministry, Ali Babacan—whose brief tenure was inconsequential—and the peripatetic academic Ahmet Davutoğlu, with his vision of Turkey as a great Muslim power, made room for themselves at the table on virtually every issue of import in the Middle East.[37] When they were not touching down in Arab capitals, they were hosting Arab leaders and delegations in Istanbul, the old imperial capital with its grand palaces and mosques attesting to past Ottoman greatness. Turkey's determination to be a regional leader precipitated a change in its ties with Israel. Ankara recognized Israel in 1949, though it maintained its distance, always reaffirming its political and diplomatic support for the establishment of a Palestinian state. It was not until 1993 that the countries exchanged ambassadors. Just three years later, the Turks and Israelis upgraded their ties further, dramatically expanding defense cooperation. Suddenly Israeli pilots were training in Turkish skies, and Turkish officers were taking part in maneuvers with Israel's armored forces in the Negev desert. Israeli defense firms were also awarded contracts to upgrade Turkish tanks, helicopters, and fighter planes.

As impressive as the development of these ties were, the Turkey-Israel defense cooperation of the late 1990s was the product of a particular moment in Turkish domestic politics when the military was ascendant and interests converged between Turkey's senior military commanders and their Israeli counterparts in confronting Iran, confronting Islamic extremist groups, and checking the Syrians who harbored Kurdish and Palestinian terrorists. When Erdoğan and the AKP came to power and began reining in the military under the guise of European Union–related reforms, the Israelis lost their primary constituency for the relationship. Although Ankara and Jerusalem maintained good ties for a time, the relationship began to hit the skids in June 2004 when Erdoğan called Israeli actions in the Gaza Strip "state-sponsored terrorism." A series of other events—Hamas leader Khaled Meshaal's visit to Ankara in early 2006, Israel's invasion of Gaza in late 2008, Erdoğan's verbal altercation with then Israeli president Shimon Peres at a World Economic Forum plenary in Switzerland in 2009, and the infamous Mavi Marmara incident in May 2010 when Israeli commandos killed eight Turks and a Turkish-American aboard a ferry that was trying to run Israel's naval blockade of Gaza—further undermined bilateral ties. The last event brought political, diplomatic, and security relations, but not business ties, to a halt. In their harsh rhetoric over what the Turks considered a violation of international law, they threatened naval action against Israeli warships in the eastern Mediterranean.

By the time Tunisians and Egyptians turned out in large numbers to demand political change, Erdoğan was already a popular figure in the Middle East. His forthright denunciation of Israeli actions, his political reforms, Turkey's prosperity, and his Islamist background gave him credibility across the Arab political spectrum. Early on in the Egyptian uprising, when Erdoğan called on Mubarak to listen to his people and leave office, it reinforced the notion that Turkey's leadership had unique insight into the politics of the Arab world due to cultural affinities and shared history—an idea that the AKP had been emphasizing since it came to power. Ankara had also convinced itself that Turkey had immense soft power in the Arab world, often citing as evidence of their regional leadership the large numbers of Arab tourists who flocked to Istanbul, the existence of Erdoğan posters in Palestinian refugee camps, and the preference that Arabs had developed for Turkish soap operas. On a practical level, its economic dynamism could help drive development in post-uprising countries desperately in need of investment. Turkey certainly had its share of business people willing to put money into Egypt, Tunisia, and Libya.

The AKP seemed to offer something far more profound than money, though. It provided a potential resolution to a vexing problem in Arab politics, namely, that Arab leaders, such as Mubarak, forced citizens to choose between his authoritarianism and the Islamism of the Muslim Brotherhood and all the social strictures this was alleged to have entailed. In the process, the Egyptian leader neutered all other potential tendencies. The resulting social tensions played to what had been Mubarak's strength before the January 25 uprising—ensuring stability at the end of rattan canes and metal truncheons. In the early 2000s, it seemed the AKP offered a way forward with its consensual approach that appealed to Islamists and liberals alike. For Arab Islamists, the party provided a critical lesson in how to overcome barriers to political power and while doing so remake a once-hostile public arena. For the Middle East's liberals, the AKP demonstrated that Islamists were not necessarily hostile to liberal ideas and progressive political reforms.

These reasons explained the considerable buzz in Ankara and Washington about the so-called Turkish model. Publicly, the Turks were reluctant to embrace the term, preferring *inspiration* and *example*. In the mid-2000s, the Bush administration invoked the Turkish model during what was dubbed the "global war on terror" and the White House's big push for democracy in the Arab world.[38] Given the profound unpopularity of the United States and especially Bush among Turks, Ankara feared that Washington's reference to the Turkish model would taint Turkey at precisely the moment Turkish leaders were seeking better ties in the Arab world. The AKP also recoiled at the idea because two decades prior the Turkish model referred to something entirely different. In the 1980s, Turkey's elite and a grab bag of American and European Cold Warriors regarded the Turkish military's robust presence in the politics of the country as the best way of ensuring Turkish democracy, which was no democracy at all. During that era, that the officers repressed pious Turks, Kurds, and leftists mattered little as long as Turkey's Western orientation remained secure.

Still, after the 2011 uprisings, senior Turkish officials acknowledged privately that Turkey under the AKP was indeed a model from which the Arabs were learning how to build more democratic and prosperous societies; in time, they overcame their reservations and began using the term themselves. In a piece for Al Jazeera's English-language website, one of Erdoğan's senior advisors, the George Washington University–educated İbrahim Kalın, reflected on how Ankara cultivated its influence in the region:

> This engagement policy has paid off in several ways, in the process raising Turkey's profile in the region. Arab intellectuals, activists, and youth leaders of different political inclinations have taken a keen interest in what some describe as the "Turkish model." Turkey's stable democracy, growing economy, and proactive foreign policy have generated growing appreciation of the country's achievements, which has augmented its "soft power" in the region.[39]

This, of course, was to be expected from someone so closely connected to the highest echelons of the AKP, but it reflected the way in which the Turks viewed their place in the Middle East more broadly. Another prominent Turk, Mustafa Akyol, who had been a leading voice in advancing the idea of liberal Islam, wrote during the summer of 2011, "The AKP's Turkey is not just an economic success ... Turkey's new system, which incorporates both secular democracy and Islamic values, offers an attractive model."[40]

Obama had been bullish on Turkey from the time he took office and included an implicit reference to the Turkish model in a speech he delivered to the Grand National Assembly in Ankara in April 2009. In private discussions administration officials were more explicit, indicating that the White House sought to hold Turkey out as a model for countries in the Muslim world. The president was so positive that Ankara could play a critical role in the Middle East after the uprisings that Erdoğan was the first person he reportedly asked to call after Mubarak fell. The president and his team were not alone, of course. A consensus among the foreign policy community was that Turkey had important lessons for Arabs as they sought to make sense of their emerging realities. In early February 2011, the London School of Economics's Fawaz Gerges declared to Reuters, "The only effective, working model in the Middle East is the Turkish model. There is nothing else."[41] Similarly, Hugh Pope, who covered Turkey for the *Wall Street Journal* in the 1990s and then ran the Istanbul office of the International Crisis Group—a nongovernmental organization devoted to "preventing and resolving deadly conflict"—told the *New York Times* this:

> Turkey is the envy of the Arab world. It has moved to a robust democracy, has a genuinely elected leader who seems to speak for the popular mood, has products that are popular from Afghanistan to Morocco—including dozens of sitcoms dubbed into Arabic that are on TV sets everywhere—and an economy that is worth about half of the whole Arab world put together.[42]

Even for analysts with a reputation for skepticism, the sense was that Turkey was in a unique position to play an important role in the Arab world. Walter Russell Mead, who had done stints at the Council on Foreign Relations and Yale University before taking up posts at the Hudson Institute and Bard College, affirmed it in his blog for *The American Interest*:

> Now that Prime Minister Erdogan . . . has defeated Turkey's secularists, he is looking to rebuild Turkey's role as the leader of the Islamic

world. In the Middle East he will have some success. The prestige of Turkey's modernization and the admiration for its democratic transition from French-style secularism to something more, well, American gives him lots of prestige—especially in the ex-Ottoman world. This is a change.[43]

Mead was hardly carried away with the romance of the moment, however. He warned—presciently—that as the Turks became more deeply involved in Arab politics, they would find little joy and copious frustration.

Elite opinion about Turkey and its role in the Middle East was perhaps best expressed in a Task Force report on US-Turkey relations that the Council on Foreign Relations sponsored in 2011 and 2012. The Task Force, composed of twenty-three regional experts and former foreign policy practitioners and had as its co-chairs former secretary of state Madeleine Albright and former national security advisor Stephen J. Hadley, struck a balanced tone, but was nevertheless optimistic about Turkish influence in the region:

> The United States and Turkey have an opportunity to cooperate in helping forge a more democratic and prosperous Middle East. The United States has already identified this opportunity and has sought to work with Turkey on "soft landings" for Arab countries that have experienced uprisings. Turkey is not only a good partner in this effort but also Washington's only partner with enough clout in enough countries in the region to play this role.[44]

The discussion on Turkey was based on two assumptions—that the country's transition to democracy would proceed apace under the AKP and that Ankara was uniquely positioned to be a positive force for democratization in the Arab world. Both propositions would ultimately prove faulty.

THE ARC OF ACADEMIA

It was not just the prominent journalists, news magazines, and think tankers who were responding to the eye-popping changes unfolding in the Middle East. For the better part of three decades, Western academia was asking some version of the following questions: Why and how do some political systems change, but others do not? Why are Middle Eastern countries so seemingly resistant to democratic change? Once change got under way in the region in 2010 and 2011, academics also began to weigh in, though they did so with a degree of nuance and caution that ran in direct contrast to the enthusiasm of the op-eds, editorials, and analyses that dominated the newspapers, opinion magazines, and policy journals.

Rashid Khalidi, the Edward Said professor of modern Arab studies at Columbia University, at one time an advisor to the Palestinian Liberation Organization, and a member of one of Jerusalem's most prominent families, offered an early reflection on the uprisings for *The Nation* magazine in March 2011. Khalidi scorned the Western media's penchant for portraying Arabs almost exclusively as "terrorists, the omnipresent bearded radicals and their veiled companions trying to impose Sharia and the corrupt, brutal despots who were the only option for the control of such undesirables" when the preceding three months had proven what Khalidi and anyone else who cared to pay attention already knew. Authoritarianism may have marked Middle Eastern politics, and the region had its share of extremists, but it was also characterized by a pluralism of ideas, ideological richness, and sophisticated debates among Arabs about the present and future of their societies. In the process of making the dramatic—and accurate point—that the Middle East is not "uniquely unsuited to democracy," Khalidi nevertheless cautioned his readers that "Nothing has yet been resolved in any Arab country."[45] He was hopeful, of course, but unlike other commentators at the time—who gave themselves intellectual alibis with trite phrases like "we still do not know yet what will happen," "anything is possible," and "history has yet to be written" before declaring that democracy had, in fact, arrived in the Arab world—Khalidi actually grasped the monumental task that lay before Arab revolutionaries. As scholars have long understood, transitions to democracy fail far more often than they succeed.[46]

The day after the Egyptian uprising began, Khalidi's colleague from the University of Illinois, Asef Bayat, published an article called "The Arab Street" in the widely read ForeignPolicy.com in which he averred that Middle Eastern leaders might very well prevail in the sudden confrontation with their own people. Yet, Bayat continued, the long-term stability of their political systems was unlikely, especially if they sought to secure political quiescence through the subsidies and social safety nets Arab states could not actually afford. Bayat argued that societies that had grown more complex and sophisticated through urbanization, increased visibility of women, and new information flows would pose an ongoing risk for the authoritarians of the region.[47]

To the trained ear, a vast literature echoed in both Khalidi's and Bayat's articles. Most of this work appeared in journals and books that few people outside academic circles ever read but nevertheless had crept into the more popular commentary about the uprisings. Khalidi's reference to prerequisites for more democratic political systems was a nod to a famous American sociologist named Seymour Martin Lipset, who outlined in his 1958 article "Some Social Requisites of Democracy: Economic Development and Political Legitimacy" the necessary political and economic development for democracies. These included a growing middle class, legitimacy and effectiveness of government, and "cross-cutting politically relevant affiliations" that serve to mitigate political tension—for example, a two-party political system.[48] Lipset was a towering figure in American social science and his article had a profound influence on the way scholars thought about the development and sustainability of democracy. For his part, when Bayat invoked "developmentalist authoritarian regimes" and "rent-subsidized welfare handouts," he was alluding to the academic work on the durability of nondemocratic political systems. He was clear that he did not think these types of political systems were stable in the long term, but his language was nevertheless derived from a strand of the authoritarian stability literature that examined what is referred to as the rentier state. In these political systems, citizens are neither taxed nor represented and the government is not accountable to them. The government derives revenues from the export of oil, but also strategic location. The natural gas-wealthy state of Qatar is a textbook example of a rentier state. Egypt, which does tax its citizens to varying degrees of effectiveness, is a rentier state in another way. Although it has modest amounts of oil and gas, the Egyptians derive strategic rent from external actors—primarily the United States—because of their location adjacent to Israel and on the Suez Canal, a vital waterway for global trade and energy security. As a result, since 1948 the United States has transferred almost $80 billion in the form of military assistance and economic aid to Egypt.[49]

Lipset's work represents one end of an arc of academic literature; work on authoritarian stability represents the other. At the time that Lipset wrote his article, Western—but particularly American—social scientists were developing theories about how societies change that came to be known as the *modernization paradigm.* These hypotheses and theories addressed a variety of issues, but the underlying assumption was that political systems in countries that used to be called "less developing" would ultimately converge with those of industrialized democracies as they adopted modern practices. The modernization paradigm fell out of favor in the 1970s primarily because, based as it was on the Western experience, it assumed that all countries developed along a similar linear path. Nevertheless, the seductive power of the theories encompassed within the paradigm and Lipset's idea of prerequisites for democratic change lived on in various forms in academic and policy debates as well as the work of columnists at major newspapers.

When it came to the Middle East specifically, the search for democracy picked up in the late 1980s. At the time, few scholars working on the region believed that the Arab world was on the cusp of democratic transitions, but an influential few certainly perceived the stirrings of democratic change. At the annual meeting of the Middle East Studies Association of North America in 1987, Georgetown University's Michael Hudson, then president of the organization, admonished his members "to be more observant of the variety and degrees of authoritarianism and democracy in the Middle East, without sacrificing our critical judgement of the region's harsh political realities."[50] Hudson was careful to distinguish between democracy, which is a type of political system, and democratization, which is a process of political change. He allowed that although no democracies were in the Arab world, the signs of "democratization are significant, but they are not exactly robust."[51] Hudson's caveated optimism was based on three developments that, from his perspective, helped create an environment conducive to progressive political change: democratization in other regions was providing a demonstration effect for the Arab world, civil society organizations were growing in the Middle East, and authoritarian political systems were reaching a point where they were incapable of managing increasingly complex societies.[52]

That rioting swept through Algeria in 1988 and protests engulfed parts of Jordan in 1989 seemed to provide evidence for Hudson's claims. It was not so much that these demonstrations occurred—though an argument could be made that civil society and international demonstration effects might have played a role—but rather the way governments responded to these challenges was a sign to some scholars that democratization was under way. In Algeria, rioters did not make explicit calls for political liberalization and democracy, though demonstrators were vocal in their demand for an end to *hogra*—arbitrary government. Shaken at the intensity of the anger of the large numbers of Algerians who turned out into the streets, Algeria's president initiated political reforms, including a new constitution—hailed as the most liberal in the Arab world—that culminated in what was promised to be free and fair elections in 1991 and 1992. The apparently wide-ranging aspects of changes in Algeria led to the conclusion that the military and political elite had accommodated themselves to democratic reforms.[53] After the 1988 riots, Algeria became a poster child for the democratization that observers had long expected but never seemed to materialize in the Middle East. Scholars pointed out that Algeria was the only country with an oil-based economy to democratize and Hudson, shedding his previous caution, declared Algeria to be "the most democratic country in the Arab world."[54] Even after a January 1992 coup d'état that nullified the elections the Islamic Salvation Front (FIS) was set to win, there was a sense among some analysts that a genuine process of democratization had been short-circuited; never mind that it had been overseen by people—notably, the army, but also the dominant civilian elite that had run Algeria continuously since it threw off French colonial rule—whose commitment to progressive political change had not previously existed.[55] The Algerian sociologist Lahouari Addi lamented the military's intervention, but remained surprisingly positive about his country's prospects. Writing in the March–April 1992 edition of the *Middle East Report*—a small, but important magazine that a group of academics ran out of a tiny office in Washington—Addi wrote, "Algeria's social elite, fearing the political dynamics that the FIS [*sic*] accession to power might set in motion, pressed the military to intervene, putting Algeria to a test that will certainly be difficult in the short term but probably productive in the long run."[56]

The response to Jordan's April 1989 food riots was similar, both by the government and by the conclusions of academic Middle East watchers. The Jordanian protests came at the end of a decade of deteriorating economic conditions. To reverse the slide, Jordan turned to the International Monetary Fund, which, in keeping with its usual practice, agreed to extend the government credit, but only if the Jordanians agreed to changes that were likely to be painful. Among the reforms were changes to subsidies on basic foodstuffs that led to steep price increases. The anger turned into three days of protests that left five people dead and almost three dozen injured.[57] King Hussein responded to the unrest quickly, sacking the government, announcing parliamentary elections (the first since the mid-1960s), issuing an amnesty for political prisoners, and allowing political parties to organize. A little more than two years after the riots, the king and the opposition agreed on "guidelines for the conduct of political party activity" that was enshrined in a national charter.[58] Observers quite rightly greeted this all as very good news, celebrating Jordan's new "relatively open political system" and "increasingly effective" political parties.[59] Another analyst referred to the early 1990s as the "Jordanian *glasnost*."[60] Jordan had an ostensible advantage over other countries because it had a

> heritage of associational life [that] has facilitated a tentative dialogue between regime[s] and opposition. Moreover, the economic crises in these countries [Tunisia and Jordan] are not as desperate as the one that brought about the collapse of the ruling bargain in Algeria. For these reasons, the "space" for fashioning new, more democratic bargains may be widening . . . in Jordan.[61]

Still other observers were more guarded in their analysis of developments in Jordan, admitting that the controlled, top-down way in which change was taking place opened up the possibility of reversals, but the country was nevertheless in "a phase of democratic development."[62]

This academic literature on democratization also looked at Morocco, Tunisia, and Egypt—the last of which Hudson called "a trailblazing case" of democratization—whose leaders had permitted various degrees of pluralism in the 1980s and 1990s.[63] Of course, not everyone was as sanguine as Hudson, but analysts tended to focus on a similar mix of countries and struck similar themes concerning democratization.[64] It was true that leaders in these countries had begun to permit a more open politics in which political parties operated relatively freely, it became easier to establish associations and nongovernmental organizations, parliamentary elections took place, and though the heavy hand of censorship in the press was not lifted it did become less burdensome for journalists and editors. There was nothing inaccurate about these observations, but they were often used to draw premature conclusions about democratization in the Middle East. How else could one conclude that Egypt in the 1980s and early 1990s was comparable to "Turkey and Israel in terms of democratization" or that Algeria's steps forward were permanent?[65]

Other scholars also regarded the apparently emerging pluralism in the Middle East positively, but they sought to place these developments in an intellectual framework to understand the process of democratic political change once it had begun and, importantly, to provide a way in which they could better predict democratization. Analysts turned to the experiences of Latin America, southern Europe (Spain, Portugal, and Greece), and Eastern Europe—regions that had experienced the so-called Third Wave of democracy of the 1980s and 1990s—as bases of comparison. Middle East experts and democratization theorists surmised that if the developments that led to political change in Latin America, for example, were present in the Middle Eastern countries, the likelihood for democratization in those places was greater. Of particular interest was what would happen if a leader lost the support of constituents who had benefited from the political system and their place in it. The idea was that if citizens organized in response to this development, it might produce a major political change. This notion was in part a reason for the voluminous work during the 1990s on the effect private, voluntary groups like legal aid societies, government watchdogs, women's organizations, human rights activists, and others—what scholars call civil society organizations—had on Middle Eastern politics.

Attention on elections was sustained. No one ever believed that staging a vote constituted a democracy, but the belief was that elections would have a dynamic effect on politics in a way that made democratic political change more likely. Elections would beget more elections, which would produce demands for additional liberalization until a transition to democracy occurred. Others investigated the viability of pacts in which the opposition and authoritarian leadership agree on a set of guarantees, privileges, and exemptions (notably amnesty) for defenders of the old political system in exchange for democratic politics. Central to the paradigm was also the idea that democracy could happen anywhere, that Lipset's prerequisites of an expanding middle class, effective governance, legitimacy, and the importance of independent political parties were actually unnecessary for countries to escape authoritarianism for democratic politics.

In time, however, the glimmers of democratization that Hudson and others identified proved more apparent than real. For its part, the transitions paradigm turned out to be interesting observations about change in parts of the world that were decidedly not generalizable to the Middle East.[66] Almost as soon as Algeria fell into civil war in 1992 after the country's senior military officers voided parliamentary election results that would have given the Islamic Salvation Front a majority in the National Assembly, Hosni Mubarak undertook a major crackdown on the Muslim Brotherhood. The same year, Egypt's almost decade-long fight with the extremists of a homegrown terrorist organization called al-Gamaa al-Islamiyya began. It was also in the early 1990s when democratization in Jordan and Morocco turned out to be more apparent.

These developments led to a new research program, especially among political scientists who asked why Middle Eastern countries were seemingly so impervious to democratic political change. They began answering this question by specifically rejecting the idea that the Arab world's democracy deficit was related to the fact that the vast majority of people who live there are Arab, most of whom are also Muslim. Few scholars ever actually made these kinds of cultural arguments, though some did. Princeton University's Bernard Lewis and Harvard University's Samuel Huntington came close with controversial arguments about the "roots of Muslim rage" and the "clash of civilizations," yet the sweeping generalizations that both scholars employed weakened their claims.[67] In 1988, a Palestinian professor of history named Hisham Sharabi published a book called *Neopatriarchy: A Theory of Distorted Change in Arab Society* in which he argued that Arab society was, by its nature, oppressive.

In making the argument, Sharabi was inviting the opprobrium of his fellow scholars, who immediately dismissed the idea that culture contributed to political outcomes.

Setting aside the cultural arguments—and the controversies they invited—scholars interested in the durability of authoritarian regimes produced a large, confusing, and contradictory but nevertheless illuminating literature on the way Middle Eastern countries worked.[68] In one important article, Georgetown University's Daniel Brumberg turned Michael Hudson's indicators of democratization on their head.[69] The authorization of political parties, staging parliamentary elections, a freer press, and an active civil society were actually intended to make authoritarian systems more stable and durable by accommodating some demands from citizens for more open politics. "Liberalized autocracies" had some formal attributes that were found in democracies, but the pillars of these political systems remained force, coercion, and control rather than individual rights and freedoms.

The counterintuitive idea of the liberalized autocracy in which Middle Eastern authoritarians skillfully manage political challenge through political openings was deeply attractive. Using the concept as a point of departure, scholars looked at the way authoritarian leaders worked to divide their opponents to diminish the impact of potential political challenges.[70] They also discovered that by legalizing civil society organizations and tying them down in regulations, leaders could render these groups ineffective.[71] Elections came to be seen not as an important step in democratization but as a way leaders produced loyal parliaments that endowed nondemocratic regimes with a gloss of popular legitimacy.[72] This was precisely what Algeria's then minister of defense, Khaled Nezzar, was referring to when, on the eve of the country's ill-fated parliamentary elections in 1991, he declared that the military sought a "just mean" in the legislature, where Islamist representation was enough to make the polling look fair and legitimate, but not enough to challenge the prevailing political order. It was not to be, however. The Islamists actually won, the military stepped in, and, as a result, the country fell into a decade of civil war that killed anywhere from 100,000 to 200,000 Algerians. The Algerian disaster demonstrated the limits of the work on liberalized autocracies. Brumberg and others offered important insights, but something was too pat and neat about their underlying claims. Scholars implicitly constructed an evil genius image of Middle Eastern authoritarians who were adept at pushing political buttons and economic levers to manipulate society, all in the service of more efficient regimes. This was hardly the case in Algeria. Of course, Mubarak, Ben Ali, Qaddafi, and Erdoğan were always seeking to ensure their survival through some combination of bribery, coercion, and ideological appeals, which required some level of manipulation, but the world was a lot messier than the literature let on. As Smith College's Steven Heydemann astutely pointed out in an influential 2009 study for the Brookings Institution titled "Upgrading Authoritarianism in the Arab World," the liberalized autocracies in the Middle East were "a product more of trial and error than intentional design."[73] Regional leaders, who were neither masters of strategic manipulation nor bumbling fools, responded to pressures as they arose, discovering ways to deflect and undermine these challenges in the heat of political contestation. The end result may have seemed coherent, but it was fundamentally ad hoc.

The failure of expected transitions to democracy in the Middle East also led to new, more rigorous analysis of the capacity of leaders to use violence and fear to ensure a regime's survival. One influential idea posited that patrimonial regimes—a system in which a leader exercises power with few, if any, checks and balances and derives support exclusively from family, ethnic group, or region—tend to survive major political challenges and crises when foreign patrons are not concerned with the force that leaders of these systems unleash on their opponents.[74] International backing was important, but scholars also identified other variables that were critical to a regime's survival, including the financial wherewithal to field well-developed security forces in the first place (which was closely connected to foreign support); military and police forces that were actually subject to political influence, cronyism, and corruption; as well as societies in which relatively few people were mobilized in opposition to the government.[75]

The recognition of international support as a critical variable in the stability of authoritarian political systems was an issue that not only popped up in the academic literature, but also made its way into policy discussions on the Middle East, especially after the Bush administration launched its Freedom Agenda. In Washington, the debate was

cast in terms of how best the United States might support democratization in the region and considerably less emphasis was put on how
the policy choices of the past contributed both directly and indirectly
to the endurance of authoritarian political systems in the region.
Of course, former secretary of state Condoleezza Rice admitted to a
packed auditorium at the American University in Cairo in June 2005
that the United States had supported dictators in the Middle East for
sixty years in the name of stability, but warned that business as usual
was over.[76] Rice's speech was a momentary exception to the rule, however.[77] That rule was economic, political, diplomatic, and military support for countries that helped the United States pursue its interests in
the Middle East. This regional political order friendly to the exercise
of American power included Morocco, Egypt, Jordan, Saudi Arabia,
the United Arab Emirates, Qatar, and Turkey (a NATO ally), none of
which could be credibly considered a democracy or even democratizing.
The American investment of approximately $30 billion in Economic
Support Funds for Egypt's economy since 1962 is not a shining example
of Washington's altruism.[78] Rather, the economic support was based
on the idea that this assistance would generate economic development,
providing an Egyptian leadership aligned with the United States with
legitimacy, thereby helping ensure the stability of Egypt's political order
even if it was nondemocratic.

The ignominious departures of Ben Ali and Mubarak; the uprisings
in Libya, Syria, Yemen, and Bahrain; and the generalized political turbulence that engulfed the Middle East in the spring and summer of
2011 seemed to completely undermine the authoritarian stability literature. What was happening in the Middle East was not supposed to
happen. An entire research program had been dedicated to explaining
how regional leaders were adept at deflecting, diffusing, and undermining political challenges, but by mid-2011 they were succumbing to
people power in surprising numbers and with unexpected speed. The
meeting with intelligence analysts and outside experts on December 13,
2010, was emblematic of the problem. The intelligence community had
actually sensed that all was not well in the Middle East but was not
necessarily confident of its analysis. As a result, officials sought an external review of their thinking. The only problem was that having spent
the better part of the previous decade concerned with explaining why

authoritarian systems in the Middle East were impervious to change, the gathered academics and regional specialists could not imagine that these regimes were actually unstable.

The apparent failure of analysts to grasp what was happening in the Middle East in the run-up to the uprisings called for a reassessment of the way scholars approached their study of the region. The Henry L. Stimson Center, a small think tank in Washington, DC, then under the leadership of Ellen Laipson, a former deputy director of the National Intelligence Council, commissioned a study titled "Seismic Shift: Understanding Change in the Middle East." The report looked at the variance between how journalists, nongovernmental organizations, the private sector, international organizations, academics, and think tankers viewed the region before Ben Ali and Mubarak fell and how the subsequent political tumult across the region proved almost everyone spectacularly incorrect.

Laipson asked Gregory Gause, then of the University of Vermont and subsequently Texas A&M University, to write the postmortem on the academic community. Gause was the perfect person to undertake the Stimson Center's reassessment. He straddled the academic and policy communities extremely well. It was not unusual to walk into a meeting at the Pentagon or State Department and see Gause just off the plane from Burlington ready to offer advice to policymakers. He was also a leading advocate of the idea that Middle Eastern political systems were generally stable. This was welcome when it came to his specialty, Saudi Arabia and the Arab states of the Persian Gulf. The tendency among journalists and the policy community was to get whipped up into a frenzy over "potential crises" and "coming instability" if a Saudi leader sought treatment in Europe or the United States for some undisclosed ailment or if a demonstration in the predominantly Shia Eastern Province of Saudi Arabia—where the majority of the country's oil is located—turned violent. The expected crisis never seemed to happen, however. Although Gause regarded stability as a salient feature of Middle Eastern politics, he was always up front that he was likely to be correct in his analysis until the day he was not.

In the Stimson Center study as well as a shorter piece that appeared in the June/July 2011 edition of *Foreign Affairs*, Gause argued that Middle East specialists had given short shrift to the role of militaries

in politics, had misconstrued the influence of neoliberal economic reforms, which they argued strengthened regional authoritarians when
the exact opposite seemed to have happened, and overlooked the power
of a renewed sense of pan-Arabism.[79] He was quite correct that militaries had not been a central focus of the work on the Middle East, having
fallen out of favor in the 1970s given the practical research challenges
associated with working on organizations that were not inclined toward
transparency. Those few studies that did exist tended to place far too
much emphasis on the connection between the officers and regime stability.[80] After all, the Tunisian and Egyptian military high commands
moved against their leaders, seemingly undermining the notion that
the officers stood in the way of democratic transitions.[81]

Gause also made a strong point about the impact of neoliberal economic reforms that Middle Eastern leaders undertook in the 1990s and
2000s. Typically this included floating the exchange rate, privatization,
loosening protections on labor (to the extent that they existed), and
liberalizing trade, all in an effort to make countries both competitive
and attractive to international investors. The authoritarian stability
literature regarded economic reform as a way of tying the economic
interests of the business community, an important pillar of political
support, more closely with the prevailing political order. Scholars rea-
soned that if business leaders were benefiting from economic liberalization, they were considerably less likely to demand political change. Yet
Gause pointed out that though neoliberal reforms may have helped
certain groups close to Middle Eastern leaders reap significant financial benefits, the crony capitalism, graft, and the widely held perception of a large and growing gap between the wealthy and poor bred
profound resentment among the working class in particular. Although
economic grievances alone did not cause uprisings in the Middle East,
they certainly played a role in creating an overall environment of misery
well before people took to the streets in late 2010 and early 2011. Had
analysts working within the authoritarian stability framework not
overlooked the effect of neoliberal reforms on groups other than elite
supporters of the regimes, they might have had better insight into the
political risks associated with these changes.

Finally, Gause criticized analysts for ignoring a latent sense of pan-
Arabism that helped produce the communal wave of protest across the

region. Pan-Arabism was from another era, the stuff of black-and-white newsreels featuring Gamal Abdel Nasser inspiring the masses across the region from atop a building in Tahrir Square. It had been some time since scholars had given the idea that in the Arab world, where people share a language and generally accept a set of myths about a common history, political and social developments can have a dynamic effect across borders from North Africa to the Levant and from there to Iraq and the Arab states of the Persian Gulf. Gause may have been onto something. Analysts have grown perhaps too fearful of being labeled Orientalists to make arguments tinged with references to culture. Ironically, Arabs are not. Yet it is hard to say with any certainty that a sense of ethnic-cultural-linguistic-historical solidarity influenced the way in which Arabs perceived their chances of bringing down dictators after Tunisia's Ben Ali was driven from power.

Gause warned that analysts might very well look back and determine that the authoritarian literature was accurate given that no country in the region had, as of his writing in the spring of 2011, become a democracy. His caveat was important, but the whole undertaking suggested that in the moment of enthusiasm surrounding the sudden explosion of people power in the Middle East, a lot of journalists, editors, government officials, and analysts expected—either explicitly or implicitly—that transitions to democracy would follow. This was only a few months after two dictators had fallen, which came only a few months after the encounter in Northern Virginia between intelligence analysts and outside experts who had determined that stability was the dominant trend in the region, which, in turn, came after decades worth of work on the durability of authoritarian systems when expected democratic transitions did not materialize in the late 1980s and early 1990s. Since the exhilarating days of early 2011, authoritarianism has proven far more resilient than many expected. This durability hardly implies stability, however. Body counts and bombings are now the daily fare for many Middle Easterners. Those who have been spared the worst of the violence still endure political turmoil, economic decline, and uncertainty in societies that are fragmenting along ethnic, sectarian, and ideological lines. It was not supposed to be this way. How and why did this happen?

2

Bread! Freedom! Social Justice!

WITH THE EXCEPTION OF a handful of people, few in the United States had ever heard of Sidi Bouzid until late December 2010. Located in the north central region of Tunisia, 175 miles due south from the capital Tunis, it is a city of a little more than 120,000 people. Other than being the seat of the governorate that goes by the same name, it has little going for it. Its white-washed buildings and dusty streets could be any secondary town in the region that has too little of everything—jobs, education, government services. Unlikely as it may seem, Sidi Bouzid has a place in twentieth-century American history. On Valentine's Day 1943, a force from Germany's 10th and 21st Panzer divisions overwhelmed elements of the American II Corps in the Battle of Sidi Bouzid. A few days later, American forces were again routed fifty miles to the west at Kasserine Pass, where they had regrouped. When it was all over, between 2,000 and 2,500 American soldiers had been killed and at least that many were missing. These engagements were the first between American and German forces in World War II. They were an important moment for US forces. The lessons and scars the inexperienced American officers took from Sidi Bouzid and Kasserine paved the way for future victories.[1] Of course, the collapse at Sidi Bouzid was not of the same scale or importance as, for example, Dunkirk, Pearl Harbor, or the German blitz through the Ardennes. It is likely for this reason that the war in North Africa, dubbed Operation Torch, and the sacrifices made there are often an afterthought. Despite the presence in

Tunisia of an American military cemetery with 2,841 graves, the entire campaign—the fighting in Sidi Bouzid included—has faded from American collective memory of World War II. Almost seven decades after the American defeat there, however, the city became central to the mythology of the "new" Middle East.

It was in Sidi Bouzid that Tunisia's so-called Jasmine Revolution and what came to be known erroneously as the Arab Spring began. Almost immediately on his death in early January 2011, Mohammed al-Bouazizi—the twenty-eight-year-old fruit and vegetable seller whose act of self-immolation triggered the Tunisian uprising—became a composite sketch of a dissatisfied generation and a martyr for those of all ages who dreamed of a democratic future. That Bouazizi subsisted on the only work he could find, lived in a modest provincial city, and was allegedly slapped by a policewoman for failing to heed her warnings about lacking proper permits are all anyone who never paid attention to Tunisia before needed to know about the man. With his death and the month-long demonstrations it initiated, Bouazizi became the personification of the Arab youth bulge. Although the demographic included females, the way the media and policymakers used the term always referred to that large pool of unemployed but often educated young men who have no prospects for a job and thus no dowry for a wife. In the all too simplistic discussion of this phenomenon among pundits and journalists, these people are left seething in their humiliation, destined to become terrorists or economic migrants living in Parisian *banlieues*—suburbs that have become notorious for their alienated and angry immigrant communities. Bouazizi was actually an outlier in this narrative. He chose to kill himself, though he was not the first young Tunisian to set himself on fire. Bouazizi's suicide came at the right, albeit unpredictable, moment. His story offered coherence to the subsequent uprisings that moved west to Algeria then swept east to Egypt and Bahrain before doubling back across North Africa to Libya and Morocco and then finally looping into the heart of the Levant, where Syria's political ferment became a slaughter. Yet the way that observers imagined the frustrated and financially stressed Tunisian fruit seller as a representation of what ailed the Middle East obscured the messy interplay of economics, human dignity, and democracy.

ECONOMIC GRIEVANCES?

According to any number of commentators who popped up on the cable news networks, National Public Radio, Al Jazeera, and the BBC, the reason Bouazizi killed himself and the explanation for why millions of Arabs (as well as large numbers of Turks some years later) turned out in the street demanding change were economic grievances. This was deeply appealing on a number of levels. First, the Middle East has many Bouazizis—millions—and to the extent that economic pain was a common thread in the regional tumult, it was an easy template for understanding why young people in Sidi Bouzid, Cairo, Benghazi, Sanaa, Manama, and even in Istanbul were out in the streets. Second, if Bouazizi's grievances and those of protesters throughout the region were primarily economic, a set of straightforward policies that would mitigate the problems facing young Middle Easterners was easy to imagine. Yet the role that economics played in the story that began in Sidi Bouzid in December 2010 is somewhat different from the one-dimensional emphasis on material grievances that was offered up as the uprisings were happening. There had long been economic struggles in Tunisia, Egypt, Libya, Turkey, and elsewhere in the Middle East as leaders developed legitimacy for their regimes through economic progress, which had been uneven. The mass demonstrations were, however, far more complicated affairs than the mere protests of a given economy's losers, especially since the uprisings occurred at a moment of relative prosperity. Rather, the downfalls of Ben Ali, Mubarak, and Qaddafi as well as the 2013 challenge to Erdoğan's rule fused the economy—or more precisely the perception of it—with demands for justice, respect, and representative government.

Despite the vast differences among these countries, they had, at a level of abstraction, followed similar trajectories. In each place, a major event occurred—a coup (Egypt and Libya), independence (Tunisia), victory in a war of independence (Turkey)—that marked the passing of the old order. Despite heroic official histories, new political and economic orders did not materialize fully formed but were the result of trial-and-error efforts to deal with complex problems. In Tunisia, Egypt, Libya, and Turkey, new leaders confronted, among other difficulties, economic underdevelopment. Their answer was state-directed development that over time gave way to neoliberal economic reforms.

These transitions were hardly smooth. The arc of economic development and economic policymaking in all four countries reveals considerable suffering when the state was the primary economic actor and
later when leaders turned toward free markets and liberal economies.
Lost in all of the commentary about economic grievances, however,
was that Tunisia, Egypt, Turkey, and even Libya were widely regarded
as either success stories, attractive emerging markets, or countries with
significant economic potential. If that was the case, how had economics
become such a popular, if not entirely powerful, explanation of what
drove demands for change in the Middle East?

After Zine al-Abidine Ben Ali came to power in a palace coup in
November 1987, Tunisians and foreign observers had considerable hope
that the former police general, interior minister, and prime minister
would usher in a period of political and economic reform. The French-
language press, which referred to Ben Ali's coup as *l'événement*—the
event—emphasized how the change in leadership represented the re-
assertion of Tunisian dignity, did not disrupt the country's stability,
and represented a spirit of renewal and purification.[2] Along with the
overwrought rhetoric about the coming of a "truly democratic" society,
the Tunisian media expressed confidence that Ben Ali, as the leader
of a new generation, would inject dynamism into a society that inefficient state bureaucracies had come to dominate. Nowhere had this
been more apparent than in the economy.

Since independence in 1956, the Tunisians had built an economy in
which the state was the central actor. Bureaucrats allocated resources,
determined prices, and nurtured the development of large state-owned
companies in diverse sectors of the economy. This approach had less
to do with ideology than with necessity, however, because the private
capital that existed simply did not have the capacity to spur industrialization and economic development. Instead, Tunisia, like many
newly independent states in the mid-twentieth century, embarked on
what development economists call *import substitution industrialization*. The goal was exactly what the name implied: to displace imports
with domestically produced goods in an effort to develop a domestic
manufacturing base that over time would provide the capacity for more
sophisticated production of intermediate goods—inputs that were necessary for making other goods—and machinery.[3] Through high tariffs,

other preferential arrangements, and the investment of state resources, Tunisian economic planners sought to nurture local industries and spur the rapid transformation of an economy from one geared toward serving colonial interests to one that served national purposes.

The centralization of the economy served the interests of Tunisia's founding president, Habib Bourguiba, who sought to build a political system in which he and his political party, the Destourian Socialist Party, were paramount.[4] Despite the effort associated with state-directed development, Tunisia's economic performance was modest at best. A decade after independence, growth in gross domestic product (GDP) varied from 3.45 percent in 1966 to 0.16 percent in 1967 before spiking in 1968 to 10.41 percent, contracting again in 1969 to 4.75 percent and in 1970 to 4.67 percent. Inequality remained high throughout the early years after independence, with a third of the population living in poverty.[5] As a result, by the early 1970s, Bourguiba began a new approach to the economy that sought a balance between state planning and the private sector. Import substitution industrialization was not altogether abandoned and the state continued to play a lead role in the economy, but the private sector would now be given a greater opportunity to grow. To that end, the government made it easier for firms in the textile, semi-finished products, and light industrial sectors to do business both at home and abroad. Planners also put emphasis on developing the tourism sector, given Tunisia's excellent beaches, favorable climate, and proximity to Europe.

Even with the early problems associated with state-directed development, a relatively large middle class—by regional standards—emerged and the country enjoyed a period of economic stability. It was not to last, however. A serious economic downturn in the early part of the 1980s laid bare underlying economic challenges associated with distributing income to a growing population, an underdeveloped private sector, and large numbers of inefficient state-owned enterprises that had become a burden on the state. As a result of a foreign exchange crisis during the summer of 1986, in which Tunisia came perilously close to running out of money to pay for imports, the government announced a set of reforms called the Plan de Redressement Économique, or Economic Recovery Plan. Despite its less than sensational title, the initiative was far-reaching, aimed at essentially relieving Tunisian bureaucrats from the economic management of the country.[6] Specifically, the plan entailed a series of budget cuts that slashed investment in, and subsidies for, public sector firms. At the same time, major infrastructure projects were shelved. The government also sought to make Tunisia more attractive to both foreign and domestic investors by lifting restrictions on imports, exports, and profits; revising the investment law; and offering incentives for firms to set up operations in parts of the country that were less developed than the northeastern coastal region. Also, prices on manufactured goods, food, medicine, and gasoline were deregulated. Central to the reform plan was the proposal to privatize "all nonstrategic public companies" and to use the revenues from the sale of these firms to restructure the remaining state-owned sector.[7] To offset the pain of these changes, the government increased the minimum wage. All of this met the approval of the International Monetary Fund (IMF) and the World Bank, which, when the reforms were made law, provided the government with a $150 million loan.[8]

The plan seemed to have set the stage for Tunisia's economic growth of the 1990s and early 2000s, when the IMF and World Bank held the country out as an example of economic reform and growth.[9] Tunisia's average annual GDP growth rate in the two decades between 1986 and 2005 was a healthy 4.11 percent. Per capita income grew during that period from $967 to $2,458 and inflation on consumer products averaged 4.70 percent, though after 1995 it was no higher than 3.73 percent, falling as low as 2 percent in 2001 and 2005.[10] Real GDP grew steadily between 2005 and 2007 before a 2.5 percent falloff in 2008. As a result of the global economic downturn, however, Tunisia's GDP contracted in both 2009 and 2010, though overall it grew at a modest 3.04 and 3.51 percent.[11] Throughout this period, per capita income trended upward, increasing almost $1,000 from $3,190 to $4,150.[12] Rates of inflation, from a low of 2 percent to about 5 percent in 2008 before pulling back by half a percentage point in 2010, were manageable for Tunisian consumers, especially because their incomes were rising.

Since Ben Ali's fall, the World Bank, journalists, and Tunisian activists have uncovered a vast network of corruption connected to the former leader's extended family and their associates.[13] These revelations tend to reinforce the notion that income inequality was a significant problem in Tunisia. This is not the case. The most extensively used and easily interpreted measure of the difference between wealthy and poor—the Gini coefficient—reveals that in the years leading to the uprising, the level of inequality was moderate. A Gini value of 100 indicates total inequality, values of 50 and above are considered high inequality, and values between 30 and 50 are categorized as moderate. In Tunisia, the Gini coefficient hovered in the mid-30s in the five years before the uprising.[14] Among countries in the Middle East and North Africa for which data are available, Tunisia's level of inequality was in the middle range below Israel, Qatar, and Morocco, but above Egypt, Jordan, and Iraq.[15] Tunisia and the rest of the Arab world are similar to East Asia, South Asia, and Europe in this area and compare favorably with Africa, Latin America, the Caribbean, and the United States, where inequality is significantly higher.

For all of the apparent economic stability that Tunisia's macroeconomic performance produced, the country had a stubbornly high unemployment rate. Between 2006 and 2008, about 12.4 percent of the country's labor force was out of work. According to the World Bank, it increased almost a percentage point in 2009 before dropping slightly to 13 percent in the twelve months prior to the uprising. The reasons for this are varied, of course, but are in part related to Tunisia's small industrial base and that its most important sectors—mining, agriculture, and services (mostly tourism)—are cyclical and, in the cases of mineral extraction and food production, capital intensive. Yet even taking the country's employment problem into consideration, the statistics indicate that Tunisia's overall economic condition on the eve of the 2010 uprising was not all that different from others in the broad category of countries that the World Bank calls upper-middle income.

Egypt's story was in ways similar to Tunisia's, though the state management of the economy came about for different reasons. The young lieutenant colonels, majors, wing commanders, and captains who came to power in a coup d'état on July 23, 1952, were not socialists, though at least one of them claimed to be. The Free Officers, as they called themselves, actually had little in the way of an economic or political agenda beyond ridding the country of foreign influence and corruption.[16] Unlike Tunisia, Egypt had a well-developed private sector whose leading figures had long been involved in the political and economic life of the country. Before the coup, a number of political parties directly represented Egypt's private interests, including the Wafd Party—the word *wafd* means "delegation," and the party was founded by national-ist leaders who sought to represent Egypt at the post-World War I Paris peace conference in 1919. The party still exists, long outliving offshoots and other parties of the era. At the time, the Wafd had a mass following based on its agitation against the British presence in the country, but the Wafdists and other allegedly liberal parties could also at least lay claim to speak on behalf of an influential sector of society. Thus, in the fight to consolidate their power after deposing King Farouk and abolishing the monarchy, the Free Officers targeted these parties and the private interests they represented through a combination of land sequestration and nationalization of industries.[17] It helped that landowners presided over a system that was a modern analogue of feudalism, that the old elite was often corrupt and cooperated with the monarchy, and that many businesses were in the hands of Greeks, Italians, Armenians, Jews, and Lebanese—all of whom were well integrated in Egyptian society. Thus the destruction of private interests fit seamlessly with the Free Officers' nationalist narrative about ridding the country of a corrupt monarchy and uplifting the people.

Despite almost immediate land sequestration, widespread national-ization of the economy did not begin until July 1961, when Gamal Abdel Nasser, the leader of the Free Officers who had become president in 1956, issued decrees that brought the economy under direct state control. The government assumed full ownership of all banks and insurance compa-nies. In addition, fifty heavy industrial and shipping concerns were also nationalized. The decrees enjoined public utilities, textile manufactur-ers, food processors, department stores, hotels, and a variety of other businesses to cede anywhere from 10 to 50 percent ownership to the government.[18] The scale of the nationalization was significant, but a siz-able portion of the economy remained in private hands. That changed in 1964 with additional decrees that brought more of the economy under state control, including firms that had been only partly nationalized in 1961 and those that had avoided government takeover altogether.[19] Nasser's state-centered approach to economic development proved ben-eficial, at least initially. Overall, GDP increased dramatically in the early 1960s before declining sharply in 1966. Income per capita also improved modestly and steadily throughout the decade before declining in 1966, though it rebounded in 1968 and 1969.[20] The plight of the Egyptian worker was markedly improved—at least for the gainfully employed. Even so, in the fifteen years between the coup and the June 1967 war, the income of Egyptian workers in the professional, technical, commercial, and clerical sectors of the economy nearly doubled.[21] Also, by the mid-1960s, the wealthiest Egyptians' share of national income declined 10 percent, and the bottom 60 percent increased its share by 12 percent. These economic changes coincided with a dramatic expansion of educational opportunities. Whereas before the coup fewer than half of school-age children received a primary education, within a decade 90 percent of urban children and three-quarters of rural children were enrolled in school, though educational standards fell.[22] And by the late 1960s, the life expectancy of all Egyptians increased by three to four years. By all accounts, Egyptians were wealthier, healthier, and better educated thanks to reforms that the Free Officers, and Nasser himself as president, undertook. Egypt's economic performance was, of course, relative. Taken as an aggregate, the economy's overall growth rate was no better than 4 percent, the increase in per capita income was a modest 2 percent, and the country remained deeply in debt.[23] Still, in comparison with the half century before the Free Officers seized power, when the country's wealth was concentrated in the hands of very few, Nasser and his associates were able to generate enough economic development to address a variety of social and economic ills, giving the regime a powerful normative appeal on which to continue their efforts to build a new Egypt.

Over time, Egypt's version of state-directed development hit its limits. By the mid-1960s, even as the Egyptian government was taking over additional private property, Nasser and his advisors were forced to rethink their approach to economic policy. State-directed development proved costly. Because savings and investment rates were low, the Egyptian government financed its economic activities with external loans. In addition, foreign assistance from the Soviet Union decreased after its leader Nikita Khrushchev was pushed from power in October 1964. Growing military expenditures in the 1960s only added to the pressure on public finances.[24] The foreign borrowing and public indebtedness resulted in a balance of payments crisis—meaning Egypt simply did not have the finances to pay its creditors. By 1968, the challenges of managing an increasingly complex economy, and poor economic performance, led Nasser to reverse his position and gave the private sector a greater role in the economy.[25] Major change would have to wait until Anwar al-Sadat's presidency, after Nasser's death in September 1970.

Building on the prestige he garnered from the Egyptian military's redemptive performance in the October 1973 war, when the armed forces crossed the Suez Canal and breached Israel's defenses on its eastern bank, Sadat began to deepen the policy changes he started soon after he succeeded Nasser. Moving with purpose to make the Egyptian presidency his own, he cleared away Nasser's remaining supporters and issued the October Paper—actually issued in March 1974 but named October to draw on the heroism of the 1973 war—in which he charted a new course for Egypt's economic and social development. The most important innovation of the document was the *infitah*, or opening. After two decades of state-directed development, Sadat now proposed greater emphasis on the private sector and foreign direct investment.[26]

Even with all the important changes, however, the new economic opening "did not usher in a period of unfettered capitalism."[27] A vaguely socialist discourse remained part of the Egyptian leadership's public pronouncements and the state would continue to be the country's primary economic actor.[28] For example, government employees identified investment priorities—exports, technology, and services— and an investment authority housed within the Ministry of Economy screened all projects before obtaining approval from other applicable government agencies. At first, the *infitah* produced positive results. Macroeconomic indicators such as GDP, balance of payments, and overall domestic production all showed healthy gains between 1974 and 1977.[29] Yet Egypt's economic opening also coincided with increases in the country's trade deficit. This was an unintended consequence of the *infitah*'s success in forging a wealthier society and the development of a consumer culture. The Egyptians would have found it difficult to finance such an expansion but for the economic assistance they were receiving from abroad, especially from the United States, which was providing Egypt with almost $1 billion annually in economic support.[30] In addition to the problem of the trade imbalance was Egypt's heavy public indebtedness, a legacy of the egalitarian ethos of the Nasser era, during which the prices of basic goods were kept artificially low through subsidies. This may have been good social policy, but it put a strain on the government's budget, which was likely to get worse in a country with 2 to 3 percent annual population growth.[31] In January 1977, at the advice of the IMF, Sadat proposed reducing—but not eliminating—these subsidies.

Egyptians responded to subsidy reform with an outpouring of anger. Across Egypt, people took to the streets to protest the proposed changes. Sadat was forced to deploy the military in order to restore order. The Bread Riots, as they became known, had a profound effect on Egyptian economic policymaking for the following three decades. Sadat's vice president and successor, Hosni Mubarak, long resisted the kinds of reforms—such as changes to subsidies, privatization, floating the exchange rate, modifying price controls, loosening trade restrictions—that were typical of IMF structural adjustment programs. To be fair, over the course of the 1990s, Mubarak oversaw the introduction of a value-added sales tax, reduced subsidies on energy, decreased the number of goods that were banned for export, depreciated the pound, and agreed to sell off a little more than 300 state-owned companies. These were important changes, but they were episodic and almost always happened only after a bruising battle between Egyptian and IMF officials.[32]

In the end, though, it was not the IMF that provided economic relief for Egypt in the 1990s but rather Saddam Hussein and the Iraqi invasion of Kuwait. Egypt was justly rewarded for its deployment of 35,000 soldiers and officers to Saudi Arabia as part of Operations Desert Shield and Desert Storm. The United States, Arab Gulf states, European countries, Australia, Japan, and Canada wrote off, canceled, or otherwise forgave $30 billion of Egyptian debt.[33] Relieved of this burden, Cairo was able to qualify for loans at lower interest rates than would have previously been possible. The resulting injection of new financial resources "eased the pressure on the Egyptian budget."[34]

The debt relief of the 1990s provided some respite for Egypt's economic policymakers, but the economy continued to struggle. By 2000, per capita income was $1,461. That was almost double what it had been in 1990, but then it declined by about $400 during the following four years. Egypt also consistently fell short of absorbing the approximately

850,000 people who entered the job market each year.[35] Apart from them were the approximately 17 percent of the population living in poverty.[36] After two decades of resistance to American and IMF advice, Mubarak, by then entering his third decade in power, grudgingly accepted the necessity for thoroughgoing economic reforms. In late 2003, Egypt's senior economic decision makers convinced Mubarak to scrap a crawling peg exchange rate, in which the value of the Egyptian pound was permitted to fluctuate within a band of rates, and announced a free-floating system.[37] This was deeply controversial. The proponents of scrapping the crawling peg argued that the change would go a long way toward resolving the country's perennial problems of unemployment and underemployment because the cheaper pound resulting from floating the exchange rate would attract foreign investment to what was hoped would be a more globally competitive economy.[38] Critics of the proposal argued that despite the necessity for the Central Bank to expend valuable resources to maintain the value of the currency within a specified range, "[a relatively] expensive pound offered social benefits, which gave Egyptians purchasing power that they would not otherwise enjoy."[39] The proponents of exchange rate liberalization won the day, however, even if the Egyptians never actually undertook a free float. Instead, they opted for a managed float exchange rate, where Egypt's monetary authorities allowed the currency's value to adjust to market forces, but used the Central Bank's reserves to defend the pound's value when necessary. The Egyptians also ramped up their efforts to privatize the economy, which was another controversial move. Since the nationalizations of the 1950s and 1960s, the state-owned sector provided a range of social benefits that were critical to their workers and managers and thus, Egyptian officials had long believed, a source of social stability.[40] Still, the state-led sector was a significant drain on state resources. After Mubarak appointed a new government of technocrats and business executives in 2004—the dream team, as the pro-government press dubbed them—privatization began in earnest. Between that year and 2009, the Egyptians privatized 191 companies, netting the government about $7 billion. This was a significant increase over the rather tepid efforts of 1991 to 2003, when 210 companies were sold off, generating $3.1 billion for state coffers.[41]

The combination of changes to the exchange rate, privatization, Egypt's investment laws, and other reforms produced sustained macroeconomic growth over the last half of the 2000s. Analysts who had grown used to mostly bad news from Egypt were surprised at the record gains in foreign direct investment, significant growth in GDP, and per capita income. Growth rates were consistently above 4 percent, reaching as high as 7.2 percent in 2008 before contracting in 2009 along with most of the global economy. Even so, Egypt continued to grow at 4.7 and 5.2 percent in the two years before the uprising of January 25, 2011. Along with GDP growth, per capita income saw significant gains. In 2005, Egyptians earned on average $1,200 (in 2015 dollars) annually; by 2010 their incomes had increased by $1,471.[42] According to the World Bank and the Standardized World Income Inequality Database, the country's Gini coefficient was in the low 30s, meaning that Egypt's income inequality was in the moderate to low range. In 2007, foreign investors poured more money into Egypt than ever before, totaling $11 billion.[43] Even with the apparent economic progress, however, Egypt still grappled with large numbers of unemployed and underemployed people. Inflation also remained a perennial problem. In 2005, inflation in the price for consumer goods was almost 5 percent, climbing as high as 18 percent in 2008 before falling to about 11 percent in 2010. Gains in per capita income helped offset the rate of inflation, but that was only as long as the good economic times continued. Despite a generally mixed picture, Egyptian officials were positively buoyant about what they believed they had achieved. In 2006, the minister of finance declared confidently that Egypt was on the verge of sustainable economic development, which would create a cycle of foreign investment, employment, and international competitiveness. For all the self-satisfied rhetoric, it was actually hard to see the changes that the numbers from Egypt's Central Agency for Public Mobilization and Statistics reflected. Even the most influential of Egyptians harbored concerns that the good economic news masked serious problems.

One afternoon in the early fall of 2010, Taher Helmy sat behind his large desk on the twenty-first floor of the North Tower of Cairo's Nile City building and became visibly irritated. Taher is one of Egypt's most prominent attorneys. Among his many accomplishments, he was the first Arab lawyer admitted before the US Supreme Court. His Helmy, Hamza and Partners is an affiliate of the large international firm Baker & McKenzie, of which he is also a senior partner. Taher's father, Samir, was a colonel in the army engineering corps in the 1950s who strongly supported the

Free Officers. In the mid-1960s, he served as a reformist minister of industry and quietly began rolling back some of the most harmful aspects of Nasser's nationalizations. On October 6, 1981, along with Sadat and eight others, the elder Helmy—by then a deputy prime minister—was gunned down and killed during the parade commemorating Egypt's crossing of the Suez Canal in the October 1973 war. Although his father identified with the uncompromising nationalism and anti-colonialism of the Free Officers, Taher's worldview seemed to be more complex. He too is a proud Egyptian, but Sadat's *infitah* and turn toward the United States had a far greater impact on him than Nasserism. From 2003 to 2007, he served as the president of the American Chamber of Commerce in Egypt, which made perfect sense given that his demeanor, haircut, and voice evoked more midwestern Republican senator than Egyptian pharaoh. In keeping with both his position and his image, his policy preferences skewed heavily toward free market enterprise, promoting privatization, streamlining the bureaucracy, and instituting a 15 percent flat tax as the ways to unlock Egypt's prosperity. The source of Taher's discomfort that day was his concern not only that the legacies of state-directed development were still with Egypt, producing inefficiencies and holding the country back, but also that the reform program had left middle- and lower-income Egyptians out of the process. Looking out of his enormous office windows with their commanding view of the Cairo sprawl, Taher remarked, "This country has so much potential. Our economy could be like Turkey's." It was an odd and not-so-odd thing to say.

Although Tunisia, Egypt, and Libya were all at one time under the suzerainty of the Ottoman Empire, modern Turkey's political history was considerably different from the House of Osman's former North African domains. The Turkish Republic was established on October 29, 1923, not as a result of decolonization but rather of defeat and then rebirth. The Allied victory in World War I triggered the end of the Ottoman Empire that for 600 years had ruled—with varying degrees of efficacy—a vast territory that encompassed the Balkans, much of the Mediterranean Basin, and most of the Middle East. The Armistice of Mudros, which Ottoman representatives signed on October 30, 1918, aboard the British warship HMS *Agamemnon*, brought an end to the Empire's participation in the Great War and opened up Anatolia— the Turkish heartland—to the colonial pretensions of the victorious

British, French, Greeks, and Italians, who imposed the division of this territory in the 1920 Treaty of Sèvres. Turkish nationalists, notably an accomplished colonel named Mustafa Kemal and a group of like-minded officers from the Ottoman military, raised an army to resist both the Allies and the sultan. Their subsequent victories over those who sought to establish an Armenian state in eastern Anatolia—the French and then the Greeks—led to the 1923 Treaty of Lausanne. A few months later, the Republic of Turkey was declared. It was a triumphant moment for Mustafa Kemal, later known universally as Atatürk (Father of the Turks), and his followers, but the new country's leaders were also immediately confronted with the reality of a war-ravaged, desperately poor, and largely agrarian country.

The military officers and civilian professionals who were the republic's new elite regarded themselves as vanguards of social transformation. Consequently, they introduced modern agricultural technology, developed railroads, nationalized private firms, and established state-owned banks to finance industrialization and other enterprises to meet Turkey's basic needs. This statist economic approach of the 1930s, which was a direct response to the failure of the laissez-faire economics of the first years of the republic, is often described as a third way between socialism and capitalism. Yet it was, initially at least, less of a mixed system and instead placed the state at the center of the economy.[44] The shock of the worldwide economic crisis that began with the stock market crash on October 29, 1929, in New York gave the upper hand to elites within Turkey's ruling Republican People's Party (better known as CHP, its Turkish acronym) who supported an all-encompassing statism that would insulate the economy from the global business cycle through autarky. Others in the party regarded statism as a necessary but temporary stage in the country's economic development given the underdevelopment of the private sector and its inability to finance industrialization.[45] In this way, Turkey at independence was no different from Tunisia and Egypt.

The results of Turkey's experiment with statism were mixed. By the late 1930s, the Turks had made some progress establishing a consumer goods sector, which saved valuable foreign exchange, but large public investments in the statist economy and the increasing number of bureaucrats to go with it placed pressure on the government's budget.[46]

The German invasion of Poland in September 1939 and the eruption of World War II frustrated Ankara's goal of pushing into a new stage of state-directed development that included the production of intermediate goods like chemicals, steel, and cement. The Turks signed a Treaty of Friendship with Nazi Germany in 1941 and continued to do business with its largest trading partner, but this did little to slow the country's wartime economic slide.[47]

During the war, Turkey suffered from high inflation and shortages of basic goods such as bread, which had to be rationed in early 1942.[48] The government responded by bringing public companies under greater control through the imposition of price controls and oversight from the ministries. In the agricultural sector, the state forced farmers to sell their crops to the government at fixed prices.[49] These efforts failed to address the problem of scarcity, encouraged hoarding, and had an adverse effect on the performance of the industrial sector, compounding Turkey's already challenging economic circumstances.

The 1950s would bring significant political and economic changes in Turkey. In 1946, Turkey's president, İsmet İnönü, ended single-party politics when he authorized the establishment of the Democrat Party. The new party won a parliamentary majority in the 1950 general elections, bringing the CHP's almost three-decade dominance to an end. On assuming office, the Democrats greatly deemphasized statism, leaving the industrial sector to private concerns and reinvigorating agriculture, which the CHP's planners had long neglected. Between 1950 and 1953, Turkey's economy grew at 10 percent. The economy then ran into trouble. The borrowing that went into the development of agriculture and infrastructure created large budget deficits and the end of the conflict on the Korean Peninsula, in which 15,000 Turks fought, meant an end to the economic stimulus that went with it. For all the dynamism of the economy between 1950 and 1953, foreign direct investment was scant and exports languished because of an overvalued lira. As a result, Turkey found itself in a foreign exchange crunch, forcing the government to impose restrictions on imports to conserve hard currency. By 1958, the situation had become so dire that Ankara was on the cusp of a liquidity crisis.[50] Unable to borrow funds from international markets, the government devalued the lira, cut spending, and lifted restrictions on imports in an effort to make Turkey more competitive, spur economic activity, and rationalize the government's balance sheet.[51]

In late May 1960, a group of thirty-seven mostly junior military officers representing different factions within the officer corps ousted Prime Minister Adnan Menderes. Plotting and conspiracies within the military had been common throughout much of the previous decade, but the immediate reason for the coup was the officers' discontent with the authoritarian drift of the Democrats, the deleterious effects of the party's economic policies, its threat to the officers' specific view of Turkish morality, and the disrespect with which Menderes and other Democrat leaders treated the military.[52] Menderes and his ministers of finance and foreign affairs were hanged in September 1961, two months after a new constitution came into force that restructured the Turkish polity. These changes coincided with a new approach to the economy, which in a number of respects resembled the statist period of the 1930s.

The new order, which the CHP led after it garnered the most votes in the October 1961 general elections, included import substitution industrialization. The government empowered a new bureaucracy, the State Planning Organization (SPO), to oversee planning in both the public and the private sectors and across industries. Initially, the new, more intensive approach to state-directed development showed some promise. At the end of the first five-year plan, which lasted from 1968 to 1972, Turkey's economy had experienced significant growth. Yet the overall growth picture obscured continuing significant problems. Despite investment in the industrial and intermediate goods sectors, the country was still importing more than the SPO wanted, putting a strain on the Central Bank's reserves of foreign currency. To avoid a balance of payments crisis, Ankara turned to the IMF in 1970 to help stabilize the economy. In return for that assistance, the Turks were required to undertake liberalizing reforms, though the program was abandoned after a military coup in March 1971.[53] As a result, Ankara continued to confront the same problem over and over again. The technocrats at the SPO never succeeded in pushing down imports, meaning that Turkey was forced to burn ever-increasing amounts of precious foreign exchange to pay for them. This was a common problem with countries undertaking import substitution industrialization. As economies grew more complex, bureaucrats proved unable to use the fiscal and administrative tools at their disposal to meet their goals.

As if managing the Turkish economy was not hard enough, in 1979 a popular revolution overthrew the shah of Iran. The dramatic events taking place next door destabilized the Turkish economy. The significant decline in Iran's oil output, reducing global supply by 7 percent, and the speculative hoarding as a result produced a severe price shock.[54] In the twelve months between April 1979 and April 1980, the price of a barrel of oil more than doubled, from $15.85 to $39.50. The price spike widened the balance of payments deficit in Turkey, which must import all of its energy resources, disproving the idea among planners that they could insulate Turkey from events outside of Ankara's control. Yet Turkey's economic troubles in the 1970s were not just a function of revolutionaries in Tehran and oil traders in New York. A series of weak coalition governments pursued populist economic agendas as politicians such as the CHP's Bülent Ecevit, Süleyman Demirel of the Justice Party, and the Islamist Necmettin Erbakan, who led the National Salvation Party, jockeyed for public support ahead of elections. The consequences were dire: high inflation, too much debt, poor investments in infrastructure, shortages of basic goods, and persistent balance of payments problems. After Demirel became prime minister in November 1979, his minority government undertook austerity measures and turned to the IMF for help.[55] Although he faithfully implemented the reforms, it was already too late.

Turkey's economic problems coincided with a sharp deterioration in domestic stability and security. In the last half of the decade, almost 5,000 Turks were killed in violence between leftist and rightist political forces that the governments of the time seemed impotent to stop. Confronted with dual crises—security and economic—Turkey's senior military command took matters in their own hands on September 12, 1980. The generals dissolved Demirel's government, suspended the constitution, closed parliament, disbanded political parties, and banned party leaders from politics. Like the 1960 military intervention, the officers sought to restructure the state and fix a listing economy. Far outside the realm of their expertise, the commanders turned to a former senior official at the SPO—also a World Bank consultant and the principal economic advisor to the ousted Demirel—named Turgut Özal. He became deputy prime minister in the junta-controlled government under the leadership of retired admiral Bülent Ulusu. Given free rein to deal with Turkey's economic woes, Özal sought to mitigate the adverse effects of both import substitution industrialization and the short-term, politically driven economic policies of the latter half of the 1970s.[56] He liberalized trade, restructured the country's debt, instituted a free-floating exchange rate, and held down wages while lifting price controls. In addition, he imposed discipline on organized labor, which had contributed to the chaos of the previous half decade. Striking workers were ordered back to work and labor slowdowns were banned. Özal provided tax relief to low-wage workers and the corporate sector, but raised income taxes on farmers, professionals, and small entrepreneurs.[57]

Özal's stewardship of the economy under the generals was short-lived. In June 1982, he was forced to resign after the failure of the rather large financial firm Kastelli threatened tens of thousands of small investors. The crisis was not of Özal's making, though he took the blame. He returned the following year when his newly formed Motherland Party won the most votes in the first post-coup elections and continued his neoliberal reforms. Özal's sterling reputation as architect and steward of Turkey's economic recovery obscures a far more mixed record. Between 1980 and 1990, Turkey's per capita income doubled and growth returned, but growth rates, especially in the years immediately after the coup, were not high enough to absorb all the new entrants to the labor market. Under Özal's watch, unemployment increased. The number of bankruptcies reached a record high because firms did not have the financial wherewithal to obtain credit after Özal oversaw a sharp rise in interest rates.[58] Perhaps Özal's greatest contribution to the Turkish economy was the political stability he provided between November 1983, when he was first elected prime minister, and his untimely death in May 1993, about halfway through what would have been a single seven-year term as president of the republic. In the following decade, Turkey had seven coalition governments composed of parties that were, at an ideological level, seemingly incompatible. Personality conflicts also hampered political comity, and corruption among senior officials was endemic. In 1996, Turkey embarked on its first experiment in Islamist-led government, which lasted only a year before the military, with the help of the media, academics, civil society groups, and the other political parties, brought it down. The weakness of the governments of the 1990s was reflected in the public indebtedness, persistent high levels of unemployment, and runaway inflation of the era.

Things did not improve in the new century. In November 2000, Turkey experienced a severe banking crisis over questions about the health of the financial sector. The story is complicated but the basics are fairly straightforward. Banks closed their lines of credit to Turkey's weak financial institutions, prompting foreign investors to sell off Turkish equities and treasury bills. With the interbank lending market closed to them, vulnerable Turkish banks sold their own portfolios of government equities to raise much-needed cash. This fire sale slashed the value of government-issued securities, which in turn raised doubt about the ability of the government to continue to finance public debt. Consequently, capital fled the country, banks dumped securities to meet their obligations, and the Central Bank ceased to extend credit to banks in an effort to conserve foreign exchange reserves. This confluence of events pushed the interbank lending rate to almost 900 percent.

Within a month, the IMF stepped in with a $10.5 billion stabilization package, yet the crisis was not over. In February 2001, a spat between the country's president and prime minister about rooting out corruption in the banking sector precipitated a loss of confidence in the country's leadership and its ability to implement the IMF stabilization program. A sell-off on the Istanbul stock exchange and speculative attacks on the Turkish lira, soaring interbank interest rates, and a rapid decline in the Central Bank's foreign currency reserves ensued.[59] Having brought the economy to the precipice, the government was forced by necessity to float the lira, which would—it was hoped—create an environment for the emergence of a more competitive, export-oriented, and thus attractive (to foreign investors) economy. This would take time, though. In the meantime, average Turks suffered. The devaluation of the lira that came with the new exchange rate regime produced higher prices for consumer products and shortages in basic goods and medicines. With much diminished purchasing power, people stopped buying practically everything. Unemployment, which was at 6.3 percent in the last quarter of 2000, jumped to 8.4 percent by the end of 2001, and to 10.4 percent in 2002 as a result of the crisis.[60] Overall, the economy contracted by 5.7 percent in 2001.[61] In one poignant moment in April of that year, an Ankara florist threw his empty cash register at Prime Minister Bülent Ecevit, who throughout the crisis seemed befuddled by the country's accumulating economic problems.[62]

It was only after the prime minister and his coalition partners appointed Kemal Derviş as minister of economic affairs and the treasury in March 2001 that a coherent plan to address the downturn developed. Derviş, an accomplished academic economist and senior official at the World Bank, quickly undertook sweeping deregulation and reforms. His goals were to "disinflate the Turkish economy, strengthen fiscal accounts, and reform the structure of the Turkish economy."[63] The severity of the economic crunch, Derviş's prestige, and his broad mandate allowed him to pursue structural changes to the Turkish economy with vigor and, importantly, without political interference. He focused his attention on rooting out corruption within state-owned financial institutions that had led to a collapse of confidence in Turkey's banking sector; "enhancing the transparency of economic management"; giving the private sector a greater role in economic restructuring, which meant speeding up privatization of the telecommunications, aviation, electricity, sugar, and steel industries; improving debt management; reducing government spending; using monetary policy under the new floating exchange rate to combat inflation aggressively; seeking a social compact on economic change; and strengthening the social safety net.[64] To support all of this, Derviş negotiated with the IMF to supplement an existing 1999 emergency funding agreement called a stand-by arrangement. This gave Ankara access to an additional $6.4 billion in what are called special drawing rights. These are assets whose value is based on the US dollar, the Japanese yen, the euro, and the British pound sterling that can be traded among members of the IMF for currency.

Derviş's efforts to rescue the economy were not enough to salvage the electoral prospects of Ecevit (who had become seriously ill but refused to resign), his party, and his coalition partners. In November 2002, the Justice and Development Party (AKP), founded fifteen months earlier when a group of reformers broke from Turkey's Islamist old guard, won 34 percent of the popular vote. Owing to the particularities of Turkish electoral law, this was enough votes to give the AKP a parliamentary majority and a single-party government. Once in power, the AKP and its leadership kept their populist impulses in check and proved to be good stewards of the economy. With the exceptions of weak growth in 2008 and an almost 5 percent contraction in 2009, Turkey's real GDP grew between 5 and 9 percent in the decade after the AKP came to power. This growth coincided with significant income per capita gains, which in 2002 was $3,576 and by 2011 reached $10,604. Inflation came down from 47.2 percent to a manageable 6.5 percent, which was a boon to Turkish consumers whose incomes were rising. With all this growth, however, unemployment remained stubbornly high, hovering around 10 percent for most of the AKP era despite a brief spike in 2009 to 14 percent.[65] Income inequality fell slightly, though it remained at the higher end of the moderate category, but not all that different from wealthier, moderate-income countries. With the exception of the obstinate problem of unemployment, the 2000s was the longest uninterrupted period of economic growth since the early 1950s, which had lasted only three years. The AKP could lay claim to a decade of economic expansion, which is one important reason Turks kept giving it a parliamentary majority with larger percentages of the popular vote. By virtually all measures, Turkish society was wealthier, healthier, more mobile, more connected to the world, and was enjoying the benefits of better infrastructure than ever before.

The Turkish experience runs parallel, in important ways, to Tunisia and Egypt, and there are also some general similarities between those countries and Libya. In one crucial respect, however, Libya's economic development is more comparable to the countries of the Persian Gulf than to its North African neighbors or Turkey. Libya sits atop Africa's largest proven reserves of oil and the fifth largest deposits of natural gas on the continent.[66] Hydrocarbons account for two-thirds of the country's GDP and 96 percent of government revenues. Among other major producers only Saudi Arabia and Kuwait are comparable to Libya, with 90 percent and 83 percent of their revenues based on oil rent, respectively. By the World Bank's standards, in the five years before the uprising against Muammar al-Qaddafi, Libya was an upper-middle-income country and Libyans were earning between $9,300 and $14,200 annually.[67] That is an estimate, however. No one actually knows for certain given the notorious inaccuracies of the Libyan government's statistics.

The September 1969 coup d'état that ended King Idris al-Sanusi's eighteen-year monarchy heralded a four decade experiment with Qaddafi's so-called popular democracy. Having initially failed to break the power of traditional tribal leaders and the small elite that dominated

Libya during the monarchy, Qaddafi declared a "popular revolution" in the spring of 1973 in the port city of Zuwara, about sixty miles west of the Libyan capital, Tripoli. From that moment on, all existing laws were abolished and replaced with revolutionary edicts, "perverts and deviationists" were purged, the bourgeoisie and bureaucracy were eliminated, weapons were distributed to the people to protect the revolution, and a cultural revolution to rid the country of foreign ideas was initiated.[68] In addition, the people were to be in charge through popular committees that would be responsible for virtually everything from local governance and management of state agencies to overseeing private interests. The exceptions to Libya's new politics were foreign policy, the military, the police, intelligence services, and the oil sector. Given the importance of hydrocarbons to the economy and the recognition among Qaddafi and his fellow military officers on the Revolutionary Command Council that specialized skills and knowledge were required to run the oil sector, the Libyan National Oil Corporation was carefully insulated from the "continuous revolution" that marked the country's politics.[69] The revenue stream from hydrocarbons also needed to be protected because that was the way Qaddafi would finance his vision.[70]

Setting aside the specific areas walled off from the popular revolution, inherent problems were associated with the assumption of responsibility by popular committees for a variety of functions related to the governance of the country. Among them was the resulting chaos and confusion over who was responsible for what and the damage this wrought on state-owned enterprises and the agricultural sector.[71] The full articulation of what the popular revolution meant—the "supervision of the people by the people"—emerged in 1976 with the publication of Qaddafi's famous *The Green Book: The Third Universal Theory*.[72] Toward that end, the second part of the volume, "The Solution of the Economic Problem: Socialism," set out a radical vision. Between 1976 and 1978, all housing that did not have residents was nationalized, apartment prices were reduced by 30 percent, and confiscated housing was given to the poor.[73] Revolutionary committees—a new structure created in 1975 to be the ideological vanguard and shock troops of the popular revolution—seized private businesses both large and small. In the place of traders and retail establishments came large state-run supermarkets. Industry—with the exception of the oil sector—was handed over to basic production committees within each firm, which were charged with running every aspect of the business. The private practice of the professions was outlawed. Individual farmers were forced into subsistence farming and all available agricultural land was put into the hands of the government.

Given the dramatic increases in oil prices that bookended the 1970s, the Libyan government was able to make the kinds of investments it did, such as foolhardy infrastructure and agricultural projects, which could always be covered up with the river of petrodollars that flowed into the country. Given its overreliance on oil revenues, though, the country was also vulnerable to changes in the international oil market. The precipitous plunge in oil prices in the mid-1980s produced some effort at economic reform. For example, to reverse Libya's economic declines, in 1987 Qaddafi declared that private property would henceforth be considered "sacred and protected."[74] The following year brought the publication of the Great Green Charter of Human Rights in the Era of the Masses, which served as a blueprint of sorts for the Socialist People's Libyan Arab Jamahiriyya—an Arabic word denoting a state representing the interests of the great masses; the term became associated with Libya during the Qaddafi era—in an era of low oil prices.[75] It promised to replace the arbitrary decrees and revolutionary courts that had been the norm since the early 1970s with a legal framework that included an independent judiciary and rational legal codes. These would have been salutary changes that might have contributed to economic change, but they came to nothing. Like constitutions and charters throughout the rest of the region, the document had built-in exceptions so that many of the new rights, privileges, and opportunities that Libyans were to enjoy under the Great Green Charter were simultaneously rescinded. For example, private property was sacred and protected unless it was in the public interest not to protect it.[76] Economic reforms would have undermined the ability of regime supporters to continue to profit, a risk that Libya's leader clearly could not take.

It was in the 1973 Zuwara speech that Qaddafi signaled the beginning of a new, more aggressive, and adventuresome shift in Libyan foreign policy that would have an impact on the country's economy. Although the United States purchased large amounts of hydrocarbons from Tripoli and American oil companies were important players in

Libya, the Zuwara speech was also the beginning of a confrontation between the Jamahiriyya and Washington that would last the better part of the following thirty years. The initial (and an enduring) source of tension was Qaddafi's declaration at Zuwara of a "Line of Death" across the Gulf of Sidra—also known as the Gulf of Sirte—that was well beyond the twelve nautical miles that are considered territorial waters under international law. The Libyans regarded the gulf, which stretches like a giant *U* from Misrata to Benghazi, as an inland sea and declared it off limits. This was unacceptable to the US Navy, which as a matter of principle has long protected the freedom of navigation on the high seas. The inevitable result was periodic hostile encounters between American aircraft and warships and Libyan fighter planes. After years of brinksmanship and near misses, in August 1981, American aircrews operating from the aircraft carrier USS *Nimitz* shot down two Libyan MiG-23s that had targeted the US fighters.

The dogfight over the Gulf of Sidra was not the last between American and Libyan pilots—an eerily similar confrontation occurred in January 1989 with the same result—but the status of that body of water was not the only irritant in the US-Libya relationship. In 1977, Libyan forces shelled the Egyptian border town of Sallum in what was billed as a march on Cairo to protest Sadat's efforts to forge peace with Israel and align Egypt with the United States. The Egyptians prevailed in the brief battle, but Qaddafi's bellicosity toward Egypt did not come to an end. Qaddafi also made terrorism an important instrument of foreign policy, the most dramatic of which was the December 1988 bombing of Pan Am Flight 103 over Lockerbie, Scotland, that killed all 259 people aboard. In between, Libya sought to destabilize its southern neighbors, especially Chad.[77] Qaddafi's bad behavior in the late 1970s and early 1980s prompted the Reagan administration to prohibit American citizens from traveling to Libya beginning in December 1981. This was followed four months later with bans on Libyan crude oil exports to the United States and a prohibition on hydrocarbon-related equipment sales to Libya. Additional sanctions on refined products were imposed in 1985. Then, in January 1986, the United States froze Libyan assets, banned American citizens from conducting financial transactions in Libya, and barred banks and other firms from extending loans or credit to Libya. These steps were taken in response to Tripoli's role in simultaneous attacks on the El Al, Pan Am, and TWA ticket counters at the Rome and Vienna airports that killed 10 people and wounded 117. The ratcheting up of financial sanctions had little effect on Qaddafi's behavior, however. In April 1986, Libyan agents bombed the La Belle discotheque, a club popular with American servicemen in West Berlin, killing two American soldiers and injuring another seventy-nine. Rather than introducing additional sanctions, President Ronald Reagan ordered air strikes on Tripoli that targeted military facilities, "terrorism centers," and, according to some reports, the Libyan leader himself.

The raid on Tripoli notwithstanding, Washington's Libya policy was geared almost exclusively toward confronting Qaddafi and isolating the Jamahiriyya through punitive financial measures. It turned out, however, that though sanctions were politically important (in the United States) and had symbolic meaning in the American fight against terrorism, their actual effect on the Libyan economy was negligible. Without the participation of Europe and other major powers in US policy, the Libyans found markets for their oil and came up with ways to circumvent American prohibitions on financial transactions. It was not until the early 1990s that Qaddafi would confront a concerted international effort to rein in his behavior. The triggers were the Lockerbie bombing and a similar attack on UTA (Union de Transports Aériens) Flight 772 over Niger in September 1989. After investigations into both incidents pointed to the work of Libyan intelligence, the United Nations Security Council passed Resolution 748 on March 31, 1992. The measure, which passed with ten countries in favor and five abstaining, slapped sanctions on the aviation sector, denying the Libyans spare parts as well as maintenance and engineering services. Landing rights for Libyan aircraft were revoked at airports worldwide, airlines were prohibited from flying to or over Libya, and the international offices of Libyan Arab Airlines were closed. The Security Council also prohibited the sale, transfer, and licensing of "arms and related material of all types" and banned military and technical assistance to Libya. Member states were expected to end any military advising missions in Libya, and the Security Council demanded that they "significantly reduce" their diplomatic presence in the country. Finally, Libyan nationals who had "been denied entry or expelled from other states because of their involvement in terrorist activities" were to be removed from countries where they might be found.[78] When, almost two years later, the Security Council determined that Qaddafi had failed to comply with Resolution 748's demand that "the Libyan Government ... cease all forms of terrorist action and all assistance to terrorist groups and that it must promptly, by concrete actions, demonstrate its renunciation of terrorism," broader international sanctions were applied.[79] The new measure—Resolution 883, which the Security Council passed on November 11, 1993, with eleven votes in favor, none against, and four abstentions—once again targeted Libya's ability to buy and maintain commercial aircraft parts and run its national airline. Even pilot training was prohibited. Unlike Resolution 748, Resolution 883 froze all Libyan assets—though the United Nations permitted Tripoli to sell oil and gas, the proceeds from which were to be deposited into "separate bank accounts exclusively for these funds." In an annex to Resolution 883, the Security Council listed a wide variety of items that member states could neither provide to Libya nor give Libyans the technology to produce on their own. The forbidden items made it clear that the Security Council intended to hinder Libya's ability to export hydrocarbons.[80]

Over the course of the ensuing decade, Libya's economy barely grew, per capita income fell from about $7,000 to $4,680, dipping as low as $3,710. During this time, earnings from exports decreased, the value of the Libyan dinar fell, and prices rose, though the hydrocarbon sector remained remarkably resilient.[81] Crude production remained about 1.3 million barrels per day in the mid-1990s and exports barely decreased.[82] Those firms—mostly from the former Soviet bloc—willing to enter Libya demanded a significant premium to do business there. The multilateral economic pressure brought to bear on Qaddafi beginning in the 1990s was likely responsible for Libya's opening to the West at the end of the decade. Qaddafi's willingness to hand over suspects in the Pan Am and UTA attacks was enough for some European countries to start bringing down the economic barriers that the Security Council had erected. Among the first were the Germans, who upgraded their economic ties with the Libyans in 1998, though commercial relations did not increase dramatically until 2004 when Qaddafi agreed to pay compensation for the La Belle discotheque bombing. London and Tripoli restored diplomatic relations in 1999. France's opening to Libya began in 2001, culminating in then French president Jacques Chirac's visit to Tripoli in 2004 and Qaddafi's agreement to increase compensation for families of the victims of the UTA bombings. A nuclear cooperation agreement and weapons contract followed in 2006 and 2007. It was not until 2003 when US-Libya relations officially began to thaw—though secret talks between the two governments had taken place in the late 1990s—when Libya acknowledged the existence and capabilities of its program to develop weapons of mass destruction. It took three more years before the United States and Libya restored diplomatic relations.

With the opening to the West came an entirely new economic strategy: neoliberal reforms. With significantly less zeal than accompanied his nationalizations of the 1970s, Qaddafi acknowledged that the world had changed around him and threw his support behind those among his advisors who advocated privatization, foreign investment, and integration with the global economy.[83] This change came at a fortuitous moment. When the United States reestablished diplomatic ties with the Jamahiriyya, the price of oil was about $71 per barrel. It spiked to $146 a barrel two years later before briefly falling by two-thirds in late 2008 and early 2009. By February 2011, when the uprising against Qaddafi began, oil was fetching $96 per barrel. The combination of diplomatic normalization with Washington and European capitals as well as high oil prices promised to transform Libya. That is at least what various journalists and analysts reported.[84] They seemed to be awed by Libyans, the country's oddities, and Qaddafi's apparent effort at desert authenticity. For example, both Professor Lord Anthony Giddens of the London School of Economics and Harvard's Joseph S. Nye Jr. began their Libya travel logs with a discussion of Qaddafi's tent and the Libyan leader's robes before relaying that Libya is complicated but that Qaddafi is attuned to the need for reform.[85] Giddens was especially bullish, relaying that "[Qaddafi] accepts the need to reform banking, diversify the economy, train entrepreneurs and dismantle inefficient state-owned enterprises. Impressive progress has been made toward these objectives in the past three years."[86] A consulting firm called the Monitor Group (and its Harvard Business School–tenured founder, Michael Porter) shaped much of the feel-good chatter about Libya in the mid-2000s, but posturing as a reformer was still an impressive pivot for the man behind *The Green Book*.[87] Although Qaddafi's opening to the West undermined everything he had stood for since the Zuwara speech in April 1973, economic reform and foreign investment would secure his legacy. Subsequent events would prove otherwise.

THE POLITICS OF PERCEPTION

Ain al-Sukhna, a resort town on the Red Sea, lies about eighty miles to the southeast of Cairo, which makes it an extraordinarily convenient for some of Egypt's well-heeled to maintain weekend villas there. Among the residents who could be found in and around the town's condos, manicured lawns, pristine infinity pools, and towpaths tucked between the azure waters of the Gulf of Suez and the ochre-colored hills that rise steeply from the shoreline was Hosni Mubarak's last foreign minister, Ahmed Aboul Gheit. It was also Abdel Moneim Said's getaway.

For many Western analysts interested in Egyptian security, politics, and foreign policy, Abdel Moneim's office at the Al-Ahram Center for Political and Strategic Studies—the government-funded think tank he directed for many years—on Galaa Street in downtown Cairo was always an important stop. In the 1990s and during the first decade of the 2000s, he was Egypt's most prominent foreign policy expert. This gave Abdel Moneim entrée to the world of Washington think tanks, the occasional appearance on Western news networks, and quotes in major Western newspapers. But being Egypt's top foreign policy analyst was not actually much of a boast. The political demands and pressures of the Nasser, Sadat, and Mubarak years had rendered the Egyptian professoriate deeply politicized, divided among regime apologists, Nasserist retreads, and Muslim Brotherhood activists. In between were people trying to do quality work, but they enjoyed neither the support nor the profile that Abdel Moneim had over many years. This support came precisely because he was a member of the ruling National Democratic Party (NDP) and, after its creation in 2002, an influential participant in the party's policies secretariat under the leadership of Gamal Mubarak, the former president's younger son and once-presumed heir to the presidency. In an odd twist, it was precisely because Abdel Moneim had been willing to do the government's bidding that he was able to position himself as an above-the-fray figure in Egypt's policy debates, such as they were. He was justly rewarded for his service when he was made president of the board of the Al-Ahram Foundation, the entity that owned government-affiliated newspapers—most prominently the flagship paper *Al-Ahram*—magazines, and book publishers. The purpose of this sprawling media conglomerate was to reinforce the official histories and narratives of the regime. In the heady months after Mubarak fell when Egyptians were hopeful for a democratic future, Abdel Moneim left his post at *Al-Ahram*. Rumors suggested that he was too close to Gamal Mubarak to occupy such a prominent position in the new era. There were also murky allegations of financial improprieties during his tenure as head of the foundation, though they were never proved.

On a scorching afternoon in June 2011, a reflective but hardly chastened Abdel Moneim held court in the backyard garden of his home in Ain al-Sukhna where several fans connected to the house through long extension cords pushed the hot air around. He suggested that Mubarak had been a victim of his own accomplishments, citing a growing GDP, rising incomes, infrastructure improvements of all kinds, and the introduction of what he considered important political reforms. In the 2000s, when President George W. Bush's administration began urging Mubarak to undertake democratic reforms, Abdel Moneim had played a role in trying to deflect this pressure by proclaiming Egypt to be an emerging democracy. This declaration tracked closely with Egyptian officialdom's pronouncements of the "deepening and strengthening" of democracy, claims that were obviously inconsistent with reality to virtually everyone outside the NDP's policies secretariat. In fairness, Abdel Moneim was entirely correct on one point: on the eve of Mubarak's fall, the country had changed dramatically from the one the deposed president inherited when he first took the oath of office on October 14, 1981. According to the World Bank, by 2011, life expectancy for both males and females approached developed world levels. The birth and infant mortality rates dropped significantly, and the annual rate of population growth began to level off. Immunization of children for tuberculosis, DPT (diphtheria, pertussis, tetanus), hepatitis B, measles, and polio reached from 96 to 98 percent whereas three decades earlier they had ranged from 41 to 57 percent. The age dependency ratio—a measure, albeit not perfect, of the population financially dependent on others—fell by almost a third, which reduced the overall burden on Egyptians in the workforce and the government. Almost three-quarters of the population was literate—a figure that remained too low but was still an improvement. The percentage of the population working in agriculture fell from 40 percent to 30 percent, and though the numbers for industry remained largely constant, gains in the service sector were large. Almost the entire population had access to electricity. In 1981, landline telephone connections in Egypt numbered only 430,000; the number reached almost twelve million in 2008 before settling back to about nine million two years later—no doubt a result of the mobile phone revolution.[88] This is not to suggest that Mubarak was a great man, as his supporters insist, or that these changes would not have happened without him, but Egypt was hardly stagnant in the twenty-nine years, three months, twenty-eight days, and six hours that he ruled.[89]

In his assertion that Mubarak's success presaged his undoing, Abdel Moneim was also channeling arguments that the economist Mancur Olson Jr. and the political scientist Samuel Huntington had advanced in the 1960s. Olson, writing in 1963, challenged the then-prevailing assumption in scholarly and policy circles "that economic growth leads toward political stability and perhaps even peaceful democracy."[90] The evidence, he argued, strongly indicated a negative correlation between rapid economic growth and the distribution of income, which produces social dislocation especially in poor countries with weak social safety nets.[91] For his part, Huntington pointed out that because the gains associated with rapid growth are unevenly distributed, large numbers of people are actually left poorer in the short run, stoking grievances that the political class is unlikely to address because they are the ones who disproportionately benefit from the economic changes. The result is instability.[92] Both arguments hinged on the idea that Abdel Moneim had echoed, which was that economic growth "awakens people to the possibilities of further improvement and thereby generates additional discontent."[93] Olson's insight into the political dynamics of rapid change went further, indicating that it is not just the losers from economic growth who are potentially destabilizing but also the winners who harbor rising expectations about the future. This was precisely what Abdel Moneim meant when he averred that it was Mubarak, not democratic activists, bloggers, the Muslim Brotherhood, or anyone else, who had made the

January 25 uprising possible. The upper- and upper-middle-class youth who had formed the core of the opposition to the regime throughout most of the 2000s were responding to the increased political, social, and economic opportunities of the Mubarak era.[94]

In the abstract, an Egyptian precedent for Abdel Moneim's argument existed. In the late nineteenth and early twentieth centuries, British consul generals, especially Lord Cromer, who governed Egypt from 1883 to 1907, undertook a range of reforms intended to improve the well-being of the population that had a profound socioeconomic effect on Egyptians and unintended political consequences for the British.[95] For example, agricultural reforms led to greater prosperity among Egypt's rural farmers and peasants. This in turn afforded their children greater access to educational opportunities in secondary, professional, and technical schools, which were also expanded at the behest of the British. Egypt's nationalist politicians emerged from this new class of professionals, technocrats, and relatively wealthier farmers.[96] The Egyptian experience is consistent with the idea that economic development can give rise to social forces that demand political change, especially in nondemocratic societies.[97] Still, in the hopeful moment just after Mubarak's fall, Abdel Moneim's argument seemed like the desperate self-justification and rationalization representative of unrepentant thinking common among supporters of the old order who were, like Mubarak, out of touch with Egypt's reality.

The problem was, of course, that Egypt, Tunisia, Libya, and Turkey offered many versions of reality. Regardless of what the data said—or whether they were accurate—what governments were telling their citizens about their lives and the way citizens were experiencing it were not the same. It was not just the governments, however. Tunisia stands out as a case that the World Bank and IMF held out "as a role model for other developing countries."[98] In a retrospective written a few years after Ben Ali's fall, World Bank analysts recognized this failing and acknowledged that "beyond the shiny façade often presented by the former regime, Tunisia's economic environment was and remains deeply deficient."[99] This was, for instance, the reality of workers in the Gafsa basin—where they engaged in wildcat strikes, sit-ins, hunger strikes, and other forms of protests during the first six months of 2008.[100] The unrest surrounded the Gafsa Phosphate Company's decision to award well-paying jobs to less qualified but politically connected individuals. The prolonged display of anger over hiring practices came against the backdrop of complaints about the lack of opportunity and corruption that reflected the rigged nature of Tunisia's economy. The security services eventually put down the demonstrations and authorities made large numbers of arrests. In 2009, Ben Ali pardoned those who had been imprisoned. Although the events of 2008 were not the first time the Gafsa basin was the scene of unrest, it seems that the Tunisian leadership was confident in its ability to bring enough force to bear to contain it and regarded the protests as a phenomenon specific to the particularities of the region. Tunisia was prosperous, after all. This is why Ben Ali seemed so surprised when, two years after the Gafsa demonstrations, the wave of protests that began with Sidi Bouzid overwhelmed him in January 2011. Ben Ali's desperate efforts to quell the unrest and his deer-in-the-headlights appearances on national television only emboldened protesters, revealing how little he understood about Tunisia beyond the positive macroeconomic indicators that his government trumpeted. On December 28, Ben Ali told Tunisians, "The use of violence in the street by a minority of extremists against the interest of their country is not acceptable." He then added plaintively, "It [the protests] will have a negative impact on creating jobs. It will discourage investors and tourists (to visit) which will hit jobs."[101]

The situation was similar in Egypt. The former first lady, Suzanne Mubarak, was reportedly in a state of shock over the uprising, and in the immediate aftermath of her husband's fall placed furtive phone calls to her courtiers asking, "Doesn't anyone see the good we did?" Her husband's minister of industry and trade between the fall of 2004 and early 2011, Rachid Mohammed Rachid, defiantly declared some months later, "The reality, at the end of the day, is, you had a growing economy. Nobody can debate this. Now, if you watch Egyptian television, if you listen to Egyptian officials, they say it never existed. But I can tell you, when the government left, our finances were in good shape."[102] The problem for Rachid, the Mubaraks, Ben Ali, and their supporters was a simple yet hard-to-grasp reality: the numbers did not matter.

This perception of economic stagnation was less prominent in the Libyan uprising against Qaddafi and secondary in Turkey's popular explosion in mid-2013. In Libya, however, the prevailing sense in the eastern part of the country, which was the cradle of the February 17 up-rising, was that it was less privileged than the western part of the coun-try, where Qaddafi's base of support was stronger.[103] It may very well be that this state of affairs angered Libyans in Benghazi, especially given that most of Libya's oil reserves are in the east or central-east of the country. Still, in Libya and Turkey, constructing the mythology of the uprising was considerably more difficult than in Tunisia, where it rose easily from the circumstances and death of Mohammed al-Bouazizi.

Indeed, as compelling—and easy to grasp—as the suggestion that economic issues were at the heart of the uprisings may have been, the dynamics of these sudden demonstrations of people power were far more complicated.[104] No doubt people's perceptions of what was or was not in their wallets were critical, but these issues were also part of a broader, multilayered, and more complex set of complaints that actually make it difficult to distinguish among economics, politics, and identity.

DEMOCRACY?

On Sunday, April 26, 1998, Barbara Crossette of the *New York Times* posed the following question in a 1,500-word article in the paper's Week in Review section: "Why has democracy—or at least popular pressure for it—not surged across the Arab world, where one-fifth [*sic*] of the world's people live, in the last decade of the 20th century?" Despite considerable time and attention to answering the question, no one really knew, which was especially vexing given how important demands for representation and justice were in the public discourse in ideologi-cally diverse Middle Eastern societies.

Of course, if there was a country in the region (other than Israel) that many observers held out as democratic, it was non-Arab Turkey. This was accurate only if one defined the concept in narrow terms. It is true that Turkey has had eighteen free and fair parliamentary elections since 1946, when then president İsmet İnönü acceded to demands from dissidents within the dominant Republican People's Party to end single-party rule.[105] It is also true that political institutions like the Grand National Assembly have had greater meaning than their ana-logues in the Arab world and that Turks have internalized democratic practices and ideas. The most salient manifestation of this has been a willingness to defy Turkey's military establishment at various times. For example, in a 1986 referendum that would determine whether party leaders banned after the 1980 coup could return to politics, the military signaled that it preferred a "no" vote, but Turks voted overwhelmingly in favor. Four times over the course of four decades—in 1960, 1971, 1980, and 1997—Turkey's senior military officers had dismissed governments they were duty-bound to serve. And though they handed power back to civilian politicians—a fact often used to bolster claims that Turkey is a democracy—each time they reengineered the institutions of the state in ways that the officers hoped would close off channels through which opponents of the system could pursue their agendas.[106] For example, after the military's 1971 intervention, the commanders oversaw amendments to Turkey's 1961 constitution that reined in a variety of political rights and established barriers to political participation for certain groups. After the 1980 coup, the military oversaw the development of an entirely new constitution intended essentially to protect the state from the individual. In the three decades since that constitution was approved in a referendum, a consensus has emerged that for the country to be truly democratic, the constitution must be replaced. Although military and civilian elites sought to enforce a drab political conformity, a cacophony of voices—leftist, rightist, secularist, religious, liberal, Kurdish, and Alevi to name just a few—demanded a more democratic and open society. Besides being fed up with craven, feckless, weak, and corrupt politicians who had made a mess of the economy by the early 2000s, the Justice and Development Party's appeal was based on the promise that it could advance Turkish politics beyond the procedural democracy of elections and expand individual and political rights as well as the rule of law. It turned out that the party's commitment to democracy was more apparent than real, which is why the parallels between the uprisings in the Arab world and Turkey's Gezi Park protests in 2013 are, despite differences in scale, so striking. The widespread purge of President Recep Tayyip Erdoğan's opponents after the failed coup d'état in July 2016 only reinforced the fact that Turkey's political pathologies were similar to those of its neighbors.

When the protests in Tunisia surged north from Sidi Bouzid to the capital and converged on November 7th Square (since renamed January

14th Square) demonstrators called on Ben Ali to "Leave!" Photographs of Tunisians of all stripes bearing signs in Arabic simply reading "*Irhal!*" or in French declaring "Ben Ali! *Dégage!*" immediately became part of the country's new political iconography. Others, more powerfully emotive (and entertaining) in Arabic than in English, revealed a complex picture of the grievances that Tunisians harbored: "Bread and water; Ben Ali no!" and "O Ben Ali, o coward, the Tunisian people cannot be disgraced!" and "Tunisia, Tunisia, free, free; Ben Ali out!" In Egypt, the creativity of demonstrators knew no bounds. Aside from the generic cry that "the people want the fall of the regime," some of the most memorable moments during those eighteen days in Tahrir Square were when protesters rose up seemingly as one and thundered across the landscape, "Raise your head up high: You're Egyptian!" and "Bread! Freedom! Social justice!"—the latter betraying the open secret of Egypt's broken social contract. In Tripoli and Benghazi, Libyans taunted Muammar al-Qaddafi: "Hosni Mubarak has fallen, the turn of his neighbor has come!" and "A nation that birthed Mukhtar has the right in what it chooses!" and "O Qaddafi, o despicable one, Libyan blood is not cheap."[107] A little more than two years later and 1,000 miles across the Mediterranean, protesters in central Istanbul mocked riot police with chants of "Let's see you use that pepper spray." Demonstrators also bellowed "Jump, jump, [he] who doesn't jump is Tayyip"—meaning Erdoğan—producing a cinematic silhouette of tens of thousands of Turks leaping against the high wattage lights fixed atop of large, imposing looking armored riot control vehicles. The Gezi Park demonstrations were an environmental protest that evolved into a statement about crony capitalism, but also about democracy. One of many signs hoisted in the park as police gathered to clear it read simply, "In democracies, police do not attack squares. We want democracy." Much of Turks' anger was captured in song, however. The group Kardeş Türküler produced lyrics like "Enough with the headstrong decrees and commands . . . Oh my, oh my, we've had enough . . . Oh my, oh my, we're really fed up!" The band Duman also captured the sentiments of the Gezi protests when they sang:

> You have pepper spray, you have tear gas, you have batons and strong kicks, *eyvallah*. Attack me without being ashamed. My eyes are

burning, but I'm not repressed, we are not fewer. I tell you that I'm still free, still right, still human, do you think I'll give up?[108]

Suffused within the slogans across all four countries were ideas about economic fairness and democracy that protesters implicitly understood to be inextricably linked. In neither Tunis nor Cairo nor Tripoli nor Istanbul did protesters specifically demand the establishment of democratic polities in any kind of formal sense, but it was implicit in their calls for freedom, social justice, and economic opportunity. The people who appeared in the squares of the Middle East—not just in Tunisia, Egypt, Libya, and Turkey—had lived under rules, laws, and decrees that did not reflect their interests, but the interests of those who held power. Thus economic grievances were also grievances about politics. Yet something else was also at work in the demonstrations across the region. Intertwined with demands for freedom, economic opportunity, and democracy was an embedded belief that the fundamental fairness of more open and just political systems would deliver demonstrators something that was sorely lacking in the status quo: dignity.

KARAMA!

The slap across Mohammed al-Bouazizi's face in Sidi Bouzid; Khaled Said's death at the hands of police in Egypt's second city, Alexandria; the arrest of human rights lawyer Fathi Terbil in Benghazi; and the unknown young woman in the red dress who was pepper sprayed at close range in Gezi Park together reflected the unseemly disdain for citizens that the authoritarian political orders of the Middle East bred. The policemen and women (in the case of Bouazizi) did these things because the political and legal environments in which they operated were permissive. Only rarely, if ever, was anyone held accountable in Tunisia, Egypt, Libya, and Turkey unless it was for political reasons. The arrogance of power and its flipside, powerlessness, were critical to the uprisings in which dignity was a common and central theme.

In the post–World War II era, Western academics and intelligence analysts made much of the importance of personal dignity in the national character studies that were in vogue at the time. The idea was that if one understood a country's national character, one could understand its foreign or domestic policies. This led to hilariously pseudoscientific conclusions like "The Arab's need to project his self in a form completely acceptable to the harsh judgments of society renders his face, his dignity mask, a type of surrogate as thought of in the philosophy of Jung, one in which he wraps the very essence of his being."[109] Indeed, maintaining face was allegedly so crucial to Arabs that no such thing as truth in Middle Eastern societies existed, in contrast, of course, to the West, where "a fact is an objective absolute." The "Arab mentality," according to a 1964 article by Peter Naffsinger that appeared in the Central Intelligence Agency's in-house journal *Studies in Intelligence*, "treats fact and truth as relative, to some extent a projection of the mind for the benefit of the self or ego. With this subjective processing the facts become what the Arab wants to believe is true."[110] Perhaps the best-known book of this genre was *The Arab Mind*, published in 1973 and written by Raphael Patai, who was born in Hungary but spent his formative years in Israel teaching cultural anthropology at the Hebrew University of Jerusalem before settling in the United States in the 1950s. But it was not only Westerners who engaged in this type of cultural reductionism. Writing four years earlier, before Naffsinger put pen to paper to write "Face among the Arabs," Sanai Hamady, a naturalized American of Lebanese birth, wrote *Temperament and Character of the Arabs*. These authors tried to make the case that Arabs were, at social and cultural levels, not just different from Westerners, but actually inferior. The argument could also run the other way. In 1967, the Egyptian geographer Gamal Hamdan produced a four-volume work called *The Character of Egypt: A Study in the Genius of the Place*, arguing that the country maintained a singular place within humanity and implied that, regardless of their circumstances at any given moment, Egyptians were destined for greatness.[111] It is true that Egyptians have long had a sense of their place in history, referring to Egypt as *umm al-dunya*—mother of the world—but Hamdan's narrative went well beyond this playful boast.

Scholarly work on national character and psychology fell out of favor in the latter decades of the twentieth century, but reductionist ideas about Islam, tribal society, and Bedouin culture continue to seep into academic and policy discussions as well as media reporting on the region. Refrains about "the Arab street" conjure images of rampaging wild-eyed mobs in stark contrast to the consensus-based politics of other regions. Questions about the ability of Arabs and Muslims to embrace modernity are common in even allegedly sophisticated fora and publications. Some of the blame lies with the West's Middle Eastern interlocutors who are often Westernized, secular, but not necessarily liberal elites who betray their disdain for their own societies when they claim that Arabs are "not ready for democracy," implying that tribal and religious affiliations are obstacles to the development of modern societies in the Middle East.

Anthropologists, sociologists, political scientists, historians, and others are cognizant—perhaps at times too cognizant—that their work on the region can be used to caricature Arabs and Muslims. After all, to suggest that some sort of cultural exigency concerning dignity is specific to Middle Eastern societies and determines Arab and Muslim behavior suggests an exceptionalism that does not exist. Dignity is important in every society. In the United States, the civil rights movement, women's demands for equal pay in exchange for equal work, and gay marriage all concern nothing less than dignity. The West may have different social, political, and cultural norms than the Middle East, but dignity remains as critical in Europe and America as it does in Arab and Muslim societies.

In the context of the Arab uprisings and Gezi Park protests, the demand for dignity—like economic grievances—was bound up in political systems that demeaned people. The call for dignity among Arab publics in 2010 and 2011 was a damning statement about the people's relationship with the state as citizens, individuals, and collectively as Tunisians, Egyptians, Libyans, and others. Alaa al-Aswany, an Egyptian dentist and author of the searing social critique of the late Mubarak period *The Yacoubian Building*, captured the sentiment well when he declared, "This revolution happened for dignity. We used to dream that the simplest citizen in Egypt would be treated as a human being with rights and dignity."[112] Supporters and spokespeople for the Egyptian, Tunisian, and Turkish governments would always challenge arguments concerning the scarcity of political rights, circumscribed personal freedoms, and official arrogance that compromised personal and collective dignity with a barrage of factoids that included the existence of regularly scheduled elections and multiple political parties, the number of opposition publications, formal checks and balances, and a variety of practices and institutions that resembled those that existed in democratic polities. Except that none of these countries were democracies and to the extent that their constitutions may have granted citizens a variety of rights, responsibilities, and freedoms, these hallmarks of democratic politics were simultaneously rendered null and void through a variety of decidedly restrictive rules, decrees, and regulations. For its part, Qaddafi's direct democracy was a blatant ruse in which Libyans had no actual rights and were subject to the political whims of the leader and his informal network of regime supporters.

Having little in the way of political rights, the leadership and elite simply left the great reservoir of masses to fend for themselves. This varied across countries, of course. The Turkish government under the Justice and Development Party (AKP) was undoubtedly responsive to the needs of Turks, which played a significant role in its electoral success. From Istanbul to Lake Van, the AKP poured resources into infrastructure, transportation, housing, and health care that transformed the way Turks worked and lived. This is why, after the Gezi Park protests began, Turkey experts from Ankara to Brussels to Washington rolled their eyes when CNN asked if Gezi Park was "Turkey's Tahrir Square?" Strip away CNN's desire to drive up ratings by linking one dramatic news story with another (even if they were two years apart) and the Tahrir Square–Gezi Park analogy was not all that bad. It is true that despite huge crowds in Istanbul, Izmir, and Ankara, the number of people protesting against the AKP was small in comparison with the Egyptians in Tahrir or even the people in support of then prime minister Recep Tayyip Erdoğan. At the same time, the Gezi protesters sounded familiar themes about the arrogance of power, police brutality, and crony capitalism heard elsewhere. In a revealing moment, Bülent Arınç, a founder of the AKP and the rare figure who at times publicly, albeit tepidly, disagreed with the prime minister, referred to demonstrators as marginal elements of society. Others went further than Arınç, calling protesters "terrorists." Regardless of how they were described, the implication was clear—they deserved the punishment that the riot police were meting out to them in the form of tear gas, water cannons, and batons.

The threat to redevelop Gezi Park certainly attracted its share of Turkish hippies of all shapes and varieties as well as members of the hard-core left, but the large protests that resulted when the police moved in to remove people who had been camped out there was a mixture of young, old, Turks, Kurds, Alevis, affluent, poor, and people of many different professions. During one memorable moment, pharmacists—looking distinguished in white lab coats—took to İstiklal Caddesi (Independence Avenue) in support of the Gezi protesters. Other professions were represented as well, if not as organized as the pharmacists. If a characteristic dominated, the demonstrators seemed to be predominantly secular, though the media made a big deal of a small presence of people calling themselves anti-capitalist Muslims. Overall, the crowd was most certainly not the radical fringe. It was more accurate to say that they were a cross-section of groups that had been marginalized under the AKP, unable to contest politics both because the opposition parties were terrible and because those in charge had the country wired in their favor. When people finally had enough of "headstrong decrees and commands," in the words of Kardeş Türküler, and found their collective voice in the form of the Gezi protests, the government and its supporters did not treat them with the respect of fellow Turks, but rather as a fifth column. The result was 7,000 injured and 5 killed. The brutality of the police was such that, on June 13, mothers descended on the area to shield the protesters and collectively rebuke the authorities for the way they were treating their children. Then president Abdullah Gül and even Arınç seemed to realize that unleashing the full fury of the riot police was unwise and made conciliatory statements, especially while Erdoğan was on an official visit in North Africa, but the prime minister overruled them, ordering authorities to bring the protesters to heel through force.

Erdoğan did not solely respond with violence. Pro-government news media at first ignored the protests but then gave the demonstrations full coverage, if only to counter what the AKP-affiliated press believed to be the bias in the coverage of CNN, the BBC, the *New York Times*, the *Wall Street Journal*, and the *Financial Times*. A virtual army of pro-AKP Twitter trolls waged an online war against protesters, their supporters, journalists, and analysts. They echoed what the prime minister and other ministers were saying—that protesters were terrorists and that the US ambassador to Turkey, Zionists, Islamophobes, and the "interest rate lobby" were manipulating events. According to Finance Minister Mehmet Şimşek, "This mischief making naturally effects [*sic*] financial markets. Their aim is to make our country weaker but the macro fundamentals are solid."[113] It was shocking that someone with a background that included stints at UBS Securities, the US Embassy in Ankara, and Merrill Lynch would make such conspiratorial claims, but coming from one of the officials responsible for the Turkish economy, it reinforced a narrative that the AKP was seeking to embed in the minds of its supporters. The people protesting were in cahoots with foreign forces seeking to do Turkey harm.

At a massive rally—easily dwarfing the Gezi protest—in support of Erdoğan on June 16, 2013, the prime minister hammered away at the idea that those who had gathered on the other side of the city to raise their opposition to him and the AKP were not authentically Turkish. The solidly middle-class throngs wore Erdoğan masks, T-shirts, and scarves; cheered the police; and heaped scorn on the Gezi demonstrators. Among the many expressions of support articulated during the event, one in particular stood out. A man in the crowd held a large yellow sign that read "*Bugün günlerden Türkiye!*" (Today is our day, Turkey!). This could be read in many ways, but in that context he seemed to be suggesting precisely what Turkey's leaders had been saying, that those who had come out to support the ruling party were part of Turkey, those battling riot police were not and thus did not deserve respect.

For all of the ways the Turkish government demeaned those who dared to criticize its leaders, it was still better than Egypt, where the leadership signaled to its 91 million citizens that it cared little about their well-being. This was certainly related to the legendary inefficiency and incompetence of Egypt's bureaucracy, but also to the Egyptian elite's thinly veiled disdain for ordinary Egyptians. Between 2002 and Mubarak's ouster, Egypt experienced a series of natural and manmade disasters, including train fires, bus collisions, ferry sinkings, building collapses, and rock slides that killed about 1,500 people. Whether these incidents were preventable remains a matter of dispute, but what happened afterward is revealing about what average Egyptians were forced to endure. When, in September 2008, a side of the Muqattam Hills collapsed on Duweiqa—an unofficial neighborhood in greater Cairo to which services such as sewage, electricity, and running water have not been extended—the government did not mount a rescue effort. A few policemen showed up hours after the landslide and did nothing. The residents of Duweiqa were left to try to rescue their loved ones on their own. When some of them applied for assistance from the authorities to help with relocation, they were dismissed as scammers seeking to benefit from tragedy. A few years earlier, relatives of passengers aboard the ill-fated MS *al-Salam Boccaccio 98*, which sank during its overnight journey from Duba on Saudi Arabia's side of the Red Sea to Port Safaga on the Egyptian coast, descended on the ferry terminal seeking information; they were met with official indifference and the metal truncheons of riot police. Then there was astonishing malice. During the last decade of the Mubarak era, Egyptian authorities employed sexual assault to demean and degrade their citizens. In two infamous cases in 2006, Egyptian police infamously raped a well-known blogger for his coverage of protests against the regime and sodomized a microbus driver for coming to the defense of a family member who was in a dispute with officers.

The situation in Tunisia was hardly different from that in Egypt. The veneer of cosmopolitanism that Habib Bourguiba gave the country with its progressive family laws, women's rights, and connection to Europe—especially the way Tunisian elites mimicked French culture, if not French values—all endured under Ben Ali. Yet this could not obscure the fearsome police state he constructed on coming to power in 1987. Throughout much of Ben Ali's tenure, the State Department criticized the Tunisian government for, among a range of human rights issues, routine physical abuse, infringement of citizens' right to privacy, and a lack of due process.[114] Human rights organizations such as Amnesty International and Human Rights Watch consistently came to substantially the same conclusions: Tunisians were denied basic personal and political freedoms. Those who spoke out against government censorship and repression were routinely intimidated, arrested, and, in some cases, tortured. Ben Ali, who had served as head of military security from 1964 to 1974 and later as minister of interior from 1986 until his appointment as prime minister in 1987, made sure the opposition was dealt with ruthlessly. The Gafsa basin may have experienced unrest for the better part of six months in 2008, but once the decision was made to put down the demonstrations, strikes, and other forms of protest, the security services proved to be efficient. The government's use of force on people who merely wanted the government to uphold its commitments regarding rights and a social safety net was demeaning enough, but, as in Egypt, the sense was also, especially outside the capital, that elites cared little, if at all, about what happened in the secondary towns of the country's periphery. It is often the case throughout the Middle East that outside major cities, the state is barely evident beyond the presence of the police, whose job is to keep an eye on the population. As the World Bank and International Monetary Fund showered the Tunisian government with praise, Tunisians in places like Sidi Bouzid and other towns seethed. In the weeks following his gruesome suicide, the press erroneously reported that Mohammed al-Bouazizi was college-educated but forced to subsist on his produce stand. This made his story all the more heartbreaking and the unrest that followed more dramatic. Yet it was the impossibility of living a meaningful, dignified life in an environment of limited opportunity and official indifference—at best—or hostility that marked Tunisian life for people of Bouazizi's circumstances. Lacking resources and recourse, most Tunisians are forced to endure this state of affairs; Bouazizi chose not to.

If Turkey, Egypt, and Tunisia seem comparable in important ways, Qaddafi's Jamahiriyya and the idiosyncrasies of this system were also an affront to dignity and decency. The widely ridiculed but less read *The Green Book* is often held out as evidence of the Libyan leader's psychological and emotional instability. And though the book is mostly a head scratcher, Qaddafi was capable of insight. His trenchant criticism of political parties and representative democracy was at times astute. For example, in a section dedicated to exposing the party as a "dictatorial instrument," he wrote, "The parties in their struggle [with each other] resort, if not to arms, which rarely happens, then to denouncing and stultifying the actions of each other. This is a battle which is inevitably waged at the expense of the higher and vital interests of the society."[115]

The problem was that his commitment to the kind of direct democracy he outlined in *The Green Book* and the Zuwara speech was hollow. As noted briefly earlier, the Jamahiriyya was subterfuge, intended to defenestrate the Libyan state in favor of those who supported Qaddafi's 1969 takeover and, over time, developed a vested interest in the continuation of Libya's unique form of (non) governance. Like Turks, Egyptians, and Tunisians, Libyans were subjected to violence and coercion to keep them under control. This was a physical manifestation of injustice and a direct assault on human dignity, but the Jamahiriyya further demeaned Libyans in an important but considerably less obvious way. Whereas Qaddafi may have asked interesting questions and offered insightful critiques of the way politics is practiced in the West, the second volume of *The Green Book*, which sets out his vision for the radical nationalization of the economy, was downright loopy in comparison. The problem was that he and his supporters implemented this vision, which took a substantial toll on the Libyan population. It was not just the shortages and corruption that predictably resulted, however. In an environment where Qaddafi practically stamped out the private sector and hamstrung the bureaucracy, all in the service of freeing Libyans from tyranny, the same Libyans became wards of the state, dependent on it for practically everything. As Libya scholar Dirk Vandewalle relays, in time the circumstances in which Libyans found themselves sapped them of their creativity and ingenuity.[116] What could be more demeaning than that?

POLLING THE UPRISINGS

In June 2011, one of Northern Virginia's consultancies convened a meeting to discuss the results of polling that yet another Washington consulting firm had contracted another firm to do in Egypt on behalf of the State Department. The attendees were all pretty excited. This was, after all, one of the first post-Mubarak surveys of Egyptians and it was time to understand what they were thinking. With this insight, policymakers would know best how to craft and implement a policy that would help Egypt's much hoped for democratic transition. After an hour and an untold number of PowerPoint slides, the presenter informed everyone that Washington would be most successful if it focused its attention on economic development. Whatever the State Department spent on the polls, it was not worth it. Egypt did not need to have an uprising that pushed its longest-serving modern leader since Mohammed Ali Pasha (the Ottoman governor who ruled from 1805 to 1848) from power and a poll afterward to tell anyone that many Egyptians were dissatisfied with their economic prospects. Since the 1970s, economic development had been a priority for the United States in Egypt, though it was geared to building legitimacy and thus—it was believed—stability into a political system whose leaders were aligned with Washington. It did not actually work that well. With Mubarak gone, however, American policymakers would be able to start afresh. This time, Washington's economic assistance would be in the service of promoting democracy.

The polling done on behalf of the State Department was unquestionably correct. After the uprising, Egyptians looked forward to brighter days and especially greater prosperity. It was also entirely rational for the professional foreign policy bureaucracy to take the polling data and run with it. It is easier intuitively for a foreign service officer, commercial counselor, and ambassador to promote economic change and development than it is for them to encourage democracy and dignity. Also prevalent was the fast and loose notion that economic development ushered in democracy. This was not quite accurate, however. Social scientists had discovered that economic development correlates with democracy but is not a cause of it. Also, the uprisings in the Arab world and Turkey's explosion of anger at Gezi Park were contingent and complicated events. In the full-on effort to understand them, "economic grievances" presented itself as an immediately compelling and straightforward explanation.

Yet the survey did not capture—because it could not—the actual grievances common around the region. When Egyptians said they wanted bread—or *'eish*, which in Egyptian Arabic also connotes life—they were articulating that they wanted prosperity (who doesn't?) and something much more. This was not merely an Egyptian phenomenon. Throughout the Middle East and in various ways in response to differing circumstances, people were connecting the economy, the nature of the political system in which they lived, and their sense of their own dignity. That is why the Gezi protests were about more than trees, Mohammed al-Bouazizi did not kill himself solely because of economic grievances, and Libyans, who were wealthier than their neighbors, pushed Qaddafi from power. Disentangling these issues risked losing the complexity and nuance of what the demonstrations and protests were all about. This is why many observers have looked at the region since this political turbulence began and have shaken their heads in surprise, but they should not. Much more was always at stake than bread.

Yet before anyone in the Middle East could figure out how to forge new governments and more just societies, a cascade of events overwhelmed them. Instead of the light of democracy, Tunisians, Egyptians, Libyans, and Turks woke up to the darkness of violence, political turmoil, and economic uncertainty.

3

Unraveling

LIKE ANY MEGALOPOLIS, CAIRO has its share of aromas—both good and bad—but in mid-December 2011 the now-fabled Tahrir Square had the unmistakable smell of piss. Protesters had taken up residence there for the better part of three weeks.[1] They were living in makeshift tents on the grassy circle that is the focal point of the square; others had made camp on the plaza in front of the massive office building called the Mugamma that is home to 13 ministries and 20,000 bureaucrats; and still more slept on broken-down cardboard boxes atop the air vents for Cairo's Metro.[2] The stench was fitting for the standoff between the "revolution"—a polyglot group of liberals, intellectuals, and activists of all stripes—and the Supreme Council of the Armed Forces, known simply as the SCAF, which had been in charge ever since Egypt's senior commanders informed Hosni Mubarak ten months earlier that his services were no longer needed. It was not at all clear why people were squatting in Tahrir Square. Some principles were involved—justice for those killed during the uprising against Mubarak and demands that the military return to its barracks—but the languid, hippie-like atmosphere was seemingly at odds with what had transpired in Egypt after the heady days of the uprising began to fade.

Just a few weeks earlier, Egyptian security forces had killed forty to fifty people in a melee near the square on Mohammed Mahmoud Street. The rage with which the two sides went at each other was manifest in the torrents of tear gas and indiscriminate buckshot the police rained down on demonstrators and the storm of bricks and rocks that protesters threw back at them. The sit-in participants who had appropriated the square were the remnants of that shocking display of violence. Unlike the events of eleven months earlier, the face-off between those who became known as the revolutionaries and the security forces did not galvanize average Egyptians. Rather they stood by bewildered and confused, left to wonder when this struggle would mercifully come to an end so the tourists would come back, the traffic would flow just a little bit, and crime, which had spiked, would go away.

Then it happened again. In the early hours of December 16, 2011, the military police decided to clear a small number of protesters who had separated themselves from the main sit-in about a quarter of a mile to the south of Tahrir Square and were sprawled out in front of the building that housed the Egyptian cabinet. As they moved in, the soldiers were typically heavy-handed, beating up protesters before hauling them off. The raid was, of course, live-tweeted, stoking outrage among revolutionaries, their supporters in Egypt and around the world, as well as a group of soccer fanatics known as the Ultras. It was the Ultras more than any other group who had broken the backs of the police and the paramilitary Central Security Forces (CSF) in Tahrir Square on January 28, 2011, precipitating the deployment of the army's tanks and armored personnel carriers on Egyptian streets and setting in motion the end to Mubarak's rule.

Things had changed since that moment, however. In activist circles, military commanders had gone from being saviors delivering Egyptians from the corruption, stagnation, and brutality of the Mubarak family and their supporters to being the enemy, the representatives of the old order, and a counterrevolutionary force. No sooner had the Ultras and other activists descended on the area around the Cabinet Building did the chants "The people want the downfall of the field marshal" begin—a reference to Field Marshal Mohammed Hussein al-Tantawi, the minister of defense who led the SCAF. The young toughs who came primed for a fight were far less interested in the political and social issues that raged in the Egyptian press, Twittersphere, and blogs than in payback.[3] After giving the police and the CSF a beating during the January 2011 uprising, the Ultras and others had taken a drubbing in clashes with them and the military police ever since. The four-day battle on Mohammed Mahmoud Street was just the bloodiest of these confrontations.[4]

By nightfall, the fight in front of the Cabinet Building was shaping up to be a replay of what transpired on Mohammed Mahmoud Street. Soldiers, policemen, and protesters hurled rocks, glass bottles, scrap metal, broken office furniture, and Molotov cocktails at each other across a narrow no-man's land that bisected the street.[5] Periodically, the muffled pop, pop, pop of tear-gas canisters being fired would send protesters and onlookers scurrying for cover. The police once again used buckshot liberally. A makeshift field hospital was set up and a steady stream of injured was delivered via motorbike. This scene had been played out over and over again in the preceding months and seemed inspiring from a distance. Selfless, mostly young, Egyptians were literally at the barricades demanding change. Up close it hardly seemed noble. Pointless was perhaps more accurate. The people on the streets seemed interested in fighting or protesting for the sake of it.

During one convulsion of violence—the action tended to ebb and flow—an errant Molotov cocktail crashed through the windows of the Institut d'Égypte, setting ablaze books and artifacts dating back to the sixteenth century. Protesters and onlookers selflessly charged into the burning building, saving many invaluable volumes. These individual acts of bravery and goodwill were exceptions that proved no rule during the whole, deeply disturbing episode, which plumbed further depths the next morning. That was when CSF conscripts beat a young woman with such savagery that she was left splayed on the street with her abaya hiked over her head, revealing a blue bra. One of her attackers, recognizing the double humiliation he and his fellow recruits had visited upon the poor young woman, quickly tried to cover her up before moving on to pummel other demonstrators.[6] The "Girl in the Blue Bra" became a symbol of the SCAF's shocking indifference to the violence being perpetrated in Egypt's streets—a state of affairs confirmed at a post-riot press conference in which Deputy Defense Minister Major General Adel Emara promised an investigation into the incident and then blamed the victims of the security forces' wrath, calling protesters "saboteurs" and declaring, "There is no evidence that we assaulted protesters. . . . [W]e exercised enviably high levels of restraint."[7] To date, no one actually knows whether the investigation to which Emara referred ever took place and, if it did, what its findings were. When the Battle of the Cabinet Building was over, twelve Egyptians were dead.

How did Egyptians get to this twisted version of Tahrir Square?[8] They had gotten what they wanted almost a year earlier, had they not? In one of those incongruities of politics and contingent events, the day before security forces and protesters were senselessly pummeling each other around the Cabinet Building, Egyptians were going to the polls in the second round of parliamentary elections. International observers on hand declared the vote free and fair—a first for Egypt, which has a history of electoral rigging and violence. Yet the act of holding the elections was itself divisive.

The SCAF had been pushing for a quick transition. The officers' initial plan was for Egyptians to elect a new legislature in June or July 2011 and a new president in the months that followed.[9] The Egyptian military establishment had gotten out of the business of running the country after the Israelis humiliated the armed forces in three days in June 1967. In the forty-five years since, it had become part of the Egyptian officer corps' ethos to steer clear of politics and administration. It showed. Tantawi and his men had proven themselves to be shrewd during the January 25 uprising, but subsequently distinguished themselves with clumsy brutality as they sought to establish political control. Far outside of its professional competence, the SCAF claimed to be "preparing the country for democracy" but there was no actual plan. Instead, the officers issued decrees that often roiled Egypt's already unsettled politics and responded to societal demands with a heavy hand, all the while crossing the days off the calendar until they could hand over administration of the country to civilian officials, whoever they might be.

In the abstract, the officers' desire to move forward with the elections and hand the governance of the country to civilians was a good thing. Yet the SCAF's relatively swift timeline sowed distrust of the military's intentions among the cross-section of liberals, secularists, democrats, and revolutionaries. They, along with the United States, the European Union, Western analysts, human rights advocates, and democracy promoters, were calling for a delay, though they did not want too much of a delay. Egyptian activists feared that staging elections before they were ready would empower remnants of Mubarak's old National Democratic Party (NDP) and the Muslim Brotherhood, both of which were better organized and financed.

Scheduling the elections for November 28 and 29, December 14 and 15, and January 3 and 4 was the Goldilocks-like compromise, yet the head-spinning number of democratic, social democratic, and social democratic revolutionary parties were still far from ready. They had spent the months since Mubarak's fall engaged in revolutionary navel-gazing and posturing rather than the hard work of political organizing. The election results reflected it. When all was said and done, the Muslim Brotherhood's Freedom and Justice Party won a plurality of seats in the People's Assembly and the Salafi Nour (Light) Party scored a quarter of the mandates. Together the two parties controlled almost three-quarters of the parliament's 508 seats. Joining them were two small Salafi parties, Fadila (Virtue) and Asala (Authenticity), along with the Free Egyptians Party—a party of decidedly secular but not necessarily liberal economic elites that one of Egypt's wealthiest businessmen, Naguib Sawiris, bankrolled. The Egyptian Social Democratic Party made it into the legislature, as did the representatives of Egypt's old, decrepit, house-broken left, the National Progressive Unionist Party. The Wafd, which had been around since the end of World War I, was also represented. Rounding out the seats were 166 independents and 10 military appointees. Fears that the old ruling party would make a comeback never materialized, though not for lack of trying. The Ittihad (Unity) Party, a sort of NDP-lite led by a former Mubarak-era minister of health and ally of the former president's younger son and once-presumed heir, Gamal Mubarak, was wiped out at the polls.

The SCAF hailed the parliamentary elections and declared that the silent majority had spoken, but the whole exercise masked a groundswell of unease and mistrust among a population that was struggling with all the apparent change and becoming increasingly polarized. After it had become clear that both the Muslim Brotherhood and the Salafis had done well in the first round of elections, an Egyptian interlocutor quipped in disbelief over the stunning changes in fortune of Egypt's political actors, "Last year the people now winning elections were [called] terrorists and the people who won elections last year are now [called] terrorists." With few exceptions, Egyptian secularists and liberals could not quite figure out where the Salafis had come from and whom they represented. According to the Nour Party's spokespeople, this had everything to do with the fact that Egypt's elites (including the Muslim Brotherhood) only knew the denizens of upper- and upper-middle-class neighborhoods like Maadi, Zamalek, and Heliopolis as well as the increasing numbers of gated communities that sprouted around Cairo in the late Mubarak era. The Salafis, in contrast, understood the people in the humble, most underprivileged parts of the country, where they had been active providing for people in need and, in the process, preaching their way to be a good Muslim.

For their part, the bewildering array of activists with different and often competing agendas had much to answer for as well. Despite all the creativity and energy that went into bringing Mubarak down, they quickly demonstrated that, as a group, they did not know what to do with their success. Abroad, they basked in the glory of well-meaning Westerners eager to heap praise on them. At times they did themselves no favors, inexplicably handing their opponents victories through missteps, infighting, and egomania. They brooked no criticism, accusing those who dared question them as *feloul*—supporters of the old regime—which was the scarlet A of the immediate post-uprising period. If the revolutionaries and their supporters were stunned that Islamists had done so well in parliamentary elections, they needed to take a hard look at what they had done, or not done, in the preceding eleven months. They were perhaps alone in wanting to forge a more just and open society—goals that the military and the Muslim Brotherhood merely paid lip service to—but the activists and revolutionaries had lost their way in the twists and turns of post-Mubarak politics. Still, for all of their mistakes and human foibles, their goals were noble. It is for this reason that in subsequent years many of the most prominent among them have been imprisoned or driven from Egypt.

At the time, the Muslim Brothers were the only ones who seemed to fully grasp the political dynamics of post-Mubarak Egypt. In an effort to appeal to the broadest section of Egypt's newly mobilized electorate, they evinced the pragmatism of problem solvers and employed the language of reform, a tactic they had been perfecting since the 1980s.

In various charters and manifestos over the years, including a notional party platform in 2007, the Brotherhood had emphasized clean government, free and fair elections, accountability, and transparency. It was part of a broader vision for Egyptian society that was, it seemed, deeply appealing to a broad range of Egyptians. After the corruption, brutality, and indifference of a leadership that had rendered Egypt, a country that was a natural leader in the region, a second-rate power, the Brothers offered Egyptians what they had been demanding for the better part of a century—economic development, social justice, representative government, and dignity.

In Washington, where the Brotherhood worked diligently to smooth over an eight-decade history of anti-Western sentiment, there was a prevailing gullibility and willingness to believe that the Brothers could be good stewards of democracy and partners with the United States. The reasons to be skeptical, however, were sound. Leaving aside the strictly hierarchical structure of the organization that demanded obedience to its leadership, the Brothers regarded themselves as a vanguard with unique abilities to transform society. The Brotherhood's leadership also believed that electoral victories conferred upon the group a mandate that did not require consensus or negotiation with those who might not agree with them.[10]

There was no better example of this view of the world than the case Abdul Mawgoud al-Dardery made for the Brothers. Although Dardery represented Luxor for the Brotherhood's Freedom and Justice Party and was the spokesman for its foreign policy committee, he was not among the top tier or a decision maker within the Brotherhood. He was influential in one sense, however. The Brotherhood's leadership clearly saw advantages in making him a principal interlocutor with foreigners. With his sunny manner and excellent English, he was a contrast to the dour and vaguely arrogant disposition of the Brotherhood's more senior figures. Dardery seemed to quite like the United States or, at least, was well versed in its history. He could speak eloquently about democracy, weaving in references to Thomas Jefferson, the US Constitution, Abraham Lincoln, John F. Kennedy, and Martin Luther King Jr. It was rather impressive, yet it also seemed a bit forced, dialed up for the benefit of Westerners seeking to understand the Brotherhood's intentions. It was also a contrast to the NDP-like way Dardery carried himself around Luxor—greeting adoring constituents who kissed his ring, tearing around town in a car at high speeds with little regard for other traffic and the long queues for gas, or reveling in the obsequious staff who lined up to meet him in the lobby of the famous Winter Palace Hotel. After a long discussion in July 2012 that touched on US-Middle East policy, Israel, American Jews, and the Palestinians, the conversation turned to the challenges facing Egypt. Without going into detail, Dardery was confident that whatever obstacles lay in the country's path Egyptians were sure to overcome them. They had brought down Mubarak, hadn't they? Yet, in an unvarnished moment, he allowed, "If we can get rid of the *feloul* in the judiciary and the military, we can transform this country." On August 12, 2012, a month after the conversation with Dardery, the Muslim Brotherhood's Mohammed Morsi, who was just six weeks into his presidential term, sacked Field Marshal Tantawi, Chief of Staff of the Armed Forces Lieutenant General Sami Enan, and the commanders of Egypt's navy, air force, and air defense command.

The surprisingly effortless way that Morsi dispatched the man who had been minister of defense for two decades and the well-respected Enan capped what had proven to be an eventful six months. After insisting for months that it would not run its own presidential candidate in elections scheduled for the spring of 2012, the Brotherhood announced that Deputy Supreme Guide Khairat al-Shater would be its standard bearer. The announcement made an already fraught political environment edgier. The Brothers claimed they had no choice because they could not find a candidate the organization could support, but this was a cover story. Given their plurality of seats in the lower house of parliament and a slight majority in its upper house (elections for the Shura Council were held in late January and early February), the presidency was a prize that was too difficult to resist. If Shater was successful, the Brotherhood would finally control Egypt after so many years of political struggle.

At least seventeen others initially joined the race, including such marquee names as Amr Moussa, the Arab League's secretary-general and longtime foreign minister; Ahmed Shafik, an air force officer who had served as minister of civil aviation from 2002 to 2011 and then as Mubarak's last prime minister; a Nasserist throwback named Hamdeen

Sabbahi; Abdel Moneim Aboul Fotouh, a former Muslim Brother thrown out of the group for defying its leadership over his intention to seek the presidency; and Omar Suleiman, Egypt's longtime intelligence chief and—ever so briefly—vice president during the final, turbulent two weeks of Mubarak's presidency. In another development that set Egypt on edge, the Presidential Election Commission barred Suleiman, Shater, and a Salafi preacher named Hazem Salah Abu Ismail as well as a slew of other candidates of various degrees of renown. The commission offered a variety of technical reasons for the disqualifications, but Egyptians understood the decision was ultimately political. Shater, in particular, was too much of a threat to win.[11] In his place, the Brotherhood put forward Morsi. He had led the group's contingent of eighty-eight "independents"—the Brotherhood was outlawed until after the uprising—in the 2005 to 2010 parliament, a group that distinguished itself as sophisticated and scrappy legislators. Morsi, with his colorless and rough-around-the-edges persona, had little of Shater's gravitas and was thus given little chance of winning.

The polls and commentators indicated that it was a two-man race between Moussa and Aboul Fotouh. Moussa had spent time subtly distancing himself from Mubarak after being sent to the Arab League; it was believed he could capture enough of the establishment and average Egyptians to win. Aboul Fotouh portrayed himself as the candidate representing the revolution. It was not quite accurate, but he garnered support from younger Muslim Brothers who wanted to emulate Turkey's Justice and Development Party and a fair number of activists and revolutionaries to brand himself a "liberal Islamist," putting him in a position to capture a broad spectrum of the electorate. He also picked up support from the Nour Party, which had an uneasy relationship with the Brotherhood. The polls proved wildly inaccurate. Neither Moussa nor Aboul Fotouh made it out of the first round, having garnered, respectively, only 11 and 17.5 percent of the vote. Instead, the presidential race turned out to be a showdown between Morsi, who had never polled higher than 14 percent but ended up winning almost 25 percent of the popular vote, and Shafik, whose 23.6 percent was also unexpected. With the Brotherhood's Morsi up against Shafik—a representative of the old order—it was as if the dynamics of Egyptian politics had not changed.

On June 24, Morsi was declared the winner: 51.7 percent to Shafik's 48.3 percent. The Brothers and other supporters of Morsi danced in Tahrir Square. Morsi's opponents bitterly refuted the outcome. Not only did they claim that the Brotherhood purchased votes at 1,200 Egyptian pounds a family—Shafik's campaign did the same, but had fewer resources—but they also argued that the announced result was the product of Brotherhood blackmail. The day after the runoff, in the early hours of June 18, the Brothers announced that, by their count, Morsi had prevailed. For Shafik's supporters, the announcement had nothing to do with exit polls but was rather an implicit threat. Should the Presidential Election Commission declare Shafik the winner, unrest would follow. As a result, the commission and the military caved, ignominiously acceding to the Brothers. If this were in fact the case, it was consistent with the officers' desire to ensure social cohesion and stability over almost everything else—even though the SCAF often pursued policies with quite the opposite effect. Yet Tantawi and his men were not entirely ready to hand the country over to either Shafik or Morsi. Late on June 17, after the polling places closed, the military issued a decree that expanded the military's powers and prerogatives in defense and national security at the expense of the presidency.

Egypt was a strange place in the summer of 2012. A Muslim Brother was president of the country, a development that before the uprising existed only in the realm of the theoretical. Morsi made things difficult for himself when, shortly after taking the oath of office in June 2012, he announced that he wanted to bring back parliament, which the SCAF had dissolved just before the runoff for the presidential election. The Supreme Constitutional Court had recommended that the parliament be dissolved based on what the justices called "a misapplication of rules for independent candidates," which meant that one-third of the legislature held their seats illegitimately. In the eyes of Morsi's detractors, this was an early indicator of the Brotherhood's disrespect for the law and disregard for checks and balances. It was all quite rich coming from people who had been comfortable with the Mubarak era's shortcomings in these areas. The new president had a fair point about what had been done to parliament. He and his advisors no doubt believed that they were striking a blow against the judges, many of whom owed their positions to the ousted president and shared an anti-Brotherhood worldview. Perhaps Morsi believed it would galvanize demonstrations, forcing the Supreme Constitutional Court to cave in. He had, after all, secured the support of "the revolution" during his second-round election campaign in what was called the Fairmont Agreement. In exchange for the backing of a diverse array of activists, revolutionaries, intellectuals, and politicians, Morsi promised to work across Egypt's political spectrum to advance the goals of the so-called revolution and thereby prevent the SCAF from reestablishing an authoritarian political system.[12] Morsi's call for the reinstatement of the parliament had some backing, but most of it came from his Brotherhood supporters who camped outside the Supreme Constitutional Court building. The justices did not bend, however, and the People's Assembly remained closed.

Morsi may have been stymied by Egypt's most senior justices, but the new president seemed intent on making good on his rhetorical support for change, which was why his decapitation of the military command was greeted with general enthusiasm among the Brothers and the activist community. At the very least, uprooting Egypt's well-developed national security state and bringing an autonomous military establishment under civilian control would provide a more auspicious environment for democracy to flourish.[13] Major General Abdel Fattah al-Sisi— who commanded the Military Intelligence and Reconnaissance Services and was, at fifty-eight years old, the youngest member of the SCAF— became the new defense minister. Sisi had graduated from Egypt's military academy as an infantry officer the same year that Anwar al-Sadat made his visit to Jerusalem. His military career had been during peacetime, though he was deployed to Saudi Arabia during Operations Desert Shield and Desert Storm in 1990 and 1991. The 35,000 Egyptian forces there did little fighting, but Sisi nevertheless wore the Liberation of Kuwait Medal. When Morsi made him defense minister, Sisi evinced a humble tone and subtly signaled his belief that the previous eighteen months had damaged the armed forces.[14] In Cairo, speculation swirled about his alleged sympathies toward the Brotherhood. This was not so according to Robert Springborg—one of the world's leading authorities on militaries in the Middle East, but especially in Egypt. He described Sisi as certainly an Islamist, but whose loyalties were with the armed forces, not the Brothers.[15]

For the remainder of the summer and through the early fall, Egypt remained fraught. Morsi and the Brothers grappled ineffectively with Egypt's economic mess, resisted pressure from the International Monetary Fund to undertake reforms, and alternately enabled and distanced themselves from ugly protests in front of the US Embassy. Then came November 2012. For eight days beginning on the fourteenth of the month, the Israel Defense Forces pounded the Gaza Strip in response to rocket fire from the area. This was the first major flare-up of Palestinian-Israeli violence since Morsi had come to power. Washington held its breath. Since the 1930s, the Brothers had played a leading role in shaping Egypt's anti-Zionist and virulently anti-Semitic discourse. These sentiments were widely shared, but because of the Brotherhood's long campaign against Egypt's normalization of relations with Israel, a variety of observers wondered whether the 1979 peace treaty was in jeopardy.[16] The question was particularly acute as the hostilities between the Israelis and Hamas escalated. It turned out that the concern about Egypt-Israel relations was misplaced. Morsi sought to complicate Israeli military operations by dispatching the Egyptian prime minister to Gaza in solidarity with the people under fire there. He recalled the Egyptian ambassador from Tel Aviv while he and the Brotherhood's senior leaders made tough statements about Israel, but the status quo did not change. When it came to hammering out a ceasefire, the Egyptian presidency, Egypt's General Intelligence Directorate, the White House, the State Department, and the Israeli prime ministry all made important contributions. Morsi never had any direct contact with the Israelis, but he and his advisors nevertheless understood the stakes involved and worked closely with American officials, primarily from the State Department, to bring hostilities to an end.[17]

The respite turned out to be rather brief, however. The day after the Israelis and Palestinians stopped firing at each other, Morsi issued a presidential edict that shielded both his decisions and the work of the Constituent Assembly—whose membership mirrored the apportionment of seats in the dissolved parliament and that had been working to draft a new constitution since June—from judicial review. Morsi was not exactly "getting rid of *feloul* judges" as Dardery had openly suggested, but he was clearly exercising the executive's power to issue decrees to ignore the judiciary. This was a power that even his deposed predecessor did not enjoy. Mubarak, of course, did everything he could over thirty years to build a judiciary willing to do his bidding. In many respects he succeeded, but the judiciary at certain moments jealously and successfully guarded its constitutionally mandated independence and prerogatives. The Supreme Constitutional Court had consistently struck down various iterations of electoral laws that the ruling party–dominated People's Assembly kept passing to keep itself in power. In 2006, the justices and the government clashed when two judges revealed evidence of fraud during the previous year's parliamentary elections. It is important not to overstate the case; the Mubarak-era judiciary was hardly a check on executive and legislative power, but Mubarak was at times forced to abide by rulings he did not like. With his decree, Morsi—whose election international observers considered a step forward for Egypt, but not as "free and fair" as the parliamentary elections six months earlier—rendered himself accountable to no one.[18]

Morsi and the Brotherhood had a different interpretation of events, of course. In issuing the decree, the president believed he was bolstering his and the Brotherhood's revolutionary credibility. Exempting oneself from judicial review and declaring it revolutionary seemed odd, especially because Egyptians had risen up in part because social justice, dignity, and representative government required accountability. From the Brotherhood's perspective, they were working to clear out the remnants of the old regime that were impeding progress. Shielding Morsi and the Constituent Assembly from the machinations of hated judges, who were responsible for dissolving Egypt's first freely and fairly elected parliament, would play well in Tahrir, would it not? The president's expanded powers, his supporters argued, were intended to be temporary anyway—a necessary measure to ensure that the promise of the uprising would be realized.

The problem was that the surest pathway to democratic politics is to support democracy. Morsi and his Brothers had failed to grasp this concept after sixty years of suffering under strongmen; Egyptians no longer seemed willing to tolerate authoritarian detours in the name of democracy. Morsi's predecessors always played for time, too. The state of emergency, under which Egyptians had lived almost continuously since 1958, was also purportedly temporary. Mubarak, Sadat, and Gamal Abdel Nasser before them also often pursued authoritarian solutions to their problems under the guise of reform. Morsi's decree precipitated a full-blown political crisis with angry demonstrations taking place in seventeen governorates beginning on November 22. In Cairo, the protests began in Tahrir Square—to commemorate the clashes on Mohammed Mahmoud Street—before moving to the Ittihadiyya Palace on December 4, where demonstrations lasted until December 6.[19] Unlike the protests of late January and early February 2011 or any since then, the December 2012 demonstrations had a dangerous new dimension. Yes, the battle at the Cabinet Building and the Mohammed Mahmoud Street clashes combined killed about sixty people, and a showdown with the military in October 2011 left twenty-eight dead, mostly Coptic Christians. But what distinguished the protests at the Ittihadiyya Palace from others was not the body count; it was how they exposed the final rupture in the "we are all Egyptians" sentiment that had made Tahrir Square such an inspiring place two years earlier. Outside the palace were people who had flocked there to support and defend Morsi and, facing them across a narrow physical boundary, those who fervently believed he had betrayed the promise of the revolution.

This was the context of Egyptian politics in the subsequent eight months that culminated in the coup d'état of July 3, 2013. As a petition to force Morsi into early presidential elections gained traction—allegedly with the help of the secret police—the Brothers and their supporters dug in. They disparaged what was known as the Tamarrod (Rebellion) Movement as anti-democratic and anti-revolutionary while mobilizing the Brotherhood's base with an increasingly defiant message. While the Brotherhood and its antagonists were engaged in increasingly dramatic political maneuvers and statements, Egypt was running out of money, gas, and electricity. In response, the minister of defense, Major General Abdel Fattah al-Sisi, gave the government and its opponents an ultimatum: agree to work together for the sake of Egypt or there will be consequences. Rather than pursuing reconciliation, Morsi and the opposition primed their supporters for confrontation. On the evening of June 26—just four days before a planned protest to demand early elections—Morsi rallied the Brotherhood in a speech that gave no ground, reminding everyone that he was elected president, calling his opponents undemocratic, threatening to purge those who did not support him, and directing the organs of the government to go after those who he claimed had sought to undermine him.[20] The combination of Morsi's uncompromising defense of his presidency and the opposition's determination to force early elections raised the specter of violence. The June 30 protests turned out to be massive, even larger than anti-Mubarak demonstrations during the January 25, 2011 uprising. Three days later, tanks and troops appeared on Egypt's streets as another president was deposed and Egyptians yet again were promised a new era of social justice, economic opportunity, representative government, and dignity. Those promises remained unfulfilled in the ensuing years; even as Egypt's new leaders implemented their "roadmap to democracy," they also filled up prisons and body bags.

In the Turkish capital, Ankara, the news of Egypt's coup d'état was met with outrage and alarm. Turkey's then prime minister, Recep Tayyip Erdoğan, had invested a significant amount of political and diplomatic capital in post-Mubarak Egypt. He had been the first world leader in early 2011 to call publicly on the Egyptian president to listen to his people and leave. This only added to the reservoir of goodwill Erdoğan enjoyed in Egypt (as well as other parts of the Arab world). Even before the uprising, the Turkish leader and the party he led had intrigued Egypt's opposition. The Justice and Development Party (AKP), which had come to power nine years earlier, had proven that pious politicians and the secularism of the state could coexist with positive political, economic, and societal results. For different reasons, the AKP's success was deeply appealing to Arab Islamists and liberals who made the trek in ever increasing numbers throughout the 2000s to Istanbul to discover the secret to Erdoğan's success. That the Turkish leader was never shy about speaking out forcefully over what he considered to be Israeli transgressions, especially in the Gaza Strip, also helped his and Turkey's popularity in the Arab world.

Although Erdoğan angered the Muslim Brothers during a visit to Cairo in September 2011 when he emphasized the difference between personal piety and secular politics in a television interview, it was Erdoğan—along with the Qatari emir—who gave the Brothers sanctuary when Egypt's military command moved against them in the summer of 2013. Alone among Middle Eastern leaders, Erdoğan harshly criticized the Egyptian officers. He dismissed Egyptian declarations of a second "popular revolution" and Sisi's "roadmap to democracy," instead calling the military's intervention what it was—a coup d'état. Given Turkey's history of coups and suppression of Islamist politicians, Erdoğan's response was hardly surprising. It was also a setback for Turkey's position in the region. The prime minister and his foreign minister, the academic Ahmet Davutoğlu, shared a worldview in which the future of the region lay with Islamists.[21] For Turkey to lead the Middle East going forward, Ankara needed to cultivate relationships with the Muslim Brothers, Tunisia's Ennahda Movement, the Syrian Muslim Brotherhood, and even a terrorist organization like Hamas. Opposition to the coup was also a matter of principle. For the Turks, regardless of accusations that the Brotherhood bought votes or manipulated the Presidential Election Commission and the SCAF with thinly veiled threats of disorder, Morsi was the democratically elected leader of Egypt. The new order coming into place under Sisi was thus entirely illegitimate.

It was a strong and principled defense of the ideals of the so-called Arab Spring, but with the exception of the Brotherhood, it fell on deaf ears. By the time Erdoğan called for Morsi's return in the name of democracy, the Turkish leader had already lost much of his constituency of Arab liberals, leftists, and revolutionaries for whom the AKP's political project had been a source of admiration and fascination. Egypt's coup also came amid a long and hot summer of protest and violence that began over plans to redevelop Gezi Park—nine acres of trees and concrete adjacent to Istanbul's famous Taksim Square—into a shopping mall designed to look like the Ottoman-era barracks that had once stood on the site. In a variety of important ways, the AKP has been a transformative force, improving the lives of Turks in various important ways against the backdrop of a compelling vision of Turkey's future as an influential, prosperous, and democratic country. As for Erdoğan, he was wildly popular among the roughly half of the population who supported the AKP. It was easy for anyone who had ever been within five feet of him to conclude that he was among the most effective and forceful politicians of his time—only former president Bill Clinton seemed possibly more so. Erdoğan has an innate ability to reach Turks at their core. It is not just that he understands what makes his constituents tick; it is almost as if he represents every dream, wish, and desire they have ever had for Turkey and themselves. Erdoğan also seemed to be the ultimate expression of the new Turkish man—strong, emotional, pious, confident, clear-eyed, and unapologetic about Turkey's greatness. It helped that he was up against weak opposition parties that had more trouble identifying what they stood for than whom they opposed, namely Erdoğan. Taken together, it was no wonder that the AKP had dominated the political arena since 2002. In the ten elections the AKP has competed in since its founding, the party has experienced only two setbacks: the March 2009 local elections when the party underperformed, but still received almost 40 percent of the vote, and the June 2015 parliamentary elections when the party's support plummeted 9 percentage points from the previous national total. That relatively poor performance was reversed in a controversial rerun of the elections after the parties could not agree on a coalition government (discussed in greater detail in the next chapter).

Yet for all the good that the AKP had done and despite Erdoğan's obvious charisma, the party's mastery of Turkish politics also had a darker side that included patronage, intimidation, and crony capitalism. The deal was straightforward: the business community had to play by the AKP's rules or they would not have access to government contracts. Those who resisted faced the punitive power of the Turkish state. A focal point for the Turkish version of pay-to-play was the Toplu Konut İdaresi (TOKİ), the Mass Housing Administration. Its mission is an important one: to provide housing for low-income groups who are priced out of the market in Turkey's urban areas. Yet it actually provided low-cost land for developers to build luxury housing and shopping malls for newly affluent Turks. A full half of TOKİ's projects had nothing at all to do with relieving the pressure of the high cost of housing on the poor. The amount of money that sloshed through this system and the vast acreage that was at TOKİ's disposal created a powerful mechanism through which the government distributed real estate and allocated construction contracts in return for political support.[22]

The AKP's great political success did not mean, however, that it could ratchet back the patronage. The opposite was the case. As the party became bigger and Erdoğan's ambitions grew, pressure to ensure the smooth transfer of money in return for political support was continual. This was the context in which the redevelopment of Gezi Park was planned. The protesters who gathered there on May 27, 2013, to protect that shady spot in Istanbul's core were specifically opposed to the re-development of the park and, by extension, the AKP's urban planning and environmental records. These were niche issues that were sure to keep the number of demonstrators low. Yet the protests grew, especially as the government ramped up its rhetoric against the motley group that pitched tents and unrolled sleeping bags in the park. When the Turkish police attacked the demonstrators at dawn on May 30, Turks were galvanized.[23] As in Tunisia, Egypt, and Libya two years earlier, the Turkish government's resort to force had precisely the opposite of the intended effect. Rather than intimidate people and convince fence-sitters to stay where they were, the state's violence brought thousands upon thousands of people on to the streets demanding change.

The convulsions of protests lasted almost three weeks, engulfing central Istanbul, downtown Ankara, Izmir, and a host of smaller cities across the country. The punishment meted out on protesters was not unusual for Turkish security forces or, for that matter, police departments in American cities, though the mixture of water and pepper spray that police doused on demonstrators was a special Turkish cruelty. In his fury over being challenged, Erdoğan ostentatiously sought to burnish his cult of personality, attacked social media, and spun dark conspiracies about foreigners seeking to bring Turkey down. Protest leaders were detained and some were subsequently charged with terrorism. This only confirmed just how far Erdoğan and the AKP had veered from the party's early promise of an Islamist Third Way that resolved the problem of religion and politics in an officially secular political system and that could lead Turkey into the European Union—a club of liberal democracies. This was the seemingly reformist AKP of November 2002, when it was first elected, and of August 2007, when Turkish voters gave it another parliamentary majority based on a broad coalition of Turks that included religious conservatives, secular liberals, cosmopolitan elites, the middle class, Kurds, and the business elite. It was this AKP that seemed to have fascinated Saudis, Egyptians, Tunisians, and many others in the region who, sensitive to what they regarded as the West's double standards when it came to Arabs and Muslims, regarded the party's accumulation of political power as a test of the European and American commitment to democracy in Middle Eastern societies.

What its Arab admirers did not know—indeed, could not know—was that the AKP's own commitment to democracy would come under scrutiny not long after analysts and officials in the West had hailed it as a success.[24] The explosion of anger around Gezi Park and the government's use of force to put it down was not actually the moment when Ankara departed from the promising path the AKP laid in 2003 and 2004 with a series of reforms and constitutional amendments that qualified Turkey to begin European Union membership negotiations (discussed in greater detail in the next chapter). Rather, the volleys of tear gas, merciless water cannons, and metal batons of the Çevik Kuvvet Polis, the riot police, were just a visible and violent manifestation of the country's authoritarian turn that had been under way for the previous six years.

The story begins in the spring of 2007, when the Turkish military's General Staff made it clear, via a statement on its website, that the senior command did not look kindly on then foreign minister Abdullah Gül becoming Turkey's next president as the AKP had planned. In years past, civilian leaders would have backed down and sought a candidate who was acceptable to the military establishment. That is precisely the way the incumbent, a solemn Constitutional Court justice and hard-core secularist named Ahmet Necdet Sezer, had become president in 2000. Erdoğan, sensing his party's popularity and how much Turkish society had changed in the almost five years since the AKP came to power, refused to be intimidated. He called for new elections in August, which, as noted, the party won with 47 percent of the vote, and, with his party's renewed popular mandate, nominated Gül to be Turkey's eleventh president. Large-scale protests in which signs declaring "Neither sharia nor a coup, a democratic Turkey" dotted a sea of Turkish flags were primarily directed at the officers, giving Erdoğan and the ruling party momentum.

In the midst of the showdown between Erdoğan and the General Staff, the Istanbul police uncovered an alleged plot to overthrow the government.[25] This was what came to be known as the Ergenekon case, which captivated Turkey from 2007 until verdicts were rendered in 2013.[26] Initially, the investigation brought relief to Turks, especially those who called themselves liberals and who saw the case as a first step in rooting out Turkey's "deep state"—an alleged network of military, intelligence, and civilian officials along with policemen, journalists, academics, business people, and mafia figures. Working in the shadows and beyond the law, the group's goal was, Turks believed, to subvert the government and any centers of power that would challenge "the system" and this coalition's interests in it. After Ergenekon came the Sledgehammer investigation in 2010, which ensnared large numbers of senior military commanders in another suspected effort to bring down the government. Given Turkey's history of coups, the alleged schemes seemed entirely plausible. In time, however, it came to light that significant portions of the evidence in both cases were flimsy or even fabricated.[27] Ergenekon, in particular, became a conspiracy within a conspiracy, used to go after both people who could very well have been plotting to overthrow the elected government and outspoken but otherwise peaceful critics of the AKP.

In addition to these spectacles, during which large numbers of officers were arrested and civilian prosecutors armed with search warrants entered military bases searching for incriminating evidence, the government arrested journalists, often on specious charges of supporting terrorism; sued critics of Erdoğan; imposed massive fines on businesses whose owners failed to support the AKP; and intimidated social media companies like Twitter and Facebook to share data on their users. The AKP also brought pressure to bear on companies that wanted to do business with the government, encouraging them to purchase media properties that could then be counted on to faithfully report what the prime ministry wanted. The Turkish Radio and Television Corporation—Turkey's national public broadcaster—and the Anadolu Agency, the state-run wire service, were also transformed from reliable news outlets into organizations hardly distinguishable from the AKP's political operation. The result was a virtual ministry of information of pro-AKP newspapers and television stations along with an army of tweeps who spread Erdoğan's message and trolled all those who disagreed. Within this alternate reality, Erdoğan was the Büyük Usta— the Great Master—and his opponents were a parallel state made up of everyone from Zionists, international bankers, Islamophobes, the

Central Intelligence Agency, the American ambassador, CNN, social media, and, beginning in 2013, "Pennsylvania." Erdoğan's reference to the Keystone State had nothing to do with 12,787,208 of its 12,787,209 residents. The one person with whom Pennsylvania came to be associated exclusively in Turkish political discourse is a cleric named Fethullah Gülen, who lives in exile on a compound in Saylorsburg, a town about ninety miles northwest of Philadelphia.

Few Turks are neutral on Gülen and his supporters—they are either a grave danger intent on undermining the state and replacing it with a theocracy or they are liberals who strive to fuse religious belief with modernity in a way that stresses science, a variety of philosophical traditions, and coexistence. Erdoğan's war with the cleric intensified after the failed July 2016 coup d'état, which the Turkish government blamed on Gülen and the followers he was alleged to have infiltrated into the officer corps. Yet Gülen's residence in the United States—he is a green card holder—was not due to the mutual animosity between himself and Erdoğan. Rather, he left Turkey in 1999 in fear that the military would have him arrested. Until 2013, Gülen and Erdoğan were partners whose respective organizations worked together and in parallel to transform Turkish society. The two big men of Turkish politics fell out over a series of issues relating to constitutional amendments; the government's overtures to the Kurdistan Workers' Party, a group that had been spilling Turkish blood since 1984; and the closure of schools affiliated with the Gülen movement. It culminated in an alleged Gülen-inspired investigation into wide-ranging corruption among associates and family members of Erdoğan surrounding an international sanctions–busting scheme to trade gold for oil with Iran. Erdoğan responded with massive purges of the police and prosecutors and declared war on the Gülen movement's affiliated media and business interests, adding a new dimension to Turkey's already polarized and increasingly authoritarian political environment.

This authoritarian turn has made it relatively easy for critics to charge that the AKP was never and could never be a genuine force for democratic change. In hindsight, that is likely true. Erdoğan is, after all, the man who declared democratization was "like a streetcar," implying that one could disembark whenever it suited one's purposes.[28] At the same time, it would be disingenuous to overlook the AKP's first term from 2002 to 2007, when pragmatism and consensus marked Turkish politics. Controversies arose, of course, but Erdoğan seemed determined not to do anything that would unnecessarily heat up the political arena and jeopardize his ambitious agenda, which seemed to include a more open and democratic Turkey. One of Erdoğan's great achievements during this period was broadening political participation in Turkey. For as long as the Turkish Republic existed—with perhaps the exception of the 1950s when the Democrat Party dominated the political arena—Turkey's politics had been the province of the nationalist-secularist elite. This meant that resources of the state were directed in a way that privileged like-minded groups and created incentives to conform. Those who had an alternate vision for Turkey's future were delegitimized and attacked as reactionaries in the case of Islamists or, when it came to Kurds who constitute 20 percent of the population and who want recognition of their ethnic identity, separatists. Erdoğan and the AKP wrought a new political elite that was not educated at the famous high school Galatasaray Lisesi, where Turkish elites have sent their children since the Ottoman period, and Boğaziçi University—founded as Robert College in 1863, whose curriculum and campus are reminiscent of elite liberal arts colleges in the United States—or that training ground for future leaders of the Turkish bureaucracy, Ankara University. The new elite was pious, from Anatolia, and their wives wore the hijab. The AKP also had a large Kurdish constituency. Only those gullible in the extreme believed any liberal democrats were in the AKP's leadership ranks. Still, the prospect of European Union membership, a long-standing Turkish goal, created incentives for reform. The allure of Europe and what looked like the AKP's commitment to political change had the practical effect of loosening the old elite's grip and its authoritarian legacy in favor of a more open political environment.[29]

The expansion of politics, and with it the discourse about Turkish society and its future, was a welcome development. In time, however, confronted with challenges real and perceived from the military and the judiciary—which in 2008 found that the AKP sought to undermine the secular nature of the republic, but fell short of enough votes to close it—the party's leaders and their supporters did precisely what the old leadership had done. They used the AKP's parliamentary mandates to ensure that the party's opponents could neither question their agenda nor effectively contest politics. The AKP (and the secular elite) valorized elections and embedded the idea in the minds of many Turks that because elections had been consistently held without fail, Turkey was a democracy. Yet neither Erdoğan nor anyone who came before him ever embraced the principles and ideals of democracy, which necessarily compromised the assertion that the Turkish political system was democratic. Rather, they harbored a majoritarian view of democracy in which accounting for the views of the losers in the political process was not necessary. This outlook was accentuated in the AKP era if only because Erdoğan and the party had been so successful in securing parliamentary majorities, which over time would institutionalize the power of the party, creating what was essentially a one-party state. The authoritarianism of Erdoğan's Turkey was further reinforced in the aftermath of the failed July 2016 coup when the Turkish leader harnessed the outrage of his fellow citizens who firmly rejected the attempted putsch to undertake a widespread crackdown of his opponents. The government had the responsibility to bring the perpetrators of the power grab—which killed at least 240 people—to justice, but the zeal with which Erdoğan oversaw the resulting purge indicated that he intended to use the episode to reinforce his personal power. Within a few weeks of the coup, about 67,000 police officers, soldiers, teachers, bureaucrats, university administrators, and judges were arrested, suspended, or fired. Journalists and editors were also arrested as the government shut down more than a hundred media outlets.

Erdoğan was not an outlier in his illiberal and populist view that support of the masses conferred upon him and the AKP the power to advance their agenda regardless of the large number of Turks who disagreed with them. As noted above, Egypt's Muslim Brothers articulated a similar view, as did Egypt's old National Democratic Party. In Libya, Muammar al-Qaddafi had taken the idea well beyond populism to establish elaborate formal mechanisms for the Libyan people to rule directly. It was, of course, deception on a grand scale that fooled no one, though over time the world was willing to overlook the brutality of Qaddafi's Jamahiriyya and its attendant social and economic costs. By the mid-2000s, after Qaddafi renounced terrorism and gave up his program to develop weapons of mass destruction, the Libyan leader was no longer the "mad dog" of the Middle East, as President Ronald Reagan once referred to him, but an eccentric curiosity: the guy in flowing robes in the escort of female bodyguards and a Bulgarian nurse. The large tent he pitched in suburban New Jersey when he attended the annual United Nations General Assembly meeting in September 2009 was a source of oddball fascination that received considerable attention from the local New York media. It was just Qaddafi being Qaddafi.

The problem was, of course, that Qaddafi had not actually come in from the cold and rehabilitated himself. He was ready to embrace economic reforms, no longer sponsored terrorism, and respected the borders of Libya's neighbors, but Qaddafi raped his bodyguards, tortured his nurse, and remained a threat to Libyans. When hundreds of them rose up in Benghazi on February 15, 2011, in protest over the arrest of a human rights lawyer named Fathi Terbil and demanded both the release of all political prisoners and an end to Qaddafi's rule, the Libyan leader responded almost immediately with violence. Within two days, eighty Libyans were killed at the hands of security forces. Two weeks later, the country fell into civil war. In the midst of the fighting, a National Transitional Council (NTC) arose out of several rebel groups and announced itself the representative of the Libyan people. The NTC was to give coherence to the military campaign, provide services in areas that it held, and prepare for a new democratic Libya.[30] In late March, it issued its "Vision of a Democratic Libya," which solemnly declared the NTC's responsibility "to write a constitution, permit the development of political parties and civil society organizations, ensure pluralism and the peaceful transfer of power, guarantee the right to vote, and secure freedom of expression and assembly."[31] It sounded quite promising, but a war remained to be fought and won. Throughout the spring, Qaddafi and rebel forces took turns trading momentum on the battlefield. Qaddafi's advances were followed with stalemate; stalemate was followed by rebel gains, and then stalemate again. It was not until the summer of 2011, when NATO airstrikes began directly targeting Qaddafi, that rebel groups gained the upper hand permanently. Qaddafi fled Tripoli in August, just a few weeks after the NTC issued its August 3 constitutional declaration, which stated that Libya was an "independent democratic state wherein the people are the source of powers" and promised that "Libyans shall be equal before the law."[32] The declaration also envisioned a state that guaranteed the range of personal and political freedoms that are most commonly associated with the democracies of the West.[33] Libyans actually produced a draft constitution in the fall of 2015, but it was hopelessly divorced from the reality of the country's fragmentation and violence.

It is hard to determine exactly when and how Libya unraveled. Some moments provided great hope. On October 23, 2011, Mustafa Abdul Jalil, the chairman of the NTC, declared the country to be liberated. This move, along with the NTC's Vision of a Democratic Libya and its constitutional declaration, was an early effort to set the tone for what many Libyans hoped would be a transition to democracy. At the same time, profound skepticism was warranted. At a broad abstract level, Libya faced challenges similar to those in Iraq. Both included regions that had never been fully integrated into the country in a way that made sense to the people who lived there. In Libya, the eastern part of the country, which had been known to colonialists as Cyrenaica and to Arabs as Barqah, chafed under the political domination of Tripoli. It was also an economy that depended solely on oil, much of which is found in the east.

In addition, Qaddafi depended on support through an informal network of civilian officials and military officers that profited from the Jamahiriyya. He also played tribal and regional politics to elicit support for his rule. It is true that tribal affiliation in Libya was less important in major urban centers like Tripoli and Benghazi, but both tribe and place (which are often coterminous) were critical to the well-being of Libyans confronting the shortcomings of Qaddafi's economic and social policies. As a result, after the uprising began, tribal and regional affiliations imposed themselves on Libya's transition, especially in the absence of countervailing political and social institutions. Being Misratan, Zintani, or of the Qadhadhfa (around Sirte), for example, has always been a vital part of one's identity in Libya, but once the Jamahiriyya came under assault in early 2011 and chaos ensued, people looked to tribe and region for support and survival more than ever before.

More tangibly, the immediate militarization of the uprising and how quickly Libyan society fell into war suggested that the challenges of post-Qaddafi Libya would likely be fundamentally different from even the enormous challenge of democratization. Saif al-Islam al-Qaddafi—the leader's son and heir apparent—embodied this abrupt resort to violence. With his advanced degree from the London School of Economics; jargon-laden, consultant-prepared discourse on reform; leadership of the Qaddafi Foundation; and stated desire to open Libya to the world, Saif was a bit of a celebrity in the West in the mid-2000s.[34] Like Egypt's Gamal Mubarak and Syria's Bashar al-Assad—the sons of other strongmen—Saif allegedly "got it" and, according to any number of sympathetic profiles, he represented a new generation of elites who wanted to forge a kinder, gentler Middle East. It was all so wildly inaccurate. In the wee hours of the morning on February 20, 2011, Saif appeared on Libyan television and, in the culmination of what seemed to be a totally unprepared address warning people of the uncontrolled forces that would be released as a result of the uprising, which was then only a few days old, he declared, "We will not sell Libya short. We will fight to our very last man, woman, and bullet."[35] It was a chilling performance.

Then came the way Qaddafi was treated when he was apprehended and killed. On October 21, the *New York Post*—in the way only its headline writers can—declared, "Khadafy killed by a 20-year-old Yankees fan."[36] The paper identified Mohammed al-Bibi, who in the accompanying picture was wearing a grayish-blue colored version of the iconic New York Yankees baseball hat, as the gunman who ended the Libyan leader's life. For the *Post* and its reporter, Andy Soltis, it was the opportunity to add a local and humorous angle to a story of major international importance. The paper also referred to Bibi as "Mr. October," a name first bestowed on Reggie Jackson, the late 1970s Yankees slugger who tended to perform best during the Major League Baseball's October playoffs and World Series. Yet the macabre charm of the *Post*'s headline and story quickly wore off as details emerged that Qaddafi was beaten and sodomized before being shot in the head. Libyan officials blamed the humiliation and degradation of the man on youthful anger and enthusiasm, but it portended a deeper, more troubling problem that would plague Libya in the ensuing years. The combination of the utter lack of respect for basic decency—a situation for which Qaddafi was largely to blame—and the dearth of formal rules that could contain the worst human instincts contributed to Libya's descent into a multisided war.

Unlike in Tunisia or Egypt, a modicum of stability never returned in Libya. Throughout the remainder of 2011 and well into 2012, the interim prime minister, Abdurrahim al-Keib, and Mustafa Abdul Jalil, the NTC's chairman, were confronted with escalating violence among militias. Much of this focused on the competition between Zintan- and Misrata-based militias. Zintan is a town of 50,000 people about 110 miles southwest of the Libyan capital, and the Zintan Military Council, as it was officially known, captured Tripoli in August 2011, signaling the end of the Qaddafi era even if he was not captured and killed until October. As for the Misratans, they suffered much during the conflict with Qaddafi, given that Misrata—a city on the western coast of the Gulf of Sidra directly opposite Benghazi—was for a time the only rebel-held area in the western part of the country and, as a result, the city was forced to endure the full fury of loyalist forces. Consequently, forces from both places laid claims to the country's leadership in post-Qaddafi Libya. Yet the conflict that emerged after Qaddafi's death was not just a confrontation between Zintanis and Misratans. The international media routinely filed stories from Libya, reporting on violence among a dizzying array of armed groups as the interim government struggled to establish control.[37] Prime Minister al-Keib, an academic with a background in electrical engineering, bravely asserted the NTC's authority amid this violence. In early December 2011, all militias in and around Tripoli were ordered to transfer responsibility for security to government authorities by the end of the month. On Christmas Day, in an additional effort to stem the bloodletting, Keib announced that the armed forces would absorb 50,000 militiamen. Neither initiative altered the dynamics on the ground, however. The practical effect of the plan to integrate the militias into the military was merely to put militiamen on the government payroll, which attracted more people to militias.[38]

Many Libyans, of course, sought a better, more just, and representative political system. Through the daily violence, those in positions of responsibility continued working toward that goal. An electoral law announced in late January 2012 ensured gender balance on all party lists and reserved 120 (of 200) seats in the parliament-in-waiting, the

General National Congress (GNC), for independents. It was hard to grasp how officials believed the political process would arrest the fighting and Libya's fragmentation, however. There was much for democrats to like in the electoral law, but it seemed rather beside the point. On March 6, tribal leaders and militia commanders in eastern Libya demanded autonomy from Tripoli, declaring their intention to form their own parliament and security forces.

Still, interim authorities hoped that the elections for the GNC, which had originally been slated for June 19 but were delayed until July 7 over security concerns, would instill in Libyans an interest in a common, democratic future. The GNC was intended to function as the legislature while a sixty-member Constituent Assembly was charged with writing a constitution. There were many skeptics, but the initial results looked promising. Turnout was 65 percent. Former Qaddafi official and interim prime minister Mahmoud Jibril's National Forces Alliance, which the international media described as a liberal secular party but in reality was neither, won thirty-nine of the eighty seats reserved for political parties.[39] The Islamists of the Justice and Construction Party, which was an obvious nod to Turkey's Justice and Development Party, garnered seventeen. The next biggest, the National Front Party (NFP), won three. A combination of eighteen parties split the remaining twenty-one seats. A month later, after elections and the results were confirmed, the NTC dissolved itself and handed power to the new congress.

The GNC then elected Mohammed al-Magariaf of the NFP as its president and thus Libya's head of state. Magariaf had a colorful background. He had been a Libyan diplomat, serving as Tripoli's ambassador in New Delhi before defecting in 1980. The NFP was the evolution of the National Front for the Salvation of Libya, which was an armed opposition group that, under Magariaf's direction and with Central Intelligence Agency money, tried to topple Qaddafi in 1984. The plot obviously failed and, until the uprising, Magariaf lived in exile, where he continued his vocal opposition to Qaddafi. Magariaf claimed that the NFP was national, but of his three seats, two came from the east. Regardless, amid all the instability and uncertainty, Libyans had managed to put together a legitimate political process. For a moment it seemed that the country's post-Qaddafi's tribulations were not the way things had to be; however, the weakness of the GNC combined with the proliferation of militias, extremism, and a political culture that placed a premium on settling disputes by force proved to be too much.[40]

In late August, just two weeks after Magariaf became the president of the GNC, extremist groups destroyed Sufi shrines in Zintan, Misrata, and Tripoli. The chaos of post-Qaddafi Libya had not only given rise to tribal and regional militias but also provided an environment in which Islamist extremism could thrive. This was not a new phenomenon, however. Going back to the 1990s, Qaddafi had confronted extremist opposition and violence in the form of an organization called the Libyan Islamic Fighting Group (LIFG). Then, as well as in 2012, Benghazi was ground zero for jihadis, especially for a group called Ansar al-Sharia (Partisans of Islamic Law), many members of which cut their teeth waging jihad as part of the LIFG. On the night of September 11, 2012, the same day that Egyptian demonstrators tried to storm the US Embassy in Cairo in what was believed to be outrage over an anti-Islam film that a fringe American group had produced and uploaded to YouTube, a similar scenario seemed to play out at the American consulate in Benghazi. In Egypt, the only casualty was the US flag, but in Libya the attack killed the US ambassador, Christopher Stevens, and three other Americans. A subsequent investigation found that rather than a spontaneous protest over the film *Innocence of Muslims*, the Benghazi attack was a well-planned and coordinated assault by Ansar al-Sharia.[41]

The day after Ambassador Stevens's death, the GNC narrowly elected the independent Mustafa Abushagur to be prime minister. In a further sign of Libya's deepening lawlessness, on October 4, protesters from the town of Zawiyah stormed the building where the GNC convened. They were angry that Abushagur's list of minister-designates did not include their preferred candidate to run Libya's National Oil Corporation. The prime minister–elect was forced to withdraw his proposed government, which was different from the one he had previously and surreptitiously agreed to with members of the GNC. In their anger at Abushagur's attempt at a double cross, when he tried again a few days later, the GNC's delegates voted to dismiss him. Libya's legislators then turned to human rights activist, lawyer, and longtime exile in Germany, Ali Zeidan, to be prime minister. He won a narrow election within the GNC by eight votes, but that Libya had a prime minister at all was a milestone. Still, like the adoption of the electoral law and the elections themselves, the political process was disconnected from the violence enveloping the country. It was as if there were two parallel Libyas: one that was building political institutions and proceeding with a transition, and one that was at war with itself. The two only rarely met when, for example, the GNC periodically demanded the disarmament of militias, to no avail.

Zeidan, like the failed prime minister–elect before him, was subject to mob rule. In March 2013, Libya's new legislature found itself under siege over a proposed political isolation law that would prohibit Qaddafi-era officials from holding government positions in the new Libya. This was akin to the de-Baathification that the United States and its Iraqi allies put in place after Operation Iraqi Freedom and the unsuccessful attempt by Egypt's Muslim Brotherhood–dominated People's Assembly to bar members of Mubarak's National Democratic Party from government service. After twelve hours, the opponents of the draft law went home, but the next day supporters of the measure staged their own siege, demanding its passage. The legislation was adopted in early May, forcing the resignation of, among others, Magariaf, who despite having spent the previous thirty-three years in, at times, violent opposition to the Libyan leader, had been a Qaddafi-era diplomat. The rationale for the new law was obvious: to prevent the return of the old political order or some version of it. That said, it was also a way for the law's primary proponents, the Islamists of Libya's Justice and Construction Party, to even the political playing field after they had underperformed in the previous summer's elections.[42]

As Libya staggered from crisis to crisis and from violent episode to violent episode throughout 2013, the GNC decided to extend its mandate to the end of 2014. The move produced protests in the streets and, on February 14, 2014, someone named Khalifa Haftar appeared on television, demanding the dissolution of the GNC and the establishment of something he called a presidential council. He had been a general in Qaddafi's military and was a commander in 1987 when the Libyan military was ignominiously driven from north-central Chad.[43] Haftar and his men were forced to surrender and ended up in a

Chadian prison, where he languished after Qaddafi publicly disowned the troops he sent into battle. After Chad freed him, Haftar aligned himself with Magariaf's National Front for the Salvation. Soon afterwards, he moved to suburban Northern Virginia close to the Central Intelligence Agency's headquarters, where he was rumored to be employed. Like many others who had spent years in exile, Haftar returned to Libya not long after the uprising against Qaddafi began. Libya's leadership dismissed Haftar's Valentine's Day television address as bluster, but such was the disorder and confusion of post-Qaddafi Libya that the general had raised an army without the prime minister or others knowing about it. In the spring he went after Ansar al-Sharia Libya and other groups in Benghazi in what he called Operation Dignity. By that time, Libya had been through two prime ministers and a prime minister–elect in three months, including Zeidan, who was ousted in March, and Abdullah al-Thinni, the former defense minister who was only supposed to serve as a caretaker for two weeks but who resigned five days after taking office following an attack on his home. Other Libyan officials convinced him to stay on until a new prime minister was elected. That person was a businessman named Ahmed Maiteeq, but he never took office because the first deputy speaker of the GNC challenged the legality of the election. In one of the few positive moments when law prevailed over lawlessness after Qaddafi's fall, Libya's Supreme Court upheld this challenge, forcing the GNC to try once again to find a prime minister.

The dysfunction within the GNC convinced Libya's politicians that their prospects would improve with a new legislative body. On June 25, 18 percent of eligible Libyan voters went to the polls and handed a victory to liberals, secularists, and those who supported a federal Libya composed of autonomous regions. In response, Islamist, Berber, and Misratan militias supporting the parties that lost launched an attack on Tripoli's airport and rival Zintani forces (nominally allied with Haftar), dubbed Operation Libya Dawn. With Tripoli under increasing fire, the new Chamber of Deputies, known more commonly as the House of Representatives, was forced to convene elsewhere. Its members chose Tobruk, a city on the Mediterranean coast about 600 miles east of the Libyan capital. At the same time, the losers in June's election—primarily Islamists from the Justice and Construction Party—reconvened the

GNC and elected a new prime minister, Omar al-Hassi. The GNC then declared that it, not the House of Representatives, was Libya's legitimate government.

The summer of 2014 proved to be an important moment in Libya's fragmentation. The country had two governments each claiming legitimacy. It also had two armies that supported these respective governments—but that did not answer to them—and between the two armies were various, competing militias.[44] The governments of Turkey and Qatar lined up in support of the GNC, whereas the United Arab Emirates and Egypt offered diplomatic, financial, and military support to the House of Representatives and Haftar. This all had the effect of crystallizing the conflict and establishing clear lines of division. Each side claimed not to want to divide the country, but their actions—intended or otherwise—did precisely the opposite, hardening divisions in a conflict that seemed destined to continue for longer than anyone cared to consider. In this static chaos, extremism thrived with a dizzying array of groups. After the declaration of the Islamic State in the summer of 2014, there was considerable concern among officials in Washington and European as well as Arab capitals that the group would infiltrate Libya. These fears seemed to be coming true when terrorists beheaded twenty-one Egyptian Coptic Christians on a Libyan beach in early 2015. It was a big story because it was the same gruesome manner of death that Abu Bakr al-Baghdadi's men had delivered to two Western journalists, James Foley and Steven Sotloff, in Iraq. Although the killing of the Egyptians prompted increased media attention on the Islamic State's growing presence in Libya, the group was far from the only extremist organization operating in the country. There was, for example, Ansar al-Sharia, whose leader, Abu Khalid al-Madani, was careful to emphasize his group's independence, though some of its members worked with the Islamic State in Benghazi and other places in northeastern Libya while maintaining some ties to al-Qaeda of the Islamic Maghreb.[45] Then there were the significant number of lesser known groups operating in Libya of which there is only incomplete information. It seems clear, however, that organizations like the February 17 Brigade—an Islamist group that had been charged with protecting the American consulate in Benghazi when it was attacked in 2012—Libya Shield 1, the Abu Salim Martyrs Brigade, Ansar al-Sharia Derna, Ansar al-Sharia Benghazi, and the Souq al-Jumaa Brigade will continue to have a considerable impact on Libya's security environment.[46]

Late in 2015, however, came a faint glimmer of hope. The previous year, the Spanish diplomat Bernardino León led a United Nations effort to help Libyans find a way out of their turmoil. He managed to launch talks, but as was true of the political process that the NTC, the GNC, and the House of Representatives have overseen, the negotiations seemed removed from Libya's reality. Neither General Haftar nor his opponents were willing to participate as both the conflict and the León talks dragged on. Yet, by December 2015, León's successor, Martin Kobler, was able to secure an agreement from representatives of the House of Representatives and the GNC to form a Government of National Accord. The complicated agreement included the establishment of a nine-member presidential council made up of the prime minister, five deputy prime ministers, and three senior ministers. The House of Representatives would constitute the lower house of parliament and the members of the GNC would become the upper house of a bicameral legislature, and all armed groups would be demobilized. On December 13, 2015—two days before representatives of the two Libyan governments were to sign the agreement—at a press conference in Rome that included Kobler and the Italian foreign minister, Paolo Gentiloni, US Secretary of State John Kerry declared, "Libya is a diverse country, but there is no inherent reason whatsoever that the Government of National Accord [GNA] cannot succeed in bringing the country together and in having the groundwork for permanent institutions that will respect the rights and interests of all be put in place." Diplomats being diplomats often accentuate the positive, but Kerry's view of Libya's future was extraordinarily optimistic given both the country's past and its violently contested present.[47] Since then, Libya's unity government has struggled—despite significant international support—to survive. The same forces that conspired to undermine previous post-Qaddafi governments have done the same to the GNA. Unable to generate legitimacy and the authority that goes with it, the government is irrelevant to many among the range of other important

Libyan political actors from would-be strong men and Islamists to militias, tribal leaders, and extremists. Even those who have served the GNA do not expect it to survive.

The hopeful tone of America's senior diplomat in December 2015 was misplaced when it came to Libya, but the country's neighbor to the west, Tunisia, was a different story. On December 21, 2014, Tunisians elected Beji Caid Essebsi to be their new president. The election capped off an extended political season that had begun eleven months earlier when the parliament approved a new constitution, continued in October when Tunisians voted for a new parliament (the Assembly of the Representatives of the People), which was followed quickly by the presidential race. The successful conclusion of these milestones suggested to many that Tunisia was a bright spot in a region that had few. The country had a civic culture and a determination to grapple peacefully with crimes of the past—embodied in an elaborate transitional justice apparatus—that seemed to give it an advantage over its neighbors to the east who were grappling with internal conflicts and political uncertainty.[48] Five days after Essebsi was elected, he published an op-ed in the *Washington Post* titled "My Three Goals as Tunisia's President." The country's new leader "hit all the right themes, emphasizing Tunisia's 'openness, tolerance, and moderation' and vowing to 'strengthen [his country's] young democracy at a time when hopes for democracy elsewhere in the region are failing to take root.'"[49] Yet Essebsi also employed unmistakably coded language to damage the prestige and legitimacy of Tunisia's Islamist Ennahda Movement, signaling that his commitment to consensus might not go much further than the page on which his words appeared.

Early in the article, Essebsi wrote, "It was trade and exchange with Europe—in particular, with France and Italy, Tunisia's closest Mediterranean neighbors—that opened the country to the Enlightenment."[50] In the context of Tunisia's post-uprising politics, evoking the Enlightenment, which was an age of reason and tolerance, Essebsi was drawing a clear distinction between himself and his party, Nidaa Tounes, and Rachid al-Ghannouchi, who led Ennahda.[51] Ghannouchi had not served in any official capacity after returning from exile in London on the heels of Zine al-Abidine Ben Ali's 2011 fall, but he had been the leader of Tunisia's Islamists since

1970.[52] To some, he was the voice of a liberal, pragmatic Islamism that emphasized consensus, compromise, and democracy. To others, he was a dangerous radical who had never relinquished his goal of taking over the state. To them, Ghannouchi's temperate discourse and gentle manner were part of a strategy to leverage Tunisia's democratic practices to advance an anti-democratic agenda. Although Essebsi and Ghannouchi had established a dialogue and, according to each of their spokespersons, a respectful working relationship for the good of the country, the new president seemed to be in the latter camp. His op-ed implicitly suggested that whatever Ghannouchi might say about tolerance, peace, and democracy, "the Ennahda Movement, by dint of its Islamism, harbored a worldview hostile to Enlightenment ideals."[53]

Essebsi also referenced Sadiki College in his op-ed. The bilingual high school, which was established in 1875, has been a training ground for Tunisia's elite. The new Tunisian president informed his readers that Sadiki graduates had forged an independent Tunisia and "brought to their task a commitment to anchor the young republic in modernity. They instituted universal education, gender equality and separation of religion and state."[54] The message was quite clear. Essebsi and Nidaa Tounes have embraced modernity; the misogynist Islamists of Ennahda have not.

The eighty-eight-year-old Essebsi's outlook seemed like a milder version of Turkey's official state secularism, made more acceptable by the warm revolutionary afterglow of Ben Ali's fall.[55] Even though many observers—American and European officials, analysts, and journalists—took the successful conclusion of the presidential elections and Essesbi's assumption of the office as a positive sign, the Tunisian leader was signaling that he had little interest in building an inclusive, pluralist political system. A relatively broad-based government was established that included Nidaa Tounes, the Free Patriotic Union, a party called Afek Tounes (Tunisian Aspiration), a number of independents, and Ennahda. Although the Islamists had initially been excluded, the electoral math that went into government coalition building made it impossible to keep them out.

If Nidaa Tounes's victory and an unsuccessful effort to sideline Ennahda was as bad as Tunisia was going to get, then the country's transition was proceeding, by any objective measure, quite well. Among these metrics were Tunisia's own. In the months following Ben Ali's flight from Tunis to Jeddah, demonstrations and anger buffeted the post-uprising political process, and in what was a paradigmatic case of heightened expectations giving way to frustration, Tunisians chafed at what they perceived to be the slow pace of change. The free and fair elections held in October 2011 for a 217-seat National Constituent Assembly (NCA) attenuated some of this anger. Turnout was a healthy 52 percent, Ennahda garnering a plurality of votes. A new interim coalition government was established that included Ennahda and two secular parties, the Congress for the Republic and the Democratic Forum for Labor and Liberties, better known as Ettakatol.

This establishment of the "Troika government" was important for two reasons. First, in the months following Ben Ali's departure, old order figures still dominated Tunisian politics. This included the interim president, Fouad Mebazaa, who had been president of the Chamber of Deputies, and the acting prime minister, Mohammed al-Ghannouchi (no relation to Rachid al-Ghannouchi). The first interim government lasted only twenty-four hours: four appointees promptly resigned over the inclusion of six members of Ben Ali's Democratic Constitutional Rally (in French, the Rassemblement Constitutionnel Démocratique, or RCD). Prime Minister Ghannouchi's tenure lasted only five weeks when, in late February, none other than Beji Caid Essebsi replaced him and remained prime minister until the October 2011 elections. The interim government had taken some positive steps, however: dissolving the RCD, disbanding the State Security Department of the Ministry of Interior, and establishing the Higher Political Reform Committee "tasked with amending the [country's] legal framework to ensure a free, fair, transparent, and pluralistic presidential election" as well as the Independent High Authority on Elections to ensure the integrity of the electoral process.[56] The interim government then merged the Higher Political Reform Commission with the Committee to Protect the Revolution to form the High Authority for the Achievement of the Objectives of the Revolution. These committees were important in bridging the Ben Ali era to the transitional period, but the government that came into being after the NCA elections proved a more tangible sign of the change for which Tunisians had been hoping. This was also reflected in Mebazaa's replacement with the physician and human rights activist Moncef al-Marzouki as interim president. Second, the seating of the NCA, which was to draft a new constitution, held out the promise that the transition would gain some momentum.

Whatever hope Tunisians harbored that the NCA would provide coherence and direction for the country was quickly dashed, however. There were persistent questions about the relationship between Ennahda and Islamist extremist groups, fostering mistrust on all sides. In addition, the newly elected legislature proved to be inefficient, rife with infighting, and unnecessarily secretive. Throughout this period, the government struggled to maintain its footing. In an extraordinarily tone-deaf move for a government that owed its existence to popular protest, the Ennahda-affiliated minister of interior, Ali Laarayedh, banned demonstrations in March 2012. When Tunisians defied the ban on April 9—Martyrs' Day, the annual commemoration of those who died on that day in 1938 protesting French colonial rule—the police responded with violence. Laarayedh rescinded his injunction on protests two days later, but the damage was done. That the minister based his initial decision on a Ben Ali–era law and that the police responded with force on a day of nationalist import was a significant political affront. Then, on September 14, 2012—just three days after the American ambassador in Libya was killed in an attack on the US consulate in Benghazi and protesters in Cairo scaled the large security walls at the US Embassy—the Tunisian police were slow to respond to Salafi-led protests that led to an assault on the US Embassy in Tunis and the torching of the American School of Tunis. This may very well have been the unintended consequence of the political pressure the government felt after Martyrs' Day. Yet the police intervened only after protesters breached the embassy building, raising questions among Tunisians about the government's relationship with violent groups, even as Marzouki and other officials expressed regret and vowed to arrest the ringleaders.

The attack on the embassy was an ominous sign that not all was well in Tunisia, but the political environment grew even more tense five months later when Chokri Belaid, the secretary-general of the National Democratic Movement, was assassinated outside his home on February 6, 2013. The killing was shocking, but not wholly unexpected. Belaid, a trenchant critic of the Islamist camp and a committed secularist, had received multiple death threats in the preceding months. Belaid's leftist, Third Worldist, and—in particular—secular worldview placed him in the crosshairs of Islamist extremists. He had been a vocal foe of both Bourguiba and Ben Ali, though the latter released him from prison in 1987. Belaid's death was met with accusations of Ennahda's complicity with extremists. Huge crowds turned out to his funeral to pay their respects two days after the crime. The crisis brought a temporary suspension of the NCA and a call from interim prime minister Hamadi al-Jebali for a nonpolitical government of technocrats. Although Jebali came from Ennahda, the party's leadership rejected the idea because, according to its vice president, Abdelhamid al-Jelassi, "the prime minister did not ask the opinion of the party," forcing the prime minister's resignation.[57] Ali Laarayedh became the new prime minister and a subsequent reshuffling of ministerial portfolios produced independent ministers of interior, justice, and foreign affairs.

The kind of extremism that led to the attacks on the American embassy and Belaid's assassination was not supposed to be a problem in what was widely regarded as a secular and Westernized Tunisia. Yet Habib Bourguiba's secularism was not without its challengers. He kept up the pressure on Tunisia's Islamists, especially Ghannouchi and his Mouvement de la Tendance Islamique (Movement of Islamic Tendency, a precursor to Ennahda). Ben Ali initially relaxed Bourguiba's approach but quickly resumed arrests of Islamists, their prosecution, and worse, in the name of fighting Islamist militancy, though this was broadly understood to be a justification for the security services to undermine his political opponents. Mubarak had pursued a similar strategy in Egypt in his effort to bring the Muslim Brotherhood to heel. Yet the Egyptians actually had an extremist problem. The al-Gamaa al-Islamiyya and other jihadi organizations waged a low-level insurgency in Egypt that targeted tourists, Egyptian officials, and intellectuals in the 1990s. When the violence came to an end, about 1,300 people had been killed. Tunisia had a problem with a spate of terrorist attacks in the mid-1980s and while it was terrible for the victims, it hardly compared to the blood spilled in Egypt. Yet the relative absence of extremist violence in Tunisia did not mean that Tunisia or Tunisians were immune from extremist ideologies. Two Tunisians, Abu Iyad al-Tunisi and Tarek Maaroufi, planned the assassination of Ahmed Shah Massoud, the West-leaning commander of Afghanistan's Northern Alliance, two days before the September 2001 attacks on the United States. Ben Ali's Tunisia actually provided fertile ground for extremist worldviews to take root. It was a regime that generally neglected large parts of the country, such as Sidi Bouzid and the *bidonvilles,* or shanty towns, around Tunis, leaving a large reservoir of people susceptible to radical ideologies. More generally, to the extent that repression is an important factor in radicalization, it is hardly surprising that when the jack boots of Ben Ali's security services were lifted after the uprising, extremists would seek to take advantage of a new, more permissive environment.

The violence was widely suspected to be the work of a group that called itself Ansar al-Sharia Tunisia, the origins of which were found in Ben Ali's prisons in the mid-2000s. The group's founders, most prominently Abu Iyad al-Tunisi, were pardoned and released from prison in the spring of 2011.[58] Like Hamas in the West Bank and the Gaza Strip or Lebanon's Hezbollah, Ansar al-Sharia Tunisia has used a combination of proselytizing and social services as a mechanism of political mobilization. This allowed Tunisi and other members of the group to dissemble when suspicion was cast upon him and his group for spilling blood. In response, he claimed that Ansar al-Sharia Tunisia was only concerned with preaching and the distribution of religious books, not abetting violence. During the immediate transition period, Ennahda's Ghannouchi apparently believed that his own prestige could moderate the group, which was preferable to a direct confrontation and the risk of civil strife. Ghannouchi got this conflict, anyway. Until the attack on the US Embassy in Tunis, Ansar al-Sharia Tunisia activists mostly made themselves a nuisance, demonstrating at art shows, declaring movies blasphemous, intimidating university administrators over Islamist-style dress, and hoisting the Black Standard—the flag that al-Qaeda and other extremists used—atop the clock tower at January 14th Square in downtown Tunis.[59] Then they assassinated Chokri Belaid and, on July 25, suspects believed to be associated with them shot Mohammed Brahmi, the leader of a small, secular, leftist political party, outside his home.[60]

The response on all sides of the political arena further deepened fissures among Tunisians. Ennahda condemned the assassination and

the government quickly designated Ansar al-Sharia Tunisia a terrorist organization. This effort to demonstrate resolve did little to ame-
liorate the Troika's critics. The Tunisian General Labor Union, known
by its French acronym UGTT and one of Tunisia's most important
political players, called for a general strike the day after Brahmi was
killed. Tunisians accused Ennahda of fingering Ansar al-Sharia Tunisia
so quickly in an effort to deflect from the government's failures and
the Islamists' responsibility for helping to create an environment that
made the assassinations of both Brahmi and Belaid possible. Within
the Ennahda-dominated National Constituent Assembly (NCA),
forty-two members resigned, signaling their lack of confidence in the
government. An umbrella group called the National Salvation Front
that included Belaid's National Democratic Movement, Brahmi's
People's Movement, and Nidaa Tounes organized large demonstrations
against Ennahda and the NCA. The existence of Tunisia's version of the
Egyptian Tamarrod campaign aided the momentum for these demonstrations. Launched in either late June or early July 2013, by the time
Brahmi was killed the group had collected 200,000 signatures in its
effort to dissolve the NCA—and thus the government—as well as the
presidency. It seemed that Tunisia was going the way of Egypt, where
just three weeks earlier the military ended Mohammed Morsi's tumul-
tuous presidency.

And then, just as journalists and analysts had begun pumping out
"Tunisia on the Brink" and "Tunisia on the Brink?" articles, op-eds,
and blog posts, Houcine Abassi determined otherwise.[61] The leader of
the UGTT appealed to his counterparts at the Tunisian Confederation
of Industry, Trade, and Handicrafts, the Tunisian Human Rights
League, and the Tunisian Order of Lawyers to form a coalition civil
society group that could leverage their prestige to deescalate the crisis
and find a way forward that preserved the promise of the Jasmine
Revolution. What became known as the National Dialogue Quartet
shepherded a process that, in October 2013, culminated in the leaders of twelve political parties affixing their signatures to a roadmap to
guide Tunisia's transition.[62] The document left the NCA in place but
required the establishment of a new technocratic government and an
independent electoral commission. It also called for the completion of
a new constitution. It was an extraordinary moment. Ennahda and the

other members of the three-party coalition bowed out, making way for a new government. Although Tunisia remained tense, the roadmap and the Quartet's commitment to dialogue and consensus building gave life to Tunisia's transition and produced the January 2014 constitution and the subsequent parliamentary and presidential elections.

Exactly two years after the roadmap was signed and 2,300 miles from Tunis, the staff at Sturegatan 14 in Stockholm, Sweden, prepared a press release that, for many, vindicated their belief in Tunisia's democratic future. The text read in part, "For its decisive contribution to the building of a pluralistic democracy in the wake of the Jasmine Revolution in 2011" the Nobel Peace Prize would be awarded to the National Dialogue Quartet. Tunisians rejoiced. It was vindication that authoritarianism did not have to be the Middle East's past, present, and future—something that sophisticated observers of the region believed, but that had never actually lined up with the data. The team at the Nobel Foundation dutifully outlined the singular role the Quartet had played in foiling a descent into violence and the implications of its work concerning the relationship between Islamists and secularists, the importance of national identity, and the role of civil society. Yet the Nobel Committee's announcement also had an aspirational quality. In the last line of the almost 700-word press release, the Nobel Committee acknowledged that "More than anything, the prize is intended as an encouragement to the Tunisian people, who despite major challenges have laid the groundwork for a national fraternity."[63] The committee's implicit recognition that all was not well in Tunisia was artfully crafted because, as of October 10, 2015, the date of the press release, the country was not as firmly on the path to democracy as perhaps many hoped.

Much had gone right in Tunisia, especially after the unionists, lawyers, human rights activists, and business community stepped in during the summer of 2013 when the country seemed to be heading down Egypt's path of repression and violence. The resulting constitution and seating of a new parliament and president were edifying, hope-inducing experiences. Despite a legacy of mistrust, outreach and willingness to cooperate remained among some Islamists, Bourguibists, republicans, and remnants of the Ben Ali era. Rachid al-Ghannouchi went so far as to address Nidaa Tounes's party congress in early 2016 to assure its members that Ennahda did not seek to press its political advantage after Essebsi's party split (discussed in the next chapter). This was reassuring, but Ennhada saw no reason to exploit Nidaa Tounes's problems. The party members were proving to be self-destructive without Ghannouchi's help.

The new constitution, in particular, represented an important change. The similarities between the 1959 document and the one that replaced it were strong, but the drafters had taken great care to alter the balance of power in the political system, particularly as it pertained to the executive. The president retained the prerogative to dissolve parliament, remained the commander-in-chief of the armed forces, appointed senior military, diplomatic, and judicial officials, and approved laws, but the prime minister was no longer the head of state's errand boy.[64] The head of government was empowered to "determine the state's general policy," albeit without encroaching on the president's mandate.[65] This gave the prime minister the power to maintain full administrative control of the apparatus of the government to implement the policies of the government. The prime minister merely needed to advise the president on these issues.[66] Like the 1959 constitution, the parliament was endowed with the responsibility to hold the executive accountable and conduct oversight through written and oral questions.[67] The independence of the judiciary was also reaffirmed.[68] Still, it seemed that the 2014 constitution could be effective only so long as the people who swore to uphold it internalized its guiding principles and ideals. Constitutions throughout the Arab world often resembled those found in democratic polities, but none of them were democracies. These documents always emphasized the independence of the judiciary and the oversight responsibilities of legislatures, but leaders often ignored these provisions. And, like constitutions from around the region, Tunisia's included the phrase "in accordance with the law" or similar formulations, which had often been used as an escape clause for authoritarians who used restrictive legal codes to rescind rights that constitutions extended.[69]

What made the potentially regressive use of law particularly worrying in Tunisia were the security challenges the Nobel Committee mentioned in passing in its press release. They were, of course, referring to terrorist attacks in March and June 2015 that killed fifty-eight people.

Given the mistrust, demonstrations, and threat of widespread instability that resulted after the assault on the US Embassy in 2012 and the assassinations of Chokri Belaid and Mohammed Brahmi the following year, the government's response to the new bloodshed was restrained but also troubling in the way it resurrected Ben Ali–era laws and security provisions (discussed in the next chapter). Against the backdrop of the deterioration of security and its impact on tourism, the economy continued to struggle with high unemployment, low investment, and slow growth.

The Nobel Peace Prize provided a respite from uncertainty that hung over Tunisian politics, but it was brief. A little more than a month after the announcement and two weeks before the National Dialogue Quartet received its award on December 10, 2015, a bomb ripped through a bus carrying members of the presidential guard, killing twelve. The following spring, terrorists attacked Ben Guerdane, a town of 80,000 near the Libyan border. When the clashes ended two days later, thirty-six extremists were dead along with twelve soldiers, and seven civilians. In response, Essebsi extended the state of emergency that had been in place since late November 2015. Despite the generosity of the United States, the International Monetary Fund, the World Bank, and the European Union, which collectively poured more than $10 billion in loans and direct assistance to Tunisia, the economy continued to falter, growing a measly 1 percent as the energy, tourism, and phosphate sectors hovered just above collapse. In keeping with the pattern that Tunisians had set since Ben Ali's fall, there were also bright spots, notably the peaceful establishment of a new government in the summer of 2016 after the previous one fell to a no-confidence vote in parliament. However, Tunisia's new head of government—reportedly an in-law of the president—faced all the same daunting challenges as his predecessor.

More than five years after Mohammed al-Bouazizi's self-immolation, the best that anyone could say about Tunisia's transition was that it was fragile. The country seemed to conform to every cliché about the so-called Arab Spring concerning the "challenges ahead" and that the "hard work was just beginning." That Tunisia had not ripped itself apart like Libya or experienced the resurgent authoritarianism of Egypt was worth celebrating, if only briefly.

Journalists, columnists, analysts of Middle East politics, and government officials have at times expressed a humbled awe at the magnitude and scale of the instability and uncertainty that has rocked the region. Much of this has to do with the conflicts in Syria and Iraq as well as the emergence of the Islamic State and its ability—despite its relatively small numbers—to influence the politics of the Middle East, Europe, and the United States. There is also a palpable sense of disappointment that is linked to the barricades that went up at various moments in Tunisia, Egypt, and Libya in 2011 and somewhat later in Turkey. The powerful narratives that emerged from the uprisings created expectations that were wholly unwarranted. This is not to suggest that democratic change is beyond the capacity of Middle Eastern societies. This was an underlying theme of the "Arab (or Islamist) Winter" commentary when violence and instability followed the uprisings. Still, Egypt's authoritarianism, Turkey's reversal of democratizing reforms, Libya's fragmentation, and Tunisia's vulnerable and tentative progress were always the more likely outcomes than successful transitions to open and democratic systems. The question is, why?

4

What Went Wrong?

EVEN BEFORE THE PARTY that began in Tahrir Square around 6:00 P.M. on February 11, 2011, wound down more than a day later, Egyptians pulled out their brooms and set about cleaning up the area. This sudden burst of civic and national pride represented the new day that so many believed had dawned on the Nile. Tahrir Square had become "the Square" and even though it remained home to a Hardee's, a Kentucky Fried Chicken, sidewalk bookstalls, and a wide variety of sketchy looking travel agencies, the previous weeks had given Tahrir, which means *liberation*, a new symbolism. Not everyone was overjoyed and brimming with that anything-is-possible sense of satisfaction, however. Diehards wanted to stay in Tahrir after President Hosni Mubarak's fall, unwilling to believe that the military would usher in an era of democracy and justice.[1] They were a distinct minority. The rest of the country—or at least the estimated millions who had joined the demonstrations—had either been carried away in the moment or actually did believe that the Supreme Council of the Armed Forces (SCAF) would, as its officers promised, "protect the revolution." Even if the commanders were dissembling, the thinking went that they would be forced to respond to the collective demands of the Egyptian people. Among the vast majority of activists, liberals, and instigators of Mubarak's fall, the military really had no choice but to "prepare the country for democracy."[2] If they did not, they would face the wrath of the revolutionaries. In their amazement at and joy over Mubarak's ouster, this view seemed entirely reasonable, but that small group of purists who wanted to continue demonstrating turned out to be particularly prescient.

In retrospect, it all seems so obvious. The platitudes of Egypt's senior military command, which included the slogan "the army and the people are one hand," were just that—banalities intended to obscure what was actually happening. Similarly, when in late 2014 Tunisia's Beji Caid Essebsi declared his desire—as opposed to what he was forced to do by circumstance—to work in partnership with the Islamists of the Ennahda Movement, he was dissimulating. He just did not have the numbers to impose his party's will on the country. In Libya, interim governments pursued a political process despite the shooting outside their windows that made a mockery of it. All the while, in the country that was supposed to be a model for the Arab world, Recep Tayyip Erdoğan was undermining the checks and balances in Turkey's political system. Still, when political contestation intensified, blood began to flow, and democratic change seemed less and less certain, some analysts believed that these problems were not indicators of failure but rather part of a long, painful process of democratic change. Middle Eastern countries were actually tracking closely to others that had undergone transitions to democracy.[3] The modern archetype of this "it will get worse before it gets better, but it will get better" analysis is, of course, France, where it took a very long time for a stable democracy to emerge after the revolution of 1789. The French experience allegedly provided insight and lessons about the likely trajectories of Middle Eastern states. Although the effort to generalize from one region to another is important to understanding the way the world works, it can go only so far lest observers lose sight of the important historical, cultural, and political particularities of the different cases they study. Late eighteenth- and early nineteenth-century France, for example, is unlikely to tell analysts much about the trajectory of early twenty-first-century Egypt or Libya.[4] The purpose of comparison is not only to discern common political developments across regions and eras but also to understand why outcomes in one region may not necessarily occur in another. Other analysts looked at the statistics from revolutions past and calculated the average time it took for stability to return—about five years.[5] Notes of caution were embedded in all of this commentary.

After all, the number of countries that failed to make a transition to democracy outnumbered the successes, but in the words of one sophisticated scholar of comparative political systems, "the Arab Spring has largely followed gross patterns in democratization from the past century or so."[6] The data may have suggested that the indicators were pointing in the right directions, but reality suggested otherwise as an unprecedented scale of violence, fragmentation, and generalized uncertainty buffeted the region.

For political partisans within the United States, the Middle East's tribulations could be traced to the failures in Iraq, whether it was the "original sin" of George W. Bush's invasion or Barack Obama's decision to withdraw in December 2011. Yet Iraq's wars, Syria's destruction, the sectarian overlay of these conflicts, and the "success" of the self-declared Islamic State did not explain why Egypt, Tunisia, Libya, or even non-Arab Turkey look the way they do. Leaders in these places might claim that extremism is the reason, but without denying the threat Egyptians, Tunisians, Libyans, and Turks face, terrorism is a convenient excuse. More to the point, the failure of democratic development or, in Turkey's case, the reversal of liberalizing reforms, contributed as much to the ghastly moment in the Middle East as Syria's barrel bombs and Jihadi John's butcher's knife.

THE REVOLUTIONS THAT NEVER WERE

It has become common for observers to refer to the uprisings in the Arab world as the "Middle Eastern revolutions of 2011," or some variation on this phrase. The iconic scenes of Middle Easterners defying authorities and gathering in public spaces to demand change intuitively evokes the term *revolution*. Besides, revolution carries with it a certain romance—people rising up to depose longtime rulers and in their place caretakers or new leaders stepping in and promising to pave the way for prosperity, representative government, and dignity. That Tunisians, Egyptians, and Libyans use *thawra*—revolution—to describe events that occurred during the winter of 2010 and 2011 highlights the intuitive nature of the term. Yet were the Middle Eastern revolutions actually revolutions?

Scholarly work on revolutions is necessarily large. Historians have spent years shedding light on the French, Russian, and Chinese revolutions as well as those that were important but have had significantly less impact on subsequent global events, such as the Iranian and Algerian revolutions. Americans, of course, are well versed in their own successful revolution of 1776. Beyond straight historical narratives about who, what, when, and where, social scientists have dedicated themselves to developing general theories of revolutions, endeavoring to develop a common set of causes to explain this phenomenon regardless of where it occurs. The literature sprawls across areas related to collective action, the socio-psychological aspects of violent rebellion, economic grievances, class, and the process of modernization. Scholars know a lot about revolutions, both their minute details as well as possible causes (even as they remain manifestly unpredictable phenomena).[7] At a basic level, scholars tend to agree that revolutions have occurred when contenders for power displace present holders of power, which tracks closely with an intuitive sense of the term that ends up in the commentary and discussion of politics in the Middle East since 2011. This notion has the benefit of simplicity and parsimony, but does not quite capture the astounding political and social disruption of revolutions.

In 1979, a sociologist named Theda Skocpol published *States and Social Revolutions: A Comparative Analysis of France, Russia, and China.* It was the result of her dissatisfaction with prevailing social scientific explanations of revolution, which were "derived . . . from models of how political protest and change were ideally supposed to occur in liberal-democratic or capitalist societies." Skocpol also bemoaned the fact that scholars often described revolutions based on categories and terms of a previous revolution. Thus the analysis of the Russian Revolution was a function of analysis of the French Revolution and the examination of the Chinese Revolution was done against the backdrop of what happened in Russia in 1917.[8] Skocpol's work is rooted in *structures*, the term social scientists use when referring to "patterned relationships beyond the manipulative control of any single group or individual." The great contribution of her work is to delineate how these structures—for example, the relationship between peasants and landlords—contributed to revolutions in France, Russia, and China.[9] The conception of revolution in *States and Social Revolutions* also adds an important dimension to the literature that clarified when analysts look at a revolution or some other disruptive phenomenon. For Skocpol, revolutions require "mutually reinforcing" changes to the prevailing political and social orders simultaneously. This is what makes social revolutions distinct from rebellions, which do not result in changes to political and social structures, and also different from political revolutions, which involve the transformation of the political system but not of social classes.[10]

Skocpol's work is not without its critics. In a March 1985 essay for the *Journal of Modern History*, William Sewell takes Skocpol to task for asserting that ideology could offer no explanation for the divergent outcomes of revolutions. Sewell freely admits that the worldview of the revolutionary does not determine the orientation of regimes after the revolution, but he does see an important place for ideology in the determination of certain outcomes. He points specifically to the "consolidation of private property in France" and its "abolition in Russia," for which structural analysis could not adequately account.[11] Clearly, the ideology of the relevant political actors during respective revolutionary upheavals matters. If Skocpol is too radical in giving short shrift to the power of ideas, her work is nevertheless illuminating even well beyond her cases. Her definition of revolution is demanding, given its requirement for the simultaneous mutually reinforcing transformations of political and social structures, but like any good definition it sheds new light on the issue at hand and raises the possibility of discovering new facts about revolutions. Her work is thus particularly apt when it comes to understanding what did and did not happen in the Middle East in 2010 and 2011. Skocpol's analysis makes clear that what are commonly referred to as the revolutions in Tunisia, Egypt, and Libya were not revolutions at all.

Before turning back to the 2011 uprisings, it is important to clarify that even if Tunisia, Egypt, and Libya had experienced social revolutions, this would not necessarily have led to democracy. In Russia, China, and Iran, social revolutions led to bloodier and more radical forms of authoritarianism than before. The critical point about the Middle Eastern uprisings is to understand that what was left behind after leaders departed is central to discerning why countries in the region look the way they do. The uprisings left some countries stuck between an old, discredited political order and a hoped-for, yet unattainable, democratic political system, with nondemocratic forces benefiting from the contested political space in between. The failure to sweep away ancien régimes left the forces of progressive political change vulnerable to better organized and well-financed opponents—Islamists, generals, extremists, the old guard and their allies.

The social and political legacies of authoritarianism certainly had an impact on Egypt's post-Mubarak politics and even Tunisia's more encouraging transition. In Turkey, the Gezi Park protests reflected strikingly similar grievances to those that Arabs had articulated a few years earlier concerning corruption, the concentration of power, brutality of the police, and the rigged nature of political systems. And although graffiti appeared in and around Taksim Square demanding that then prime minister Recep Tayyip Erdoğan resign, there was no question that he would not. Unlike Tunisians, Egyptians, and Libyans, Turks would have to use the ballot box to try to push Erdoğan and his Justice and Development Party from power—no easy task. For their part, Libyans faced an entirely different problem from others around the region. In toppling Muammar al-Qaddafi, Libya may have come closest to a social revolution, but what was left behind was just as salient for the country's future as it was for Tunisia and Egypt. Qaddafi's Great Socialist People's Libyan Arab Jamahiriyya—the "Great" was added in 1986 after the US bombing of Tripoli—established elaborate structures through which the people could exercise direct democracy. Decision making and power were supposed to flow effortlessly up and down as well as across basic popular congresses, people's committees, unions, syndicates, and the General People's Congress. Because the masses were intimately involved with each component of the overall structure, the Jamahiriyya was the perfect expression of direct democracy. In the grandiose way that is typical of Qaddafi's *The Green Book*, the Libyan leader declared, "In this way, the problem of the instrument of governing is, as a matter of fact, solved and dictatorial instruments will disappear. The people are the instrument of governing and the problem of democracy in the world is completely solved."[12]

In practice, the "Authority of the People" that *The Green Book* outlined was not just confusing to understand but it was also a sham.

Power rested in the hands of Qaddafi and a small group of collaborators and associates even though, as of 1979, they had no actual formal titles or roles.[13] That year, Qaddafi and his closest advisors resigned from the General People's Congress to devote themselves exclusively to "guiding the revolution."[14] For the remaining three decades, Qaddafi's leadership was—in Libya's official narrative—based on the alleged consensus of the people, though he occupied no official office. Political control was ensured for a time by shock troops called revolutionary committees and a number of overlapping internal security agencies, but the underlying informal system of power was based on the loyalty of senior military officers, high-ranking bureaucrats, the immediate Qaddafi family, and tribal politics. Each of these groups developed a vested interest in the perpetuation of the Jamahiriyya's parallel system, in which the formal structures of government were separate from actual exercise of power. It was so Qaddafi-specific that when the system failed, it bequeathed nothing—at least nothing useful—to those who wanted to build a more just and democratic society.

Nevertheless, some aspects of continuity connected Qaddafi's Libya and the new Libya. The government continued to pay salaries of members of the bureaucracy and the Supreme Court continued to exercise some authority, but the overall political vacuum left in Qaddafi's wake created an environment conducive to militia violence and the fragmentation of the country. Virtually all of the media reporting concerned with Saif al-Islam al-Qaddafi's February 20, 2011, appearance on Libyan television focused on his "last man, woman, and bullet" comment, but the younger Qaddafi seemed to understand Libya far better than those who subsequently opined that the country's dearth of political institutions was a potential advantage for its democratic development.[15] Before that dramatic moment when Saif threatened bloodshed, he warned that unless Libyans endeavored to settle their differences, the country would be consumed with violence for "forty years before there is an agreement."[16]

Under these circumstances, it was laudable that Libyans got as far as they did with the July 2012 elections for the General National Congress, the seating of a new government, and the establishment of a committee to write a constitution, which produced a draft in the fall of 2015. Yet as the previous chapter emphasized, violence overwhelmed the country, rendering the formal political process in Libya irrelevant. In the absence of political institutions to help bridge Qaddafi's long rule to a new era, Libyans coalesced around tribes and clans for protection and the provision of services. This was not necessarily new, but after the collapse of Qaddafi's political control, these groups came into open and often armed conflict with each other. The result was precisely as Saif had predicted when the uprising was only a few days old.

In some ways, Libya was the mirror image of its neighbor to the east. Although Hosni Mubarak was no longer president, the country remained very much Mubarak's Egypt. As Vice President Omar Suleiman informed the country on February 11, 2011, that "the president . . . has decided to leave his position . . . and has entrusted the Supreme Council of the Armed Forces to administer the nation's affairs," the man himself was aboard a plane headed for a villa in Sharm el-Sheikh, the resort town at the southern tip of the Sinai Peninsula. He would remain holed up there until August, when he and his two sons, Alaa and Gamal, were put on trial in Cairo. Owing to his age, reports alleging ill health, and respect for the office he once held, the former president was sent to a military hospital in Maadi—a wealthy area of greater Cairo—and his sons were remanded to a large complex called Tora Prison, just south of the Egyptian capital. If anything symbolized the change under way in Egypt, it was the Mubaraks in the dock awaiting trial. Hosni was charged with conspiring to kill protesters, selling gas to Israel at below market prices, corruption, and embezzlement; Gamal and Alaa were accused of corruption, embezzlement, and insider trading. They were not alone, however. Among the most prominent servants of Mubarak who occupied cells at Tora Prison were the former prime minister and the former ministers of the interior, housing, tourism, and information. Some of the biggest and most influential business tycoons who came to dominate the ruling National Democratic Party were also in legal jeopardy. Those who understood what was in store once the military deployed in Tahrir Square on January 28 fired up their Gulfstreams and Learjets and headed for exile in Beirut, Dubai, Doha, London, and Madrid.

On one level, the changes were stunning. Mubarak had been around for so long it seemed he might never leave. It was hard to imagine the country without him. Some Egyptians were overjoyed at his departure and subsequent incarceration but could not quite grasp what had transpired. One journalist kept asking a foreign friend to explain over and over again how it was that Mubarak fell and that his intelligence chief and vice president (for all of ten days), Omar Suleiman—who had a Darth Vader–like reputation among Egyptians—could not save him. Despite the collective and giddy disorientation the uprising produced, the sudden and dramatic personal reversals of the Mubarak family, the arrests of some members of the business elite, and the exile of others obscured the fact that the political and social structures of Egyptian society that marked the previous three decades (and earlier) remained intact.

Egypt's ruling elite remained the ruling elite, the business elite was unchanged, and the status of the middle and lower classes continued to be what it was on January 24, 2011—the day before the uprising began. The judiciary was untouchable. In addition, many of the ministers who served under the SCAF in the eighteen months between Mubarak's ouster and Mohammed Morsi's election had served the fallen president in one capacity or another. It is true that during his brief presidency, Morsi pushed out the minister of defense, the chief of staff of the armed forces, and the commanders of the navy, air force, and air defense command. Less than a week before he relieved Field Marshal Mohammed Hussein al-Tantawi and other senior military officers, Morsi fired the head of the General Intelligence Directorate, the commander of the Republican Guard Corps, and the governor of North Sinai, and then ordered the field marshal to sack the head of the military police. The proximate cause of Morsi's fury was a terrorist attack on Egyptian forces in Sinai near the Gaza frontier that killed sixteen Egyptian border guards. It seemed clear that he was using the incident to clean house, but the replacements were no different from the officials who had been sacked. They were not Brotherhood people, but people who came from within the system. No better example of that was the man who became minister of defense, Major General Abdel Fattah al-Sisi, who was a product of the military establishment that Tantawi had led for the previous two decades. The best that could be said was that the Egyptians respected the lines of authority and heeded the demands of the president, but it made little or no difference overall. The dismissals were personnel moves that younger, ambitious officers enabled.

Had the changes at the Ministry of Defense led to a transformation of civil-military relations (in favor of the civilians) they would have been revolutionary.

Whereas Egypt's military and intelligence officers seemed to begrudgingly accept Morsi's authority—at least for the time being—the same could not be said of its police generals. As much as it was widely understood that the Ministry of Interior was badly in need of reform, Morsi both needed and feared the police generals. They were the difference between quiet, safe streets and chaos. In a counterintuitive way, lawlessness—or the threat of it—was the Ministry of Interior's insurance policy against being purged and its officers prosecuted. If Morsi had tried to remove senior ministry officials, others would have made sure that Egyptians' sense of security—already faltering—would diminish further and that much of the blame would fall to the presidency. He was forced instead to make little more than a few cosmetic changes to the Ministry of Interior, risking a political price with Egyptians who regarded it as a symbol of brutality and oppression.

The only visible difference in Egypt was the replacement of National Democratic Party (NDP) loyalists with those of the Brotherhood. The new group was inexperienced, and during its brief tenure it could not match the smarmy wheel-greasing that the NDP had perfected, though it was not for lack of trying. When Abdul Mawgoud al-Dardery learned that his guest was unable to secure a seat on the 6:00 P.M. flight from Luxor to Cairo and was instead scheduled to be aboard the 3:00 P.M. departure, he sent an assistant as his emissary to EgyptAir's office to fix the problem. When the assistant returned empty handed, Dardery sent him back, but to no avail. Slightly embarrassed, he apologized that he could not make the visit longer. It was a switch that the once-ruling NDP operatives who previously controlled Luxor would have more than likely accomplished with little trouble. Perhaps Dardery's failure was a sign of growth; Egyptian business concerns, especially large and important ones like EgyptAir, would no longer tolerate political pressure in the service of personal demands. Maybe Dardery's effort to change his guest's flight reflected an exaggerated sense of his self-importance. These were certainly possibilities, but that he believed he could exert pressure on the airline by dint of who he was and whom he represented—not the people of Luxor, but the Muslim Brotherhood— indicated something important about Egypt in the post-Mubarak era. It was not as "post" as having the former president in custody might suggest. The Brotherhood saw itself in the same privileged light as the NDP. Once more, under Morsi the cast of characters may have changed, but not actually by that much. In 2012, Luxor's governor was a Morsi- appointed retired diplomat, but his deputy was a police general. By way of comparison, under Mubarak the governorates were in the hands of retired military and police officers. The July 2013 coup brought another shift, but the new people represented the interests of those who were restoring a version of the political order that had been in place from the time the Free Officers came to power until Mubarak departed.

By the fifth anniversary of the uprisings, it was clear to virtually anyone with even a passing interest in the region that change had not really come to Egypt. Like Mubarak, the only thing civilian about President Sisi was the suit he put on in the morning. Egypt's social structures—broadly speaking, society's prevailing economic and power relations—remained remarkably the same. Tunisia, in contrast, was sig- nificantly more confusing. The rapturous reporting on the National Dialogue Quartet, its Nobel Peace Prize, the Islamist Ennahda's Rachid al-Ghannouchi, and the "one Arab Spring success story" was interspersed with bad news about terrorism, a deteriorating economy, and a seeth- ing countryside. Tunisia had undoubtedly made progress, especially in comparison with Egypt, but the residue of the Ben Ali era threatened to have a negative effect on the country's political development.

When Zine al-Abidine Ben Ali fled Tunisia for Saudi Arabia on January 14, 2011, it seemed as if virtually all of the country's eleven million people were happy to see him go. His Tunisia was a fearsome police state married up to a "what's mine is mine and what's yours is mine" outlook of the president's inner circle and his extended family. The rage with which Tunisians attacked and looted Ben Ali–affiliated properties and homes after the president's departure was probably the wrong way to begin what was supposed to be a new era of democracy and the rule of law, but it was entirely understandable. Yet even as the former president and his notorious wife, Leila Trabelsi, were tucked away in Jeddah and members of their extended family were in exile in

Doha and Montreal, a far larger group of economic and political elites stayed put.

Tunisia's business leaders may have been forced to keep a lower pro-file—at least for a time—but like the early Habib Bourguiba period, when circumstances rather than ideology dictated the adoption of state-directed development, transitional governments more than six decades later were forced to reconcile themselves to Tunisia's existing commercial elite. They had the necessary capital to invest in Tunisia and jumpstart an economy that was wobbly in the political uncertainty after the uprising. The ties between Ben Ali–era elites and transitional governments did not sit well, however. A week after the funeral of Chokri Belaid—the leftist politician assassinated in February 2013—the powerful Tunisian General Labor Union (UGTT) took the oppor-tunity to press an Ennahda that was already on the defensive by calling a general strike. The UGTT leadership was dismayed that Ennahda and its partners in government were too cozy with big business.[17] That the government was courting this group in the first place suggested that despite the uprising Tunisia's social order had not actually changed very much. The dominant class under Ben Ali remained a powerful force despite his being holed up in Saudi Arabia.

Tunisia is not Egypt, but even there the staying power of social forces whose interests lay in the old political system seemed robust. When Essebsi founded Nidaa Tounes in 2012, it was to provide a focal point for supporters of the old order. A considerable contingent of Ben Ali's Democratic Constitutional Rally (RCD) figures and supporters were thus within its ranks. After Belaid's death and the accusations of Ennahda's complicity with or tolerance of extremist groups, a few small secular parties on the left and unionists coalesced under Essebsi's lead-ership. This only underscored what Nidaa Tounes was all about: un-dermining and weakening Ennahda. It was hardly an easy partnership given that the party was actually a front made up of multiple politi-cal factions that had little in common save their antipathy toward the Islamists. In time, this would prove to be Nidaa Tounes's weakness, but in 2013 and 2014 the party was Tunisia's most effective political force. In the October 2014 parliamentary elections, Nidaa Tounes won 37.5 percent of the popular vote, which was good enough for 86 of the 217 seats in the awkwardly named Assembly of the Representatives of the People. Ennahda followed with almost 28 percent of the vote and sixty-nine parliamentary mandates. The remaining seats were divvied among a variety of smaller parties and independents that garnered less than 5 percent of the vote.

Less than a month after the parliamentary elections, Tunisians went back to the polling stations and cast their vote for president. After failing to win more than the 50 percent needed to forestall a runoff, Essebsi beat Moncef al-Marzouki—the incumbent who had the tacit support of Rachid al-Ghannouchi—by 11 percentage points. Between owning the largest bloc in parliament and the presidency, it seemed that Nidaa Tounes had taken a step toward restoring the old political order, or at least some version of it. At that moment, the lesson of the so-called Jasmine Revolution indicated that it was possible to move from a system that had only sham elections—Ben Ali's last presidential election produced 90 percent support for the incumbent—to one in which elections were real even if they did reward many of the same people who had held political and economic power all along.

Essebsi emerged from Tunisia's political season with supreme confidence. By law, he could no longer lead Nidaa Tounes, but the party had done what it was created to do—provide an alternative to Ennahda. The man to whom Essebsi turned to form a new government was Habib Essid, an agricultural economist with degrees from the University of Tunis and the University of Minnesota. He was a political independent, but only because Ben Ali fell and the RCD was abolished. During the Ben Ali years, Essid held senior posts in the Ministries of Agriculture and Interior and served as minister of interior during Beji Caid Essebsi's tenure as interim prime minister in 2011.

Essid initially sought to form a government that excluded Ennahda. This was a controversial and provocative move, though Essid was forced to back down after the ensuing uproar made it clear that he would not get the 109 votes of confidence in parliament to establish a government. Instead, on February 5, 2015, he brought forth a broadly based government that included nine independents (including the prime minister), six Nidaa Tounes ministers, and two mandates each for the small Free Patriotic Union and Afek Tounes. Ennahda was granted a single government portfolio—the Ministry of Vocational Training and Employment—and three minister of state positions.[18] The government received unanimous support from the parliament. It was a positive moment that averted a potentially destabilizing crisis, but it also exposed the intentions of Nidaa Tounes and its allies, whose first inclinations were to ignore the high-minded rhetorical commitment to consensus that had become part of Tunisia's political discourse. The inability of Nidaa Tounes to impose its will on the political arena and keep Ennahda out of the government might be good for the development of democracy in Tunisia, if only because stalemates force parties to work together in ways that reinforce compromise. This was something that in time Essebsi came to realize, and so when Essid lost a vote of confidence in July 2016, the new Tunisian government under Youssef Chahed better reflected the balance of political forces in the country. This was good news, but given Tunisia's difficult social, economic, and political circumstances, this type of political equilibrium is also vulnerable to disruption from unanticipated events.

THE "STICKINESS" OF INSTITUTIONS

It is hard to have a conversation about the Middle East in Washington or in university conference rooms without a discussion of institutions—a term that is often confused with institute. Unlike institutes, institutions do not have doors, offices, and people who work within them. The venerable Brookings Institution should actually be named the "Brookings Institute." Institutions are frameworks for social action like rules, laws, decrees, and regulations. They shape people's expectations and behavior in a society. For some time, analysts have imagined that one of the markers—and thus a major problem—of Middle Eastern countries was weak institutionalization. That seems to be true when it comes to a country like Libya, where Muammar al-Qaddafi left an institutional blank slate. Yet the image of an inadequately institutionalized Middle East runs counter to what analysts know (or should know) about places like Egypt, Tunisia, or Turkey. Those countries are robustly institutionalized, though it is not actually the number of institutions that count. It is their nature that matters, which in the Middle East has been authoritarian. The origins of political institutions lie in struggles over power. For example, Egypt's Gamal Abdel Nasser "discovered" laws, rules, regulations, and decrees that helped him and the Free Officers prevail over their opponents as they sought to consolidate their power in the early 1950s. Those institutions have lived on in one form or another ever since.[19] In other words, they are "sticky." And because institutions in any society reflect the interests of those who have political and economic power, leaders can be expected to leverage the prevailing rules of the political game to keep, maintain, and reinforce their privileged positions. Patterns of politics in the Middle East indicate that when leaders confront political challenges, they crack down on their opponents and then reengineer or revise institutions in an effort to forestall future challenges. Yet these changes are based on a state's existing laws, decrees, rules, and regulations that then shape the direction and quality of that evolution. This is why it is so important to understand how the non-revolutions of the region have profoundly affected the political trajectory of the Middle East. In Tunisia and Egypt, the uprisings pushed leaders from power but left authoritarian institutions intact that are vulnerable to the manipulation of an elite who want to preserve their power. In Turkey, the Gezi Park protests did not push Recep Tayyip Erdoğan from power but reflected anger and frustration at the way he and his Justice and Development Party fell back on authoritarian measures and manipulated the institutions of the state for their political advantage.

In Tunisia, the challenge of extremism highlighted the way both the instrumentalization and stickiness of institutions can affect politics. On March 18, 2015, two terrorists stormed the Bardo National Museum in Tunis and killed twenty people, including seventeen tourists. The museum, which features artifacts from Tunisia's Hellenistic and Roman past, is among Tunis's top tourist attractions. The bloodshed there raised two related concerns. The first was obvious: Tunisia had a terrorism problem. The attack on the American embassy in 2012 and two political assassinations in six months in 2013 had heightened awareness of the brewing problem of extremism, but the attack at the museum revealed that the country remained vulnerable. About three months after the museum attack, a twenty-three-year-old named Seifeddine Rezgui Yacoubi wandered onto the beach along Tunisia's eastern Mediterranean shore near the resort town of Sousse. He looked like anyone else that

day in that place, wearing swim trunks and carrying a large beach umbrella. Yet instead of spending the day enjoying the warm surf and sand,
he pulled out an AK-47 rifle that he had obscured with his umbrella
and raked the beach with gunfire. When it was all over eleven minutes
later, thirty-eight tourists, most of them British, were dead. Another
thirty-nine were injured. The government deployed more than 1,000
police officers to protect tourist sites and vowed to build a 100-mile
long fence along Tunisia's 285-mile border with Libya, which it claimed
had become a source of guns and terrorists. An additional aspect of the
government's response raised a second and more serious long-term concern about Tunisia's political trajectory. The centerpiece of the government's counterterrorism strategy was Organic Law number 22 of 2015,
titled "Relating to the Battle against Terrorism and the Suppression
of Money Laundering," which resurrected a number of Ben Ali–era
measures that had been used against his opponents during the former
leader's twenty-four-year rule.

In keeping with the new Tunisia, the law begins well enough, emphasizing constitutional rights and human rights. It also references a
number of international agreements and charters concerned with the
protection of individual and political liberties.[20] Yet aspects of the 100-
page law ran counter to the more just and democratic society Tunisians
had demanded. The Tunisians had a legitimate fight on their hands,
but activists expressed concern that the measures used to fight terrorists
would be turned on peaceful opponents of the government. Among
the most objectionable was the extension of time a suspect could be
detained without charge from six to fifteen days. During this detention, the accused would not have the right to consult with an attorney
or to meet with family members. As Human Rights Watch and others
pointed out, this situation was ripe for abuse.[21] Serious questions arose
about due process as judges were given the power to shield the identities of victims from the accused thereby denying them the right to
mount a basic component of criminal defense: the right to confront
one's accusers. In addition, Article 52 of the law granted authorities per-
mission to use "special investigative techniques" to monitor the communications of suspected terrorists.[22] These powers were subject to a
court-issued warrant and came with penalties if they were abused, but
given the pervasive surveillance of the Ben Ali era and the problematic

nature of these security investigations in even the most sophisticated democracies, granting sweeping powers to the Ministry of Interior's intelligence directorates seemed like a step backward. The law also included the death penalty for a wide variety of acts that resulted in the loss of life and rape. The Tunisian state had not put anyone to death since 1991, but the law's provision for the punishment, combined with the heightened state of anxiety over the security of the country, opened the possibility that this quarter-century freeze would come to an end.[23]

Perhaps the gravest concern about the anti-terror legislation was its overly broad definition of what constituted terrorism. Article 13, for example, identifies specific acts such as releasing chemical and biological agents into the water supply as terrorism, which it surely is. At the same time, the law indicated that vague offenses, such as causing damage to private and public property including infrastructure, were also terrorism.[24] Tunisians could be charged with terrorism under these provisions in a variety of scenarios when they were not engaged in any action that meets a reasonable definition of terrorism—demonstrating against the government being a notable example. Sure enough, in late April 2016, the Tunisian government accused 157 civil society organizations of links to terrorism. Critics charged that the government's evidence for this accusation was vague, at best. In a corollary to this expansive definition of terrorism, the Tunisian legislature also made it a crime to glorify terrorist acts.[25] As abhorrent as it might be for individuals to admire and applaud terrorism, the parliament set back Tunisia's democratic aspirations when it implicitly made speech and thought a crime. These were the ways that governments in the region repressed political opponents and justified widespread abuse of human rights.

Tunisia's recent history indicated ample precedent for the way the government leveraged laws, rules, regulations, and decrees to suppress its adversaries. Modern Tunisia's first president, Habib Bourguiba, for example, demonstrated little tolerance for Islamists. At his behest, Rachid al-Ghannouchi spent the years between 1980 and 1984 in prison and, in 1987, was arrested again along with eighty-nine other Islamist leaders on charges of "inciting violence and seeking to change the nature of the state."[26] Ghannouchi and a number of others were initially sentenced to death, though the courts reduced Ghannouchi's sentence to life imprisonment. However, then prime minister Zine al-Abidine Ben Ali, of all people, saved him. On November 7, 1987, Ben Ali pushed the ailing Bourguiba from power, promising a new reformist era in Tunisian politics. In early 1988, the country's new leader ordered Ghannouchi and the thousands of his supporters who had been arrested in Bourguiba's waning days released from prison.[27] Ben Ali then issued a national pact that marked a change in the orientation of both Tunisia's nationalist narrative and foreign policy, in part emphasizing the country's Arab and Islamic heritage. This was an important signal of an ostensibly more inclusive political environment, though the 1956 Personal Status Code—which provides for the rights of women in marriage, divorce, custody, and inheritance—remained sacrosanct.[28]

The positive environment, which was reinforced with Ben Ali's declaration that the "people deserve an advanced and institutionalized political life, truly based on the plurality of parties and mass organization," was nevertheless short-lived.[29] Although the parliament passed a law authorizing the creation of political parties, the government took no action on Ghannouchi's application to legalize Ennahda (which until that time had been known as the Islamic Tendency Movement).[30] Because it remained illegal, Ennahda ran independent candidates in the 1989 general elections. They garnered only about 15 percent of the overall vote, but the Ennahda independents did particularly well in both the south of the country and the suburbs surrounding Tunis, far outstripping the popular support for every other party save Ben Ali's. Based on these results, Ghannouchi demanded that the government recognize Ennahda as a political party. When the government refused, Ghannouchi, sensing an increasingly hostile environment, left Tunisia for exile in Great Britain (via Algiers and Khartoum). From the safety of London he insinuated that the Islamists would continue their efforts not just for legal recognition, but also to take over the political system.[31] Ghannouchi's provocative statements combined with the recent memory of a number of terrorist attacks staged during the summer of 1987 was all that Ben Ali needed to repress Ennahda and position himself as the defender of Tunisia's secular orientation against the challenge of militant Islam.[32] In the ensuing years, Ghannouchi's followers confronted harassment, arrest, and at times torture. Ghannouchi was himself sentenced in absentia to life in prison in 1992.

Times had changed since both the Bourguiba and Ben Ali era, but how much? Some factions within Nidaa Tounes were profoundly uncomfortable with any accommodation with Ennahda. After Abdel Fattah al-Sisi removed Mohammed Morsi from power in Egypt in July 2013, Essebsi himself implied that he would welcome an "Egyptian solution" to Tunisia's Islamists (though he was later quite critical of developments in Egypt under Sisi).[33] That did not happen, but it was clear how the anti-terrorism law could be brandished against not only violent extremists but also peaceful competitors to those in power. Even before the law's passage, the government had begun taking special measures against suspected extremists. According to some reports, in 2015 the government had swept up as many as 100,000 people in anti-terror dragnets that did not offer adequate protection for the accused.[34] This in and of itself should have raised questions about the quality of Tunisian politics, but given the country's international status as the one Arab Spring success story only a few bothered to point this out. When the measure went before the legislature, it passed overwhelmingly with 174 votes in favor. Yet one in five of Tunisia's lawmakers either abstained or failed to show up to vote, implicitly registering their opposition to the sweeping legislation. All sixty-nine of Ennahda's deputies voted for the law. They were either confident of the democratic progress Tunisia had made and therefore believed that safeguards built into the legislation requiring court orders for surveillance, the penalties for abuse of that power, and the authorities' commitments to constitutional principles would carry the day, or they were constrained politically to vote for the law, lest they be accused once again of complicity with extremists.

When a suicide bomber killed twelve members of the presidential guard in November 2015, Essebsi declared a month-long state of emergency in the country and a curfew in the capital. The response once again was a round of arrests and an appeal to national unity, but in Tunisia's difficult security environment it remained entirely unclear whether public expressions of national solidarity and the leadership's vows to deal with the problem were merely superficial or were the discursive bases for deliberalization in the name of security. For its part, Amnesty International accused "the government [of] . . . us[ing] the] emergency laws to trample on human rights."[35] With the anti-terrorism measures, Tunisian authorities certainly had the tools to achieve that goal if they chose to do so. It seemed hard to believe given the way Tunisians had previously refused to give in to the divisions and polarization that play into the hands of authoritarians promising to stamp out extremism and establish order. Yet there was reason to be concerned. It was not so much Essebsi's vow in response to the Bardo National Museum killings to "exterminate" a "savage minority," but rather the combination of law, the outlook of Essebsi and Nidaa Tounes, and historical precedent that made it entirely plausible that fighting extremism could derail Tunisia's much hoped for democratic transition.[36]

Tunisia's anti-terrorism law was not the only example of the way the Ben Ali era crept back into Tunisian politics. In the summer of 2015, Essebsi presented a draft financial reconciliation law to the government that would allow business leaders and civil servants who were guilty of financial crimes to pay back money they embezzled—with interest—in exchange for amnesty. Essebsi and the government presented the law both as part of Tunisia's transitional justice process and as a way to spur badly needed investment, especially after the toll the Bardo and Sousse attacks took on the tourism industry.[37] The draft law generated a significant backlash, however. To Tunisian democracy activists, the measure was nothing more than a backdoor way of letting the corrupt, bootlicking, high-class grifters of the Ben Ali era back in the game, not prudent economic policy. Even so, in the spring of 2016, parliamentarians guaranteed the law's passage, which was forwarded to the legislature for consideration a few months later. The anti-terrorism law and draft financial reconciliation measure fell within the context of a broader effort under way among regional leaders to leverage political institutions that were a threat to the democratic aspirations of societies agitating for change. Often these measures were promulgated under the guise of reform or, as Essebsi and his allies claimed when they sought to grant amnesty to the corrupt, to ensure justice. Tunisia was hardly the worst transgressor, but even in a place touted as better than the rest, the post-uprising political system was vulnerable to both the way elites leveraged political institutions and the stickiness of rules, laws, regulations, and decrees. It was Turkey, a country where the Gezi Park protests shared features with the uprisings in Tunisia, Egypt, and Libya without pushing the Turkish leaders from power that is nevertheless an exemplary case of how the manipulation and staying power of institutions have a profound effect on a country's political trajectory.

On a warm afternoon in early April 2013, just a few months before the protests over Gezi Park exploded, Okan Altıparmak was in fifth gear as he walked and talked through the Kadıköy neighborhood on the Asian side of the Bosphorus Strait. His soliloquy had probably gone on for the better part of three hours and combined such varied, but closely linked, subjects as the Turkish soccer club Fenerbahçe, Prime Minister Recep Tayyip Erdoğan, the ruling Justice and Development Party, the cleric Fethullah Gülen, and the utter perfidy of Fenerbahçe's rival, Galatasaray. Okan had an encyclopedic knowledge of Fenerbahçe and its inner workings, but he was not your standard Turkish soccer nut. He hailed from soccer royalty. Okan's father, Ogün, was a team legend who led the Turkish league in goals in 1970 and 1971. When Ogün made the short walk from the club's headquarters to its home field at Şükrü Saraçoğlu Stadium, the masses gathered around him as flashes from smartphone cameras blinded. Okan's younger brother was also a standout for Fenerbahçe in the 1990s. As for Okan, he was no slouch. He played "the beautiful game" at Northwestern University near Chicago, where he majored in economics. After graduating, he headed to Los Angeles to live out every young Turkish man's dream, spending the late 1980s and most of the 1990s in California before returning to Istanbul in 1998. The years in Chicago had a lasting impact. Turkish is a vowel harmony language, meaning that when Turks speak English, it tends to produce a kind of sing-song accent. Okan was the exception to this fast and loose rule. He was the only guy in Istanbul whose (flawless) English was peppered with a Midwestern lazy *a*. It was an endearing trait that at times produced an "Is he Turkish or American?" kind of tension, especially when he wore his Chicago Bears jersey. He was without a doubt soccer-obsessed, but he was also a sophisticated and deeply knowledgeable observer of Turkish politics. As he ambled down Bağdat Caddesi—Baghdad Avenue, which fans refer to as Fenerbahçe's Citadel because its stadium is located on that street—he commented "football [soccer] is one of the few outlets where Turks can express themselves freely."[38]

The anger and irony in Okan's tone reflected how much Turkey had changed and then changed again since October 6, 2004, when the

European Commission recommended that Ankara begin negotiations to join the European Union. Until that time, European leaders were unwilling to seriously consider Turkish membership because of a range of problems, including Turkey's human rights record, the outsized role of the Turkish military's General Staff in politics, Turkey's occupation of northern Cyprus, and Ankara's support for the Turkish Republic of Northern Cyprus, which no other country recognizes. There was also Turkey's suppression of ethnic Kurdish cultural rights, the war between the Turkish state and a terrorist group called the Kurdistan Workers' Party (PKK), and a long list of economic issues.[39] More than anything, the Europeans seemed skittish about admitting a large, overwhelmingly Muslim country into their midst. This was the cultural issue that every Turk acknowledged but many Europeans denied. For their part, Turkish leaders were resistant to compromise on Cyprus—the southern half of which is an internationally recognized government and a European Union member state since 2004—and were quick to invoke special circumstances when it came to the military's place in the political system. The Turks were also wary of relinquishing some of their sovereignty in favor of Brussels.

Neither side had an interest in bringing Ankara's efforts to an end, though. The Europeans were content to let the process continue, never believing they would actually have to make a decision about Turkish membership, and the Turks were unwilling to let Europe off the hook. As a result, Turkey's integration with Europe proceeded at a glacial pace. Spurts of progress punctuated the ambivalence of both sides, however. A 1996 Customs Union agreement provided an important link between Turkey's economy and that of Europe, and in 2001, Brussels and Ankara agreed to an Accession Partnership for Turkey. The following year, the Turkish parliament passed three "harmonization" packages that made important changes to the penal code, the codes of criminal procedure, and the anti-terror law. The legislation also abolished the death penalty in peacetime, strengthened freedom of expression, and permitted broadcasts in Kurdish.[40]

After the Justice and Development Party (AKP) came to power in late 2002, it passed an additional five reform packages between January 2003 and July 2004. This was a significant shift from Turkish Islamist parties of the past, who regarded Ankara's effort to integrate with Europe as a form of cultural abnegation. The reformists who founded the AKP rejected this idea and at the time of their election claimed that membership in Europe was consistent with their values.[41] The changes they introduced fell under broad categories of the judiciary, human rights, economics, minority rights, and the functioning of political parties. The reform packages also included a series of changes that diminished the military's autonomy and its ability to influence politics, an issue with which the European Commission consistently expressed concern in its annual reports on Turkey's progress toward meeting membership requirements. The practical effect of the eight reform packages—three that the previous government passed in 2002 and the AKP's five harmonization bills—was substantial. The European Commission recommended that Ankara begin membership negotiations, though its endorsement was hedged.[42] By Europe's own metrics, Turkey had taken steps to "achieve stability of institutions guaranteeing democracy, the rule of law, human rights and respect for and protection of minorities, the existence of a functioning market economy as the capacity to cope with competitive pressure and market forces within the Union," but it had not fulfilled these requirements in their totality.[43] The European Commission argued that the negotiation process itself would spur further reforms. Despite the European Union's caveats, it was a moment of tremendous optimism. It had been forty years since Turkey signed an association agreement with what was then the European Economic Community with the goal of becoming integrated into Europe. That negotiations were to begin was an acknowledgment of the important liberalizing changes that the Turks had undertaken.

It was not to be. Almost as soon as Turkey began membership negotiations, they ground to a halt over mostly French and Cypriot objections. Turkey's reforms subsequently faltered. On the face of it, the European Union's lack of enthusiasm seems to be directly linked to political reversals in Ankara, but Turkey's deliberalization likely had less to do with Brussels than with the political opportunities Erdoğan and the AKP perceived in their effort to transform the country in a way that did not conform to European Union standards. Because political institutions are sticky, the way in which the AKP manipulated laws, regulations, rules, and decrees for its political ends would have a profound effect on Turkey's future development. Okan—who had never been a supporter of the AKP—was surely exaggerating at the time about the inability of Turks to express themselves freely, but not by a lot. As of 2013, much of what was once the country's vibrant and free, if not always responsible, press existed in a profoundly repressive environment in which a significant percentage of media outlets were in the hands of AKP supporters and used to advance the goals of the ruling party. This was accomplished in a variety of ways that included coercion but also manipulation of government rules and regulations.

It was a problem that had been in the making for some time. In 2007, for example, the Savings Deposit Insurance Fund (SDIF) took over *Sabah* newspaper and ATV Television over legitimate concerns that their former owner, who had been involved in a bank failure, retained an interest in these properties. Given the SDIF's responsibility to recover assets on behalf of depositors, this was an appropriate step.[44] The problem came when the SDIF turned around and sold the properties in a sole-bid deal to a firm called Çalık Holding, the chief executive officer of which was none other than Erdoğan's son-in-law. *Sabah*, which had grown critical of the prime minister before the sale, became a reliable supporter of the AKP afterward. Then there was the case of Doğan Media Group, which was assessed a $2.5 billion tax fine in 2009 for overstating losses at certain properties to minimize its tax exposure. No specific evidence pointed to Erdoğan or AKP pressure on the Revenue Administration to go after the firm, but the affair was tinged with politics. Aydın Doğan, the group's owner, was a fierce critic of Erdoğan and the AKP. His flagship newspaper, *Hürriyet*, closely followed allegations that AKP operatives in Germany raised money for charity among the country's large Turkish population and then funneled these funds to Erdoğan-friendly business concerns in order to buy media properties. The fine was reduced when Doğan agreed to sell off another newspaper, *Milliyet*, which under new ownership became significantly less critical of the government.

Those journalists and editors who refused to bend to the AKP's will lived in fear of arrest or shutdown. According to the Committee to Protect Journalists, Turkey ranked fifth in 2015—after China, Egypt, Eritrea, and Iran—in the number of journalists jailed with at least fourteen. All of those charged worked for publications that were critical of the AKP. The editors of the Gülen-affiliated *Zaman* and its

English-language counterpart *Today's Zaman* were arrested in October 2015 on charges of "establishing and leading a terrorist organization" and "attempting to destroy the Republic of Turkey or preventing it from doing its duties" in one case and for insulting Erdoğan—who had become president of the republic in August 2014—in the other.[45] Also in October 2015, riot police stormed the headquarters of another Gülen-affiliated firm, the Koza-İpek Media Group, after a court ordered it seized on the grounds that it was involved in financing terror and disseminating terrorist propaganda. A month after the raid on Koza-İpek, the editor and the Ankara bureau chief of the unambiguously secularist and nationalist *Cumhuriyet* were jailed for "knowingly and willingly aiding an armed terrorist organization," membership in a terrorist organization, and "obtaining and exposing secret documents of the state for the means of political and military espionage."[46] The cumulative effect of the government's manipulation of tax, banking, and anti-terrorist laws was to create a virtual ministry of information that sought to inculcate in the minds of Turks the AKP's version of reality.

Erdoğan's ability to secure friendly media properties or to go after Doğan Media Group was a function of the AKP's mastery of much of the bureaucracy whose ministers and directors had an interest in doing the then prime minister's bidding. The plight of the editors of *Zaman*, *Today's Zaman*, and *Cumhuriyet* indicates that, as time went on, Turkey's leaders were able to instrumentalize the courts for their political ends. After Turkey's chief prosecutor charged the AKP in March 2008 with being a center for anti-secular activity, the judiciary became an urgent issue for the party's leadership. When the Constitutional Court ruled on the case later that year, seven out of eleven justices found enough evidence to support the charge and voted to close the party. That was just one vote short to carry out a ban, however. Instead, the AKP was forced to pay a fine of $20 million.[47] "This was too close a call for Erdoğan. The AKP's genealogy included four parties that had been closed as a result of either a coup or a court order; he was determined never to allow his party to meet the same fate."[48]

Toward that end, on September 12, 2010, Turks were asked to vote in a referendum on a constitutional amendment that gave the government greater freedom to appoint new judges and fill vacancies on the bench. The proposed change was undertaken in a way that virtually ensured its passage. First, the date of the referendum coincided with the anniversary of the 1980 coup d'état, which produced the constitution, written at the behest of the junta, that Turks were being asked to amend. The symbolism was hard to miss because the vote was trumpeted as another step in the AKP's drive to forge a more democratic Turkey. Second, the amendment on the judiciary was rolled up neatly with other proposed changes, including hard-to-oppose provisions for the protection of children's rights, freedom of residence and movement, the right of appeal, right to petition, and right to acquire information, into a single package on which Turks were simply asked to vote yes or no. The amendment passed by a wide margin—of the 77 percent of eligible voters who cast a ballot, 58 percent voted in favor and 42 percent opposed. In the summer of 2016, the AKP-dominated Grand National Assembly passed legislation to make it even easier for the party to place supporters on the bench.

One need not look too hard to find instances where the Turkish leadership used the judiciary and prosecutors for its political advantage. Two of the most spectacular, the Ergenekon and Sledgehammer cases— which ensnared large numbers of military officers and civilian critics of the government—actually occurred before the 2010 amendment that allowed the AKP to pack the courts. Since then, the most important (though underreported) example is the legal jeopardy that those who investigated and brought corruption charges against figures within or close to the AKP leadership now find themselves. On the morning of December 17, 2013, Turks awoke to the news that four government ministers and some of their children were under suspicion for bribery and influence peddling. Charges were also leveled against the chairman of the state-owned Halkbank for his role in helping Turkish business interests skirt international sanctions on Iran. The other prominent person taken into custody was the construction and real estate magnate, Ali Ağaoğlu. His arrest coincided with the detention of officials from TOKİ, the Mass Housing Administration. As chapter 3 describes, TOKİ had been used as a vehicle for the AKP's patronage machine. The arrest of Ağaoğlu and TOKİ officials suggested that prosecuters believed they had enough evidence to break it. A few months later, a shocking audio recording surfaced in which someone believed to be the

Turkish leader was heard instructing his son to move tens of millions of dollars from the homes of members of the Erdoğan family where the money had been hidden.

At the time, the corruption investigation represented the single biggest challenge to Erdoğan and the AKP since they came to power in 2002—bigger than both the military's effort to block Abdullah Gül from becoming president in 2007 and the 2013 Gezi Park protests. As a result, within a week of the initial investigation, Erdoğan sacked more than fifty police commanders, reassigned judges and prosecutors, declared the inquiry a "dirty operation," and claimed that Fethullah Gülen was orchestrating the entire sting via the alleged parallel state that he and his supporters had established within Turkey's bureaucracy. The prime minister's effort to frame the corruption investigation as a Gülenist plot to overthrow the state was not just rhetoric but also part of a larger strategy to undermine the charges and to leverage the legal system to exact retribution on the AKP's opponents.

In response to the crisis, Turkey's parliament voted to establish a fourteen-member Corruption Investigation Commission to determine whether the ministers should be referred for prosecution.[49] Because the AKP held nine of the seats, the outcome of the commission's work was never in doubt. On January 5, 2015, all nine AKP members of the commission voted against referral on the grounds that the allegations against the ministers were part of an attempted Gülenist coup. A few weeks later, the Grand National Assembly, where the AKP held 327 seats, affirmed the parliamentary commission's recommendation. The charges against the ministers' sons, Ali Ağaoğlu, an Iranian-Turkish businessman involved in Halkbank's affairs, and the TOKİ employees were all subsequently dropped. In a twist, the AKP gave sweeping powers to Criminal Courts of Peace to investigate the police officers and prosecutors who had brought the charges against the ministers and others.[50] The enhanced prerogatives of these courts were reminiscent of the State Security Courts that the AKP had abolished in its European Union reforms a decade earlier. Still, Erdoğan and his supporters justified this move on the basis of protecting the state from an organization—the Gülenists—that was bent on overthrowing it. The Gülenists were not the good guys they portrayed themselves to be among foreigners and in the international media, but the evidence of AKP wrongdoing was overwhelming. The charge that the corruption allegations were actually a Gülenist coup attempt was intended to obscure what was actually happening: the ruling party had used the combination of its dominant position in the Grand National Assembly, parliamentary procedure, and anti-terrorism measures to turn the scandal to its advantage and exact revenge on its opponents.

The saga of Turkey's June 2015 general elections is important not only because what Erdoğan and the AKP did was so brazen, but also because it is the logical consequence of the party's effort to leverage institutions of the Turkish state to make any effort to contest its political power extraordinarily difficult. It is true that the AKP was better organized than its opponents, that its leader is charismatic, and the party has an appealing vision, but the way it has manipulated institutions since at least the mid-2000s may ultimately be more consequential to Turkey's trajectory, resulting in the party's ability to deftly turn defeat into victory. On June 7, 2015, almost 84 percent of eligible voters turned out in what some members of the press called the most important general election in more than a decade.[51] Much was at stake given now president Erdoğan's determination that Turkey should have a new constitution with a strong presidency. Under Turkey's prevailing arrangements, the president—who is supposed to be apolitical—enjoys a range of powers that include accepting or rejecting legislation, ratifying international treaties, appointing the chief of staff of the armed forces, and selecting the prime minister from the party with the largest number of seats in the Grand National Assembly, but the locus of authority in the political system is the prime ministry.[52] Erdoğan wanted to change that and the fastest way of doing it was by winning a two-thirds majority of 367 seats in the parliament, which could approve a new constitution outright. The next fastest way was securing at least a 330-seat majority, allowing the AKP to take a new constitution directly to the people in a referendum. Anything below that number would require negotiations in the parliament, which had previously not gone Erdoğan's way.

When the results began trickling in that evening, opponents of the AKP threw themselves a huge celebration. After garnering nearly 50 percent of the vote in the 2011 parliamentary elections, the party ceded

9 percentage points and sixty-nine seats. The AKP did not even come close to the coveted majority that Erdoğan desired, meaning that the party would need to find a coalition partner to continue governing—something it had never had to do. The AKP still commanded the largest number of seats by a significant percentage, but it no longer seemed so invincible. The results reflected a rare political miscalculation on Erdoğan's part. Beginning in 2014, he had tacked hard to the nationalist right to cover himself and the AKP after pursuing peace with the Kurdistan Workers' Party (PKK), something that was anathema to Turkey's nationalist camp, which had a hard time even acknowledging the distinct ethnicity and culture of the Kurds. In the process, however, Erdoğan pushed the AKP's large constituency of religious Kurds into the arms of a Kurdish-based party called the Peoples' Democratic Party (HDP), which easily surpassed Turkey's 10 percent threshold for parliamentary representation by about six million votes in the June 2015 general elections.[53] The morning after the results were announced, Erdoğan issued a written statement that seemed statesman-like, encouraging the political parties to work together to ensure stability in what was apparently a new era in coalition government. The AKP's comeuppance, according to some analysts, demonstrated the resilience of Turkey's democratic institutions.[54] It was a nice story, but considerably overly optimistic.

Erdoğan offered the sitting prime minister, the AKP's Ahmet Davutoğlu, the task of trying to put together a coalition government—a process the president had every intention of and interest in undermining. Article 116 of Turkey's constitution requires the formation of a government within forty-five days after the president taps a party leader, almost always the one with the largest number of seats in parliament, to form one.[55] Not surprisingly, none of Davutoğlu's coalition talks went anywhere. This was in part because of the slash-and-burn campaign tactics of the president and his advisors, who worked hard to tie Kurdish politicians to the terrorists of the PKK. As a result, the HDP immediately ruled out a coalition with the AKP. Davutoğlu's problems were also the result of poor political judgment. The Nationalist Movement Party (MHP) leader, for example, preferred making demands such as curbing Erdoğan's influence to which the AKP could never accede, rather than negotiating. The MHP was also under the impression that the president was greatly diminished, and as a result, it was time for the opposition to press its ostensible advantage. The nationalists had added twenty-seven seats to their 2011 total, but the AKP still controlled more than three times the number of MHP mandates.

Beyond the bad blood between the AKP and the Kurds or the incompetence of MHP, another, larger issue was at play. Erdoğan and members of the AKP wanted to play out the clock and take their chances with a new election. As early as June 8, when Erdoğan was sounding conciliatory, Burhan Kuzu, an AKP parliamentarian and advisor to the president, told the BBC's Turkish service, "No government will emerge from this scenario. Not even a coalition . . . Early elections look inevitable."[56] As the weeks went by, it became clear that Erdoğan, with his near constant refrain about the need for stability and the problems associated with weak coalition governments of the past, sought to derail coalition talks. He more than implied that this kind of instability at a time when Turkey was battling the PKK and confronting the threat of the self-declared Islamic State was dangerous. Erdoğan did not start the bloodshed with either group, but the fighting between Turkish security forces and the PKK, which picked up during coalition talks, certainly worked to his advantage. The Turkish leader had zeroed in on the HDP and its eighty seats in the Grand National Assembly as the reason the AKP was denied its fourth parliamentary majority. The bloodshed provided an opportunity to hammer away at the idea that the HDP was no different from the PKK. Last-ditch efforts at a coalition government including the AKP and the Republican People's Party came up empty over both philosophical differences and Erdoğan's desire to rerun the elections.

On August 23, Davutoğlu was forced to admit defeat. He established a provisional government and scheduled new elections for November 1. All the polling indicated that Erdoğan had made another grave error and that the outcome of the rerun election would be exactly the same as the June results. Analysts surmised that the president would never be able to recover politically from the blow, ending his fanciful quest to establish a strong presidency.[57] As the sun went down on November 1, the only things that seemed fanciful were the pre-election analysis and polls. The AKP won 49.4 percent of the popular vote and a 317-seat majority, reversing almost all of its losses in the June elections. As the returns came in, one of Erdoğan's advisors tweeted a photo of a relaxed-looking president grinning like a cat that had just swallowed the canary. Erdoğan was still thirteen seats from what he needed to transform Turkey's political system, but he remained committed to forging a presidential system. Given his and the AKP's capacity to bend the laws, regulations, rules, and decrees that governed various aspects of Turkey's political life to their advantage, Erdoğan's opponents would be foolish to count the president out. In the short term, the markets rejoiced and the press reported that stability had returned to Turkey. The larger story was bleaker, revealing the extent to which Erdoğan and the AKP had manipulated Turkey's political institutions. The November 1 elections simply did not need to be held. They took place only because Erdoğan did not like the outcome of the June elections: he made sure of both a new election and an outcome more to his liking. The way in which Turkey's leaders manipulated the institutions of the state combined with the sticky quality of these laws, regulations, rules, and decrees does not bode well for the country's political development.

The abortive coup of July 2016 only reinforced these authoritarian political dynamics. Upon his dramatic return to Istanbul after a harrowing night of violence in that city and the Turkish capital, Erdoğan, who had been vacationing in Marmaris, a tourist resort on the Mediterranean coast in the Turkish southwest, vowed to rid society of those he deemed responsible for the failed power grab. That is precisely what he did. As the government announced a three-month state of emergency, the Turkish leader oversaw the apprehension of the coup plotters and many thousands more. Among the most shocking developments was the pressure brought to bear on the Turkish media. By late 2016, about 140 journalists had been jailed and the credentials of another 300 had been revoked. Even members of parliament were not immune as the authorities arrested eight representatives from the largely Kurdish HDP, including the party's two leaders, who were accused of supporting terrorism. The widespread crackdown, which the AKP fused with a devastatingly effective narrative about saving democracy that tapped into the collective shock and trauma Turks experienced as a result of the coup attempt, only enhanced Erdoğan's personal power and buttressed the strength of the party. In the aftermath of the entire episode, there was no need for the constitutional change and "executive presidency" that Erdoğan coveted. Turkey looked more like an elected autocracy than ever before.

This was not the model for the Arab world that the policy community, government officials, and journalists often invoked in 2011 and 2012. Far from it. In some cases what Erdoğan had done was positively Mubarak-esque, but with "better" results. When the Turks clamped down on social media, forcing Twitter users and others to use virtual private networks, and proposed a range of new restrictions on social media, an Egyptian diplomat in Washington marveled, "How does he [Erdoğan] get away with it? How come there is no revolution in Turkey?" The parallels did not end with the Mubarak era, however. It was ironic that Erdoğan and Egyptian leader Abdel Fattah al-Sisi took every opportunity to criticize each other because they were engaged in similar political projects and often used similar tactics.

Both leaders were, for example, among the foremost jailers of reporters. Like Turkish journalists, their Egyptian counterparts were often arrested and charged (when they were charged at all) for offenses related to terrorism or aiding a terrorist organization. As the Committee to Protect Journalists (CPJ) emphasized, no actual evidence justified these allegations unless one considers journalism, which is often critical of governments, to be a crime. The well-publicized case of three Al Jazeera journalists—Mohammed Fahmy, Baher Mohammed, and Peter Greste—who were sentenced to three years in prison and held for thirteen months before being released in 2015 comes to mind, but at least 25 other journalists remained in detention as of late 2016.[58] Then there is freelance photographer Mahmoud Abou Zeid, more commonly known as Shawkan. On August 14, 2013, Shawkan was taken into custody after covering the security forces' crackdown on the pro–Mohammed Morsi sit-in at Rabaa al-Adawiyya Square. According to the CPJ, Shawkan was in the square on behalf of the London-based photo and video newswire Demotix. Even though no evidence linked Shawkan to the Brotherhood, he remained in pretrial detention in Tora Prison through 2016—exceeding 1,000 days. An even less well-known case is that of Saeed Abuhaj, who was picked up in al-Arish in northern Sinai in November 2013 and charged with "incitement, participating in a demonstration, and using arms against the police."[59]

Abuhaj, who is a bureaucrat at the local tax office, was video recording Muslim Brotherhood demonstrations for the online Sinai Media
Center, to which he was a regular contributor. In Sisi's Egypt, the mere
act of taking photos or video of demonstrations, especially those involving supporters of the Muslim Brotherhood, turned journalists into
terrorists. At the same time, the legal jeopardy in which members of
the media found themselves was not terribly different from the restrictions they confronted during the Mubarak period, when Egypt was
under a state of emergency, which placed the country under military
rule, if not martial law.

On November 25, 2013, Adly Mansour, the chief justice of the
Supreme Constitutional Court who had been acting head of state
since the coup, promulgated a protest law that severely restricted the
ability of Egyptians to stage demonstrations. This was a particular
affront given that it was street protests that contributed to the two
"revolutions" of January 25, 2011, and June 30, 2013. The ostensible
reason for the restrictions on freedom of assembly in the so-called
new Egypt related to the Muslim Brotherhood's sit-in that Shawkan
was covering. The demonstration—and a smaller one in another part
of Cairo—began on June 28 as a counter-protest to what anti-Morsi
forces were planning for June 30. It came to a bloody end six weeks
later when the police and presidential guard moved in, killing at least
800 people. The need for security, which was a real issue, was merely
an excuse for the protest law. The other reasons were political. If the
Muslim Brotherhood, for example, was permitted to demonstrate, the
protests would, just by dint of happening, highlight the illegitimacy of
Sisi's coup. Next was the stark reality that massive street protests had
brought two presidents down in the space of thirty months, something
that those who engineered and supported the military's intervention
never wanted to happen again.

It was not enough to clamp down on the press and proscribe street
demonstrations. Hosni Mubarak had taken these measures yet he still
faced the wrath of millions. Many had a sense that Sisi believed—along
with his collaborators in the General Intelligence Directorate, the
Ministry of Interior, and the judiciary—that Egypt's longtime strongman was not so strong, that he did not actually have the stomach to
do what was necessary to ensure political control. This was especially

so when it came to the Muslim Brotherhood, which Mubarak handled by oscillating between repression and accommodation.[60] Sisi pursued a different strategy using Mubarak's tools. Thus more journalists were in jail in 2016 than at any time since international watchdogs began keeping tabs, and violations of the protest law were dealt with severely. Mubarak's riot police beat up their share of people, but showed no mercy under Sisi.

Egypt's nongovernmental organizations (NGOs) confronted a similar dynamic. These organizations had long been the bogeymen of Egyptian leaders, who regarded the array of groups dedicated to political and individual rights in particular to be subversive and routinely cast them as agents of foreign influence. Consequently, the authorities repeatedly sought to limit their activities. Under Law 84 of 2002, the government restricted the ability of Egyptian civil society organizations to raise money and made it more difficult for them to operate. Central to the law was a requirement that all NGOs—between 16,000 and 19,000 organizations—register with the Ministry of Social Affairs. During the Mubarak period, this registration requirement gave the government the opportunity to reject applications from a variety of long-standing groups dedicated to human rights, workers' rights, housing rights, and combating torture. Egypt's NGOs were also prohibited from engaging in political activity, though NGO staff did not know where politics began or ended and thus feared that an overly broad definition of the term would place them in legal jeopardy. Nongovernmental organizations were permitted to accept donations, but they were prohibited—without exception—from receiving money from abroad. A 2014 amendment to the penal code made it possible to receive the death penalty for doing so.[61] Also, if the organization received funding of 20,000 Egyptian pounds (about $2,500) or more from a single source, the NGO's board was required to submit the details of the donation and supporting documentation to a registered auditor. Violation of these provisions would result in fines equal to the amount of the gift or jail time.[62] The law also gave the Ministry of Social Affairs the broad authority to dismiss the boards of NGOs, seize an organization's assets, and revoke its license.

Sisi did not seek changes to the NGO law. Instead, he oversaw its rigorous enforcement along with other measures, notably those contained in the 2015 anti-terror law that defined a terrorist act as any effort to

> prevent or impede public authorities, agencies or judicial bodies, government offices or local units, houses of worship, hospitals, institutions, institutes, diplomatic and consular missions, or regional and international organizations and bodies in Egypt from carrying out their work or exercising all or some of their activities, or resists them or disable the enforcement of any provisions of the Constitution, laws, or regulations.[63]

Egypt, like Tunisia, had a terrorism problem. After Mubarak's fall, violence in the Sinai Peninsula—which was home to a variety of extremists, gun smugglers, human traffickers, and drug mules—surged. Central authority had never been particularly strong in the Sinai, except for places that the government actually cared about such as Sharm el-Sheikh and its resorts, but the 2011 uprising further weakened Cairo's grip. When the military removed Mohammed Morsi from power, the violence increased. Jihadi groups attacked Egyptian forces and government facilities in the Sinai as well as more populated places like Ismailiyya and Cairo with greater frequency. An allegedly al-Qaeda-connected extremist group emerged during this period called Ansar Beit al-Maqdis (Partisans of the Holy House, meaning Jerusalem). In time, the group would swear an oath of allegiance to the Islamic State and changed its name to Wilayat Sina (the Sinai Province). By 2016, terrorism in northern Sinai became a full-blown insurgency that had taken the lives of between 700 and 2,000 security personnel and untold numbers of civilians and terrorists.

At the same time, the Egyptian authorities used this war to justify the repressive measures they had adopted since Sisi came to power. Like Tunisia's anti-terrorism measure, the intention was to define terrorism so broadly that virtually anything an organization did that the government did not like could be classified as a terrorist act. The provisions of the legislation interlocked with those of the protest, nongovernmental organizations, and press laws, which made it easier to criminalize routine political activities. This led to the government's closure of 434 NGOs for their alleged ties to the Muslim Brotherhood, which the government designated as a terrorist organization in December 2013.[64] The goal was not just to dismantle the Brotherhood, though that was of supreme importance. Egyptian authorities also sought to instill fear among members of boards and staffs of Egypt's NGO community, some of whose members were determined to highlight the routine violation of human rights, corruption, hypocrisy, and incompetence of the government.

Of course, Sisi and other Egyptian officials insisted that whatever measures they had taken were done to combat terrorism, ensure stability, and advance democracy. They could point to the "road map to democracy" Sisi issued the day of the July 2013 coup and how Egyptians had fulfilled all of its elements, including the most important—reviewing the 2012 constitution, which led to the adoption of a new document in January 2014; the election of a new president; and after a long delay the selection of a new parliament, called the House of Representatives, in the fall of 2015. Mission accomplished. Yet having satisfied the conditions of the roadmap hardly indicated that Egypt was a democracy or was democratizing. Certain aspects of the constitution were problematic and the presidential election suffered from low voter turnout, but it was parliamentary elections that drove home how Egypt's leaders leveraged the political institutions of the state to ensure the outcomes they sought.

To suggest that Egypt's electoral procedures are complicated is an understatement. The seats of the 596-member unicameral legislature are filled in the following ways: the president appoints 28 members, 120 members are elected from lists for four districts on a winner-take-all basis, and the remaining 448 members are chosen to represent 205 electoral districts that each have from 1 to 4 seats.[65] It seems unlikely that the law was written to produce an inclusive, broad-based parliament, especially given that Sisi had more than once indicated that the role of the legislature is to support the government. The decision to use the winner-take-all system for the 120 members chosen from four districts was designed to overrepresent one party at the expense of others because the list that won a majority of votes in a district was awarded all the seats in that district. As the US-based NGO Democracy International explained in its preliminary report on the conduct of the elections, "unlike traditional list systems in other countries, where seats are allocated based on the proportion of votes that each list receives, the list portion of the system in Egypt is not a basis for encouraging representation of minority political parties or viewpoints. Rather, the Egyptian system has the opposite effect."[66] This was a diplomatic way of saying that the system was essentially rigged. In theory, any party could enjoy the advantages of the winner-take-all system, but this was unlikely to be the case in an environment where a favored party enjoyed resources that others did not. As it turned out, the pro-Sisi For the Love of Egypt alliance won all 120 seats in the winner-take-all districts.

The election of the remaining 448 members seemed designed to sow as much confusion among voters as possible, thereby depressing turn-out, which always favors well-organized and resourced organizations. Voters were asked to vote for as many candidates as there were seats in each district, but because the numbers were different in different districts many voters did not know how many people they were sup-posed to vote for. The rules required an exact match of votes and seats, so that if a citizen voted for three candidates in a district with four seats, that ballot was disqualified. When the Egyptian parliament was finally seated on January 10, 2016, about three and a half years after the Supreme Council of the Armed Forces dissolved the old Islamist-dom-inated People's Assembly, the new House of Representatives seemed immediately doomed to irrelevancy. It was composed overwhelmingly of Sisi supporters who seemed intent on being a rubber stamp for the presidency, precisely what Egypt's old People's Assembly had been for Mubarak. This echo of the past is likely also to be the House of Representative's present and future given the stickiness of institutions. Even if—as has been the case in the past—the Supreme Constitutional Court strikes down electoral laws, the new iterations have been based on old laws, all of which are written in a way to give those in power a political advantage.

The lowly prospects for Egypt's new parliament reflects a pattern of politics in Egypt. Consider, for example, the way Egypt has sought to corral nongovernmental organizations. Law 84 of 2002 is a direct de-scendant of Law 153 of 1999, which is a further iteration of Law 32 of 1964. It may be true that in six decades between 1952 and 2011 much has changed in Egypt, but these changes took place within the context of existing institutions and previous institutional innovations. And because the formal and informal (or uncodified) rules of the political system did not break through five years of turbulence, Egyptian politics will more likely resemble a version of its past than the inspiring future the instigators of the uprising had dreamed of. In 2016, it may be Abdel Fattah al-Sisi's Egypt, but that is an innovation of Mubarak's Egypt, which was built on Sadat's Egypt, which was in turn an evolution of Nasser's Egypt. In Tunisia, the counterterrorism law—sections of which have been recycled from the Ben Ali era—and financial reconciliation measures that will absolve corrupt elites of their crimes pose a potential threat to democratic progress in ways that are less pronounced than in Egypt, but nevertheless reflect a similar dynamic. In Turkey, the ability of the ruling party to harness institutions reversed the liberalizing progress of 2003 and 2004 and set the country on an authoritarian path. At a level of abstraction, the Turkish political system is just as undemocratic in 2016 as it was in 1996.

What was left after the uprisings and how elites (or competing groups of elites) sought to leverage this detritus only tells part of the story of the region. This is because despite the best efforts of leaders to gain control over societies and impose their will through the manipulation of the institutions of the state, Tunisians, Egyptians, and Turks who want to live in just and democratic societies still agitate to realize this dream. The inevitable results are hotly contested political arenas in which coercion and violence have increasingly become the norm. Libya, which has not figured into this part of the analysis because of its dearth of institutions, is nevertheless exceedingly violent. It is precisely this bloodshed that represents the broader failures of the Arab Spring and Turkey's thwarted transition. Flowing directly from these breakdowns is another potent factor that reinforces the region's instability, uncertainty, and violence: identity.

WHO ARE WE?

When the uprisings around the Middle East began, it seemed that protesters had broken the fear that rulers had imposed on their own people. Yet popular demonstrations were not new—in Egypt in 1968, 1972, and 1977, in the Syrian city of Hama in 1982, in Tunisia in 1984 and 1988, and in Algeria in 1988, to name just a few—but those in 2010 and 2011 were demonstrably different in a single way: longtime dictators were forced to flee. This was unprecedented, but the demands heard around the region echoed an earlier era. Beginning in the late nineteenth century, Arabs and Turks had been asking fundamental questions about themselves: Who are we? What kind of governments do we want? What is the proper relationship between religion and society? Is modernity—defined in terms of Western institutions and ideals—compatible with our values?

In the 1950s and 1960s, new Arab leaders such as Gamal Abdel Nasser, Houari Boumédiène in Algeria, Habib Bourguiba, and Hafez al-Assad in Syria guided (with an iron fist) the modernization of their societies. Central to this project were the development of official narratives concerning the anti-colonial struggle and economic progress under the new, independent order so as to "resolve questions about nationalism, identity, and citizenship."[67] Yet the Arab leaders who came to power after the first wave of decolonization eventually became a conservative old guard who replaced revolutionary ardor with tired platitudes. Few in the Middle East today remember the independence, nationalizations, and reforms that briefly produced educational opportunities and some social mobility. Instead, the vast majority of Arabs, whose median age is under thirty, have experienced official indifference to failing social contracts and the brutality of security services to keep them in line.[68] This is not to suggest that coercion and fear were new phenomena in the region over the last three or four decades. Egypt's Nasser built the archetypal Middle Eastern police state. Yet Nasserism—a set of vaguely socialist and nationalist ideals—was extraordinarily compelling. This was made more so because it conformed to a reality that Egyptians actually experienced, if only briefly, between 1956 and 1967. Nasser's nationalization of the Suez Canal in July 1956 thrilled thousands precisely because it interlaced nationalism, dignity, and identity: "The Suez Canal," Nasser said at the time, "was one of the facades of oppression, extortion and humiliation. Today citizens, the Suez Canal has been nationalized . . . Today, citizens, we declare that our property has been returned to us. The rights about which we were silent have been restored to us."[69]

The forlorn banner strung from light poles in Tahrir Square during Hosni Mubarak's 1999 election campaign—it was actually a referendum—exhorting Egyptians to support the president, "For the sake of stability and development," paled in comparison. Nevertheless, Mubarak and other elites continued to define national identities through a mixture of Arab nationalist mythologies, economic nationalism, anti-colonialism, and the importance of Islam as both a religion and civilization. All the while, they applied the International Monetary Fund's neoliberal economic reforms, survived in part on assistance from the West, purchased copious amounts of weapons from the same countries, and regularly consorted with Western leaders and the titans of the multinational business world. Where was Amr Moussa—formerly Mubarak's foreign minister, then secretary-general of the Arab League, and the arch-nationalist of the song "I Hate Israel, but I Love Amr Moussa"—when Egyptians converged on Tahrir Square to demand change on January 25, 2011? Attending the World Economic Forum in Davos, Switzerland, with the global economic elite.

When Arabs chased Zine al-Abidine Ben Ali, Hosni Mubarak, Muammar al-Qaddafi, and Yemen's Ali Abdullah Saleh from office, and threatened the ruling Al Khalifas in Bahrain and the Assads in Syria, they gave themselves opportunities to redefine who they were. Egypt's Abdel Fattah al-Sisi had an opportunity after millions turned out on June 30, 2013, to challenge Mohammed Morsi and the Muslim Brotherhood's vision for Egypt, but all he has offered has been a narrow vision of what it means to be Egyptian, one in which the conflict with the Muslim Brothers is central. Suddenly, in Egypt, to support the Brotherhood is not to be authentically Egyptian, denying the important role the Brothers and Islamists, more generally, have played in forging a major part of Egypt's national identity in the twentieth century. When Hassan al-Banna founded the Brotherhood in March 1928, he was responding to what he and his small group of followers at the time perceived to be the pernicious effect of secularism buffeting Egyptian society, whether it was the orientation of the universities, the cultural milieu that celebrated secularism, or direct attacks on the religious orthodoxy of his time.[70] The success of the Brotherhood indicates how Banna's message about the centrality of Islam in resisting the depredations of foreigners tapped into the widely held resentments and frustrations of many Egyptians. The intellectual debates during this period revolved around identity. Was Egypt a Hellenic-Mediterranean country or was it a predominantly Eastern and Muslim one whose values and principles were fundamentally different from those of the West?[71] By the latter part of the twentieth century, the Islamists won the debate.[72] When the Egyptian government began to afford the Brotherhood an opportunity to operate in the educational and cultural spheres in the mid 1970s, the Brothers often framed the discourse on what was acceptable in the realms of art, literature, and intellectual inquiry.[73] When their activism seeped too far into politics, Anwar al-Sadat and Mubarak repressed them, but in many ways the Islamists carried the day. Egyptian elites and others continued to live secular lifestyles, but the Brotherhood's political and social criticisms, which were framed in religious terms, forced Egypt's leaders to use religious imagery, symbols, and language in an effort to stave off the group's challenge. That the call to prayer can be heard in Cairo's Metro or that the government acquiesced in the declaration that a prominent Cairo University professor was an apostate because he applied modern literary criticism to the Quran suggests the importance of religion and the role of the Brotherhood and the Salafis in forging Egypt's modern identity.

In Tunisia, President Beji Caid Essebsi resisted the desire of some within Nidaa Tounes who regarded Egypt's effort to dismantle the Brotherhood as a model, but he was not above dismissing the importance of religion and the role of the Islamist movement in the collective identity of Tunisians. The secularization of Tunisia had an impact on the country, which was clear from the prevailing worldviews of the elite, powerful union leaders, and leftist groups that had shaped the country's politics and culture with its decidedly Francophone flair. Institutionally, the 1956 Personal Status Code, which was a reflection of this secular sensibility, was untouchable. This was Habib Bourguiba's legacy. At times Tunisia's former president for life could not hide his hostility toward pious Tunisians and the religious activism of Rachid al-Ghannouchi and his colleagues. It was Bourguiba and Bourguibism that shaped Essebsi's outlook, which he revealed in a quip to the *New York Times* that he was not at all worried about Ennahda because it had become "Tunisiafied."[74] He used the term again when, in May 2016, Ennahda announced that it was eschewing the Islamism of its past and in an effort to broaden its appeal, rebranding itself a party of Muslim Democrats. Essebsi's implication was clear. To the Tunisian president, the Islamist current was actually foreign to the country and its political and social experience. Islamist groups from other parts of the Middle East without doubt influenced Tunisia's Islamists—indeed, some observers continue to ask questions about the nature of the relationship between Ennahda and the Muslim Brotherhood—but Ennahda can trace its lineage back almost fifty years to a group called the Quranic Preservation Society; the country even had a history of religious

intellectual production and debate before then.[75] In implicit acknowledgment of the importance of Islam in society and the societal fissures
that Bourguiba's secularization produced, Ben Ali signaled an important shift. Not long after coming to power, he went on the pilgrimage
to Mecca and permitted the *azan*—call to prayer—to be broadcast over
the radio. His 1988 National Pact placed an emphasis on Islam in public
life.[76] Yet for Essebsi, it was as if the Zaytuna Mosque and University—
which the University of Tunis absorbed in 1961—played no role in the
development, intellectual capital, and identity of modern Tunisians.

These changes and swings from one leader to the next underline
what scholars have discovered about the socially constructed nature of
identities, which makes them subject to the manipulation of politicians and their opponents. Egypt's Nasser did not have a particular
commitment to religion and spent a good deal of effort bringing religious forces, from the Muslim Brotherhood to al-Azhar University and
mosque, to heel. Yet when Sadat came to power he called himself "the
believing president." The shift had everything to do with each leader's
political needs—the consolidation of power—but under different political and social circumstances. As a result, Nasser emphasized a mix
of Arabism and republicanism, whereas Sadat, without ever eschewing
Arab nationalism, emphasized Islam. Sadat may have, indeed, been a
believer. His *zabiba*—the calluses that develops on the forehead from
prostrating fervently during prayer—suggested this was the case. At the
same time, Sadat also understood that to outmaneuver his Nasserist
opponents who sought to keep him weak, he needed to widen his base
of political support. Religion was available to him. He therefore emphasized Islam and eventually reached out to the Muslim Brotherhood,
allowing them greater sway in the educational and cultural spheres.

The scholarly literature on identity is quite large, spanning political science, anthropology, history, sociology, and psychology, and is
closely connected to concepts like citizenship, nationalism, and collective memory.[77] As implied, identity is not something with which
people are born but rather something they develop over time in response to a wide variety of variables that include socioeconomic circumstances, education, ethnicity, religion, place of birth, history to
which they are exposed, and politics. As a consequence, individuals
have a repertoire of identities, which they emphasize at different times

and in different circumstances. Nobody explains this better than Yasser Elguindi, whose Twitter handle is @AbuelGamecock. Of course clever handles are not in short supply on the microblogging site, among them @HebronJames, @BlogsofWar, and @TweetsInTheMiddle East, but Yasser's is not just clever. Whether intentionally or not, his handle captures perfectly the multiple identities individuals employ as they negotiate their way through the modern world. Yasser is a proud Egyptian, an equally proud American, and a supporter of his beloved University of South Carolina football team, the Gamecocks. Thus his handle's nod to his Egyptian birth, Arab heritage, and South Carolinian upbringing.

Yasser's Twitter handle is a further iteration of the informal lesson on identity that he offered friends at a rooftop party in the late spring of 1995 in Washington, DC. The gathering was inside the Beltway, and Yasser—who is now a successful energy analyst but at the time was a graduate student at the Johns Hopkins School of Advanced International Studies—and a gaggle of friends were standing in a circle discussing some weighty event in the Middle East. It might have been about negotiations between Israelis and Palestinians or sanctions on Iraq—Washington's twin obsessions at the time—but whatever it was that everyone was discussing, it was not as interesting as Yasser's response to some good-natured ribbing concerning what "the Egyptian" thought about these issues. In response he smiled and said, "You know, when I am with my Egyptian friends, I am American. When I am with my American friends, I am an Arab. And when I am among Arabs, I am first and foremost, Egyptian." In those few lines, Yasser perfectly articulated the idea of identity being a social construct, contingent on time, place, and circumstance. It is also hotly contested. Identity is what the culture wars that buffet the United States at various decibels at different moments, particularly during presidential campaigns when politicians seek to manipulate identities for their advantage, are all about. The same is true in Europe, where the troubling rise of neo-fascist parties— to advance an exclusivist political agenda—mythologize what it means to be French, Austrian, or British in contrast to recent arrivals from South Asia, the Middle East, and the Balkans.

When the Great Socialist People's Libyan Arab Jamahiriyya came to an end in 2011, not much was in place to prevent a country that had been held together with petrodollars and force from fragmenting. Citizens of the country thought of themselves as Libyan—they knew of nothing else—but in the chaos of the uprising and the post–Muammar al-Qaddafi period, many sought safety and security in city, town, and tribe, which are often coterminous. People may have long relied on these connections to get along given the depredations of living in the Jamahiriyya, but the crumbling of the country gave them an even greater incentive to seek shelter in these ties. They are social constructs that are part of people's multifaceted identities, which is why, when Qaddafi fled Tripoli, it made perfect sense that he made his way to his hometown Sirte, where the al-Qadhadhfa tribe is well represented. As the conflict that quickly enveloped the country after protests became a full-blown uprising in February 2011, being Libyan made less sense than being Misratan, Zintani, or Zawiyan, to name just a few, for those seeking shelter from the chaos. This made Saif al-Islam al-Qaddafi's television appearance not only rambling, incoherent, and threatening, but also prescient.[78]

Beyond the tendency of people to seek safety in tribe and region, the multilayered political conflicts battering the country combined with the lack of political institutions and effective authority only strengthened tribalism and regionalism. Consider the competition between Zintanis, who liberated Tripoli, and Misratans, who suffered greatly during the eight-month civil war. Theirs is a conflict over power resources, and grievances defined in a specific way—Zintanis versus Misratans—tends to reify these identities. More broadly, since the end of Qaddafi's regime, Libya's ostensible leaders have exercised little in the way of real power. The so-called Libyan National Army is under the control of General Khalifa Haftar, who is accountable to no one as he prosecutes a war against Islamists and revolutionaries in the eastern region of the country. Two competing parliaments and various other forces contend for power. When central authority is incapacitated, militias, tribes, towns, and Islamist groups wield power.[79] In their own discrete ways, these forces undermine what it means to be Libyan. The 2015 United Nations–brokered Government of National Accord was supposed to overcome these centripetal pressures. Even with considerable international support, it is hard enough to imagine its success. Given Libya's panoply of problems, but given also the way regional and tribal identities have come to the fore at the expense of a specifically national, Libyan sensibility, the effort seemed doomed from the start.

Unlike Libya and other countries in the Middle East, Turkey is never included among those that observers consider to be artificial entities. The country "may not owe its existence to colonial administrators in Paris and London, but it was very much the product of someone's imagination: Mustafa Kemal Atatürk. He forged an ethnonational state out of a piece of a multiethnic and multicultural empire where one had never existed."[80] For this state-building project to succeed, it was necessarily suffused with myths about Turkishness as an ethnic marker, the linkage between Turks and the land, the Turkish language, and what it meant to be a Turk, not to mention the ethnic cleansing of Greeks in Turkish territory (and Turks in Greek territory). The loyalty of citizens would thus necessarily shift from a political religious establishment that ruled over a predominantly Muslim domain to a nation of Turks and a state whose rulers derived their legitimacy from the defense of Turkishness and their commitment to progressive ideals and science.[81]

Turkishness and the set of ideals that came to be known as Kemalism, which served as the ideological foundation of the new republic, never achieved the broad acceptance as a legitimate system of belief as is commonly assumed. If they had been, there would have been little need for the ostentatious efforts to reinforce Kemalism throughout the country in the form of portraits, busts, and paeans to the glory of the Turkish nation attributed to Atatürk in every town and village square throughout the country. There are many in Turkey, especially those of a previously dominant political class, who embraced Atatürk's ideas, but others have resisted them, and still others have remained ambivalent. Consequently, Turks have often asked similar questions as others in the region about who they are.

Throughout the republic's history, the demands of Turkishness have alienated Kurds, whose identities are "wrapped in separate mythologies about language, land, and ethnicity, all of which the official narrative of the republic denied."[82] Many Kurds are well integrated into Turkish political, social, economic, and cultural life, but there is an inherent friction between Turkishness and Kurdishness, the most obvious of which is the war between the Kurdistan Workers' Party (PKK)—an ethnic-based terrorist organization—and the Turkish state that has been under way since 1984. At its base, the fight is a struggle between two national-isms and the identities linked to them.[83]

The other deep fissure in Turkish politics revolved around religion. For the break from the Ottoman Empire and the consolidation of the new Turkish Republic to be successful, Atatürk had to disestab-lish Islam. Abolishing the Ottoman caliphate as he did in 1924 was a historic step, but it was not enough. A massive cultural shift was also required. Toward that end, Atatürk instituted the use of the Latin script, European numerals, surnames, and the Gregorian calendar. He also criminalized the fez. Along with the caliphate, Atatürk abolished the office of the Sheikh al-Islam, a powerful position whose incumbent played an important role in education and religious affairs; the Ministry of Religious Affairs and Pious Foundations; and religious schools. Sufi brotherhoods, known as *tariqat*, were outlawed and their lodges closed. In 1928, Article 2 of the 1924 Constitution, which identified Islam as the religion of the state, was deleted.[84] Atatürk's project of seculariza-tion ironically placed the state at the center of religion, from where it policed the public arena by proscribing certain religious activities and beliefs while prescribing others.

For those to whom Atatürk's secularizing reforms did not make sense, their opposition was not just a matter of personal piety. After all, one could be a fervent believer in the new republic as long as religion did not enter the public sphere—politics, education, media, and the arts—in any way. This was not an accommodation that pious Turks were willing to make for two related reasons. First, the official narrative that connected secularism with progress and faith with backwardness had consequences for the pious who confronted institutional discrimination. Second, when Turkey's Islamist movement developed in the late 1960s and early 1970s, its leaders sought to fuse religious ideals and principles with other spheres, including politics, education, business, and culture. Part of their resis-tance to Kemalism was the Islamist view that the elite's effort to embed Western ideals and institutions in Turkey was needlessly emulating alien ideas and values that were inconsistent with a Muslim society.[85] These competing conceptions of Turkish identity have largely defined the pa-rameters of political discourse since the republic's founding.

Inasmuch as a culture war is at the heart of Turkish politics and Turkey is often portrayed as a country with two societies—one secular and the other religious—living in parallel, these categories are not as clear as this rendering suggests. Turkey's Islamists are nationalists who accept the terms of the republic even as they have sought to accommodate it to their own political needs and vision. At the same time, the republican elite have used religion for their own ends. The most relevant example is the way the military—routinely described in the Western media as staunchly secular—promoted Islam as a specific part of a broader "national culture" in the 1980s to establish political control over a society in which violence between leftist and rightist groups killed thousands before the 1980 coup d'état took place.[86] The idea, called the "Turkish-Islamic synthesis," was, at its base, about identity.[87]

Yet it was not until the Justice and Development Party (AKP) came to power that Turks could explore their religious identities more freely. This was unsettling to the party's opponents and was made more so not just by the AKP's electoral success but also by the way these victories advanced "Muslimhood" in Turkey.[88] Conventional accounts that label the AKP as Islamist, placing it in the company of the Muslim Brotherhood, do not adequately capture the nature of the party. The Muslimhood of the AKP is less targeted and more diffuse than the Brotherhood's Islamism, and though it certainly belongs within the general classification of Islamist groups, the AKP's underlying philosophical concerns and agenda are somewhat different from those organizations. This is a function of the AKP's interpretation of both the Ottoman and the republican experience. The party shares with Islamist groups the idea that society's deviation from religious values has had a deleterious effect on it. In Turkey's case, this deviation came in the form of Atatürk's inauthentic reforms that placed the country within the ambit of a West that did not accept Turks as equal partners. Ankara's natural place was instead as a leader of the Muslim world, which is consistent with the AKP's benign view of the Ottoman period. Domestically, Muslimhood comes across in both the AKP's style of politics and a social setting in which a pious sensibility flows effortlessly and naturally through all aspects of society without undermining the secular nature of the republic. The party has sought to limit alcohol consumption and secularists have raised alarm over the perception that an increasing number of Turkish women are donning the hijab in response to implicit pressure to conform to the AKP's religious values, but the party is not interested in the transformation of Turkish society through religious dictates. Rather one of the great accomplishments of the AKP—and a source of its electoral success—has been the way in which the party has paved the way for Turks to explore and express their Muslim identity in ways that would have been unthinkable and unsafe in the past.

The AKP has successfully fostered a religious sensibility because the notion that Turkey is a secular society is a myth. According to the 2012 Pew survey of Muslims worldwide, "97 percent of Turks believe in God, 67 percent of Turks say that religion is very important in their lives, 44 percent of Turks attend mosque at least once a week, and 42 percent pray multiple times a day."[89] The following year's survey revealed that 70 percent of Turks contend that it is necessary to believe in God to be moral, and 76 percent of Turks say their lives reflect the *sunna* and *hadith*—the practices and sayings of the Prophet Muhammad.[90] Under these circumstances, "the AKP has merely buttressed and extended these social and cultural dispositions" that already existed within Turkish society.[91]

The problem, of course, is the considerable resistance to the AKP's project. Even given the large numbers of Turks self-identifying as believers or who regard religion as important to them, the AKP has never been able to capture an outright majority of Turkey's popular vote. Although Erdoğan garnered 52 percent of the vote in his 2014 presidential elections, the party's high-water mark was 49.83 percent in the June 2011 elections.[92] Multiple variables account for electoral outcomes, of course, but Turkey's history of culture wars and a political strategy of polarization based in part on identity are part of the explanation. Erdoğan and the leaders of the AKP have worked assiduously to cast their opponents as not authentically Turkish in that "solidly middle class with conservative values" way of the party's core constituency. Opponents of this newly authentic idea of what it means to be a Turk are "marginals," in league with foreigners who want to bring Turkey to its knees, and terrorists. When, in May 2013, resistance developed among secularists and businesses to an AKP plan to restrict the sale of alcohol to certain hours and prohibit its sale near schools, Erdoğan asked the party's parliamentary faction, "Given that a law made by two drunken [people] is respected, why should a law that is commanded by religion be rejected by your side?"[93] An uproar ensued given what seemed to be Erdoğan's implicit insult of Atatürk and his longtime deputy, İsmet İnönü, both of whom could consume copious amounts of alcohol. If this was not enough, Erdoğan was clearly drawing the line between God-fearing good Turks and those who preferred the illegitimate legacy of two alcoholics. Although the AKP may have resolved the problem of Islamist politics in an officially secular political system, identity remained a raw issue. Erdoğan governed the Turks who voted for the AKP and reflected the party's Muslimhood and intimidated those for whom this shift made no sense. He did this as elucidated above by leveraging the institutions of the state, which, especially after the May 2013 Gezi protests and the December 2013 corruption scandal, were deeply polarizing. As Samuel Huntington declared in his famous and controversial 1993 essay "The Clash of Civilizations?" Turkey is "torn," but, contrary to Huntington, the state of affairs was not related to the nature of Islam but instead to the manipulation of Turkish identity for political gain.[94]

Turkey illustrates a dynamic also under way in Egypt and Tunisia, where Sisi and Essebsi had both emphasized a specific idea of what being Egyptian and Tunisian meant. For the Egyptian president, the state and privately owned pro-government media made it easy to saturate the airwaves with messages connecting the Muslim Brotherhood with terrorism. In addition, the government drove home the message that the Brotherhood was no different from al-Qaeda, the self-declared Islamic State, and Boko Haram, and thus had no particular commitment to Egypt's well-being. The Brotherhood's discourse had had a pan-Islamic aspect, but this was not the problem. The Brothers were actually good nationalists whose opposition to Egypt's strategic relations with the United States, its ties with Israel, and how those relationships rendered the country a "second-rate power" were an indictment of the establishment that returned with the July 2013 coup d'état.[95] This was why in Egypt's angry and polarizing nationalist discourse the Brotherhood was grouped with the worst of the worst. Its leaders flirted with jihadi imagery, to be sure, but the Brotherhood's supreme guide was no Ayman al-Zawahiri—the al-Qaeda leader who had deemed the Brotherhood too moderate during the formative period of his radicalization. The linkage between the Brothers and the most violent extremists created a vicious rhetorical circle, rendering it hard to imagine any eventual accommodation with the Brothers. For example, on coming to power, Sisi had promised stability and prosperity. Yet both remained significant challenges given the insurgency in the Sinai that at times reached out and shook Cairo and drove tourists away. Egyptian officialdom and its cheerleaders in the media explained that instability and economic problems had nothing to do with the quality of Egypt's politics but were instead directly related to terrorism, meaning the Brotherhood, which only further reinforced specific ideas about the alleged alien nature of the Brotherhood's worldview.

In Tunisia, the passage of a new constitution gave hope that a "normal politics" about jobs, infrastructure, education, and foreign policy would mark Tunisia's future, but the electoral success of Nidaa Tounes later in the year suggested that identity politics still lurked in the political arena. Essebsi had been more sophisticated than his Egyptian counterpart in this dangerous game, but his goal was also to render his chief opponents inauthentically Tunisian. Beyond the electoral math that forced him to include Ennahda, a year after his triumphant victory, Nidaa Tounes, the primary vehicle for the secularist elite—whether Bourguibists, remnants of Ben Ali's Democratic Constitutional Rally, or the left—split. The crackup was the culmination of rivalries that go back as far as 2013 but broke into open intraparty political warfare during the summer of 2015. Multiple, overlapping circles of controversy revolved around Hafedh Caid Essebsi, the fifty-three-year-old son of the president, including a power struggle with the party's secretary-general, Mohsen Marzouk—a leftist activist—that contributed to Nidaa Tounes's precipitous slide.[96] Yet the problem ran deeper, revealing the underlying ideological contradictions within the party that made it extraordinarily difficult for anyone to manage its structures once Beji Caid Essebsi became president.[97] These tensions came to a head in early November 2015 when thirty-two members of Nidaa Tounes's parliamentary delegation resigned, accusing Hafedh of a power grab within the party. The resignations reduced the party's parliamentary representation, leaving it with the second largest number of seats in the parliament behind Ennahda. Other resignations followed and, in what continues to give even the greatest cynic a modicum of hope, Nidaa Tounes did not bring the government down. Optimists argued that even the meltdown of the party with the most parliamentary seats could not derail Tunisia's transition to a more democratic political order. It was a good sign, but Nidaa Tounes's troubles do not themselves resolve the conflict over identity that has simmered since the Bourguiba era. The party's split was not only about Hafedh's perceived power grab but also Marzouk's opposition to working with Ennahda, a position that the Tunisian General Labor Union and its decidedly secular leadership largely shared. When Ennahda shed its Islamism, it was unclear whether the change was actually about broadening its popular support (after Nidaa Tounes's crackup, Ennahda held the most seats in parliament) or, given Tunisia's problem with extremism and the historic mistrust between Islamists and secularists, fear. In all, however, the struggle over identity in Tunisia and other parts of the region may not necessarily play out between secularists and Islamists per se but rather could involve other forces with an appealing vision of not what it means to be Tunisian or Egyptian or Libyan or Turkish, but rather how to be Muslim.

In Libya, people have sought safety in region and tribe. Turks are engaged in a familiar three-way battle involving Turkish nationalism, Kurdish nationalism, and Islamism. Egypt's leadership has sought to reinvent a national identity in an all-out effort to defeat not just terrorism but also its primary competitor for power, Islamism. Identity politics lurks behind Tunisia's modest political progress as well. Not coincidentally, the struggles seem familiar. This is the consequence of new leaders who have not offered a vision that satisfies the questions about identity that Tunisians, Egyptians, Libyans, and Turks all have. Instead, these new leaders have sought to impose their will on their populations through the manipulation of institutions, exclusivist answers that do not make sense to large numbers of people, and violence. These are the failures of the pre-uprising period being replicated in the post-uprising era, accentuated only because the efforts to recreate or reinforce the authoritarian politics of the past are incomplete. Into this breach have come political entrepreneurs offering their vision of the future with emotionally and materially satisfying notions of identity. None has been more potent than Abu Bakr al-Baghdadi.

In June 2014, Americans rediscovered Iraq after the country had been relegated to Around the World round-ups located on page A27 of the newspapers of record, if the country was being covered at all. Two years before, the *New York Times* began reducing its coverage of Iraq. The paper's Baghdad bureau chief, Tim Arango, departed for Istanbul where he set up a bureau with the intention of covering Iraqi politics on an "as needed" basis. The Gezi Park protests and the tear gas and water cannons of Turkish riot police that came with it no doubt seemed tame in comparison to the improvised explosive devices and mortars of Iraq's many extremists. Yet when a group that called itself the Islamic State of Iraq and Syria stormed into the northern Iraqi city of Mosul and easily defeated the military and police units there, laid siege to a small heterodox religious community called the Yazidis, threatened the Iraqi-Kurdish capital of Erbil, beheaded James Foley and Steven Sotloff, took an amount of territory in Iraq and Syria that equaled the size of Maryland, and declared itself to be a revived caliphate named the Islamic State, Arango was back in Iraq. He and many other journalists then spent the better part of the next year explaining the Islamic State to the world.

As is true of all major events, there was a crush of commentary from all directions concerning the who, what, where, when, why, and how of the self-proclaimed Islamic State. Some of this work was quite good; the rest was mostly derivative of the interesting work, but often with a political edge. Among the best was from the group of scholars and analysts who had been following—some obsessively—the jihadi phenomenon for years.[98] Collectively, this work clarified much of what pundits and commentators had to say about the Islamic State by usefully complicating the issue. Less expert analysts and journalists often made the claim that the Islamic State was an outgrowth or offshoot of al-Qaeda. This was true and not true all at the same time. As William McCants reports in his stunningly detailed book, *The ISIS Apocalypse*, Abu Musab al-Zarqawi, who became the leader of what would later be called the Islamic State, sought out Osama bin Laden and Ayman al-Zawahiri in Afghanistan in 1999. Accounts differ on whether Zarqawi ever met bin Laden and if he did, what exactly transpired, despite a consensus that al-Qaeda's leadership did agree to "coordinate and cooperate" with Zarqawi. McCants is careful to point out that Zarqawi was not offered membership in al-Qaeda and that even if one had been forthcoming, he would have rejected it.[99] The confusion about the relationship between the Islamic State and al-Qaeda was directly related to the name that Zarqawi and his followers used—al-Qaeda of Iraq—in the early years after the American invasion of Iraq. The name suggested that the group was part of, sanctioned by, and loyal to bin Laden and Zawahiri, but it was not that straightforward. Zarqawi's group ran through a series of names starting in 1999 with Monotheism and Jihad before declaring itself in succession to be al-Qaeda of Iraq, the Consultative Council of the Mujahideen, the Islamic State of Iraq, and then the Islamic State of Iraq and Syria.[100] At least initially Zarqawi had an interest in subordinating his organization to al-Qaeda—declaring itself a part of al-Qaeda in 2004—but as McCants and others make clear, much to the chagrin of bin Laden and Zawahiri, he operated independently of them. This autonomy was reinforced four months after Zarqawi was killed in an American air strike in 2006 when his successors declared the Islamic State of Iraq without bothering to inform al-Qaeda's leadership.[101]

The ambivalent relationship between the two groups was the result of both Zarqawi's ambition to surpass al-Qaeda as the locus of transnational jihad and the significantly different diagnoses of what ailed the Muslim world and the prescription to cure it. For bin Laden and al-Qaeda, the problem was corrupt, immoral, non-Muslim governments that enjoyed the generous diplomatic, financial, and military support of the United States. If Washington was forced to withdraw its support for Hosni Mubarak's Egypt and the Al Saud royal family in Saudi Arabia, they would fall, paving the way for governments and societies that hewed closely to their fanatical interpretation of the Quran, the *sunna*, and the *hadith*. Zarqawi saw things differently. In addition to his unyielding sectarianism, which bin Laden and Zawahiri resisted for fear of alienating ordinary Muslims, Zarqawi believed that the problem lay not solely with government, but rather with societies that had strayed from Islam.[102] The remedy was to take over territory and declare a state in which God's law would be enforced. Bin Laden and Zawahiri also sought such a state but believed a period of preparation was necessary. Zarqawi and his followers believed otherwise. For them the declaration of a state—the Islamic State—was part of an end-of-days narrative that al-Qaeda's leaders did not share.[103]

The standard account of the Islamic State emphasizes the importance of Iraq and Syria in its rise and success. By all measures this is true. After the US invasion of Afghanistan, Zarqawi made his way from there to northern Iraq, where he linked up with the Kurdish extremist group, Ansar al-Islam (Partisans of Islam). He also began organizing cells to go into action once American forces crossed the border and began their dash to Baghdad. The chaos of post-Saddam Iraq, of which Zarqawi's group was both a symptom and a cause, rightly points to the centrality of Iraq in the Islamic State's genesis story.[104] Zarqawi and his followers perpetrated some of the earliest and most spectacular attacks in the early days of the American occupation, including the bombing of the United Nations compound, the Jordanian embassy, and the Imam Ali Mosque, a Shiite shrine.[105] His goal was to ignite a war with Shia Muslims by killing them and those whom Zarqawi and his group believed to be their collaborators. What better place to do that than Iraq? A decade later, the Islamic State of Iraq and Syria would prey on the alienation of Sunnis in a Shia-dominated Iraq under then prime minister Nouri al-Maliki.

The brutal conflict in Syria that evolved after Bashar al-Assad militarized a peaceful uprising also provided opportunities for the Islamic State. The group muscled its way into Syria, once again outmaneuvering al-Qaeda and its affiliate, Jabhat al-Nusra, and changing its name to the Islamic State of Iraq and Syria to reflect its expanded ambitions. It was from eastern Syria that Islamic State fighters and Anbari tribes would engineer the takeover of the Iraqi city of Fallujah in January 2014 and then stage its bold assault on Mosul six months later.[106] For all of the importance of Iraq and Syria to the Islamic State's story, neither conflict actually created the Islamic State. That may seem obvious knowing what analysts know about its history, but the political discourses in places as varied as the United States, Turkey, and Saudi Arabia suggest otherwise. Iraq and Syria were opportunities the group's leaders seized to advance their agenda, but even then, it was not even all that successful. For six years after Zarqawi's death, the organization was moribund. As Cole Bunzel reports, things had gotten so bad for the group that the US military discounted the bounty it had put on its leaders.[107] In January 2012, when it was still called the Islamic State in Iraq, Baghdadi, the group's leader, went so far as to declare for anyone willing to listen that it was making a comeback. This rebound did happen, but more than two years later and for reasons that simultaneously did, and did not, relate to those blood-soaked countries.

All the confusion about the Islamic State and its relationship to al-Qaeda, its gruesome violence and repression, and who exactly was behind it led to much speculation about the group's goals. In March 2015, a journalist named Graeme Wood sought to settle these questions in the *Atlantic* magazine. As of late 2016, his article "What ISIS Really Wants" had surpassed twenty million page views. Wood reveals in great detail the ideological and theological underpinnings of the apocalyptic vision of Baghdadi and his followers. It is a scary story. On an intellectual level, one can understand the grievances associated with Hamas's violence and why the Lebanese terrorist organization Hezbollah does what it does. Even Osama bin Laden outlined specific grievances that one could grasp no matter how horrific his and al-Qaeda's methods were.[108] The Islamic State has been harder to comprehend because the vision of its leaders is a cosmic sort. According to McCants, bin Laden's deputy, Sayf al-Adl, describes Zarqawi as "want[ing] to bring Sunni Islam back to 'the reality of human life.' "[109] The only way he and his successors determined to do this was through the establishment of a state, which they sought to forge through violence. This was not particularly unusual. Throughout history, state-making has often been violent.

Wood's article was met with a variety of criticisms. His suggestion that the Islamic State is "medieval" gives short shrift to the fact that the group was a product in part of a conflict over modernity.[110] Scholars and analysts zeroed in on what they believed to be Wood's suggestion that the Islamic State was "an inevitable product of Islam."[111] It is not. Others took him to task for suggesting that the Islamic State was religious in nature and that it had a theology. It is and does. The theoreticians that shape the Islamic State's worldview anchor the group's methods and mission in a particular interpretation of Islamic texts. That those readings have been contested by Muslims—scholars and otherwise—around the world does not necessarily undercut the claim that the Islamic State is religious. This set off a debate in scholarly and policy circles whether one can fairly call the Islamic State *Islamic*. This issue remains unsettled and has at times veered into the esoteric, but the question remains critical. After all, without the theological justification for its existence, what would the Islamic State be? It would have little allure. The beheadings, crucifixions, and wholesale murders have been so much the focus of the West that it is often lost that this horrific violence is in the service of a bigger project intertwined with religion and identity, which was why it is so appealing to a wide variety of people.[112]

Part of the astounding success of Wood's article is the way it frames the debate about the Islamic State. In Washington, in particular, two questions dominate the discussion: "What does the Islamic State want?" and its corollary, "How do we deal with it?" Lost in the effort to provide good answers is a third question: "What does the Islamic State offer?" It is the flip side of the question about what the group wants, but it is just as important in trying to figure how to deal with the specific challenge that the Islamic State presents. Before even answering, though, a caveat is in order. Among the varying estimates of people who have traveled to the group's capital in Syria, Raqqa, and other places to fight on behalf of the Islamic State, among them without a doubt are sociopaths motivated purely by their desire to kill people and engage in other kinds of violence. At the same time, the Islamic State had been successful in attracting adherents and capturing and keeping territory (for a time) because of the present moment of capacious failure in the Middle East. The vortexes of violence that are Syria and Iraq today have certainly helped the Islamic State's cause, but the group's resurgence also coincides with the broader region's spiral into violence, instability, and uncertainty. The Arab Spring was supposed to give way to transitions to democracy that many hoped would approximate the AKP's Third Way, which would do much to ease the complex and multilayered political, social, and economic pressures that Middle Easterners have been grappling with for a long time. Not only do the problems of the region persist, but they have grown more acute against the backdrop of the ruins of the Arab republics, the revolutions that never were, the Muslim Brotherhood's disastrous rule in Egypt, resurgent authoritarianism, limited economic opportunities, and the fragmentation of major countries in the region.

Under these circumstances, the Fertile Crescent has become fertile ground for the Islamic State. In the tragedy that has become the Middle East, people are becoming disoriented and unmoored. The modest progress that Tunisian elites have made in resolving their differences is laudable, but in the country's periphery—towns such as Sidi Bouzid—alienation has been a defining characteristic of life. Egyptians were suffering from political whiplash after having been through what seemed like thirty years' worth of political events in the two years after Mubarak's fall, and then having to do it again after the military intervention that ousted Mohammed Morsi. Libyans were confronting the question of how one could be a Libyan when there is hardly a united Libya. Turkey is stable by comparison, but the reality is that the country is at war with itself in both the metaphorical and literal sense. Instability, violence, and uncertainty seem only to intensify questions about society and an individual's place in it. At this difficult moment, many Tunisians, Egyptians, and Turks draw support from a deeply felt nationalism and its symbols; Libyans look to their city or tribe. Yet nationalism, city, and tribe are by their nature exclusivist. What does one do when one is, for example, a Muslim Brother, a Kurd caught in the crossfire, or an alienated young man from somewhere other than a capital city? The Islamic State has an answer.

Baghdadi's call from his Iraqi base, Mosul, was violent but also something much bigger. For those looking for a sense of place, belonging, and citizenship, the Islamic State was a call to arms in the service of a grand religious project, especially after Baghdadi declared the establishment of his caliphate in June 2014. To live in accordance with the imagined original community of believers seemed to give some people meaning that they lacked in places where other experiments in the organization of government and society had either failed or were deeply unsatisfying.[113] What looks like nihilistic violence to so many around the world has a point within the bounded world of the Islamic State. As Jessica Stern and J. M. Berger relate, the marauding and pillaging of Baghdadi's forces has all been in the service of upending the irreligious and amoral societies and building a religious ideal.[114] The conflicts and contradictions of modernity are seemingly resolved within the Islamic State. People would no longer be divided based on arbitrary boundaries and, at least in theory, it is easier to be a good Muslim within the Islamic State by dint of living within a territory where God's law reigned supreme. As for the end-of-days aspect of Baghdadi's vision, ushering in the appearance of the Mahdi—a figure in Islam whose arrival will signal that Judgment Day is upon humanity—is something to which one can productively devote oneself in the Islamic State. The reality of life within the Islamic State is, of course, much different from this prophecy, as the intrepid reporters from the online citizen journalism site Raqqa Is Being Slaughtered Silently indicate, but people still make the pilgrimage there in search of meaning and identity.[115]

The people who made their way to the Islamic State's territory remains quite small. Estimates range from 20,000 to 30,000 (according to the Central Intelligence Agency) to as many as 100,000, and not just from the Middle East or the broader Muslim world. Paris, London, Brussels, and Denver (though on a much smaller scale) are also places from which people come to the Islamic State in search of meaning.[116] Still, it is primarily a Middle Eastern phenomenon whose "achievements" seemed beyond imagination. The irony is that the topplings of Zine al-Abidine Ben Ali, Hosni Mubarak, and Muammar al-Qaddafi were supposed to be a rebuke of extremist ideologies in favor of democracy and, with a little help, something akin to the Justice and Development Party's Turkey might emerge in the Arab world. People in the Middle East rose up because they wanted bread, social justice, and dignity, not extremism. It never dawned on anyone that the Islamic State was offering a version of the same. This may be why, despite whatever democratic progress Tunisia has perhaps made, an estimated 3,000 Tunisians have nevertheless gone off to fight on behalf of the Islamic State.

The story of the present Middle East is not about the specific leaders, the incompetence of oppositions, or the utter perfidy of extremists. They obviously have played an important and devastating role in the tragedies that have beset the region, but had it not been Beji Caid Essebsi, Abdel Fattah al-Sisi, or Recep Tayyip Erdoğan, those roles would have been played by others. The Arab Spring and Turkey's liberalization never really were. The conjuncture of uprisings, but not revolutions, and the institutional environments begat instability and violence, accentuating identity politics in the region, producing more bloodshed and thwarting the dream of democratic transitions. Authoritarianism in Egypt is resurgent, Turkey is a case study in the reversal of liberalizing reforms, and Libya is a paradigmatic example of fragmentation, leaving only Tunisia, where promise and despair oscillate. In the overall context of the contested, unstable, uncertain, violent politics of the region, a question remains for outsiders: what do we do about it?

5

"Getting the Middle East Right"

ON A SUNNY WEDNESDAY morning in early June 2011, the Saban Center for Middle East Policy at the Brookings Institution convened a symposium on the Middle East. It was a fairly large gathering, which was not terribly surprising given the speed of apparent change in the region. Tunisia's Zine al-Abidine Ben Ali was gone, Egypt's Hosni Mubarak had repaired to Sharm el-Sheikh, a war was under way in Libya, and Bashar al-Assad was in the process of militarizing the uprising in Syria. The political turbulence was not confined to these four countries, however. With the exceptions of Qatar and the United Arab Emirates, every country in the Arab world had experienced unrest in the preceding seven months. The Saban Center's director at the time, Ken Pollack—a veteran of the Central Intelligence Agency and the Clinton White House as well as the author of eight books—called the meeting of mostly Washington-based Middle East hands to brainstorm about the region and US policy. One of Pollack's books helped shape the public discourse leading up to Operation Iraqi Freedom; yet another less-noticed volume argued that the Middle East was headed toward a period of coups, internal strife, wars, and general instability.[1] The objective of the meeting was to figure out how to forestall such a dystopian future. Since the uprisings began, the effort (and a good deal of posturing) to make sense of why they were happening and what would come next had been tremendous.[2] Yet very little systematic thinking had focused on how Washington's policy toward a region that had been based on the predictability and stability of authoritarian leaders should change.

The day's agenda included panels on countries already in transition, how to foster reform in other places, the prospects for failing states, and how non-Arab regional actors were responding. Much of the formal and informal discussion focused on Egypt, a country in which the United States had invested close to $80 billion since 1948. To many of the gathered experts, Washington now had an opportunity to liberate itself from the outmoded policies and sunk costs associated with the Mubarak era. These sentiments were not new. In the years before Egypt's January 25 uprising, Americans and Egyptians had come together at various times to figure out how to invigorate a relationship that officials in both countries called strategic but that had little sense of purpose. For all of the expertise brought to bear on the issue during the 2000s, the proposals lacked imagination. The most often discussed three alternatives included maintaining the approach that had sustained the Egypt-Israel peace treaty, ensured open access to the Suez Canal, and kept the Islamists on the defensive; promoting democracy; and shifting the relationship from one defined by aid to one in which trade was the centerpiece. None of these satisfied all the constituents of the relationship, so bureaucratic inertia preserved the status quo. The meeting at Brookings did not generate any new ideas, but a number of the participants asserted that with Mubarak gone and the Supreme Council of the Armed Forces promising "to prepare the country for democracy," Washington had an opportunity to "get Egypt right."

It was entirely understandable that the policy community perceived change under way in Egypt and other parts of the Middle East as a chance to begin anew. Yet it also seemed out of step with what was transpiring in the region and the actual limits of American power. Arabs had risen up to demand dignity, representative government, and economic empowerment in response to the problems and contradictions they experienced within their own societies. The United States had few diplomatic tools and little in the way of financial resources to help make Arab dreams of more open, just, and prosperous societies a reality, though this state of affairs seemed lost in the conversation at Brookings that imagined Washington as an influential player in the Middle Eastern political transitions. It was entirely unclear that

Middle Easterners, especially Egyptians, wanted American help. In Tahrir Square, the United States was not a major preoccupation of protesters. And after Mubarak fell, Egypt's activists, liberals, democrats, and revolutionaries were not necessarily interested in assistance from the United States. To them, Washington had been Mubarak's primary ally and enabler. At another meeting that spring, Ahmed Maher—a founder of the April 6th Youth Movement, which had been a creative opponent of the Egyptian leader—suggested that the United States continue its assistance to Egypt as penance for supporting Mubarak for almost thirty years.[3] It is true that Libyans looked to NATO for protection from Muammar al-Qaddafi and Tunisians welcomed whatever assistance well-meaning foreigners, including representatives of the US government, had to offer, but external powers were not central to the uprisings.

It was a special conceit of the policy community—both inside and outside the government—that the United States had a role to play in Arab efforts to build new societies and political systems after the uprisings. These sentiments may have been misplaced, but they came from a good place: the belief in democracy as the best form of governance, that for too long Washington supported authoritarian leaders and looked the other way when those allies violated human rights, that democracies would generate greater wealth and more inclusive prosperity, and that democratic partners were better and more appropriate allies for the United States. It was hard to argue with these assertions, though democracy in the Middle East would not necessarily have made the region's countries better partners. Egyptian activists had argued that democratic government, which would actually reflect the will of the people, was the best way to resist what they regarded as predatory American policies in the Middle East. For their part, the Muslim Brotherhood believed that the close ties between Washington and Cairo had weakened Egypt and compromised its regional leadership role. Egypt was perhaps a special case. By the time Mubarak fell, the United States had become a negative factor in Egypt's domestic politics.[4]

More broadly, a general wariness prevailed about America's promotion of democracy in the region. This was to be expected of authoritarian leaders who did their best to resist and deflect the policy, but the mistrust ran both broader and deeper. Washington's history of unfailing support for Israel and regional dictators was a source of outrage for many in the Arab world. People in the region had long admired the United States, its principles, and its ideals, but could not understand the gap between the way Americans lived at home and Washington's conduct in the world. The 2003 invasion of Iraq only accentuated the ingrained suspicion of American aims in the region and led people to conclude that the Freedom Agenda was a backdoor effort to remake societies and undermine their collective identities. This was all being done, Arab critics charged, to the benefit of American "interests," which in the Arabic—*masalih*—can have negative connotations. In the mid-2000s, discussions in the Arab world about democratic change and American efforts to encourage reform were invariably met with either accusations about the supposed neoconservative guiding principle of "creative destruction" or outright derision given the disasters that had befallen Iraq. After the revelation of the US military's systematic abuse of prisoners at Iraq's Abu Ghraib prison, American visitors to the region were put in the odd position of having to listen to lectures from Middle Eastern officials about the importance of upholding human rights. Many Arabs craved democracy and sought various kinds of support from the United States, but leaders and their allies sought to shape a discourse that made these activities and the people who participated in them illegitimate. It was a credit to American policymakers that they continued to promote democracy in the context of this opposition.

The record during the Bush years was not all bad, however. At the time, it seemed that the president's forthright call for freedom and democracy had an effect on the politics in the Arab world in indirect and complicated ways. It placed regional leaders on notice that Washington was paying close attention to domestic political developments in their countries, which forced Arab leaders to position themselves as reformers, if only to relieve American pressure for change. This tactical accommodation of US demands in turn allowed activists, who for so long had worked on the periphery and at the mercy of the Arab world's well-developed national security states, to pursue their agendas in new and more meaningful ways. This, in turn, helped alter the prevailing public discourse in the region, which suddenly seemed to focus on political reform. Concerned about the new narratives they had been forced to let loose on their societies, leaders sought to balance against it. Almost by reflex, they tried to change the subject, declaring that reform could not take place until the Palestinian-Israeli conflict was resolved. When that did not work, they sought to appropriate the language of reform. When this strategy failed to deflect increasingly bold demands for change, state security services stepped in. Many journalists, editors, bloggers, and activists suffered—in some cases, more than ever. But perceptions had changed. The gap between what the regimes felt obliged to say and what they actually did grew larger and larger. Arab authoritarians could neither roll back the new discourse nor stop the growing recognition of their rank hypocrisy. It was this new perceptual reality that helped set the stage for the uprisings.

Given the prevailing political context in the region during the 2000s, did the actual programs of the Freedom Agenda make a difference? Did the US-Middle East Partnership Initiative, a refocusing of some United States Agency for International Development (USAID) projects on good governance and democracy promotion, and broad multilateral efforts like the (unfortunately named) Partnership for Progress for a Common Future with the Region of the Broader Middle East and North Africa have any measurable impact, let alone a decisive one, on Arab politics? Perhaps, or perhaps not. Despite some clues, there is really no way to know. An internal USAID study of the agency's democracy and governance programs in Egypt found that many did not achieve their objectives.[5] Mubarak resisted these efforts, which of course made their proximate failure more likely, but he fell anyway.

In addition to the US government, an array of organizations such as the federally funded National Endowment for Democracy, its affiliated International Republican Institute (IRI), and the National Democratic Institute (NDI) have long been dedicated to promoting democratic change around the world. These groups had worked in parts of the Middle East for years but sought a more active profile in the region with Bush's "forward strategy of freedom." Among other things, these organizations offered on-the-ground training for activists in election monitoring, party organization, and political advocacy. In April 2011, a few articles in the *Washington Post* and the *New York Times* suggested that NDI- and IRI-sponsored programs must have been effective because

some of the activists involved in uprisings around the region had participated in them. The efforts of NDI, IRI, and others seemed worthy, but
"there are no good metrics for determining how effective democracy
promotion programs, whether governmental, quasi-governmental, or
private, have been in the Middle East."[6] Regardless of this uncertainty,
the consensus among Middle East watchers was that the uprisings had
created new openings for the United States to help the people of the
region build democracies.

The day at Brookings may not have broken new ground, but there
was no shortage of articles and reports offering advice to the Obama
administration about what to do. Even well before the uprisings the
policy community had been thinking about political change in the
Arab world. In late 2004, the Council on Foreign Relations (CFR) convened an Independent Task Force to study reform in the Arab world.
The following spring it produced a report titled *In Support of Arab
Democracy: Why and How.* The twenty-six specialists with expertise in
a variety of areas including Middle East politics, economics, education,
public diplomacy, and religion under the direction of former Secretary
of State Madeleine Albright and former Congressman Vin Weber, a
Republican from Minnesota, offered a detailed set of recommendations
for the American and Arab governments that captured Washington's
collective mindset on democracy promotion. The task force called on
the Bush administration "to encourage" Arab leaders to develop public
"pathways to reform," promote change on a country-by-country basis,
"support the political participation of any group or party [including
Islamists] committed to abide by the rules and norms of the democratic process," pursue political and economic reform simultaneously,
and make the quality of relations with the United States conditional in
part on reform. An additional grab bag of suggestions included improving public diplomacy, fostering educational reform, and making the
Middle East more attractive to foreign direct investment.[7] Similarly, in
2010, the United States Institute of Peace (USIP) convened its own blue
ribbon commission to look at the issue. The report was prescient about
the potential for instability in the region, yet like CFR's Independent
Task Force, USIP's experts strained to propose practical suggestions.
For example, the report called on the Obama administration to "deploy
a mix of private and high-level public diplomacy to encourage ruling

elites to replace short-term tactical reforms with long-term programs that build the legal and institutional infrastructure for democratic representation."[8] Middle Eastern countries were very much in need of the legal and political reforms, but how "private and high-level public diplomacy" was going to help make it happen remained entirely unclear, especially given that Arab leaders had been clear that they were not interested in democratic change beyond cosmetic changes designed to put off American policymakers. The underlying logic of these reports was the notion that Washington could convince Arab leaders that if they did not make changes, they would confront challenges to their rule. This hunch turned out to be correct, but at the time Arab leaders refused to take steps that they believed amounted to little more than reforming themselves out of power.

After the uprisings, analysts labored even harder to find constructive policy recommendations for American policymakers, but the complexity of politics in the region left this work wanting. For example, one idea was that the United States should play the role of a global catalyst that would bring together the resources and expertise of Europe, the Persian Gulf countries, and rising powers such as Brazil and others to invest politically and financially in Middle Eastern transitions to democracy.[9] This was an evolution of the notion that the United States needed a "Marshall Plan for the Middle East," which had come up from time to time in Beltway discussions about the region since the attacks of September 11, 2001.[10] The global catalyst idea was attractive in part because it was multilateral, which avoided reinforcing the impression that Washington was engaged in the same international social engineering project that it launched in the 2000s, but under a different president. Yet working with partners in other parts of the world was hardly an innovation. The reports of both CFR and USIP had suggested it. In 2004, with its partners in the Group of Eight, the Bush administration launched the Partnership for Progress to coordinate democracy promotion with its European, Canadian, and Asian partners. After the uprisings, there was actually not much new to say about multilateralism despite general agreement within the policy community of the need for a multilateral component to American efforts. All that one prominent group of analysts could muster on the issue was that "Both the United States and European countries have a role to play in trying to steer competing Arab elites away from acrimonious and ultimately sterile ideological debates and toward more practical problem solving."[11] The analysis of what was happening in the Middle East and why was often quite good, but the recommendations these articles, reports, and books offered were frustratingly nebulous.[12]

When it came to specific countries undergoing change, the policy recommendations were no more incisive. On Libya, for example, one expert recommended in 2011 that "USAID, the State Department, and the Department of Defense should design now a package of multiyear U.S. civilian and military assistance focused on capacity building for the new Libyan government, its military, and its civil society."[13] This recommendation was reasonable but hopelessly overtaken by events as Libya fragmented. When it came to Egypt, many of the suggestions echoed what the policy community had offered before Mubarak fell, including American support for local nongovernmental organizations, promotion of good governance, conditioning aid on political reform, and broadening "strategic dialogues" with Egyptians from various sectors of society.[14] In Tunisia, recommendations ran from security sector reform (a good idea) to "engaging" with all parties, especially the Islamist Ennahda Movement, as a way both to promote democracy and "restore American credibility in the region."[15] Everyone who weighed in on what Washington should be doing in response to the Arab uprisings was smart and accomplished, some with years of US government experience at various levels. That they strained so hard to offer policy recommendations that seemed workable and could possibly make a difference in the Middle East said a lot less about them and much more about the nature of the challenge they were addressing.

Turkey also figured prominently in the conversation, so much so that in April 2011, the producers of National Public Radio's program *All Things Considered* aired a mash-up of interviews conducted in the preceding four months during which experts had emphasized the importance of Turkey in the aftermath of the Arab uprisings.[16] Another one of CFR's Independent Task Forces indicated that "The United States and Turkey have an opportunity to cooperate in helping forge a more democratic and prosperous Middle East."[17] This idea was consistent with the White House's position that Turkey was well placed to lead the region after the uprisings and be a model for Arab political systems.

Then prime minister Recep Tayyip Erdoğan's declaration early in the Egyptian uprising that Mubarak should heed the call of his people for change, combined with the Turkish leader's undeniable popularity in the region, led administration officials to believe that the Turks had special insight into the Middle East—a message that Turkey's Justice and Development Party (AKP) had been emphasizing well before the uprisings.[18] All the intense interest in the prospect of Turkey's shaping Arab political systems and economies tended to overshadow the deteriorating Turkish political environment, however. By no means did the entire foreign policy community share the sunny optimism about Erdoğan's Turkey.[19] A good deal of commentary and analysis concerned the AKP's efforts to dominate the Turkish political arena, but the overwhelming tendency was to cast these concerns as an implicit form of Islamophobia, a blatant misreading of Turkey's democratic transition, challenges that could be overcome with diplomacy, or problems outweighed by the opportunities Turkey presented.[20] The Obama administration was not unaware of these problems but chose to give them less public attention than they deserved, preferring to communicate concerns privately.

Part of the policy problem US officials confronted was the speed of change taking place and the competing political pressures associated with them. Mubarak had been in power for almost thirty years but was brought down after eighteen days of protest. This occurred after years in which the collective wisdom believed that he would die in office and that power would pass to his son or his intelligence chief.[21] Much of Washington's approach to Egypt was based on this expectation. Yet it was the NATO intervention in Libya that would become the paradigmatic example of the policy challenges that the rapidly changing environment of the Arab uprisings produced. A compelling humanitarian case was to be made as Muammar al-Qaddafi threatened that he was mobilizing his forces to crush Benghazi, in addition to pressure from NATO allies—notably, Great Britain and France—to take military action quickly, but the Pentagon was also wary of yet another conflict after a long decade in Afghanistan and almost that much time in Iraq. President Barack Obama's 2008 run for office was predicated in part on withdrawing the United States from two costly wars, not getting the country involved in what could be another one. Then again, how could the administration be faithful to the "New Beginning" with the Muslim world that the president announced in his June 2009 speech at Cairo University and stand idly by as Qaddafi killed his own people? The resulting policy—a no-fly zone in which Washington provided its unique military capabilities to allies who lacked them—helped save Benghazi and bring down Qaddafi, but then Libyans were left largely to their own devices in trying to stabilize their country, few in the West (or anywhere else) having either the resources or the fortitude to deploy large forces in support. Detailed reconstruction plans—that the British government took the lead developing—were impossible to carry out effectively without stability in Libya and an international commitment to nation building.[22]

In an effort to give direction to Washington's approach to the Middle East, on May 19, 2011, Obama made the short trip from the White House to the State Department. There, on the eighth floor in the ornate Benjamin Franklin Room with its commanding southern views of the Lincoln Memorial and the Potomac River, the president delivered a speech to America's diplomatic corps and civil servants who, more than any others, would be charged with carrying out US policy in a radically changed Middle East. Among Obama's speeches, his remarks that day will not likely be held up among his best. Despite some promising rhetorical flourishes, it was far from inspiring, and his effort to link Mohammed al-Bouazizi to Rosa Parks fell flat. The speech was notable both for what the president left out—Saudi Arabia—and for what he included—the Arab-Israeli conflict, despite its manifest irrelevance to the issues at hand. In between Obama declared:

> We have the chance to show that America values the dignity of the street vendor in Tunisia more than the raw power of the dictator. There must be no doubt that the United States of America welcomes change that advances self-determination and opportunity. Yes, there will be perils that accompany this moment of promise. But after decades of accepting the world as it is in the region, we have a chance to pursue the world as it should be.[23]

It would thus be the policy of the United States to "promote reform across the region, and to support transitions to democracy."[24] Like a lot of recommendations the policy community had previously offered, few specifics were attached to these platitudes. For example, Obama announced that the United States welcomed "working with all those who embrace genuine and inclusive democracy" and would "oppose" those who sought "to restrict the rights of others, and to hold power through coercion and not consent."[25] These declarations sounded suspiciously like the executive summaries of think tank reports and, as with those summaries, it remained entirely unclear what any of these words meant and how they would be operationalized.

Obama then pivoted to how Washington would support democratic change through economic development. This included a more detailed discussion of debt relief, the announcement of an enterprise funds intended to invest in small and medium businesses in Tunisia and Egypt, and the encouragement of entrepreneurship, among a number of other initiatives. It was no surprise that this part of the speech had more coherence. The economic goals Obama laid out were not only tangible, but diplomats also had clear ideas based on years of experience about how to go about achieving them. In contrast, promoting democratic change was amorphous and the policies aimed at advancing more open and just societies were unproven.

In one particularly important passage of the speech, the president implicitly cautioned his audience about the limits of American policy. This was consistent with an overall theme of the Obama presidency that emphasized rightsizing a US foreign policy that had become badly overextended.[26] Because the president's words were interwoven with statements that George W. Bush could have uttered about "pursu[ing] the world as it should be," it was initially hard to detect the call for restraint, but this passage was the most important of the speech: "Of course, as we [promote reform and support transitions], we must proceed with a sense of humility. It's not America that put people into the streets of Tunis or Cairo—it was the people themselves who launched these movements, and it's the people themselves that must ultimately determine their outcome."[27] Obama then outlined a series of principles that should guide US policy—nonviolence, free speech, freedom of assembly, tolerance, the rule of law, and the right to choose one's leaders.[28] More than anything else that Obama said that day, his admonition about humility without abdicating America's values was most consistent with what was actually happening on the ground in the Middle East. The uprisings were a source of pride and dignity, in particular. Tunisians, Egyptians, Libyans (even though Qaddafi had not fallen yet), and others were experiencing a moment of tremendous empowerment. And although he was consistent with his Cairo speech that Washington was ready to help, Obama was also signaling to those who saw opportunity for democracy promotion in the ousters of Ben Ali and Mubarak that he preferred a significantly lighter touch.[29]

Even so, it was hardly that the United States shut down its efforts to promote democracy. In the weeks and months after the Tunisian and Egyptian uprisings, American officials were on the ground offering assistance, "but quietly"—in the case of Egypt—as the *Washington Post* reported.[30] The White House and the State Department shifted gears from trying to understand what was happening in the Middle East to providing support for those working in the region to translate the promise of the uprisings into democracies. Yet a certain ambivalence about US policy prevailed, revealing a philosophical debate within the administration that was never resolved, at least as far as the Arab uprisings and subsequent tumult in Turkey were concerned. In both word and deed, it seemed clear that Obama was inclined toward realism in foreign policy. His mantra, "Don't do stupid shit," was an off-color way of reinforcing for him and his advisors what was really important—balancing the ambitions of other countries, exercising American power judiciously in the service of national interests, and maximizing American strength.[31] An element of "do the opposite of what Bush did" was also a part of the administration's approach to the world. At the same time, much of what Obama did—whether the "reset with Russia," commitment to withdraw from Iraq and Afghanistan, outreach to Iran, or reinforcement of ties with countries in Asia—was a retrenchment borne of the realist concern that the foreign policy the administration inherited in 2009 included commitments that sapped Washington's power. In the Middle East, the administration sought a policy that focused on American interests in the narrow way they had traditionally been defined—ensuring the free flow of energy resources out of the region, helping guarantee Israel's security, preventing any single power from dominating the region, countering terrorism, and preventing the proliferation of weapons of mass destruction. The way Obama chose to help bolster Israeli security and check Iran's drive for nuclear technology raised considerable hackles, but it did not reflect a fundamental shift in the way American officials defined core US interests in the region.

Obama's realist inclinations nevertheless coexisted with a policy that did nothing to alter the bureaucracy it inherited that was charged with promoting democracy. Still, there was a lack of enthusiasm about this project. Funding for USAID programs in the Middle East initially fell at the same time the Obama administration requested that Congress appropriate larger sums for democracy and good governance initiatives through other State Department offices such as the Middle East Partnership Initiative. Those requests leveled off in 2011 and subsequently fell after 2012. As for the Bureau for Democracy, Rights, and Labor (also within the State Department), Congress consistently granted more resources than the administration requested for its work in the Middle East.[32] Within the White House there were senior members of the National Security Council staff who had supported policies that promoted democratic change in their academic careers and/or prior government service. The same was true at various levels of the State Department, where political appointees, civil servants, and foreign service officers dedicated considerable time and effort to the issue. In what seemed like a compromise between his predispositions and the advice of his advisors, Obama indicated that the United States would support democratic change, but Washington was not going to push it.

The president proved to be as good as his word. When the uprisings happened, the administration accepted the outcomes that people in the streets produced. The White House's rhetoric about "being on the right side of history" was perhaps politically necessary against the backdrop of inspiring events, but had the unintended effect of making it seem as if the United States actually had a choice about what was transpiring in cities and squares far from Washington in the Middle East. It did not. Tunisia had been an afterthought of American foreign policy until the uprising that dumped Ben Ali; it took some time before the US Embassy in Tunis fully understood the magnitude of what was happening after Bouazizi's suicide on December 17, 2010.[33]

Had they grasped the threat to Ben Ali's rule, American diplomats or anyone else could not have done much. Even the French, who had close diplomatic, financial, and military ties with the Tunisian government, were no more than onlookers as Ben Ali came undone. Some commentary at the time of Egypt's uprisings and revisionist analyses since have suggested that the Obama administration "dumped" Mubarak, implying that American support could have saved the Egyptian president.[34] Once the Egyptian military deployed on January 28, 2011, however, Mubarak had little chance of remaining in power. The confluence of the Supreme Council of the Armed Forces' interests in stability and preventing Gamal Mubarak, the president's son and presumptive heir who had never served in the military, from becoming the next president and those of demonstrators demanding "the end of the regime" ensured that the Egyptian president's days in power were rapidly coming to an end. Like Egypt's top military brass, the Obama administration spent two weeks after the tanks and armored personnel carriers arrived in Tahrir Square trying to devise a dignified exit for Mubarak with the least amount of bloodshed.

FROM PRINCIPLE TO PRAGMATISM

The president's nod to values in his May 2011 speech was to be expected. Any American president is going to have to say something about values when somewhere in the world people rise up and demand dignity and freedom. The exception was the Obama administration's silence during Iran's uprising two years earlier. This decision had an inherent logic. The White House feared that full-throated American support for Iranian protesters would provide an opportunity for hard-liners in Tehran to delegitimize the demonstrations as yet another American effort to undermine Iran. This made sense, but as the aftermath of the Arab uprisings unfolded, the Obama administration demonstrated a pattern of forsaking the core values the president himself outlined at the State Department to preserve working relationships with the leaders of the Middle East. Under different circumstances, that might have been the most prudent approach, but in the unstable, uncertain, and politically variable environments in which Washington was operating, it proved damaging. Even in relatively stable Turkey, the administration did itself no favors.

When then secretary of state Hillary Clinton visited Egypt two weeks after the Muslim Brotherhood's Mohammed Morsi took the presidential oath of office, protesters greeted her at her hotel with chants of "Mo-ni-ca! Mo-ni-ca!" A day later, demonstrators threw tomatoes, water bottles, and shoes in the direction of her car as she arrived to open a new US consulate building in Egypt's second city, Alexandria. Though small in number, the demonstrators seemed to represent a far larger group of Egyptians seething over the turn of events that placed a member of the Muslim Brotherhood in the Ittihadiyya Palace. The crude, sophomoric, and shameful displays of anger directed at Clinton were based on the canard that the Obama administration not just supported Morsi's candidacy for Egypt's presidency but also brought pressure to bear on election officials to declare him the winner. It was a bizarre allegation given the Brotherhood's illiberal worldview that included healthy doses of anti-Americanism, anti-Semitism, and anti-Zionism, along with the decades of mutual hostility between the organization and the United States. Certainly an argument could be made that for exactly these reasons the Obama administration should have opposed the Brotherhood and Morsi. Yet such an approach would have placed Washington in the awkward position of opposing the outcome of elections after Egyptians had risen up in part because they wanted their country's electoral process to mean something. In early 2006, after pushing for Palestinian elections, the Bush administration refused to deal with a victorious Hamas. The policy achieved nothing. Hamas remained in power—at least in the Gaza Strip—and the United States was widely denounced for liking elections only when its friends won them. Instead, the Obama administration chose to accommodate itself to the results and outcomes that Egyptians produced.

It was the only reasonable approach for Obama to take given the Egyptian search for a democratic political system. It would also free the United States from falling into the same trap it had with the former president, Hosni Mubarak, in which Washington became identified specifically with the Egyptian leader. The White House and the State Department wanted to establish a working relationship with Egypt's new leadership. As Secretary Clinton noted in her remarks at the consulate in Alexandria, however,

> I want to be clear that the United States is not in the business, in Egypt, of choosing winners and losers, even if we could, which of course we cannot. We are prepared to work with you as you chart your course, as you establish your democracy.... And we want to stand for principles, for values, not for people or for parties but for what democracy means in our understanding and experience.[35]

This statement represented all the right instincts about Egypt, which is why it was so mystifying to many in Egypt that the actual conduct of American policymakers turned out quite different. Public commitments aside, the administration placed working relationships ahead of principles and values, which made it seem as if Washington was, in fact, "choosing winners."

Whether Morsi intended to amass so much power or not, the effect of his November 2012 decree was the same, providing an excellent opportunity for the Obama administration to emphasize the values that both the president and the secretary of state had articulated. The State Department's spokesperson, Victoria Nuland, offered a milquetoast statement expressing the "concerns" of "many Egyptians and the international community" about Morsi's actions. She also called on "all Egyptians to resolve their differences over these important issues peacefully and through democratic dialogue."[36] Nuland's counterpart at the White House referred inquiring journalists to her statement and reiterated the role the Egyptian leader played in helping negotiate a ceasefire between Israel and Hamas.[37] The reluctance of the American government to take Morsi to task for what many saw as a power grab fueled Egyptian suspicions that Washington was once again willing to trade stability for authoritarianism. It also provided further evidence for those Egyptians inclined to believe that the United States was invested in the success of Morsi and the Muslim Brotherhood. This perception actually went back as far as the mid-2000s at the height of George W. Bush's Freedom Agenda, but it became more commonplace as the United States tried to navigate the uncertain and contested political environment of post-uprising Egypt. This made for some ugly moments during the massive demonstrations that preceded the July 3 coup, during which the American ambassador was called a "bitch" and an "ogre" and Obama was called a "supporter of terrorism."

By the time the military ousted Morsi in July 2013, considerable mistrust had built up between Washington and Egypt's senior military officers, who were wary of US intentions. Once again, though, Washington abdicated the values that Obama articulated in 2011. In its effort to accommodate a political outcome that was purely of Egyptian making, the administration studiously avoided calling the military's intervention a coup, which it surely was. To the commanders and their supporters, this four-letter word became an anti-military epithet associated with the Muslim Brotherhood. The Obama administration wanted to sidestep section 508 of the 1961 Foreign Assistance Act, which requires the suspension of aid to governments that had come to power by coup. Washington did register its disapproval some months later when Obama delayed the transfer of twenty F-16 fighter planes, ten Apache helicopters, 125 M1A1 tank kits, and twenty Harpoon missiles. This was an uneasy compromise between principle and pragmatism, however. Although the Egyptians complained bitterly—despite already having the fourth largest inventory of F-16s in the world, thirty-four Apache helicopters, and large numbers of M1A1 tanks in storage—the freeze was actually done in a way to avoid damaging their national security, especially given that the administration maintained all levels of specific counterterrorism aid. Nevertheless, that Obama did not unconditionally welcome the coup and support Major General Abdel Fattah al-Sisi once again reinforced the notion that the United States was pro-Brotherhood. The situation was made worse, however, because the Brothers and their supporters regarded Washington's reluctance to identify the military's action as a coup d'état, demand Morsi's return to the presidency, and cut military assistance completely as an indication that the Obama administration supported Sisi's takeover.[38] The inevitable result was the worst of all possible worlds: across the board hostility toward the United States.

Of course, the White House could not be faulted for the competing narratives that emerged from the summer of 2013. The problem came with the Obama administration's unwillingness to be forthright about first-order principles like nonviolence, rule of law, and a variety of personal and political freedoms. Without any clarity about what the United States stood for, Washington became unwittingly ensnared in the high-stakes struggle over identity in which Egyptians were engaged. In the process, it hurt everything the United States wanted to do in Egypt, from counterterrorism to technical assistance for ministries, which were gummed up not just because of Egypt's usual bureaucratic lethargy but also out of mistrust and the malice it bred. There is no guarantee that the Obama administration would have avoided this problem had the president and other senior officials been consistent with his May 19, 2011, speech, but it certainly would have helped Washington avoid the general distrust and anger that every player in Cairo held toward the United States.

A similar dynamic was under way in Turkey. As deliberalization proceeded, Washington remained mostly quiet. Determined to rebuild ties with Ankara after a tension-filled five years following the US invasion of Iraq, Obama delivered an address to the Turkish Grand National Assembly in April 2009 and spoke of "Turkey's strong and secular democracy" and the "common values" between Turkey and the West.[39] The new American president was fulsome in his praise for what the Justice and Development Party (AKP) had achieved but also encouraged the Turks to broaden and deepen the reforms they had previously undertaken. Prime Minister Recep Tayyip Erdoğan became an important interlocutor for Obama in the year after the Arab uprisings began. The thirteen telephone calls between the American and Turkish leaders during that period became an informal measure of US-Turkey relations. The interaction between the president and prime minister was so frequent that American diplomats began referring to Obama as the Chief Turkey Desk Officer—a reference to country desk officers at the State Department who coordinate policy.[40] Yet the new dawn in Washington-Ankara ties coincided with troubling domestic changes in Turkey to which the administration tended to demonstrate a studied indifference.

Invariably, the White House rejected suggestions from Turkey analysts, editorial boards, and members of Congress that Obama publicly criticize the Turkish leader. First, the Turks were sensitive to what they regarded as interference in their domestic affairs. Second, public chastisement did not seem to work. Secretary Clinton's July 2011 comments in Istanbul concerning press freedom fell on deaf ears. When the American ambassador, Frank Ricciardone, did the same shortly after taking up his post in the summer of 2011, Erdoğan called him a "novice" who did not know the country (despite his previous service there and his fluent Turkish). When the ambassador broached the issue again two years later, other AKP officials reacted angrily, accusing Ricciardone of exceeding the limits of what was appropriate diplomatic behavior.[41] In March 2013, Clinton's successor as secretary of state, John Kerry, rebuked Erdoğan for his assertion that "Zionism is a crime against humanity." The Turkish leader treated America's top diplomat with pouty disdain at a subsequent meeting and never retracted his statement. Finally, the administration had enjoyed previous success airing differences with Erdoğan privately. Relations between Washington and Ankara had grown tense in the spring of 2010 over Turkey's efforts—along with Brazil—to negotiate a nuclear deal with Iran and Turkish opposition to sanctions on Iran in the UN Security Council. Also, Turkey-Israel relations were in a deleterious state after a confrontation at sea in late May between activists aboard a Turkish ferry trying to run the Israeli blockade of the Gaza Strip that left eight Turks and a Turkish American dead; this was of serious concern to the Obama administration. Rather than snubbing the Turkish leader at the annual summit of the Group of Twenty (G20) of the largest economies, as a variety of outside experts suggested to senior American officials, Obama decided to meet with Erdoğan. In the privacy of a Toronto hotel room, the two leaders reportedly set aside diplomatic niceties and hashed out their differences, which placed ties on a more constructive path for the next two and a half years.[42] During that time, the administration seemed to treat warnings from Turkish opponents of the AKP about Erdoğan's troubling illiberal approach to politics as little more than the complaints of elites who failed to compete effectively in the political process.

By the time the Gezi Park protests broke out in May 2013, however, it became increasingly difficult for the administration to overlook what had been happening in Turkey. The rate of phone calls between Obama and the Turkish prime minister slowed. They did have a conversation on June 24—three weeks after the demonstrations began—in which, according to the White House's summary of the call, "the two leaders discussed the importance of nonviolence and of the rights to free expression and assembly and a free press."[43] The State Department did little more than reiterate its concern about the violence; it informed the press that Secretary of State John Kerry had been in touch with his Turkish counterpart, and "called for calm."[44] Over the following eighteen months, subsequent phone calls dealt with Syria, Egypt, Iraq, counterterrorism cooperation, Erdoğan's presidential election, refugees, the US commitment to Turkey's security, Cyprus, the G20 summit, and Turkey's tense relations with Russia. In one call, in February 2014, Obama mentioned the rule of law, likely in response to the corruption scandal rocking Turkey at the time.[45] None of the calls with Obama or the intermittent and mild US government statements had an impact on Erdoğan.

In Istanbul and Ankara, Turkish journalists and activists concluded that the subdued response from the White House to the Gezi Park protests was directly related to Washington's strategic ties with Ankara rather than the principles for which the United States stood. It was an easy critique in the anger over tear gas, water cannons, and arrests, but it was also true. Among American policymakers, ties with the Turks were extremely important. Policymakers had grown used to telling themselves that Ankara's proximity to some of Washington's most pressing foreign policy concerns made it indispensable. The record of Turkish indispensability was actually rather mixed because Washington and Ankara differed on a variety of issues related to Iraq, Syria, Israel, Hamas, and Egypt. Nevertheless, having no choice but to work with Turkey, and in the absence of any alternative to Erdoğan and the AKP within the country, officials placed faith in their ability to encourage and cajole the Turks to cooperate, realizing that criticizing Erdoğan on the illiberal turn in Turkish domestic politics would jeopardize the already existing areas of cooperation with the Turks.[46]

One of the points on which the United States wanted Turkey's cooperation was the March 2011 intervention in Libya. The US government justified Operation Odyssey Dawn on humanitarian grounds, specifically a concept called *responsibility to protect*—often referred to as R2P. The basic premises of the concept are straightforward: states have a responsibility to protect their citizens; if they cannot, the international community must assist them; if a state is the perpetrator of mass atrocities, the international community has a responsibility to intervene to protect the population under threat.[47] Humanitarian intervention was not unprecedented in American foreign policy, but it was applied unevenly. In 1992, the United States and other countries intervened in Somalia on humanitarian grounds but failed to stop the genocide in Rwanda a few years later. At the end of the decade, Washington and its NATO allies took military action in Bosnia and Kosovo for the same reasons, though only after about 200,000 had been killed.[48]

The military operation in Libya, which the French and British governments first proposed, proved controversial within the administration. The secretary of defense, Robert Gates, and the uniformed military were opposed, whereas other influential figures such as Secretary Clinton, Susan Rice—who represented the United States at the United Nations and who later became the National Security Advisor—and Rice's successor in New York, Samantha Power, argued in favor. Supporters won the day and on March 19, 2011, the Libya intervention began. It was a very big story. The West had stood on the sidelines when Tunisians and Egyptians rose up, but in Libya, NATO countries along with forces from Qatar and the United Arab Emirates undertook operations to protect Libyans that, in effect, also amounted to regime change.

In time, however, the actual intervention and its underlying rationale received far less attention than the events of September 11, 2012, when the American ambassador in Libya, Christopher Stevens, and three others were killed in an attack on the US consulate in Benghazi. After ten congressional committees, including one by the Select Committee on Benghazi, investigated the incident, *Benghazi* became a watchword for scandal and negligence. This was unfortunate because it obscured the actual failure that lay elsewhere. The international reconstruction plans for Libya that had been developed in the spring of 2011 were abandoned as soon as the Europeans and the United States recognized the magnitude of such an undertaking in a chaotic security and political environment. There are good reasons to question the wisdom and applicability of R2P, but once the intervention took place, the Obama administration and its allies were obliged to continue the mission to its logical conclusion. Instead, they betrayed the very principle that the United States and Europeans invoked to justify their collective intervention. They entered the Libyan conflict to rescue people, but once

Qaddafi had fallen, those countries left the very same people they had just saved to the mercy of the violent forces pulling the country apart. At least in Egypt and Turkey an argument was to be made that abdicating values in favor of a pragmatic policy served the national security interests of the United States. What was the argument in Libya? There was none. Abandoning principle in 2011 as Libya descended into chaos forced Washington and its allies five years later to confront the possibility of another military intervention in Libya, this time to attack affiliates of the self-declared Islamic State and other extremist groups.

Tunisia, by contrast, looked very good in comparison with Egypt, Turkey, and Libya and, as a result, the country became of great importance to the United States. The irony was that few in Washington had ever thought about Tunisia or North Africa more broadly until it dawned on them a few days before Zine al-Abidine Ben Ali was toppled that he might fall. Yet because Tunisia's transition proceeded relatively better than those of other countries, Washington became even more invested in its success. The desire to support Tunisia was without a doubt for the benefit of Tunisians, but it was also part of a broader democratization agenda. The thinking went that if Tunisia's transition to democracy was truly a success, it would be a powerful model and would have a demonstration effect on other societies. The idea came from the academic literature on the spread of war, democratization, and the role international linkages play in both. Scholars had established that international demonstration effects did exist, especially in the "diffusion" of war, as did waves of democratization. Like a lot of ideas and concepts that first appeared in the pages of specialty academic journals, international demonstration effects lost some nuance and complexity in policy discussions.[49] The focus on Tunisia as the demonstrator of democracy got the concept backward. The literature indicates that "a high proportion of democratic neighbors facilitates democratization" rather than a single apparent democratizer among countries with authoritarian systems doing so.[50] One study also found that societies needed to be receptive to change for an international demonstration effect to be possible in the first place.[51] In other words, if Tunisia was going to rub off on Libya or Egypt or Algeria or any other country in the region, political actors in those countries would need to be amenable to the lessons of Tunisia's transition. They were not. Still, the United States became invested in

Tunisia because it was good for both the many Tunisians who wanted to live in a democracy and the purportedly dynamic effect its success would have on the rest of the region. Consequently, President Beji Caid Essebsi enjoyed the extraordinarily rare privilege of sharing a byline with an American president and Tunisia was bestowed the designation of major non-NATO ally in an effort both to validate what Tunisians had accomplished and to show others in the region the benefits of positive change.[52] For President Barack Obama and his advisors to agree to coauthor with his Tunisian counterpart, they had to overlook what Nidaa Tounes stood for, or at least what factions of it stood for, and the willingness of Essebsi himself to play identity politics, albeit neatly intertwined with jargon about democratic change. On Essebsi's visit to Washington, one American official relayed that any question about the Tunisian president's commitment to democracy on these grounds was "trying too hard to find a dark cloud around the silver lining."[53] The Tunisian transition was shaky to the point that these kinds of protestations seemed forced, to say the least. Yet the country's problems, which became clear not just with the terrorist attacks of 2015 but also with the violent protests that swept through parts of the country on the fifth anniversary of Ben Ali's departure, were to the policy community more reasons the United States had to "get Tunisia right."

WHAT LEVERAGE?

As democratic transitions in the Middle East faltered, the policy discussion tended to focus on what kind of leverage the United States could bring to bear to shape the choices of governments in the region. In Tunisia, the Obama administration clearly pursued a "more honey than vinegar" approach to encourage change. It was unclear, however, how much difference a coauthored op-ed and an upgraded alliance status would mean. Between 2012 and 2015, Washington committed $700 million in direct assistance to Tunisia. The Tunisians also received an additional $142 million in aid in 2016. There were also loan guarantees from the United States that allowed the Tunisian government to raise up to $500 million on international capital markets at preferential rates. Taken together this financial support underlined the importance American officials attached to helping the country's shaky transition become a success story.[54] In addition, between 2014 and 2016, the IMF, World Bank, and European Union extended slightly more than $10 billion worth of loans to Tunisia. This assistance represented an important international commitment to the country's success, but an open question remained of whether the Tunisian government could put it to good use given its inability to do much of anything.[55] With Libya, the conversation about leverage was largely irrelevant. None of the political actors there had the kind of relationship with the United States that would allow Washington either to provide or to withhold any meaningful financial, diplomatic, or military assistance to make much of a difference. The Central Intelligence Agency had reportedly cut ties with General Khalifa Haftar in the 1990s.

That left Turkey and Egypt, where the United States had longstanding strategic relationships that could surely be used to alter the behavior of Turkish and Egyptian officials. Yet, in both cases, either considerably less leverage was available to the United States than many believed or American officials were unwilling to pay the price for using it. Washington's economic and military assistance to Turkey is minimal, devoted mostly to helping Ankara deal with the Syrian refugee crisis, a US-based military education program, counterterrorism, and nonproliferation. Like Egypt's military, the Turkish air force was well stocked with F-16 fighter planes and other weapons systems purchased from the United States, though the Turks have their own defense industrial base. There was precedent for the United States to use its security relationships with these countries to make a political point. After Turkey's 1974 invasion and occupation of Cyprus, the US Congress embargoed arms sales and military assistance to Ankara. The embargo was lifted during the Carter administration, but not because of any change in Turkish policy. About 30,000 Turkish troops remain on the northern side of the island to protect the Turkish Republic of Northern Cyprus—an international pariah. In 2015, some members of Congress expressed concern that the precision munitions Ankara sought for its F-16s would be used against Turkey's Kurdish citizens in the government's fight against the Kurdistan Workers' Party (PKK). That concern did not result in any congressional action to block the sale of these weapons after Ankara played the "you are asking us to help fight the Islamic State, but won't sell us bombs" card.[56] And, as noted, the United States was more often than not reluctant to speak out to protest Turkey's deliberalization. Ankara was deemed too important to a variety of US policy priorities, most important of which, beginning in 2014, was the fight against Abu Bakr al-Baghdadi's caliphate. The United States coveted the use of Turkey's İncirlik airbase, which is much closer to eastern Syria and Iraq than are bases in Qatar, Kuwait, and the United Arab Emirates and aircraft carriers in the Persian Gulf. After a year of negotiations, the Turks granted American and allied forces access to İncirlik and other bases. Clearly, Washington did not want to do anything to jeopardize those negotiations or its access to the airfields once it had them, so the Obama administration said little about Turkey's domestic politics.

Yet even had the administration been less reluctant to criticize Erdoğan's approach to domestic politics, one was hard-pressed to think of what Washington could actually do, what threat it could brandish, that might push the Turks. In early 2016, then vice president Joe Biden made an official visit to Turkey during which he met with President Recep Tayyip Erdoğan, then prime minister Ahmet Davutoğlu, a small group of journalists, an NGO activist, and a law professor. It was an important encounter because it was a very public signal that the administration recognized all was not well in Turkey. One participant expressed gratitude for the meeting as a "reminder that we were not alone in the world" and hoped it meant that the United States "will not remain silent against the gross violations of basic rights and freedoms in Turkey just because it needs Ankara's collaboration in their [sic] fight against ISIS."[57] The meeting coincided with the government's attack on about a thousand academics who signed a petition expressing their opposition to Turkish military operations against the PKK in the southeastern part of the country that were also taking a heavy toll on civilians. In his fury, Erdoğan accused the professors of "treachery" and called them a "fifth column."[58]

Providing support for Turkey's beleaguered academics and journalists was not the only or even the primary reason for Biden's trip to Ankara, however. The top of his agenda included coordinating with the Turks on the fight against the Islamic State, moving them closer to the US position on Iraq, and, importantly, convincing the Turkish government to accept the presence of Syrian Kurds at talks aimed at finding a solution to Syria's civil war. It did not work. Ankara remained steadfast in its opposition to empowering this group. For months, Erdoğan had watched with growing unease as Syrian Kurds wrested more territory from the Islamic State with the help of American airpower. In public statements, he emphasized Turkey's opposition to the emergence of an independent Kurdish entity along the Turkish border in northern Syria. Ankara regarded such a development to be an existential threat to Turkey's unity given the impact it could have on its own Kurdish population, especially as the Syrian Kurdish forces were allied with the PKK. The combination of Biden's efforts to convince Erdoğan on Syria's Kurds and his meeting with the Turkish leader's opponents prompted Erdoğan to trash the United States almost as soon as the vice president departed, declaring that "Some of Turkey's allies do not want to recognize the real terrorism threat in Turkey."[59] This type of rhetoric took on a more sinister tone after the attempted coup in July 2016 when Turkish leaders, but Erdoğan in particular, darkly insinuated that the United States and the West "support terrorism" and have sided with plotters.[60] They were able to get away with this conspiracy theory because during the AKP era, Ankara had come to believe that the United States needed Turkey more than Turkey needed the United States. This diminished Washington's ability to influence Turkish decision making, which was not substantial from the start. The country's location at the geographic center of some of the most important foreign policy concerns of the United States dating back to the Cold War, Turkey's status as a NATO ally, and the prickly nationalism of its leaders always made it difficult for American officials to compel the Turks to cooperate with Washington.

Turkey was clearly not the best place for American leverage. If any country was supposed to be responsive to American demands and threats, it was Egypt. The seven-decade American investment in Egypt included food aid in the 1940s, dramatic increases in economic assistance in the mid-1970s, and annual infusions of $1.3 billion in military aid beginning in 1987. By one authoritative account, US assistance covered most of Egypt's costs associated with procuring American weapons systems.[61] This apparent dependence bred the belief that Washington could use the money it sent to the Ministry of Defense as an instrument of behavior modification. Beginning in 2005, when Congressman Tom Lantos (D-CA), who was a founder and longtime co-chair of the Congressional

Human Rights Caucus, proposed shifting $325 million from Egypt's military assistance to the economic support it received from Washington, seven efforts were made in eleven years to cut or withhold this aid; none had been made in the previous two decades. Each of the proposed measures was based on the premise that threatening something as important as security assistance would compel the Egyptians to undertake reforms. At the very least, it would signal to Cairo that Washington was serious about promoting democracy and implementing a foreign policy consistent with the values and ideals that Americans lived by at home. The proposition was never tested, however, either because bills never made it out of committee or because the George W. Bush administration signed waivers attesting to potential damage to US national security by withholding military assistance to Egypt.[62]

Proponents of leverage often invoked the case of Saad Eddin Ibrahim, an Egyptian-American academic and democracy activist who won his release from an Egyptian prison after Bush refused to consider Hosni Mubarak's request for supplementary security assistance. Was this a one-off event or could the copious amounts of aid the United States had supplied to Egypt be used to promote change? Some advocates of what was referred to as conditionality thought so, arguing that Washington's reluctance to use aid as leverage was needlessly hampering its ability to promote change. Fears that the Egyptians would retaliate were overblown. Would Egypt really deny the US military overflight rights if Washington withheld or cut aid? After the July 2013 coup, the debate over the continuation of aid grew more intense given the legal and moral concerns associated with American taxpayer assistance to Egypt's new military leadership.[63] These arguments made sense, but they often failed to take into consideration or downplayed two important factors. First, Washington actually received something for its investment in the Egyptian armed forces, namely, fast-track access for its warships through the Suez Canal and other logistical support that proved valuable to US military efforts in Iraq, in Afghanistan, and later against the Islamic State. Under these circumstances, the Department of Defense—an important interest group—and members of Congress who regarded the war against terrorism as Washington's top priority remained reluctant to risk picking a fight with the Egyptians over democracy. Second, and more important, to the extent that Egyptians framed the post-Mubarak political struggle in terms of identity, the stakes became critical. The political forces in the country involved in the battle had their own conception of an allegedly authentic Egyptian way of life and worldview they were fighting to preserve. Under these circumstances, it was hard for external actors, even those thought to be uniquely influential, such as the United States, to say or do anything to alter the decision making of Egypt's leaders. Washington had made a strong statement condemning the conduct of Egypt's security forces after the Battle of the Cabinet Building in 2011 and noted its concern when authorities rounded up and arrested employees of various NGOs in 2012—including Americans, among them the son of then secretary of transportation Ray LaHood, who was forced to hide in the US embassy for thirty-four days. These protestations had no effect on the way Field Marshal Mohammed Hussein al-Tantawi and the Supreme Council of the Armed Forces administered the country. After the July 2013 coup, the White House docked Egypt's military aid—something no administration had ever done. This major step made no difference to the way Major General Abdel Fattah al-Sisi calculated his political interests. Repression continued. By the time the weapons systems were released to Egyptians in early 2015, it was clear that their delay made Egypt neither less unstable nor more democratic.[64] A good moral case was to be made for suspending aid to Egypt, but policymakers needed to understand that it would actually do little to alter Egypt's behavior.

In the late 1950s, Premier Nikita Khrushchev of the Soviet Union voiced concerns about the treatment of the Egyptian Communist Party; Egyptian president Gamal Abdel Nasser, however, brushed these off as a violation of Egypt's sovereignty.[65] Mubarak approached George W. Bush's push for democratic change in much the same way. This problem has only been accentuated during the Sisi era. Egypt may be paradigmatic of this problematic dynamic, but the situation is also present in Turkey, Tunisia, and Libya, hampering any effort by America—or any other power or combination of them—to have an effect on these internal struggles or the path these countries eventually follow.

LITTLE TO DO ABOUT A LOT

The level and scale of violence buffeting the Middle East has been unprecedented. The actual or potential failure of four states—Libya, Syria, Iraq, and Yemen—the related matters concerning the exercise of Iranian power, the threat of the Islamic State, and resurgent authoritarianism have led to calls from places as disparate as Jerusalem, Riyadh, Abu Dhabi, and the United States Congress for "American leadership." It was hard to know exactly what this meant, especially because in the United States these entreaties were intertwined with presidential politics and President Barack Obama's effort to shape his legacy. In general, however, they revolved around different notions about how to deal with the conflict in Syria, the breakdown of the state in Iraq, rolling back Iran's influence, and combating the Islamic State. For Washington's Middle Eastern allies, American leadership meant bringing down the Assad regime, unconditionally supporting Abdel Fattah al-Sisi in Egypt, and eschewing a nuclear deal with Iran.

Obama was not prepared to pursue these policies because, from his and his advisors' perspectives, they amounted to "stupid shit" that did little to advance what had become Washington's policy priority in the Middle East: combating the Islamic State. Still unwilling to commit large ground forces to the fight, the administration securitized its relations with those in the area. Two problems were inherent to this approach, however. First, most of its allies in the region were decidedly ambivalent about fighting the Islamic State. Saudi Arabia and the United Arab Emirates were more engaged in prosecuting a war against Houthi tribesmen in Yemen whom Riyadh and Abu Dhabi insisted were doing Iranian bidding. Both Saudi and Emirati officials warned of the Hezbollah-ization of Yemen and as a result focused their military resources and diplomatic attention there.[66] The clerical establishment in Saudi Arabia bolstered the war effort with anti-Iran—actually anti-Shia—propaganda that at times tracked closely to the Islamic State's discourse. The Jordanians stepped up their air strikes against the Islamic State when it burned a Royal Jordanian Air Force pilot alive after his F-16 fighter plane crashed in Syria in late 2014, but the tempo of Jordan's operations decreased with time. Egypt wanted to combat the Islamic State, but it intended to combat only the group's affiliates in the Sinai Peninsula and Libya. When it came to Syria, the Egyptians actually supported Russia's intervention on behalf of Assad, calculating that this was the best way not only to defeat the extremists but also to forestall a post-Assad Syria in which that country's branch of the Muslim Brotherhood could likely play an important role. As far as the Turks were concerned, Kurdish nationalism, which the Syrian conflict boosted, was a more immediate threat than the Islamic State. In addition, Ankara argued that Washington's anti–Islamic State strategy was not enough. From the Turks' perspective, the best way to defeat Abu Bakr al-Baghdadi's caliphate was regime change in Syria, where the Islamic State had fed off the chaos and bloodshed of the civil war. Ankara needed to be cautious; it was geographically close to Raqqa and Mosul, and it had permitted extremists to flow across its border with Syria and back in its effort to harm the Syrian government. If Turkey committed itself to the fight against the Islamic State, it would be an easy target for retaliation.

Second, Washington's air strikes against the Islamic State and its coordination with friendly forces on the ground—mostly Iraqi and Syrian Kurds, as well as elements of the Iraqi Security Forces—were critical to countering the threat that Baghdadi's forces represented, but these measures alone could only degrade the group's military capacity. That in and of itself was a good thing, but defeat was an entirely different story. Even if it had been US policy to "make the sand glow," the political and theological nature of the problem of the Islamic State made the statement empty rhetoric. The military component of the fight against the Islamic State was critical in keeping the group at bay and rolling back its territorial gains, but the Islamic State could only be defeated in the realm of ideas. As the United States itself proved when it killed Abu Musab al-Zarqawi, al-Qaeda of the Arabian Peninsula's Anwar al-Awlaki, and Osama bin Laden, warheads and bullets are extraordinarily effective and efficient ways to kill people, but they do not kill sentiment. It is hard to imagine what message the United States can bring to bear in this intra-Muslim and intra-Arab struggle that could contribute to the group's defeat. Washington has proven that it can fight ideological battles—the United States defeated Nazism and communism—but that does not mean it can play the same role in the war of ideas with the Islamic State. Without a doubt, the United States stands for important and universal values, but it is ill-equipped in the ideological campaign against the terror group largely because American policymakers have proven time and again that they do not understand the Arab and Muslim worlds. More important, Washington's vision, which is based on a specific version of the American experience, does not resonate with those attracted to what the Islamic State has to offer and is thus not a potent alternative to its grand religious and political project. In the mid-2000s, Washington's message about democracy had some impact, but never as much as supporters of the Freedom Agenda had hoped it would. The Middle East in 2005 was also a very different place from the one it had become in 2015.

That decade was critical in both good ways and bad. About half-way through, Arabs rose up and demanded economic, political, and social change. A few years later, Turks vented their anger at a leader and ruling party that emulated the politics and tactics of recently deposed Arab dictators. Roughly five years after these events, countries in the Middle East seemed no closer to democracy than before Mohammed al-Bouazizi took his own life. Since that time, American officials have wrestled with Tunisia's fragile transition, Egypt's resurgent authoritarianism, Turkey's deliberalization, and Libya's fragmentation. The result has consistently been frustration. This is because of both the nature of the problems and the expectations that Washington sets in the way it talks about them. Obama's May 2011 declaration that "after decades of accepting the world as it is in the region, we have a chance to pursue the world as it should be" captures a quintessentially American ideal about the world, Washington's role in it, and the desire to help people realize their dreams of democracy. This was the reason for the stream of unsatisfying reports, recommendations, and proposals coming from the American foreign policy establishment.

As noted, it was actually Obama who expressed caution during that moment of enthusiasm in the spring of 2011 about Washington's role in the region. When that moment morphed into one of profound pessimism, the question before officials remained essentially the same as it had been five years earlier: what should the United States do? The easy answer is to recycle the litany of "Washington musts" and the "United States shoulds," propose a regional investment bank, encourage the growth of small and medium enterprises, and devise new ways to cooperate with international partners to support change. Perhaps some of this might help, which would be a good thing, but against the backdrop of the actual political dynamics roiling Tunisia, Egypt, Libya, and Turkey, they seem beside the point. It would be better for American officials and the policy community to recognize that there is not much for the United States to do. This is a difficult proposition to accept given the turbulence, authoritarianism, and bloodshed that is the daily fare of headlines coming from these countries. Even if good news does come from Tunisia—the last refuge for optimists in an environment of failure—the overall trend is uncertainty and instability.

The underlying reasons for the parlous state of politics—the non-revolutions of the region, sticky institutions, and identity—should inform US policy in the region. Under these circumstances, it seems clear that the high-stakes struggles under way in the Middle East are so great that their resolution is well beyond the tools of American diplomacy. Consequently, the United States should not even try to resolve them. This is not a cultural argument about the suitability of Arabs and Muslims to democracy. Instead, it reflects the reality that US policy can accomplish little in a political environment where it is at best a bit player. What can the United States offer Tunisians in the bitter fight to overcome the legacies of Habib Bourguiba and Zine al-Abidine Ben Ali? Or to Egyptians who are engaged in an iteration of a struggle they have been waging since the late nineteenth century? Does Washington have the answer to Turkey's complex and connected layers of political contestation related to secularism, religiosity, Turkishness, Kurdishness, republicanism, and Ottomanism? How can Americans put Libya back together? The problems are daunting; in fact, for the United States they are too difficult, if not impossible. The responsibility for answers to them lies squarely with Arabs and Turks.

It will nevertheless be hard for American policymakers to stop talking about democracy. It is part of the American identity running from the Boston Tea Party and President Franklin D. Roosevelt's 1940 declaration that the United States "must be a great arsenal of democracy" to President Ronald Reagan's Westminster Speech in June 1982, the Clinton administration's democratic enlargement, and, of course, George W. Bush's Freedom Agenda. Yet policymakers would do well to recognize that the conditions for democratic change do not currently exist and Washington can do little to forge them from Arab and Turkish societies. As the Iraq war and the uprisings demonstrated, these conditions come from within.

The United States can do some things, however. It can uphold—at least rhetorically—the principles and values that Obama laid out in his remarks at the State Department in May 2011, along with the sense of humility he expressed that day. Had his administration emphasized nonviolence, tolerance, pluralism, accountability, and the equal application of the law, Tunisia, Egypt, Libya, and Turkey would still look the way they do, but at the barest minimum, Washington would have avoided the worst of all possible worlds in which virtually all the players in these countries harbor profound mistrust toward the United States. Current and former policymakers often protest how hard it is to be consistent, but in the tumult that is the present (and likely future) Middle East, unwavering public support for first-order principles would likely serve Washington best. This may sound suspiciously similar to some of the airy-fairy policy recommendations outlined earlier. It surely is. Emphasizing basic principles will not make Middle Eastern democracies, but it is also cost-free and consistent with American values. That is worth something in a region where people tend to view Washington as a peddler of pernicious double standards.

The United States still has an opportunity to invest in the Middle East's future, but not through the good governance and democracy promotion programs of the recent past that have not worked. Scarce resources are better spent on the kind of technical assistance programs that improve the daily lives of people. This would be hard in Libya, where central authority is fractured and likely permanently impaired, and in Turkey, where development assistance ended long ago. Investments in agriculture, education, and public health can have a profound, though often unseen, impact on politics. History is never a blueprint for the future, but it does offer insights into the present. When British colonial officials in Egypt instituted a series of administrative, agricultural, and educational reforms beginning in the 1880s, it had an important, but unintended effect, on Egypt's masses. A new technocratic class emerged. It was this group of new professionals, relatively wealthier farmers, and administrators that formed the crucible of Egypt's nationalist movement. The analogy is not perfect, but wealthier, healthier, and better-educated populations may be in a better position to demand change and, unlike the last five years, achieve it. Nothing is guaranteed, of course. The path dependencies of authoritarian institutions and identity politics will likely have a negative impact on the Middle East for years to come. These ideas for US policy are deeply unsatisfying, especially given the magnitude and scale of the problems in the Middle East. Yet in the complex reality of the region, beyond America's control, policymakers need to think small and patiently wait for the world to turn again. This leaves the bottom-line question concerning America's core interests in the Middle East—oil, Israel, and ensuring that no country dominates the region—along with two derivatives of these interests, counterterrorism and nonproliferation. Rethinking these interests or reconsidering how best to achieve them is long overdue, especially given the turbulence and tumult of the region. Yet that debate would require political will and foresight that are presently in short supply in the United States. Even if that conversation could be had, it is likely that the United States would still be committed to securing these interests but would seek to do so in different ways. In the interim, the uncertain politics of the Middle East will force Washington to improvise as it tries to salvage what it can from a fractured regional order. If the last five years are any measure, however, American policymakers will continue to find themselves in the profoundly awkward position of rhetorically supporting progressive change in Egypt while working with a military and leadership that rejects liberalizing reform, of reintervening in Libya, standing by as Turkey's Justice and Development Party continues to limit political contestation, and holding Tunisia out as a shining example of success. Of course, policymakers have a choice, but it would mean forsaking either security interests, which have always been paramount, or their public commitment to democratic development. It seems that neither the Obama administration nor its successor would be willing to make that choice.

The inevitable result will be more of the policy improvisation and contradictions of the Obama years no matter what politicians say on the campaign trail about the need for American leadership. The idea that the Middle East just needs leadership is oversold and half-baked. With the exception of Iraq, the Middle East looks the way it does because of the outcomes that people who live there have produced. The region has always been hard for outsiders to manage short of suffocating force; it is now harder. The revolutions that were not to be, a cadre of leaders intent on leveraging political institutions for their own interests, and a prevailing sense of failure and disorientation have fueled unprecedented instability and violence. These may not be "rooted in conflicts that go back a millennia" as Obama erroneously indicated in his last State of the Union address, but that still does not mean that their outcome depends on what Washington does.[67] That is because what ails the Middle East has less to do with the United States than Washington's political class and the foreign policy establishment are inclined to believe. Policymakers should get used to it because it will likely be the story of the Middle East for at least a generation to come.

6

Freedom Interrupted

JULY 19, 2012. THE line at passport control at Istanbul's Atatürk International Airport was long, way too long. Atatürk, or IST, as frequent visitors have come to know it, was once a "gloriously modern, efficient airport for a country with big ambitions. It had reached well beyond its capacity and become a frustrating slog over the past decade, though."[1] During that time Turkish Airlines had become a virtual arm of the Turkish Foreign Ministry, adding service wherever the ruling Justice and Development Party (AKP) wanted to flex its muscles or open a market, but especially throughout the Middle East, North Africa, and East Africa. The expansion pushed the arrivals and departure halls to the breaking points, but the Turkish leadership liked the idea of transforming IST into a global crossroads like the airports in London, Frankfurt, Dubai, New York, and Singapore, so the people kept coming. As difficult as it had become to navigate the sea of humanity splayed out across long hallways, eateries, and departure lounges to get to or from a flight, the airport was actually one of those places where the ethnic, religious, and national differences among travelers faded away in common pursuit of Johnnie Walker Black, Toblerone chocolate, Mavi Jeans, Dolce and Gabbana sunglasses, and Turkish delight.

The hustle and bustle of Istanbul's airport no doubt pleased the leaders of the AKP who not only saw it as an economic engine but as an expression of their worldview. Since it emerged from a split within Turkey's Islamist movement in the summer of 2001, the party had portrayed itself as open to the world, business friendly, Europe-ready, and a leader in the Arab and Muslim worlds. The Islamist old guard had also spoken fancifully about the latter goal, but in the AKP's decade-long rule it had delivered and made Ankara a player in the Middle East in ways Turkish elites had previously shunned in favor of a West-oriented approach to the world. In this newly discovered prestige, the AKP connected the Ottoman era, Turkey's present, and its future. Almost a century after the dissolution of the Ottoman sultanate in 1922, a newly confident Turkish leadership, riding high on economic and political success at home, sought to position itself as a moral force, economic driver, and political power in the Muslim, but particularly Arab, world. There was no better reflection of this than then foreign minister Ahmet Davutoğlu's declarations to the Grand National Assembly in April 2012:

> A new Middle East is emerging ... We will continue to be the master, the leader and the servant of this new Middle East. In the new Middle East the aspirations of the people and justice will rule; not tyranny, oppression and dictatorships. And we will be a strong defender of this voice. And a new zone of peace, stability and prosperity will emerge around Turkey.[2]

The Arab uprisings and the way Turkey was positioning itself to lead the region seemed to be the fulfillment of the AKP's ambitions that all the talk among Western elites about the so-called Turkish model only reinforced. In the afterglow of the uprisings, Istanbul became a place for Arabs to learn how to build new political systems. The city's hotels were jammed with conferences—the names of which all seemed to be "Turkey, the Arab World, and the Emerging Democratic Future"—in which the AKP imparted to Arab Middle Easterners the sources of Turkey's success. Wending their way through the rope line at passport control that morning was a polyglot group of Libyans, Tunisians, Egyptians, and Iraqis. A fair number of Saudis were also visiting on holiday.

About thirty minutes into the wait, an editor with *Foreign Policy* magazine emailed: "Do you want to write an article about Omar Suleiman?" It seemed a curious non sequitur. Suleiman had been very quiet since the Presidential Election Commission disqualified him from running for Egypt's president in the spring. What was the sudden interest in an article on him? "Thanks, Dave. Just landed in IST. I'd love to do something on Omar some time, but I've got some other ideas I'd like to bat around with you." The reply came almost immediately: "Steven, he is dead." The news was a little staggering, another "holy moly" moment among many during the previous eighteen months. Hosni Mubarak's intelligence chief, consigliere, and (very briefly) vice president had been a gracious host on a number of occasions in Cairo the previous few years. He was the power center and the man who was (in his own words) "responsible for the stability of Egypt." On the evening before the January 25 uprising he insisted to a group of visitors, "Tunisia can never happen here." In the hubbub of the crowded airport, with three Libyans yammering away in the background eager to attend whatever meeting to which they had been invited, Zine al-Abidine Ben Ali tucked away in Saudi Arabia, Syria burning, Yemen cracking, and a Muslim Brother set up at Egypt's Ittihadiyya Palace, Omar Suleiman's passing seemed the final and definitive marker of the end of one historical moment and the beginning of another.

Looking back, it all seems dream-like. Not just the Turkish swagger, the misbegotten Turkish model fixation, the giddy Libyans, but the entire era, if it can be called that. Egypt's Facebookers and bloggers, Mohammed al-Bouazizi, Khaled Said, Tahrir Square, brave Libyan fighters advancing on Tripoli, the Girl in the Blue Bra, and Gezi Park's girl in the red dress are of a recent but seemingly distant past—a gauzy sequence of determination, defiance, hope, and activism that has not been extinguished as much as eclipsed by political uncertainty, instability, and at times unspeakable violence.[3] In Egypt, the death of Khaled Said in 2010 at the hands of policemen embodied a police state run amok and contributed to the uprising six months later, but there have been thousands of Khaled Saids since. In Istanbul, Gezi Park seems a forlorn symbol of a country with no checks and balances on the ruling party's exercise of power. Tunisia's Avenue Habib Bourguiba, from which the Ministry of Interior keeps a watchful eye, represents a country on edge. And Benghazi, which the West saved from Muammar al-Qaddafi so that its activists and revolutionaries could build a better country, is thick with rival militias and violent extremists. New authoritarians and techno-savvy terrorists have replaced techno-savvy revolutionaries as the makers of politics in the "new Middle East."

The blame for this state of affairs does and does not lie with the likes of Abdel Fattah al-Sisi, Recep Tayyip Erdoğan, countless Libyan militia leaders and extremists, and Beji Caid Essebsi. If any of them were better people, perhaps Egypt, Turkey, and Libya would be better places. Tunisia is better but is not a success, and its advantages are tenuous. It is a terrorist outrage or some other disaster away from a setback. There was also the reality that leaders around the Middle East harbored worldviews that were antithetical to what the uprisings and the Gezi Park protests stood for. At the same time, these figures cannot be held solely responsible for the nature of politics in their respective countries. They have certainly had help from feckless oppositions, bloodthirsty extremists, and indifferent world powers. In an important way, however, no one is directly responsible. The Middle East looks the way it does because the confluence of uprisings (not revolutions), institutions or lack of them, and the search for identity and authenticity have conspired to thwart the dreams of a democratic Middle East. Sisi, Erdoğan, Essebsi, and various Libyans have both driven politics and responded to the incentives and constraints the political environment has produced, calculating their interests accordingly.

This is a difficult reality to confront, especially for those who fervently believed in the power of street politics to change their world. Just when that moment so many had been waiting for arrived in Egypt and Libya, it disappeared. The long, hot summer of tear gas in Gezi Park had little impact on the prospects of the AKP, which remains firmly in control. Tunisians avoided the brink, but terrorism and economic collapse threaten to undo what gains—no matter how modest—Tunisia has achieved. That transitions to democracy in the Middle East have failed seems obvious. Yet a valiant optimism and brave defiance remain among those activists, democrats, and liberals who live in the region and perceive positive developments where there are few or none. Hounded, jailed, killed, or on the run, their message to the world is "Don't give up on us; the revolution is not over." They still are not afraid. Much has been written about how the uprisings broke the ability of leaders to instill the fear in their populations that is central to the durability of authoritarian rule. This new courage is purportedly matched with a newfound willingness to question authority figures and the principles they espouse. This is a nice story, but it is largely ahistoric. It is true that the toppling of dictators and the region-wide nature of the unrest was unprecedented, but the uprisings themselves were not a new phenomenon in the region. The Middle East has known fear but also periodic revolts. Arabs have always found ways to critique their leaders and the political systems they oversee, whether through politics, art, satire, soccer, journalism, blogging, or some other form of protest. The trope that Arabs were docile until Tunisia's uprisings was just that, a trope.

What, then, will the Middle East look like? This is the question now being asked over muffins, bagels, and weak coffee in the conference rooms of Beltway consultancies across Northern Virginia. It is also no different from the question intelligence analysts and regional experts tangled with in mid-December 2010, just days before the Middle East that everyone had come to know seemed to come to an end. It is unclear why with the humbling hindsight of time anyone would hazard to answer this question. Predictions of stability were upended with the uprisings, which gave way to a moment of enthusiasm that rendered the Middle East's spring of 2011 to be France's 1789, Europe's 1848, or Eastern Europe's 1989. None of these analogies offered any useful insight into what was or would happen in the region. Even after the enthusiasm began to wane, when would-be reformers acted like the authoritarians they were and the body count began to rise, few imagined that countries would fail and that the dominant story of the region would be extremism rather than democracy. This did not mean that democracy would not or could never happen. Rather, the romantic and enthusiastic zeitgeist of 2011 and 2012 had shifted to a darker, more pessimistic view of what would unfold in the Middle East. That was the easy call to make with ugly authoritarian politics in Egypt and Turkey, and Libya's continued descent into chaos with multiple political and military forces vying for control. Then there was Tunisia, where people hoped all the goodwill from abroad would translate into economic opportunity, the government could break out of its immobility, the homegrown extremist problem would be kept at bay, and the armed forces would succeed in keeping out instability on the country's borders. Further afield, blood continued to flow in copious quantities in Syria, Iraq, and Yemen.

Even as there are those who remained committed to the idea that the violence, uncertainty, and malaise of the politically murky present would give way to a new dawn, there are three critical factors that challenge this faith: the non-revolutionary nature of the uprisings, the way leaders have leveraged institutions and their stickiness, and the search for identity among many in the region. The combination has undermined the dream of just and democratic political systems, and instead unleashed instability and violence.

THAT VISION THING

Egypt's July 3, 2013, coup d'état was confounding. To the great acclaim of Egyptians just a few years earlier, the military helped oust Hosni Mubarak. Egyptians then voted for Muslim Brotherhood parliamentary candidates in large numbers. They also voted—thirteen million of them—for the Brotherhood's Mohammed Morsi to be Egypt's first post-Mubarak president. They then turned out in astonishingly large numbers to oppose Morsi a year later, ushering in the military's intervention, which was welcomed in so many Egyptian quarters as something that can only be described as akin to the grace of God. In the course of thirty months, the officers had gone from saviors to counterrevolutionaries to saviors again. The esteem with which Egyptians held the officer corps was best explained by the previous six decades of hopes and disappointments as well as the polarization and near chaos that marked Egypt under Morsi and the Brotherhood. Since the 1952 coup that ousted King Farouk and established Egypt as an Arab republic, the armed forces have been Egypt's state builder, liberator, and redeemer. Almost exactly six decades later, Abdel Fattah al-Sisi and his fellow officers held out the same hopes for the Egyptians. In their self-proclaimed reset of the country's democratic transition, the officer corps promised to bring stability, prosperity, and dignity to Egypt. Whether conscious or not, Sisi's implicit and explicit references to the era of Gamal Abdel Nasser when there was a modicum of economic opportunity and national powers were telling. Egypt's past greatness was central to its future accomplishments under a new great man in uniform. One could understand why Egyptians were willing to give themselves over to Sisi and the armed forces, but his vision for Egypt was a burden because neither the past nor the future were what Egyptians imagined them to be.

As the Sisi era has unfolded, he found that the commitments he made to Egyptians upon coming to power were extraordinarily difficult to keep. A gap quickly emerged between what Sisi told people about their daily lives and the way people were actually experiencing life. The Egyptian leadership sought to compensate for this difference with a propaganda campaign that could only be described as "Sisi-mania," which went well beyond the billboards and posters of the "great man" that are de rigueur in so many parts of the Middle East to include Sisi sandwiches, Sisi candy, Sisi pajamas, Sisi lingerie, Sisi cologne, Sisi T-shirts, and Sisi ringtones. All of this went with odes to the great man in the government-affiliated press and video paeans to Sisi and the armed forces.[4] Yet had the legitimacy of the coup and Sisi's rule never been questioned, this garish and, in a way, humiliating display of obsequiousness and fealty, much of which the government itself manufactured, would not have been needed.

The Egyptians also employed various degrees and forms of coercion. The primary targets of state violence were the Muslim Brotherhood and extremists, but they were not the only ones. The significant discrepancies between Sisi's public pronouncements about stability, economic opportunity, and governance and the country's bleak reality only reinforced Egypt's authoritarianism. Students, journalists, academics, and activists of all stripes were remanded to prison for highlighting or raising their voices in protest over the state's violence, corruption, and incompetence that wasted lives and resources. The profoundly repressive state of Egypt's politics exceeded anything under Mubarak, but the underlying patterns of politics and the means of establishing control were largely the same.

At a superficial level Turkey provides a contrast to Egypt's pathological authoritarianism. The Justice and Development Party's (AKP) vision for Turkey's future was an integral component of its long successful run. The party's emphasis on Muslim values, prosperity, and national power resonated deeply with its core constituency and beyond. It was liberating for Turks to celebrate themselves and their own historical legacies in the way that the AKP deemphasized Kemalism and its obsession with Western culture in favor of a highly specific and favorable interpretation of the Ottoman era. President Recep Tayyip Erdoğan reversed the long-running narrative concerning Turkey's desire to be part of the West, essentially telling his fellow citizens that if the Europeans wanted to leave Turks knocking on the gates of Vienna, then it was their loss. It also helped Erdoğan that Turkey's other political parties proved incapable of crafting their own vision for the future, but this would have given the AKP less of an advantage had the party not also delivered. That Turks felt wealthier, perceived the growing global and regional importance of Ankara, and were permitted to explore their Muslim identities reinforced the AKP's worldview and contributed to its success. What Erdoğan told Turks—at least the pluralities who voted for his party—about themselves, their country, and their society was consistent with the way they experienced it.

Yet all was not well in Turkey. The Turkish media environment reflected the fact that the AKP's vision, despite the party's consistent electoral success, was not hegemonic. Had it been, there would have been no purpose for the virtual ministry of information that the party forged out of various newspapers and television networks that reliably reproduced Erdoğan's version of events and crowded out the remaining few outlets with alternate editorial lines. The AKP had come tantalizingly close to winning 50 percent of the popular vote in 2007, 2011, and the November 2015 redo of the general election, but it seemed unable to push beyond that threshold. Consequently, Turkey's leaders governed the almost-half of the country that voted for them and intimidated the rest. Erdoğan threatened the big business community unless they were willing to support him, hammered away at the idea that those who opposed him were either terrorists or not authentic Turks, packed the courts, purged the bureaucracy, sued his critics, and after the failed July 2016 coup d'état, widened his war on the Gülenists. It was a cruel irony that Erdoğan deployed tactics against his opponents that have roots in the political system the AKP vowed to change when it came to office in 2002.

Tunisia had not experienced the kind of resurgent authoritarianism that had become a fact of life in Egypt and Turkey, but its leaders were caught within the pressures of secularism, Islamism, and democracy that had an impact on the quality of Tunisian politics. A new constitution and successful elections in 2014 were bright spots, but those who questioned provisions of the anti-terrorism law, the draft financial reconciliation bill, or the continuing lack of opportunity confronted the heavy hand of the Ministry of Interior just as they had during Zine al-Abidine Ben Ali's rule. The flare-up of protests on the fifth anniversary of Ben Ali's departure in Tunisia's south-central region, including Sidi Bouzid, Kasserine in the west, and Bizerte on the north coast, and the security forces' response to these demonstrations underscored how little things had actually changed. A significant part of Tunisia's problem was the inability of the country's leaders to offer a powerful and widely shared vision for the country's future, which accentuated the underlying distrust among the country's political actors and their supporters.

In 2016, as Tunisia reeled from a series of terrorist attacks, Rachid al-Ghannouchi, the leader of the Islamist Ennahda Movement, declared that the answer to the extremist phenomenon was more democracy.[5] The underlying logic of his argument that a just and open political system was an elixir for extremism was straightforward, though flawed. Tunisians, who made up a surprisingly large contingent of the self-declared Islamic State's cadres, were not fighting because Tunisia needed more democracy. For the ideologically committed, both democracy and authoritarianism were fatally flawed given that both systems place human laws above God. Ghannouchi's argument worked better at a level of abstraction, however. The failures of the Middle East's uprisings to produce decent political systems and the concomitant bloodshed accentuated conflicts over identity that Abu Bakr al-Baghdadi and his followers purported to have resolved within the territory of the Islamic State. Democracy was the solution, according to Ghannouchi, because representative political systems would offer dignity, citizenship, and a sense of belonging that would blunt the appeal of the Islamic State and other groups. This would certainly be a positive development, but given the circumstances under which Ghannouchi made his statement, it seemed like the plea of a man whose worldview remained powerful but its realization frustratingly out of reach.

Tunisians had voted for his Ennahda in large numbers but gave an even larger percentage of votes to Beji Caid Essebsi's decidedly secular

Nidaa Tounes. It mattered a lot for Tunisian politics that the party imploded in late 2015 and early 2016, but its previous dynamism revealed a weakness at the core of Ghannouchi's vision: for an apparently large number of Tunisians, the linkage between Ennahda's version of Islamism and democracy did not make sense. As a result, in May 2016, Ghannouchi announced that the Ennahda Movement was no longer interested in advancing an Islamist agenda. The failure to articulate a vision was not Ghannouchi's alone, however. The European-leftist-inspired secularism of a variety of other parties and the main labor union also seemed alien to a significant number of Tunisians. Perhaps this was healthy, creating an overall balance of political forces that prevented any single group from imposing its will on others. It was also a prescription for political deadlock and policy drift, which plagued admirably broad-based but weak governments as the patience of Tunisians wore thin and cynicism crept in.

No one in Libya could offer a vision of either a centralized system of government or federalism, in which sovereignty is shared by a central government and regions, that would be acceptable to all parties concerned. The international community merely hoped for some semblance of a government in the 2015 national unity agreement. That there was a political process in Libya was a testament to the fact that some people supported unity and disliked the extremism that had become embedded in the country's landscape, but the politics had proven over and over again quite different from Libya's fragmented reality. Perhaps it would take the forty years that Saif al-Islam al-Qaddafi had warned about before an agreement could be reached among warring factions, or perhaps some group would emerge powerful enough to disarm the others. This was, after all, how the Taliban emerged in Afghanistan in the 1990s.

AUTHORITARIAN INSTABILITY

This image of the Middle East feels both old and new, but in what ways? Without a doubt Libya's fragmentation represents an important change, but it is the result of a condition that has existed in Libyan politics for some time in which the informal affiliations of tribe and region outweigh all others—a dynamic that Muammar al-Qaddafi's fall accentuated. Turkey seems just as far, if not farther, from democracy than it did two decades ago.[6] Abdel Fattah al-Sisi is not Hosni Mubarak, but the way he has sought to establish control and the nature of politics in Egypt are both reminiscent of what is commonly referred to as the old order and, in ways, exceed the coercion that was common to the previous era. Tunisia might emerge with a more just and democratic political system, but, overall, authoritarianism will likely be a persistent feature of the region more broadly.

The Middle East will also be chronically and violently unstable. This seems to be a new factor in the region, but only the scale of this instability is novel. As proponents of democracy promotion consistently argued in the 2000s, the authoritarian stability of the region was actually no stability at all. It was merely a false sense that leaders had the ability to deflect and undermine demands from below for change. Tunisia, Egypt, Libya, and Turkey have long been ideologically rich, politically contested, and occasionally quite violent. The first two factors are now manifest in spades and violence has sadly become a part of life for Tunisians, Egyptians, Libyans, and Turks. Thus, the defining features of the new era in the Middle East will be resurgent authoritarianism and sustained instability, but that should surprise no one.

For all of the analytic attention on change in the Middle East since late 2010, the underlying pathologies of politics in the Middle East remain remarkably similar to the world that existed then. The Arab uprisings and the Gezi Park protests were extraordinary moments to witness. In a variety of ways, they were deeply moving and transformative personally. After eighteen days in Tahrir Square, a passionate and dedicated member of the Muslim Brotherhood confided that he felt he had more in common with the Coptic Christians and liberal young women whom he encountered during the demonstrations than with his own organization's leadership. If only that sense of unity had lasted—but it was never actually meant to be. The awe and overwhelming sense of hope in Ashraf Swelam's question "What could be wrong?" and his own inspiring answer of "We are now free" was no match for the realities of the Middle East. What leaders left behind in their wake, the institutions available to new ones, and the still unsettled questions of identity conspired to thwart the dreams of so many. The dawn that first broke in Tunisia, promising a new era, proved to be a false one.

That activists, democrats, liberals, and would-be revolutionaries made mistakes is a given, but they were beaten almost from the start. Their collective failure was itself a product of the authoritarianism they resist. Tunisians, Egyptians, Libyans, and Turks seem to have now collectively awakened with a start to the realization that the future will likely be no better than when Mohammed al-Bouazizi struck the match.

NOTES

―――◆―――

Introduction
1. Tamimi, *Rachid Ghannouchi*, 72.
2. Malinowski, "Jefferson in Benghazi." This was an idea repeated in Washington through much of 2011 and 2012.
3. Tillman, "Sultanism or Not?"
4. Skocpol, *States and Social Revolutions*, 5.
5. Cook, "Middle Eastern Revolutions."

Chapter 1
1. Presidential Daily Brief, "Bin Ladin Determined to Strike."
2. The narrative of Bouazizi's self-immolation has come under intense scrutiny in the years since. For a greater discussion on this, see Sulaiman, "Spectacle and Soundscape."
3. Kuran, "Now Out of Never," 12–13; see also Kurzman, *Unthinkable Revolution*.
4. Kuran, "Now Out of Never," 12–13.
5. Kuran, "Now Out of Never," 22.
6. Clinton, "Recent Events in Tunisia."
7. At the time of Ben Ali's departure rumors circulated that he had hopscotched around the Mediterranean from France to Italy to Malta seeking refuge. Some speculation even suggested that he was headed to Montreal, where his daughter and son-in-law owned a home. No direct evidence attests to any of this being true. It is most likely that Ben Ali intended to go directly to Saudi Arabia all along. It is true that the Maltese government allowed Ben Ali's plane passage through its airspace and a

Foreign Ministry spokesperson is reported to have told journalists that it was headed north. This could have been a misstatement or might have been misunderstood. It is likely that the spokesperson meant to say that the plane was flying through Malta's northern airspace. If Ben Ali had sought asylum in either France or Italy, there would have been no reason for his aircraft to be in the vicinity of Malta, though passage through or near Maltese airspace is consistent with flight patterns from Tunis to Jeddah.

8. Crowley, "Daily Press Briefing."
9. Reuters, "U.S. Urges Restraint in Egypt."
10. Clinton, "Remarks," Doha, Qatar.
11. Clinton, "Interview with David Gregory"; "Interview with Chris Wallace"; "Interview with Candy Crowley"; "Interview with Bob Schieffer."
12. Obama, "Remarks by the President on Egypt."
13. Obama, "On a New Beginning."
14. Albright, Weber, and Cook, *Support of Arab Democracy*.
15. This is a large literature spanning decades. For a compilation of the contemporary debate, see Brown, Lynn-Jones, and Miller, *Debating the Democratic Peace*; Snyder, *Voting to Violence*.
16. US Department of State, "The Middle East Partnership Initiative Story."
17. Daalder and Lindsay, *America Unbound*, chapter 9.
18. Haass, *War of Necessity*.
19. Wehner, "Slap Heard Round the World."
20. Krauthammer, "From Baghdad to Benghazi."
21. Pew Research Center, "A Year after Iraq War"; University of Maryland and Zogby International, *2009 Annual Arab Public Opinion Survey*, 19–20; International Republican Institute, "IRI Iraq Index," 1.
22. More recent polling indicates that since Krauthammer wrote, the Arab view of Iraq has not improved. In a 2014 Zogby poll, large pluralities of Jordanians, Saudis, and Iraqis themselves believed that the country would be worse off in five years. See Zogby, Zogby, and Zogby, "Today's Middle East."
23. Oppenheimer, *Exit Right*, 306–7.
24. Hitchens, "The Iraq Effect."
25. Hitchens, "The Iraq Effect."
26. Beaumont, "Truth about Twitter"; Ryan, "Anonymous and the Arab Uprisings"; Tapscott, "Social Media"; Saletan, "Springtime for Twitter."
27. Kristof, "We Are All Egyptians."
28. *Economist*, "The Awakening."
29. Abu Khalil, "Review"; Abu Khalil, "Reviewed Work"; Baker, "Understanding Egypt's Worldly Miracles"; Baker, *Sadat and After*, chapter 10; Boehlert, "Media's Favorite Arab Expert"; Falk, "Imperial Vibrations."
30. Ajami, "How the Arabs Turned Shame into Liberty."

31. *Economist*, "A Golden Opportunity?"; Feldman, "Islamists' Victory in Tunisia"; Khanfar, "Those Who Support Democracy"; Gerecht, "Islamist Road to Democracy"; Roy, "Muslim Brotherhood."

32. Salamé, "Where Are the Democrats?" 3.

33. Roy, "Islam," 13.

34. Johnson and Champion, "Egypt's Islamist Riddle."

35. *Economist*, "A Golden Opportunity?"

36. Moshiri, "Interview with Rachid Ghannouchi."

37. Özkan, "Turkey, Davutoglu and the Idea of Pan-Islamism."

38. Bush, "President Discusses Democracy"; Powell, "Powell Cites Opportunities."

39. Kalın, "Turkey and the Arab Spring."

40. Akyol, "Turkey's Maturing Foreign Policy."

41. Villelabeitia, "Can Arabs Learn."

42. Thomas, "In Turkey's Example."

43. Mead, "Erdogan's Big Fat Turkish Idea."

44. Albright, Hadley, and Cook, *U.S.-Turkey Relations*.

45. Khalidi, "Arab Spring."

46. Langohr, "Too Much Civil Society," 193.

47. Bayat, "New Arab Street."

48. Lipset, "Social Requisites of Democracy."

49. Sharp, "Egypt: Background and U.S. Relations."

50. Hudson, "Presidential Address 1987," 158–59.

51. Hudson, "Presidential Address 1987," 159.

52. Hudson, "Presidential Address 1987," 161.

53. Mortimer, "Islam and Multiparty Politics."

54. Dillman, "Transition to Democracy"; Hudson, "After the Gulf War," 414.

55. Quandt, *Ballots and Bullets*; Tahi, "Algeria's Democratisation Process."

56. Addi, "Algeria's Democracy," 36–38.

57. Cowell, "5 Killed in South Jordan."

58. Jordan, "Jordanian National Charter."

59. Hudson, "After the Gulf War," 419.

60. Amawi, "Democracy Dilemmas in Jordan."

61. Brumberg, "Arab Path to Democracy?" 125.

62. Rath, "Process of Democratization in Jordan," 534.

63. Hudson, "After the Gulf War," 408.

64. Koran, Brynen, and Noble, *Political Liberalization*; Norton, "Future of Civil Society"; Abu Khalil, "Viable Partnership," 22–23, 65; Boyd, "Democracy"; Al-Sayyid, "Slow Thaw"; Esposito and Piscatori, "Democratization and Islam"; Muslih and Norton, "Need for Arab Democracy"; Brumberg, "Arab Path to Democracy?"; Lesch, "Democracy in Doses."

65. Hudson, "After the Gulf War," 410.

66. For reassessments of the transition paradigm, see Carothers, "End of the Transition Paradigm"; Geddes, "What Do We Know?"

67. Lewis, "Roots of Muslim Rage"; Huntington, "Clash of Civilizations?"

68. Stacher, *Adaptable Autocrats*; Blaydes, *Elections and Distributive Politics*; Escribà-Folch and Wright, "Dealing with Tyranny"; Magaloni and Kricheli, "Political Order and One-Party Rule"; King, *The New Authoritarianism*; Ginsburg and Moustafa, *Rule by Law*; Albrecht, "Authoritarian Opposition"; Heydemann, "Social Pacts"; Lawson, "Intraregime Dynamics"; Brownlee, *Authoritarianism*; Stenner, *Authoritarian Dynamic*; Kassem, *Egyptian Politics*; Herb, "Princes and Parliaments"; Kienle, *Grand Delusion*; Gause, "Persistence of Monarchy"; Linz, *Totalitarian and Authoritarian Regimes*; Anderson, "Dynasts and Nationalists."

69. Brumberg, "Trap of Liberalized Autocracy"; writing a decade earlier, Gudrun Krämer offered similar insights about top-down liberalization, though his "Liberalization and Democracy in the Arab World" did not have the same broad impact as Brumberg's later work. See also Linz, "Transitions to Democracy."

70. Lust-Okar, "Divided They Rule," 159.

71. Wiktorowicz, "Civil Society as Social Control," 43.

72. Posusney, "Multiparty Elections in the Arab World."

73. Heydemann, "Upgrading Authoritarianism," 1.

74. Brownlee, "Yet They Persist," 36.

75. Bellin, "Robustness of Authoritarianism."

76. Rice, "Remarks at the American University."

77. Within six months of Secretary Rice's speech, the Bush administration pulled back from its previously rather vigorous rhetorical support for democratic change in the region. The conventional view was that after the Muslim Brotherhood independents gained eighty-eight seats in Egypt's parliamentary elections, the Islamic Resistance Movement—known universally by its acronym, Hamas—prevailed in Palestinian elections in January 2006, and the sectarian bloodletting in Iraq reached a crescendo, the president and his advisors lost interest in the issue. This was plausible, but there is another interpretation. According to administration insiders, the State Department, in particular, pulled back from democracy promotion because Rice decided she would like to make a push for Palestinian-Israeli peace. To be successful, she would need Egyptian and Saudi help so she decided to ratchet down the pressure on political change.

78. US Department of State, "Egypt"; Sharp, "Egypt"; Johnson, "Egypt."

79. Gause, "Middle East Academic Community"; "Why Middle East Studies."

80. Cook, *Ruling but Not Governing*.

81. Gause, "Middle East Academic Community," 14.

Chapter 2

1. Atkinson, *An Army at Dawn*, 339–92.
2. Najar, "Dignity!"; "Young Face the Event"; "Tunisia, The Promise"; "A New Era"; Mahfoudh, "Dawn of a New Day"; "In the Street"; "Operation of Purification"; "Calm and Hope."
3. For an explanation of the origins and stages of import substitution industrialization, see Hirschman, "Political Economy."
4. Erdle, *Ben Ali's "New Tunisia,"* 74.
5. World Bank, "World Development Indicators."
6. Vandewalle, "Ben Ali's New Tunisia," 6.
7. Murphy, *Economic and Political Change*, 97–100.
8. Murphy, *Economic and Political Change*, 98.
9. World Bank, *Unfinished Revolution*, 16.
10. World Bank, "World Development Indicators."
11. Real GDP grew steadily between 2005 and 2007 before a 2.5 percent fall off in 2008. As a result of the global economic downturn, however, Tunisia's GDP contracted in both 2009 and 2010, though overall it grew at a modest 3 and 3.5 percent. World Bank, "World Development Indicators."
12. World Bank, "World Development Indicators."
13. Rijkers, Freund, and Nucifora, "All in the Family."
14. See Solt, "Standardized World Income Inequality Database."
15. No data are available on income inequality in Saudi Arabia, the United Arab Emirates, Kuwait, Bahrain, Oman, or Libya.
16. Cook, *Struggle for Egypt*, 40; Gordon, *Nasser's Blessed Movement*, 4.
17. Jankowski, *Nasser's Egypt*, 21; Hanna and Gardner, *Arab Socialism*, 132–33.
18. Richards and Waterbury, *Political Economy*, 195–96.
19. Cook, *Struggle for Egypt*, 78.
20. World Bank, "World Development Indicators."
21. Mabro, *Egyptian Economy*, 222–23; World Bank, "World Development Indicators."
22. Abdalla, *Student Movement*, 104.
23. Hinnesbusch, *Egyptian Politics*, 27.
24. Egyptian defense spending as a share of GDP rose from almost 6 percent in 1959 to a yearly average between 7 and 8 percent until 1966. In 1967, military expenditures as a percentage of GDP rose to 13 percent and reached 18 percent by 1970. Looney, "Economics of Middle East Military Expenditures"; Kenawy, "Economic Development in Egypt."
25. Waterbury, *Egypt of Nasser and Sadat*, 167.
26. Waterbury, *Egypt of Nasser and Sadat*, 128–34; Husni, "Law No. 43 of 1974," 229–61.
27. Cook, *Struggle for Egypt*, 138.
28. Beattie, *Egypt during the Sadat Years*, 141.

29. Egyptian Ministry of Economic Development, "Major Economic Indicators."

30. Hinnesbusch, *Egyptian Politics Under Sadat*, 69.

31. Cook, *Struggle for Egypt*, 141.

32. Kienle, *Grand Delusion*, 148. An eligible country could borrow up to a maximum of 140 percent of its IMF quota under a three-year arrangement, although this limit could be increased under exceptional circumstances to a maximum of 185 percent of quota. Loans under the IMF's Enhanced Structural Adjustment Facility program carried an annual interest rate of 0.5 percent, with repayments made semiannually, beginning five and a half years and ending ten years after the disbursement.

33. Cook, *Struggle for Egypt*, 161.

34. Cook, *Struggle for Egypt*, 161–62.

35. Murata, "Designing Youth Employment Policies"; Assad and Barsoum, "Youth Exclusion in Egypt," 6.

36. El Laithy, Lokshin, and Benerji, "Poverty and Economic Growth."

37. Massoud and Willet, "Egypt's Exchange Rate," 3-6.

38. Cook, *Struggle for Egypt*, 177. After the January–February 2011 uprising, the newly installed minister of manpower and immigration placed the unemployment figure at 19 percent, the number of those underemployed greater still. This was double the 9 to 10 percent that the government reported through most of the 2000s.

39. Cook, *Struggle for Egypt*, 177.

40. Waterbury, *Innumerable Delusions*.

41. Bakir, "Public Promise."

42. World Bank, "World Development Indicators."

43. World Bank, "World Development Indicators."

44. Barkey, *Industrialization Crisis*, 46.

45. Barkey, *Industrialization Crisis*, 47.

46. Bayar, "Developmental State," 775; Barlas, *Etatism and Diplomacy*, 98.

47. In 1942, the government imposed the capital levy, which was a tax on private sector profits, but not evenly. Greek-, Jewish-, and Armenian-owned businesses were taxed at a higher rate than those of Muslims. Despite the obvious advantage to one group at the expense of others, the measure soured relations between the government and the business community as a whole. The imposition of the levy had a whiff of the Nazi-inspired fascism that was attractive within influential circles of the CHP. See Ahmed, *Modern Turkey*, 70; Leitz, *Nazi Germany*, chapter 4.

48. Ahmed, *Modern Turkey*, 70.

49. Barkey, *Industrialization Crisis*, 50.

50. Bayar, "Developmental State," 777; Fry, *Finance and Development Planning*, 13.

51. Barkey, *Industrialization Crisis*, 54.

52. Cook, *Ruling but Not Governing*, chapter 5; Ahmed, *Modern Turkey*, chapter 7.

53. Celâsun and Rodrik, "Turkish Economic Development," 622.
54. Graefe, "Oil Shock."
55. The reforms were known as the January 24 Measures.
56. Öniş, "Turgut Özal."
57. Yalpat, "Turkey's Economy."
58. Yalpat, "Turkey's Economy."
59. Republic of Turkey, "Letter of Intent"; Radobank, "Turkish 2000–01 Banking Crisis."
60. World Bank, "World Development Indicators."
61. Turkish Statistical Institute, "Seasonally and Calendar Adjusted."
62. Anderson, "Lone Protester."
63. Republic of Turkey, "Letter of Intent."
64. Republic of Turkey, "Letter of Intent."
65. World Bank, "World Development Indicators."
66. EIA, "Libya."
67. World Bank, "World Development Indicators."
68. Qaddafi, *Green Book*, 216.
69. Alexander, "Libya"; Vandewalle, *Modern Libya*, 111.
70. Vandewalle, *Modern Libya*, 108–117.
71. Alexander, "Libya," 219.
72. Qaddafi, *Green Book*, 30; Vandewalle, *Modern Libya*, 101–2.
73. Vandewalle, *Modern Libya*, 106.
74. Republic of Libya, "Great Green Charter."
75. Wehr, *Hans Wehr Dictionary*, 163.
76. Vandewalle, *Modern Libya*, 142.
77. The Libyans claimed to have tribal, religious, and ethnic ties to groups in northern Chad, but it also seemed clear that Qaddafi was interested in large uranium deposits in that area (for a complete discussion of Libya's military forays into Chad, Egypt, and Uganda, see Pollack, *Arabs at War*, chapter 4).
78. UN Security Council Resolution 748.
79. UN Security Council Resolution 748.
80. UN Security Council Resolution 883.
81. World Bank, "World Development Indicators"; other sources cite slightly different income statistics. See Oskarsoon, "Economic Sanctions," 96; Day, "Economy," 796; Maddy-Weitzman, *Middle East Contemporary Survey*, 150.
82. Niblock, *Pariah States*, 64.
83. Takeyh, "The Rogue," 66.
84. For prominent examples of cliché-ridden travel writing on Libya, see Wilkinson, "First Taste" and Gray, "Tripoli."
85. Nye, "Tripoli Diarist"; Giddens, "The Colonel."
86. Giddens, "The Colonel"; see also Giddens, "My Chat with the Colonel."
87. Between 2004 and 2007, the Libyans paid Porter to help them rethink their economy. He produced at least three reports, which borrowed heavily from his work on other parts of the world, and offered the following advice

to Tripoli, "Define Libya's unique position in the world economy." For a full discussion of the public intellectuals who certified Qaddafi's reformist credentials after brief visits to Libya, see Vandewalle, *Modern Libya*, chapter 7.

88. World Bank, "World Development Indicators."
89. Cook, *Struggle for Egypt*, 295.
90. Olson, "Rapid Growth," 529.
91. Olson, "Rapid Growth," 532–36.
92. Huntington, *Political Order*, 57.
93. Olson, "Rapid Growth," 542.
94. One survey at least indicated that the emphasis on Egypt's so-called revolutionary youth was somewhat misplaced, but that economic grievances nevertheless drove the vast majority of protesters—who happened to be closer to middle age—during the January 25 uprising. Bessinger, Jamal, and Mazur, "Who Participated?"
95. Cook, *Struggle for Egypt*, 20.
96. Little, *Egypt*, 100.
97. Bellin, *Stalled Democracy*, 4.
98. World Bank, *Unfinished Revolution*, 16.
99. World Bank, *Unfinished Revolution*, 16.
100. The Gafsa basin is an industrial mining area that produces phosphates. In the year before the uprising against Ben Ali, phosphates accounted for about 4 percent of Tunisia's gross domestic product. See Industries Chimiques, *Chemical Industries*.
101. Al Arabiya, "Tunisian Leader Says Violent Protest Unacceptable."
102. Zacharia, "Mubarak Ally Watches."
103. Protests against Qaddafi began on February 15, 2011, but Libyans refer to the February 17 Revolution, which was when protesters called for a "Day of Rage" and coincided with the anniversary of the February 17, 2006, protests that were originally focused on cartoons depicting the Prophet Muhammad in the Danish newspaper *Jyllands-Posten*, which became an anti-Qaddafi protest.
104. Bessinger, Jamal, and Mazur, "Who Participated?"
105. Kalaycıoğlu, "Elections and Governance," 55.
106. Heper and Güney, "Military and Democracy"; Özbudun, "Turkey, Crises, Interruptions, and Reequilibrations."
107. Libyans were referring to Omar al-Mukhtar, who led a two-decades-long resistance to Italian colonization in the early twentieth century.
108. "The Songs of Gezi."
109. Naffsinger, "Face among the Arabs," 49.
110. Naffsinger, "Face among the Arabs," 51.
111. Hamdan, *Character of Egypt*. Amr Leheta provided invaluable interpretation of Hamdan's four-volume work.
112. Al-Aswany, "What the Military Council."

113. Dombey and Saigol, "Turkish Unions."
114. US Department of State, "Human Rights Report 2011: Tunisia."
115. Qaddafi, *Green Book*, 12.
116. Vandewalle, *Modern Libya*, 135.

Chapter 3
1. Cook, "Frankenstein."
2. Al-Najar, "Cairo Governor Dr. Galal al-Saeed."
3. Cook, *Struggle for Egypt*, 311–12.
4. There is some disagreement over the duration of the Mohammed Mahmoud protests. They lasted from November 19 to either November 22, when Field Marshal Tantawi promised to hand power to an elected civilian president in June 2012, or until November 25, when demonstrators gathered in Tahrir Square in what was billed the Friday of Martyrs to reiterate the demand that the SCAF relinquish power.
5. Cook, *Struggle for Egypt*, 311–12.
6. Cook, *Struggle for Egypt*, 312.
7. Tarek, "SCAF Hails Security."
8. Cook, "Frankenstein."
9. Brown and Dunne, "Egypt's Draft Constitutional Amendments." The initial date of the parliamentary election was unofficial and likely arrived at based on a clause in the SCAF's constitutional declaration of February 13, 2011—approved by referendum in March 2011—in which the officers stated, "The Supreme Council of the Armed Forces shall take charge of administering the affairs of the nation in a temporary manner for a period of six months or until the conclusion of elections for the People's Assembly, the Shura Council, and the president of the republic." The implication was that the first set of elections could be held as early as late June or early July 2011. As a result, in February 2011, *New York Times* Cairo bureau chief David Kirkpatrick reported a six-month blueprint and the *Telegraph*'s Richard Spence and Praveen Swami similarly informed their readers of the same.
10. For a full discussion of these points, see Trager, *Arab Fall*.
11. Khairat al-Shater was disqualified because he had been convicted of a crime during Hosni Mubarak's rule, which banned him by law from political activity for six years after his release. Omar Suleiman was disqualified because he failed to get enough endorsements for his candidacy from fifteen provinces as required by law. The Salafi candidate, Hazem Salah Abu Ismail, was disqualified because his late mother, Nawwal Abdel Aziz Nour, held US citizenship, which violated the election law that stated all candidates, their spouses, and their parents must have only Egyptian citizenship. Abu Ismail, who often railed against the United States, maintained that his mother only had a green card and was never an American citizen, but California public records and a Los Angeles voter registration website determine otherwise. Kirkpatrick, "Authorities Bar 3."

12. Abdel Rahman, "Morsi's Campaign." Specifically, Morsi told the activists, intellectuals, liberals, and revolutionaries who agreed to support him that he would assure a national partnership and a comprehensive national project to realize the aims of the revolution; would establish a presidential team and a government of national salvation that includes all political groups; would be a president who is a national and independent; would create a crisis management team to ensure the proper and complete transfer of power to the elected president; would abolish the SCAF's June 2012 decree relating to the dissolution of the parliament and its June 2012 constitutional declaration that reserved for the military sole control over national defense and security policy; would work to create an equal balance in the Constituent Assembly that would write a constitution for all Egyptians; and would ensure complete transparency with the people in all political activities.

13. Cook, *Ruling but Not Governing*.

14. Springborg, "Sisi's Secret Islamism."

15. Springborg, "Sisi's Secret Islamism"; "Sisi's Islamist Agenda."

16. Youssef, "Blame for Sinai Tension"; Katulis, "Maintaining the Delicate Balancing Act"; Wittes and Hamid, "Camp David"; Trager, "Obama's Big Egypt Test"; Pryce-Jones, "Hamas's New Strength"; Cook, "Still Think Middle East Peace"; Kirkpatrick and El Sheikh, "With Gaza Attacks"; Egypt Independent, "FJP Drafts Amendment"; *Ahram Online*, "Egypt's Morsi's Advisor"; Issacharoff, "Morsi Mulling Amendments"; IkhwanWeb, "Muslim Brotherhood Statement"; Hassen, "Fate of the Egyptian-Israeli Peace Treaty"; Satloff, "Morsi's Victory."

17. Personal communication with former US government official, December 16, 2015; December 14, 2015.

18. Carter Center, "Presidential Election in Egypt"; Electoral Institute for Sustainable Democracy in Africa, *Election Witnessing Mission Report*.

19. Cairo Institute for Human Rights Studies, "Al-Ittihadiya."

20. Morsi, "Speech"; for the text in English, see Atlantic Council, "Translation."

21. Özkan, "Turkey, Davutoglu and the Idea of Pan-Islamism."

22. Kayserilioğlu, Işıkara, and Zirngast, "Social and Economic Project"; Pérouse, "State without the Public"; Sönmez, "Turkey's Second Privatization Agency."

23. The initial Turkish press coverage of the protests varied considerably. Papers like *Zaman*—but not its English-language version, *Today's Zaman*—the mass circulation *Hürriyet* and its English mirror *Hürriyet Daily News*, and *HaberTürk*, a mainstream Kemalist newspaper with liberal leanings covered the protest from the beginning. Others like the Kemalist standard-bearer *Cumhuriyet* did not pick up the story until May 30. The right-of-center, pro-AKP *Sabah* covered the story, but it was initially focused on the participation of filmmaker and activist Sırrı Süreyya Önder and his

Kurdish-based political party, the Peace and Democracy Party. Other pro-AKP outlets like the English-language *Daily Sabah* and *Yeni Şafak* carried no coverage of the protests during their initial stage.

24. Akyol, "Turkey's Veiled Democracy"; Burns, "Future of the U.S.-Turkey Relationship"; Cook, "Cheering an Islamist Victory"; de Bellaigue, "Turkey at the Turning Point?"; *Economist*, "Lesson from Turkey"; *New York Times*, "Democracy in Turkey"; Öktem, "Harbingers."

25. Federation of American Scientists, *Turkey—Guide to Ergenekon*.

26. The Ergenekon organization was also allegedly connected to the Susurluk scandal that began with the November 3, 1996, car crash in Susurluk that involved the deputy chief of the Istanbul Police Department, a powerful Kurdish member of parliament, and the leader of the neo-fascist Grey Wolves. In January 1997, a retired naval officer and political commentator named Erol Mütercimler published an article in the newspaper *Aydınlık* in which he claimed that Ergenekon had authority over the General Staff and the National Intelligence Organization.

27. Doğan and Rodrik, "Sledgehammer Coup Plan"; "Sledgehammer Coup Allegations"; "'Back to the Future.'" See also Arsenal Consulting, "Preliminary Report"; "Preliminary Samsung"; "Preliminary Gölcük."

28. Quoted in Caldwell, "East in the West."

29. Cook, "Cheering an Islamist Victory."

30. International Crisis Group, "Making Sense of Libya."

31. NTC, "Vision."

32. NTC, "Constitutional Declaration," Articles 1 and 6.

33. NTC, "Constitutional Declaration," Part II, Rights and Freedoms.

34. Saif al-Islam al-Qaddafi was the subject of a number of sympathetic profiles in the Western media in 2009 and 2010; see Griswold, "The Heir"; Thomas, "Unknotting Father's Reins"; Grove, "Man Who Freed the Bomber"; Jamieson and Freeman, "Profile"; Solomon, "Circle of Fire."

35. Qaddafi, "Speech," 39:42.

36. Qaddafi, "Speech," 39:42.

37. Holmes, "Fighters Clash Again"; Stephen, "Libya"; Krauss, "Militias and Army"; Al Jazeera, "Deadly Factional Clashes"; Van Langendonck, "Libya Militias Taking"; and Karadsheh, "Libyan War Over."

38. Wehrey, "Libya Doesn't Need."

39. Mezran, "Can Libya's Liberals?"

40. Anderson, "Unraveling."

41. US Department of State, "Accountability Review Board Report for Benghazi," 4.

42. Anderson, "Unraveling."

43. For a detailed discussion, see Pollack, *Arabs at War*, 375–412.

44. Wehrey and Lacher, "Libya's Legitimacy Crisis."

45. Joscelyn, "Ansar al Sharia Libya."

46. Chivvis and Martini, *Libya after Qaddafi*, 30; NCTC, "Ansar al Sharia."

47. Pack, "Two Deals, No Solution."

48. Republic of Tunisia, "Law on Establishing and Organizing Justice."

49. Cook, "Beji Caid Essebsi."

50. Essebsi, "My Three Goals."

51. Cook, "Beji Caid Essebsi."

52. Tamimi, *Rachid Ghannouchi*, 31.

53. Cook, "Beji Caid Essebsi."

54. Essebsi, "My Three Goals."

55. Essebsi's apparent affinity for Kemalism was likely not a coincidence. Habib Bourguiba—whom Essebsi served loyally—held Mustafa Kemal Atatürk in high regard. See Hopwood, *Habib Bourguiba*, 84.

56. Nouira, "Obstacles on the Path."

57. *Le Monde*, "Main Tunisian Union."

58. Tajine, "Jihadist Comes Home."

59. Zelin, "Tunis Designates Ansar al Sharia."

60. Ansar al-Sharia Tunisia never took responsibility for the murders, though Tunisian investigators suspect Boubacar al-Hakim, a member of the group. Amara, "Secular Politician Brahmi"; Al Jazeera, "Tunisia Opposition Figures."

61. Maher, "Frustration Grows"; Totten, "Tunisia on the Brink"; Marks, "Tunisia in Turmoil."

62. The political figure that resisted the most was Ennahda's Rachid al-Ghannouchi, who called the roadmap a basis for discussion but was forced to sign under the collective pressure and prestige of the UGTT, the Tunisian Confederation of Industry, Trade, and Handicrafts, the Tunisian Human Rights League, and the Tunisian Order of Lawyers. See Chayes, "How a Leftist Labor Union."

63. "Nobel Peace Prize for 2015."

64. "Constitution of Tunisia," Articles 78–77.

65. "Constitution of Tunisia," Article 91.

66. "Constitution of Tunisia," Article 92.

67. "Constitution of Tunisia," Articles 95–96.

68. "Constitution of Tunisia," Title Five, Judicial Authority.

69. Cook, *Ruling but Not Governing*; Brown, *Constitutions*.

Chapter 4

1. El-Hamalawy, "#Jan25"; Neuman, "Joyful Egyptians"; Batty, "Egypt the Day After."

2. Al-Assar, public meeting.

3. Cole, "Why It's Way Too Soon"; Walt, "A Requiem"; Applebaum, "Every Revolution."

4. Cook, "Middle Eastern Revolutions."

5. Goldstone, "Understanding the Revolutions."

6. Ulfelder, "The Arab Spring."

7. Some of the most important works on the theory of revolutions include Chalmers Johnson, *Revolutionary Change*; Ted Gurr, *Why Men Rebel*; Charles Tilly, *From Mobilization to Revolution*; Theda Skocpol, *States and Social Revolutions*; and Jack Goldstone, *Revolution and Rebellion*.
8. Skocpol, *States and Social Revolutions*, xiii.
9. Skocpol, "Cultural Idioms," 87.
10. Skocpol, *States and Social Revolutions*, 4.
11. Sewell, "Ideologies and Social Revolutions," 59.
12. Sewell, "Ideologies and Social Revolutions," 32.
13. St. John, *Historical Dictionary*, 129.
14. Vandewalle, *A History*, 119.
15. Malinowski, "Jefferson in Benghazi."
16. Qaddafi, "Speech."
17. Cole, "Why Tunisia's Arab Spring."
18. Marks, "Tunisia Opts."
19. See March and Olsen, *Rediscovering Institutions*.
20. Republic of Tunisia, Organic Law no. 22/2015.
21. Human Rights Watch, "Tunisia."
22. Republic of Tunisia, Organic Law no. 22/2015.
23. Mersch, "Ineffective Counterterrorism Law."
24. Republic of Tunisia, Organic Law no. 22/2015.
25. Republic of Tunisia, Organic Law no. 22/2015, Article 30.
26. Tamimi, *Rachid Ghannouchi*, 69.
27. Tamimi, *Rachid Ghannouchi*, 69.
28. Perkins, *A History*, 194; for the English text, see Sfeir, "Tunisian Code."
29. Ben Ali, "Tunisia."
30. Republic of Tunisia, "Organizing Political Parties."
31. Perkins, *A History*, 197.
32. Ghedira, "Will Ennahda Apologize"; Botha, "Terrorism in Tunisia," 114; Dwyer, *Arab Voices*, 154.
33. Marks, "Tunisia's Ennahda," 8.
34. Mersch, "Ineffective Counterterrorism Law."
35. Amnesty International, "Tunisia."
36. Quoted in Stephen, Shaheen, and Tran, "Tunis Museum Attack."
37. Samti, "In Tunisia"; Mersch, "Tunisia."
38. Cook, "Turkey's Political Football."
39. The Republic of Turkey's Ministry for European Union Affairs maintains an online archive of all European Union progress reports since 1998.
40. Özbudun and Gençkaya, *Democratization*, 73–80; Müftüler-Baç, "Turkey's Political Reforms"; CEC, *2002 Regular Report*; Secretariat-General, "Political Reforms."
41. Gül, "US-Turkish Relationship."
42. CEC, *2004 Regular Report*; European Commission, "Commission Recommends."

43. The European Union's Conditions for Membership are available online at http://ec.europa.eu/enlargement/policy/conditions-membership/index_en.htm.

44. US Embassy Ankara, "Despite Allegations."

45. Quoted in CPJ, "2015 Prison Census."

46. Quoted in CPJ, "2015 Prison Census."

47. The AKP's 2003 revisions to Article 68 of the Turkish Constitution and the political parties law had made it harder to close a party but not impossible. It was these changes, specifically the requirement that three-fifths of the court had to vote for closure rather than a simple majority, that saved the AKP. See Algan, "Dissolution of Political Parties," 811–18, 825.

48. Cook, "How Erdogan Made."

49. The Supreme Council is actually the Constitutional Court, but it takes on the name Supreme Council to facilitate trials of government ministers.

50. Çiçek, "Top Court to Review Content."

51. Finkel, "Why Investors Are Calling"; Girit, "Turkey Election."

52. Republic of Turkey, "Constitution," Article 104.

53. Meyersson, "How Turkey's Social Conservatives."

54. Ülgen, "Turkey at a Democratic Crossroad"; Ignatius, "Why Turkey Voted"; Çağaptay, "Turkey's Election Results"; New York Times, "Democracy Wins."

55. Constitution of the Republic of Turkey, Article 116. In 1995, after the Islamist Welfare Party won 22 percent of the popular vote, the largest share of any party, its leader, Necmettin Erbakan, was poised to become Turkey's new prime minister. Yet President Süleyman Demirel turned to the Motherland and True Path Parties, which both earned about 19 percent of the vote each to form a coalition thereby blocking Welfare from coming to power. The Motherland–True Path coalition eventually faltered; in June 1996, Demirel then tapped Welfare's Erbakan to establish a government.

56. Quoted in Letsch and Traynor, "Erdoğan Concedes."

57. Tharoor, "Turkey's Election"; Çandar, "Post-Election Erdogan."

58. Committee to Protect Journalists, "Egypt's Imprisonment."

59. Committee to Protect Journalists, "Egypt's Imprisonment."

60. Campagna, "From Accommodation to Confrontation."

61. Arab Republic of Egypt, Law No. 128 of 2014.

62. Arab Republic of Egypt, Law No. 84 of 2002, especially articles 17, 21, 42, and 76. Law No. 84 was a descendant of Law No. 32 of 1964, which gave the Ministry of Social Affairs the power to oversee and regulate the activity of civil society groups. In 1999, the government replaced Law 32 with a new regulation on the activities of the NGO sector, Law 153, which was more restrictive than its predecessor. Under the new law, foreign NGOs were required to register with the Ministry of Social Affairs and the practice of registering some civil society groups as civil companies to get around the ministry's restrictions was prohibited.

63. Arab Republic of Egypt, Law No. 33 of 2015.

64. Nader, "Education Organisation Shuttered"; BBC, "Egypt's Muslim Brotherhood."
65. See Arab Republic of Egypt, Law No. 46 of 2014; Law No. 92 of 2015; Democracy International, "Preliminary Statement."
66. Democracy International, *Observing Egypt's Roadmap*, 2.
67. Cook, "Middle Eastern Revolutions."
68. Cook, "Middle Eastern Revolutions."
69. Nasser, "Public Address."
70. Mitchell, *Society of the Muslim Brothers*, 4. The attacks on religion that Banna perceived were in part the result of the disestablishment of Islam that Turkish nationalists undertook after the defeat of the Central Powers in World War I and the subsequent collapse of the Ottoman Empire.
71. The debate revolved around one of Egypt's foremost intellectuals of the early twentieth century, Taha Hussein, whose 1938 work, *The Future of Culture in Egypt*, was the subject of tremendous debate among secularists and Islamists.
72. Glicksberg, "Islamist Movement."
73. Glicksberg, "Islamist Movement."
74. Gal, "Tunisian President."
75. Waltz, "Islamist Appeal," 652; Perkins, *A History*, 144–46; Tammimi, *Rachid Ghannouchi*, 9–10; Burgat and Dowell, *Islamic Movement*; for a critique of Ghannouchi, see Kramer, "Karen Hughes"; "Rachid Ghannoushi"; and "A U.S. Visa?"
76. For a discussion of the 1988 National Pact and the political context in which it was issued, see Sadiki, "Political Liberalization"; Anderson, "Political Pacts."
77. For an illustrative list, see Lustick, "Hegemony"; Laitin, *Identity in Formation*; Aronoff, "Collective Identity"; Brubaker, *Ethnicity without Groups*; Smith, *National Identity*; Gellner, *Culture*; Anderson, *Imagined Communities*; Tilly, "Citizenship, Identity, and Social History."
78. Qaddafi, "Speech."
79. Pargeter, "Why Elections."
80. Cook, "How Happy Is."
81. Cook, "How Happy Is"; *Ruling but Not Governing*, 95; Mardin, "Religion and Secularism," 363–65.
82. Cook, "How Happy Is"; Barkey and Fuller, *Turkey's Kurdish Question*, 10.
83. Marcus, *Blood and Belief*, 38.
84. For a complete inventory of what is now regarded as the Kemalist reforms, see Toprak, "Religious Right," 223.
85. Reynolds, "Worldview," 12.
86. Şen, "Transformation of Turkish Islamism," 63.
87. For a full explanation, see Çetinsaya, "Rethinking Nationalism and Islam."
88. The term *Muslimhood* comes from Jenny White's work on Turkish identity (see *Muslim Nationalism*).
89. Cook and Koplow, "Turkey's Secularists Surrender."

90. Bell et al., *Religion, Politics and Society; Unity and Diversity.*
91. Cook and Koplow, "Turkey's Secularists Surrender."
92. For the official results of the June 22, 2011, general election, see Supreme Electoral Council of the Republic of Turkey, "Results of Turkish General Election." In November 2015, the AKP won 49.5 percent of the vote.
93. *Hürriyet Daily News*, "Two Drunks."
94. Cook, "How Happy Is"; Huntington, "Clash of Civilizations?" 42.
95. Muslim Brotherhood, "Regional Leadership"; see also *Program of the Party.*
96. Salah, "Nidaa Tounes?"
97. Petré, "Nidaa Tunis Tensions."
98. Among the most well-informed and interesting scholars on jihadism and the Islamic State phenomenon are William McCants, Aaron Y. Zelin, Daniel Byman, Steven Simon, Michael Weiss and his coauthor Hassan Hassan, Jessica Stern, J. M. Berger, Daveed Gartenstein-Ross, Thomas Hegghammer, and Thomas Joscelyn.
99. McCants, *ISIS Apocalypse*, 8.
100. Zelin, "War between ISIS and al-Qaeda."
101. Bunzel, "Paper State to Caliphate," 20.
102. Weaver, "Short Violent Life."
103. Weaver, "Short Violent Life," 27–29.
104. In an op-ed for the *New York Times* ("How Saddam Gave Us ISIS"), Kyle Orton goes much further, arguing that Saddam Hussein's embrace of Islamism during the last decade of his rule, in particular, laid the groundwork for the emergence of the Islamic State with the heavy presence of former Saddam-era intelligence operatives and military officers who embraced Salafism among its leadership. Others—such as Samuel Helfont and Michael Brill in "Saddam's ISIS?"—reject this claim, arguing that there is "no evidence that Saddam or his Baathist regime in Iraq displayed any sympathy for Islamism, Salafism, or Wahhabism."
105. McCants, *ISIS Apocalypse*, 10.
106. Bunzel, "Paper State to Caliphate," 25.
107. Bunzel, "Paper State to Caliphate," 23.
108. Lawrence, *Messages to the World.*
109. McCants, *ISIS Apocalypse*, 8.
110. Ghazal and Sadiki, "ISIS."
111. Jenkins, "What *The Atlantic* Left Out."
112. Stern and Berger, *ISIS*, 22–23. Stern and Berger explicate the *Management of Savagery*, which justified Zarqawi's violence. Translated originally for the Combating Terrorism Center at West Point, *Management of Savagery* was penned by a pseudonymous jihadi thinker who established an inextricable link between violence and the establishment of an Islamic State.
113. In their book, Michael Weiss and Hassan Hassan indicate that in their interviews with ISIS fighters, they "found that what draws people to ISIS could easily bring them to any number of cults" (*ISIS: Inside the Army of*

Terror, 153). People are drawn to cults precisely because they are in search of identity.

114. Stern and Berger, *ISIS*, 6.
115. The work of Raqqa Is Being Slaughtered Silently can be accessed at http://www.raqqa-sl.com/en/.
116. Gartenstein-Ross, "How Many Fighters?"

Chapter 5

1. Pollack, *Threatening Storm*; see also Pollack, *Path out of the Desert*.
2. Hounshell, "You're So Vain."
3. Shaikh et al., "A Generation Revolts."
4. Cook, *Struggle for Egypt*, chapter 6.
5. Office of Inspector General, "Audit of USAID/Egypt."
6. Cook, "America's Radical Idealists," 78.
7. Albright, Weber, and Cook, *Support of Arab Democracy*, 4–9.
8. Brumberg, *Pursuit of Democracy*, 3.
9. Jones, "The West, the Rest."
10. See Behrman, *Most Noble Adventure*. Behrman worked on the Policy Planning Staff of the Clinton State Department, where he was responsible for coordinating a series of scientific and educational initiatives that President Obama announced in his 2009 Cairo speech.
11. Ülgen et al., "Emerging Order."
12. Some examples include Muasher and Wilkens, "Awakening"; Satloff, "Ideas"; and Pollack et al., *Arab Awakening*.
13. Serwer, "Post-Qaddafi Instability."
14. Schenker, *Egypt's Enduring Challenges*; Hamid, "Guns and Butter."
15. McInerney, "Islamist Victory"; Exum and Stuster, "Policing Reform."
16. NPR, "Turkish Democracy."
17. Albright, Hadley, and Cook, *U.S.-Turkey Relations*, 42.
18. Personal communication with US government official, Washington, DC, February 22, 2011.
19. An illustrative list includes Hasan, "In Turkey the Right"; Altıparmak and Berlinski, "The Wikileaks Cables"; Yeşilada and Rubin, *Islamization of Turkey*; Lerner, "Losing Turkey"; Rubin, "Turkey"; Çağaptay, "Is Turkey Leaving"; Tibi, "Islamists Approach Europe"; Gurfinkiel, "Is Turkey Lost?"; Rubin, "Mr. Erdogan's Turkey."
20. This was a view that prevailed even after the Gezi Park protests. In her remarks at the annual Sakıp Sabancı Lecture at the Brookings Institution, titled "Turkey and the Transformation of the Global Political and Economic Landscape," on May 1, 2014, former secretary of state Madeleine Albright took the Turkish leadership to task for its authoritarian approach to politics but nevertheless continued to express optimism that Turkey's transformation would continue. She based this assertion on her confidence that Turks want democracy and that Ankara's partners in Europe and NATO could support

this kind of change. For pre-Gezi analysis, see Albright, Hadley, and Cook, *U.S.-Turkey Relations*; Taşpınar, "Turkey's General Dilemma"; Walker, "Will Turkey Remain"; Hale and Özbudun, *Islamism, Democracy*; Danforth, "How the West Lost Turkey"; Cook, "The Odds on Turkey."

21. Weaver, "Pharaohs in Waiting," 79–92.
22. International Stabilisation Response Team, "Libya, 20 May–30 June 2011."
23. Obama, "Remarks on the Middle East and North Africa."
24. Obama, "Remarks on the Middle East and North Africa."
25. Obama, "Remarks on the Middle East and North Africa."
26. Lynch, "Obama and the Middle East."
27. Obama, "Remarks on the Middle East and North Africa."
28. Obama, "Remarks on the Middle East and North Africa."
29. Kagan and Dunne, "Why Egypt."
30. Lally and Sheridan, "U.S. Offers Aid."
31. Goldberg, "Obama Doctrine," 73.
32. McInerney and Bockenfeld, *Federal Budget and Appropriations*, 14–17.
33. Personal communication with former US government officials, February 4, 2015, Washington, DC.
34. Ignatius, "Hillary Clinton"; Stock, "It's Obama"; Bolton, "Mubarak Understood"; Holmes, "Egypt"; Simes, "Throwing an Ally."
35. Clinton, "Remarks."
36. Nuland, "The United States' Reaction."
37. Carney, "Press Briefing."
38. Hussein, "Muslim Brotherhood"; El-Haddad, "Anti-Coup Alliance"; Perry, "Brotherhood Sees Egypt."
39. Obama, "Remarks to Turkish Parliament."
40. Personal communication with US government official, November 18, 2011, Ankara.
41. Daloğlu, "AKP Reacts."
42. Çağaptay, "Fragile Thaw"; Ignatius, "U.S. and Turkey."
43. Obama, "Readout of Call with Erdoğan."
44. US Department of State, "Daily Press Briefing," May 31, 2013; June 17, 2013.
45. Obama, "Readout of Call with Erdoğan."
46. Personal communication with US government official, March 10, 2014, Washington, DC.
47. Evans and Sahnoun, *Responsibility to Protect*, xi.
48. Appy, *American Reckoning*, 302; Cigar, *Genocide in Bosnia*, 9. Samantha Power, special assistant to the president and a senior national security aide to President Obama, has written a Pulitzer Prize–winning book in 2002, *A Problem from Hell*, in which she explored the reasons for American inaction during the genocides of the twentieth century.
49. Strand et al., "Why Waves?"; Keohane and Nye, *Power and Interdependence*, chapters 9 and 10; Levitsky and Way, "International

Linkage"; Gleditsch, *All International Politics*; Gasiorowski, "Economic Crisis"; Huntington, *The Third Wave*. For a recent study on diffusion and international demonstration effect related specifically to the Middle East, see Lynch, "Transnational Diffusion."

50. Gasiorowski, "Economic Crisis," 893.
51. Starr, "Democratic Dominoes."
52. Obama and Essebsi, "Helping Tunisia." The only other instance of presidential coauthorship also occurred during President Obama's presidency when he wrote an op-ed with India's prime minister, Narendra Modi, that also appeared in the *Washington Post*.
53. Personal communication with US government official, May 20, 2015.
54. Arieff and Humud, *Political Transition*; US Senate, "FY2016 Appropriations Bill."
55. European Commission, "EU-Tunisia"; International Monetary Fund, "IMF Survey"; Davis, "John Kerry Says"; World Bank, "IBRD Statement of Loans."
56. Personal communication with congressional staff, February 4, 2016.
57. Personal communication with a participant in a January 22, 2016, meeting US Vice President Joe Biden, February 3, 2016.
58. Erdoğan, "Remarks."
59. Erdoğan, "Kılıçdaroglu's 'Bellyaching.'"
60. Toksabay and Tattersall, "Erdogan Says Turkey's"; Fraser and Becatoros, "Turkey's Erdogan Blasts"; *Hürriyet*, "Breaking News."
61. Sharp, "Egypt."
62. Hawthorne, "Part I" and "Part II"; Cook, *Struggle for Egypt*, chapter 6.
63. A representative list includes Kaplan, "Stop Paying the Generals"; Kagan, "The U.S. Is Complicit"; Dunne, "Crisis in Egypt"; Gharib, "Cutting Aid"; Abrams, "Reacting to the Coup"; Bandow, "Cancel Aid to Egypt"; Phillips, "Time to Freeze"; Hamid, "Real Reason"; Murkhaji, "Egypt's Regime"; *Washington Post*, "More Bucks"; Boot, "Mubarak."
64. Cook, "Middle East Revolutions."
65. Freedman, *Soviet Policy*, 15.
66. Personal communication with senior Saudi official, October 25, 2015, Riyadh; personal communication with senior Emirati official, October 27, 2015, Abu Dhabi.
67. Obama, "State of the Union Address."

Chapter 6
1. Cook, "Turkey's in a Terrible Spot."
2. Ornarlı, "Davutoğlu."
3. Shapiro, "Revolution, Facebook-Style."
4. Abdel Aziz, "Catch the Sisi Mania."
5. Ghannouchi, "Tunisia Holds the Key."
6. Özbudun, "Turkey"; Cook, "Turkey's Democratic Mirage."

BIBLIOGRAPHY

———◆———

Abadi, Jacob. *Tunisia since the Arab Conquest: The Saga of a Westernized Muslim State*. Reading, UK: Ithaca Press, 2013.

Abdalla, Ahmed. *The Student Movement and National Politics in Egypt, 1923–1973*. Cairo: American University in Cairo Press, 2008.

Abdel Aziz, Lubna. "Catch the Sisi Mania." *Al-Ahram Weekly*, September 19, 2013. http://weekly.ahram.org.eg/News/4103/44/Catch-the-Al-Sisi-mania.aspx.

Abdel Rahman, Amr. "Morsi's Campaign: A Full Agreement between Nationalist Forces to Stand in Opposition to the Military's Attempts for Autocracy" [Arabic]. *Masress*, June 22, 2015. http://www.masress.com/misrelgdida/93113.

Abrams, Elliott. "Reacting to the Coup in Egypt." *National Review Online*, July 3, 2013. http://www.nationalreview.com/corner/352744/reacting-coup-egypt-elliott-abrams.

Abu Khalil, Asad. "Reviewed Work: *The Vanished Imam: Musa al-Sadr and the Shia of Lebanon* by Fouad Ajami." *MERIP Report* no. 144 (January–February 1987): 46–47.

Abu Khalil, Asad. "A Viable Partnership: Islam Democracy, and the Arab World." *Harvard International Review* 15, no. 2 (Winter 1992–93): 22–65.

Abu Khalil, Asad. "Review: 'The Islam Industry' and Scholarship: Review Article." *Middle East Journal* 58, no. 1 (Winter 2004): 130–37.

Addi, Lahouari. "Algeria's Democracy between Islamists and the Elite." Translated by Zachary Lockman and Joost R. Hiltermann. *Middle East Report*, no. 175 (March–April 1992): 36–38.

Ahmed, Feroz. *The Making of Modern Turkey*. New York: Routledge, 1993.

Ahram Online. "Egypt's Morsi's Advisor Repeats Calls for Camp David Amendment." October 4, 2012. http://english.ahram.org.eg/NewsContent/1/64/54836/Egypt/Politics-/Egypts-Morsis-advisor-repeats-calls-for-Camp-David.aspx.

Ajami, Fouad. "How the Arabs Turned Shame into Liberty." *New York Times*, February 26, 2011.

Akyol, Mustafa. "Turkey's Maturing Foreign Policy." *ForeignAffairs.com*, July 7, 2011. https://www.foreignaffairs.com/articles/turkey/2011-07-07/turkeys-maturing-foreign-policy.

Akyol, Mustafa. "Turkey's Veiled Democracy." *American Interest* 3, no. 2 (November/December 2007): 88–94.

Al Arabiya. "Tunisian Leader Says Violent Protest Unacceptable." December 28, 2010. https://www.alarabiya.net/articles/2010/12/28/131323.html.

Al-Assar, Mohammed. Public meeting, Egypt Defense Office. Washington, DC (July 7, 2011).

Al-Aswany, Alaa. "What the Military Council Did Not Hear" [Arabic]. *Al-Masry al-Youm*, October 25, 2011. http://www.almasryalyoum.com/news/details/52685.

Al-Ghannouchi, Rachid. "Tunisia Holds the Key to Defeating ISIS." *Time.com*, January 25, 2016. http://time.com/4189180/tunisia-holds-the-key-to-defeating-isis.

Al Jazeera. "Deadly Factional Clashes Erupt in Libya." November 13, 2011. http://www.aljazeera.com/news/africa/2011/11/2011111341559598501.html.

Al Jazeera. "Tunisia Opposition Figures 'Shot by Same Gun.'" July 27, 2013. http://www.aljazeera.com/news/africa/2013/07/201372611531821363.html.

Al-Najar, Ahmed al-Said. "Cairo Governor Dr. Galal al-Saeed: We Are Studying Vacating the Mugamma al-Tahrir to Relieve the Pressure of 100,000 Citizens Visiting It Daily." *Al-Ahram*, July, 3, 2015. http://www.ahram.org.eg/NewsQ/412360.aspx.

Al-Qaddafi, Muammar. *The Green Book*. Reading, UK: Ithaca Press, 1999.

Al-Qaddafi, Saif al-Islam. "Speech by Saif al-Islam Muammar al-Qaddafi" [Arabic]. YouTube video, 39:42, February 20, 2011. https://www.youtube.com/watch?v=1J_oECAgEto.

Al-Sayyid, Mustapha K. "Slow Thaw in the Arab World." *World Policy Journal* 8, no. 4 (Fall 1991): 711–38.

Albrecht, Holger. "Authoritarian Opposition and the Politics of Challenge." In *Debating Arab Authoritarianism*, edited by Oliver Schlumberger, 59–74. Stanford, CA: Stanford University Press, 2007.

Albright, Madeleine K., Stephen J. Hadley, and Steven A. Cook. *U.S.-Turkey Relations: A New Partnership*. Independent Task Force Report no. 69. Washington, DC: Council on Foreign Relations, May 2012.

Albright, Madeleine K., Vin Weber, and Steven A. Cook. *In Support of Arab Democracy: Why and How*. Independent Task Force Report no. 54. New York: Council on Foreign Relations, May 2005. http://www.cfr.org/democratization/support-arab-democracy/p8166.

Alexander, Nathan. "Libya: The Continuous Revolution." *Middle Eastern Studies* 17, no. 2 (April 1981): 210–27.

Algan, Bülent. "Dissolution of Political Parties by the Constitutional Court in Turkey: An Everlasting Conflict between the Court and the Parliament." *Ankara University Faculty of Law Journal* 60, no. 4 (2011): 811–25.

Altıparmak, Okan, and Claire Berlinski. "The Wikileaks Cables on Turkey: 20/20 Tunnel Vision." *Middle East Review of International Affairs* 15, no. 1 (March 2011). http://www.rubincenter.org/2011/08/meria20103the-wikileaks-cables-on-turkey-2020-tunnel-vision.

Amara, Tarek. "Secular Politician Brahmi Killed with Same Gun as Belaid." *Reuters*, July 26, 2013. http://www.reuters.com/article/us-tunisia-death-weapon-idUSBRE96P0G420130726.

Amawi, Abla. "Democracy Dilemmas in Jordan." *Middle East Report*, no. 174 (January–February 1992): 26–29.

Amnesty International. "Tunisia: Severe Restrictions on Liberty and Movement Latest Symptoms of Repressive Emergency Law." Press Release. New York: Amnesty International, March 17, 2016. http://www.amnestyusa.org/news/press-releases/tunisia-severe-restrictions-on-liberty-and-movement-latest-symptoms-of-repressive-emergency-law.

Anderson, Benedict. *Imagined Communities: Reflections on the Spread of Nationalism*. London: Verso, 1983.

Anderson, John Ward. "Lone Protester Taps into Turks' Anger at Economy." *Washington Post*, April 7, 2001. https://www.washingtonpost.com/archive/politics/2001/04/07/lone-protester-taps-into-turks-anger-at-economy/03803057-a52f-45e5-9d47-c6789bcce496.

Anderson, Jon Lee. "The Unraveling." *New Yorker*, February 23, 2015. http://www.newyorker.com/magazine/2015/02/23/unravelling.

Anderson, Lisa. "Dynasts and Nationalists: Why Monarchies Survive." In *Middle East Monarchies: The Challenge of Modernity*, edited by Joseph Kostiner, 53–70. Boulder, CO: Lynne Rienner, 2000.

Anderson, Lisa. "Political Pacts, Liberalism, and Democracy: The Tunisian National Pact of 1988." *Government and Opposition* 26, no. 2 (April 1991): 244–60.

Applebaum, Anne. "Every Revolution Is Different." *Slate*, February 21, 2011. http://www.slate.com/articles/news_and_politics/foreigners/2011/02/every_revolution_is_different.html.

Appy, Christian G. *American Reckoning: The Vietnam War and Our National Identity*. New York: Penguin, 2015.

Arab Republic of Egypt. Decree-Law No. 92 of 2015. "Amending Some Provisions of the Political Rights Law No. 45 of 2014 and the House of Representatives Law No. 46 of 2014." Cairo: State Information Service, October 19, 2015. http://www.sis.gov.eg/newvr/elec%20low/HouseOfRepresentativesAmendments2015-92-En.pdf.

Arab Republic of Egypt. Law No. 128 of 2014. "Presidential Decree Amending the Penal Code" [Arabic]. Cairo: State Information Service, September 21,

2014. http://www.cc.gov.eg/Images/Legislations/G/2014/09/128-2014__21-09-
2014.pdf.

Arab Republic of Egypt. Law No. 33 of 2015. "Anti-Terrorism Law." Cairo: State
Information Service, August 15, 2015. http://www.atlanticcouncil.org/images/
EgyptSource/Egypt_Anti-Terror_Law_Translation.pdf.

Arab Republic of Egypt. Law No. 84 of 2002. "Law on Non-Governmental
Organizations." Cairo: State Information Service, June 5, 2002. http://www.
bu.edu/bucflp/files/2012/01/Law-on-Nongovernmental-Organizations-Law-
No.-84-of-2002.pdf.

Arieff, Alexis, and Carla E. Humud. *Political Transition in Tunisia*. CRS Report
no. RS21666. Washington, DC: Congressional Research Service, 2015.
https://www.fas.org/sgp/crs/row/RS21666.pdf.

Aronoff, Myron J. "The Politics of Collective Identity." *Reviews in Anthropology*
27, no. 1 (March 1998): 71–85.

Arsenal Consulting. "Çetin Doğan T.C. İSTANBUL10. AĞIR CEZA
MAHKEMESİ 2010/283: Preliminary Report." Chelsea, MA: Arsenal
Consulting, March 21, 2012. https://cdogangercekler.files.wordpress.com/
2012/03/burosu_dogan-021512-preliminary-report-final.pdf.

Arsenal Consulting. "Çetin Doğan T.C. İSTANBUL10. AĞIR CEZA
MAHKEMESİ 2010/283: Preliminary Samsung Hard Drive Report." Chelsea,
MA: Arsenal Consulting, March 28, 2012. https://cdogangercekler.files.
wordpress.com/2012/03/dogan-preliminary-samsung-hard-drive.pdf.

Arsenal Consulting. "Çetin Doğan T.C. İSTANBUL10. AĞIR CEZA
MAHKEMESİ 2010/283: Preliminary Gölcük CD No. 1 and Eskişehir
Thumb Drive Report." Chelsea, MA: Arsenal Consulting, March 21,
2012. https://cdogangercekler.files.wordpress.com/2012/05/dogan-021512-
preliminary-gocc88lcucc88k-cd-no-1-and-eskiscca7ehir-thumb-drive-report-
final-with-signature.pdf.

Assad, Ragui, and Ghada Barsoum. "Youth Exclusion in Egypt: In Search
of Second Chances." *Middle East Youth Initiative* Working Paper no. 2.
Washington, DC: World Bank, 2007.

Atkinson, Rick. *An Army at Dawn: The War in North Africa, 1942–1943*. Vol. 1,
The Liberation Trilogy. New York: Henry Holt, 2002.

Atlantic Council. "Translation: President Mohamed Morsi's
Address to the Nation." *AtlanticCouncil.org*, June 28,
2013. http://www.atlanticcouncil.org/blogs/egyptsource/
translation-president-mohamed-morsi-s-address-to-the-nation.

Baker, Raymond W. *Sadat and After: Struggles for Egypt's Political Soul*.
Cambridge, MA: Harvard University Press, 1990.

Baker, Raymond W. "Understanding Egypt's Worldly Miracles." *Middle East
Journal* 66, no. 1 (Winter 2012): 163–70.

Bakir, Sherine. "Public Promise: Uncertainty Surrounds Privatization Scheme."
Cairo: American Chamber of Commerce in Egypt, January 2009. http://
www.amcham.org.eg/resources_publications/publications/business_monthly/

issue.asp?sec=4&subsec=Uncertainty%20Surrounds%20Privatization%20
Scheme%20&im=1&iy=2009.

Bandow, Doug. "Cancel Aid to Egypt." *American Spectator*, June 23, 2014. http://
spectator.org/articles/59724/cancel-aid-egypt.

Barkey, Henri J. *The State and the Industrialization Crisis in Turkey*. Boulder,
CO: Westview Press, 1990.

Barkey, Henri J., and Graham E. Fuller. *Turkey's Kurdish Question*. Lanham,
MD: Rowman & Littlefield, 1998.

Barlas, Dilek. *Etatism and Diplomacy in Turkey: Economic and Foreign Policy in
an Uncertain World, 1929–1939*. Leiden: Brill, 1998.

Batty, David. "Egypt the Day after Mubarak Quits—Live." *Guardian*,
February 12, 2011. http://www.theguardian.com/world/blog/2011/feb/12/
egypt-day-after-mubarak-quits.

Bayar, Ali H. "The Developmental State and Economic Policy in Turkey." *Third
World Quarterly* 17, no. 4 (1996): 773–86.

Bayat, Asef. "A New Arab Street in Post-Islamist Times." *ForeignPolicy.
com*, January 26, 2011. http://foreignpolicy.com/2011/01/26/
a-new-arab-street-in-post-islamist-times.

BBC News. "Egypt's Muslim Brotherhood Declared 'Terrorist Group.'"
December 25, 2013. www.bbc.com/news/world-middle-east-25515932.

Beattie, Kirk J. *Egypt during the Sadat Years*. Boulder, CO: Westview Press, 1994.

Beaumont, Peter. "The Truth about Twitter, Facebook, and the Uprisings in the
Arab World." *Guardian*, February 25, 2011. https://www.theguardian.com/
world/2011/feb/25/twitter-facebook-uprisings-arab-libya.

Behrman, Greg. *The Most Noble Adventure: The Marshall Plan and the Time
When America Helped Save Europe*. New York: Simon & Schuster, 2007.

Beissinger, Mark R., Amaney Jamal, and Kevin Mazur. "Who Participated in
the Arab Spring? A Comparison of the Egyptian and Tunisian Revolution."
(February 17–19, 2012). http://www.princeton.edu/~mbeissin/beissinger.
tunisiaegyptcoalitions.pdf.

Bell, James, et al. *The World's Muslims: Religion, Politics and Society*. Washington,
DC: Pew Forum on Religion & Public Life, 2013. http://www.pewforum.org/
files/2013/04/worlds-muslims-religion-politics-society-full-report.pdf.

Bell, James, et al. *The World's Muslims: Unity and Diversity*. Washington,
DC: Pew Forum on Religion & Public Life, 2012. http://www.pewforum.org/
files/2012/08/the-worlds-muslims-full-report.pdf.

Bellin, Eva. "The Robustness of Authoritarianism in the Middle
East: Exceptionalism in Comparative Perspective." *Comparative Politics* 36,
no. 2 (January 2004): 139–57.

Bellin, Eva. *Stalled Democracy: Capital, Labor, and the Paradox of State-Sponsored
Development*. Ithaca, NY: Cornell University Press, 2002.

Ben Ali, Zine al-Abidine. "Tunisia: The Overthrow of Bourguiba." *Al-Bab.com*,
November 7, 1987. http://www.al-bab.com/arab/docs/tunisia/declaration_
07111987.htm.

Berman, Shari. "The Promise of the Arab Spring." *Foreign Affairs* (January/February 2013): 64–74.

Blaydes, Lisa. *Elections and Distributive Politics in Mubarak's Egypt.* Cambridge: Cambridge University Press, 2011.

Boehlert, Eric. "The Media's Favorite Arab Expert." *Salon*, December 21, 2001. http://www.salon.com/2001/12/21/ajami_2.

Bolton, John R. "Mubarak Understood His Country Better than Western Know-It-Alls." *Ottawa Citizen*. Reproduced on the website of the American Enterprise Institute, July 9, 2013. https://www.aei.org/publication/mubarak-understood-his-country-better-than-western-know-it-alls.

Boot, Max. "Mubarak, Let Your People Go." *Los Angeles Times*, May 19, 2005. http://articles.latimes.com/2005/may/19/opinion/oe-boot19.

Botha, Anneli. *Terrorism in the Maghreb: The Transnationalisation of Domestic Terrorism.* ISS Monograph Series no. 144. Pretoria: Institute for Security Studies, 2008.

Boyd, Douglas. "The Democracy Agenda in the Arab World." *Middle East Report*, no. 174 (January–February 1992): 3–5, 47.

Brown, Michael E., Sean M. Lynn-Jones, and Steven E. Miller. *Debating the Democratic Peace.* Cambridge, MA: MIT Press, 1997.

Brown, Nathan J. *Constitutions in a Nonconstitutional World: Arab Basic Laws and the Prospects for Accountable Government.* Albany: State University of New York Press, 2002.

Brown, Nathan J., and Michele Dunne. "Egypt's Draft Constitutional Amendments Answer Some Questions and Raise Others." Washington, DC: Carnegie Endowment for International Peace, March 1, 2011. http://carnegieendowment.org/2011/03/01/egypt-s-draft-constitutional-amendments-answer-some-questions-and-raise-others.

Brownlee, Jason. "And Yet They Persist: Explaining Survival and Transition in Neopatrimonial Regimes." *Studies in Comparative International Development* 37, no. 3 (Fall 2002): 35–63.

Brownlee, Jason. *Authoritarianism in an Age of Democratization.* Cambridge: Cambridge University Press, 2007.

Brubaker, Rogers. *Ethnicity without Groups.* Cambridge, MA: Harvard University Press, 2006.

Brumberg, Daniel. "An Arab Path to Democracy?" *Journal of Democracy* 1, no. 4 (Fall 1990): 120–25.

Brumberg, Daniel. "The Trap of Liberalized Autocracy." *Journal of Democracy* 13, no. 14 (October 2002): 56–57.

Brumberg, Daniel. *In Pursuit of Democracy and Security in the Greater Middle East.* Muslim World Initiative Report. Washington, DC: US Institute of Peace Press, January 21, 2010. http://www.usip.org/publications/in-pursuit-of-democracy-and-security-in-the-greater-middle-east.

Bunzel, Cole. "From Paper State to Caliphate: The Ideology of the Islamic State." Analysis Paper no. 19. Washington, DC: Brookings Institution Press, March 2015. https://www.brookings.edu/wp-content/uploads/2016/06/The-ideology-of-the-Islamic-State.pdf.

Burgat, François, and William Dowell. *The Islamic Movement in North Africa.* Austin: University of Texas Press, 1997.

Burns, R. Nicholas. "The Future of the U.S.-Turkey Relationship." Washington, DC: US Department of State, September 13, 2007. http://2001-2009.state.gov/p/us/rm/2007/92066.htm.

Bush, George W. "President Bush Discusses War on Terrorism with Tunisian President." Washington, DC: The White House, February 18, 2004. http://georgewbush-whitehouse.archives.gov/news/releases/2004/02/images/20040218-2_b33s8771-515h.html.

Bush, George W. "President Discusses Democracy, Freedom from Turkey." Washington, DC: The White House, June 29, 2004. http://georgewbush-whitehouse.archives.gov/news/releases/2004/06/text/20040629-4.html.

Çağaptay, Soner. "The Fragile Thaw in U.S.-Turkey Relations." Policy Watch no. 2402. Washington, DC: Washington Institute for Near East Policy, April 7, 2015. http://www.washingtoninstitute.org/policy-analysis/view/the-fragile-thaw-in-u.s.-turkish-relations.

Çağaptay, Soner. "Is Turkey Leaving the West?" *ForeignAffairs.com*, October 26, 2009. https://www.foreignaffairs.com/articles/turkey/2009-10-26/turkey-leaving-west.

Çağaptay, Soner. "What Turkey's Election Results Mean." Policy Alert. Washington, DC: Washington Institute for Near East Policy, June 8, 2015. http://www.washingtoninstitute.org/policy-analysis/view/what-turkeys-election-results-mean.

Cairo Institute for Human Rights Studies (CIHRS). "Al-Ittihadiya: 'Presidential Palace' Clashes in Cairo, 5–6 December 2012." Cairo: Cairo Institute for Human Rights Studies, December 2012. http://www.cihrs.org/wp-content/uploads/2012/12/Ittihadiyya.rep_.CIHRS_.Eng_.Dec_.pdf.

Caldwell, Christopher. "The East in the West." *New York Times Magazine*, September 25, 2005. http://www.nytimes.com/2005/09/25/magazine/the-east-in-the-west.html.

Campagna, Joel. "From Accommodation to Confrontation: The Muslim Brotherhood during the Mubarak Years." *Journal of International Affairs* 50, no. 1 (Summer 1996): 278–304.

Çandar, Cengiz. "Post-Election Erdogan Cannot Regain Power He Lost." *Al-Monitor*, June 29, 2015. http://www.al-monitor.com/pulse/originals/2015/06/turkey-post-election-erdogan-cannot-regain-power-lost.html.

Carney, Jay. "Press Briefing by Press Secretary Jay Carney, 11/26/2012." Washington, DC: The White House, November 26, 2012. https://www.whitehouse.gov/the-press-office/2012/11/26/press-briefing-press-secretary-jay-carney-11262012.

Carothers, Thomas. "The End of the Transition Paradigm." *Journal of Democracy* 13, no. 1 (January 2002): 5–21.

Carter Center. *Presidential Election in Egypt: Waging Peace, Fighting Disease, Building Hope.* Atlanta, GA: Carter Center, May–June 2012. https://www.cartercenter.org/resources/pdfs/news/peace_publications/election_reports/egypt-final-presidential-elections-2012.pdf.

Celâsun, Merih, and Dani Rodrik. "Turkish Economic Development: An Overview." In *Country Studies—Indonesia, Korea, Philippines, Turkey,* edited by Jeffrey Sachs and Susan M. Collins, 617–28. Vol. 3 of *Developing Country Debt and Economic Performance.* Chicago: University of Chicago Press, 1989.

Çetinsaya, Gökhan. "Rethinking Nationalism and Islam: Some Preliminary Notes on the Roots of 'Turkish-Islamic Synthesis' in Modern Turkish Political Thought." *Muslim World* 89, nos. 3–4 (July–October 1999): 350–76.

Chayes, Sarah. "How a Leftist Labor Union Forced Tunisia's Political Settlement." Washington, DC: Carnegie Endowment for International Peace, March 27, 2014. http://carnegieendowment.org/2014/03/27/how-leftist-labor-union-helped-force-tunisia-s-political-settlement.

Chivvis, Christopher S., and Jeffrey Martini. *Libya after Qaddafi: Lessons and Implications for the Future.* Santa Monica, CA: RAND Corporation, 2014. http://www.rand.org/pubs/research_reports/RR577.html.

Çiçek, İzzeittin. "Top Court to Review Content of Law on Penal Judges of Peace." *Today's Zaman,* October 23, 2014.

Cigar, Norman L. *Genocide in Bosnia: The Policy of "Ethnic Cleansing."* College Station: Texas A&M Press, 1995.

Clinton, Hillary Rodham. "Interview with Bob Schieffer of CBS's Face the Nation." Washington, DC: US Department of State, January 30, 2011. http://www.state.gov/secretary/20092013clinton/rm/2011/01/155587.htm.

Clinton, Hillary Rodham. "Interview with Candy Crowley of CNN's State of the Union." Washington, DC: US Department of State, January 30, 2011. http://www.state.gov/secretary/remarks/2014/07/229508.htm.

Clinton, Hillary Rodham. "Interview with Chris Wallace of Fox News Sunday." Washington, DC: US Department of State, January 30, 2011. http://www.state.gov/secretary/20092013clinton/rm/2011/01/155589.htm.

Clinton, Hillary Rodham. "Interview with David Gregory of NBC's Meet the Press." Washington, DC: US Department of State, January 30, 2011. http://www.state.gov/secretary/20092013clinton/rm/2011/01/155585.htm.

Clinton, Hillary Rodham. "Recent Events in Tunisia." Press Statement. Washington, DC: US Department of State, January 14, 2011. http://www.state.gov/secretary/20092013clinton/rm/2011/01/154684.htm.

Clinton, Hillary Rodham. "Remarks." US Consulate, Alexandria, Egypt. Washington, DC: US Department of State, July 15, 2012. http://www.state.gov/secretary/20092013clinton/rm/2012/07/195036.htm.

Clinton, Hillary Rodham. "Remarks." Ritz Carlton Hotel, Doha, Qatar. Washington, DC: US Department of State, January 13, 2011. http://www.state.gov/secretary/20092013clinton/rm/2011/01/154595.htm.

Cohen, Richard. "We Need the Realist's Vigilant Cynicism." *Washington Post*, September 1, 2014. https://www.washingtonpost.com/opinions/richard-cohen-we-need-the-realists-vigilant-cynicism/2014/09/01/8955ac58-2fca-11e4-9b98-848790384093_story.html.

Cole, Juan. "Why Tunisia's Arab Spring Is in Turmoil." *Informed Comment* (blog), February 9, 2013. http://www.juancole.com/2013/02/tunisias-spring-turmoil.html.

Cole, Juan. "Why It's Way Too Soon to Give Up on the Arab Spring." *Los Angeles Times*, June 28, 2014. http://www.latimes.com/opinion/op-ed/la-oe-cole-arab-spring-millenials-20140629-story.html.

Commission of the European Communities (CEC). *2002 Regular Report on Turkey's Progress Towards Accession*. Brussels: European Union, October 2002. http://ec.europa.eu/enlargement/archives/pdf/key_documents/2002/tu_en.pdf.

Commission of the European Communities (CEC). *2004 Regular Report on Turkey's Progress Towards Accession*. Brussels: European Union, October 2004. http://ec.europa.eu/enlargement/archives/pdf/key_documents/2004/rr_tr_2004_en.pdf.

Committee to Protect Journalists (CPJ). "2015 Prison Census: 199 Journalists Jailed Worldwide." New York: Committee to Protect Journalists, December 1, 2015. https://cpj.org/imprisoned/2015.php.

Committee to Protect Journalists (CPJ). "Egypt's Imprisonment of Journalists Is at an All Time High." New York: Committee to Protect Journalists, June 25, 2015. https://cpj.org/reports/2015/06/egypt-imprisonment-of-journalists-is-at-an-all-time-high.php.

Cook, Steven A. "America's Radical Idealists Strike Again." *American Interest* 6, no. 6 (July/August 2011): 74–79.

Cook, Steven A. "Beji Caid Essebsi and Tunisia's Identity Politics." *From the Potomac to the Euphrates* (blog), May 20, 2015. http://blogs.cfr.org/cook/2015/05/20/beji-caid-essebsi-and-tunisias-identity-politics.

Cook, Steven A. "Cheering an Islamist Victory." *Boston Globe*, July 26, 2007. http://archive.boston.com/news/globe/editorial_opinion/oped/articles/2007/07/26/cheering_an_islamist_victory.

Cook, Steven A. "The Frankenstein of Tahrir Square." *ForeignPolicy.com*, December 19, 2011. http://foreignpolicy.com/2011/12/19/the-frankenstein-of-tahrir-square/.

Cook, Steven A. "How Erdogan Made Turkey Authoritarian Again." *Atlantic Monthly*, July 21, 2016. http://www.theatlantic.com/international/archive/2016/07/how-erdogan-made-turkey-authoritarian-again/492374.

Cook, Steven A. "'How Happy Is the One Who Says, I Am a Turk!'" *ForeignPolicy.com*, March 28, 2016. http://foreignpolicy.com/2016/03/28/how-happy-is-the-one-who-says-i-am-a-turk.

Cook, Steven A. "January 25th and the Egypt the Revolution Has Made." *ForeignAffairs.com*, January 25, 2012. https://www.foreignaffairs.com/articles/north-africa/2012-01-25/january-25th-and-egypt-revolution-has-made.

Cook, Steven A. "The Middle Eastern Revolutions That Never Were." *American Interest*, October 26, 2015. http://www.the-american-interest.com/2015/10/26/the-middle-eastern-revolutions-that-never-were.

Cook, Steven A. "The Odds on Turkey." Letter to the Editor. *Commentary*, June 1, 2007. https://www.commentarymagazine.com/articles/the-odds-on-turkey.

Cook, Steven A. *Ruling but Not Governing: The Military and Political Development in Egypt, Algeria, and Turkey.* Baltimore, MD: Johns Hopkins University Press, 2007.

Cook, Steven A. "Still Think Middle East Peace Doesn't Matter?" *ForeignPolicy.com*, November 19, 2012. http://foreignpolicy.com/2012/11/19/still-think-middle-east-peace-doesnt-matter.

Cook, Steven A. *The Struggle for Egypt: From Nasser to Tahrir Square.* New York: Oxford University Press, 2011.

Cook, Steven A. "Turkey's Democratic Mirage." *ForeignAffairs.com*, January 8, 2014. https://www.foreignaffairs.com/articles/turkey/2014-01-08/turkeys-democratic-mirage.

Cook, Steven A. "Turkey's in a Terrible Spot." *Slate*, June 29, 2016. http://www.slate.com/articles/news_and_politics/foreigners/2016/06/isis_is_just_one_problem_of_many_for_turkey_and_erdogan.html.

Cook, Steven A. "Turkey's Political Football." *From the Potomac to the Euphrates* (blog), April 8, 2013. http://blogs.cfr.org/cook/2013/04/08/turkeys-political-football.

Cook, Steven A., and Michael J. Koplow. "Turkey's Secularists Surrender." *From the Potomac to the Euphrates* (blog), August 9, 2014. http://blogs.cfr.org/cook/2014/08/09/turkeys-secularists-surrender.

Cowell, Alan. "5 Killed in South Jordan as Rioting over Food Prices Spreads." *New York Times*, April 20, 1989.

Crowley, Philip J. "Daily Press Briefing." Washington, DC: US Department of State, January 18, 2011. http://www.state.gov/r/pa/prs/dpb/2011/01/154747.htm.

Daalder, Ivo H., and James M. Lindsay. *America Unbound: The Bush Revolution in Foreign Policy.* New York: John Wiley, 2005.

Daloğlu, Tülin. "AKP Reacts to U.S. Criticism of Turkey." *Al-Monitor*, February 8, 2013. http://www.al-monitor.com/pulse/originals/2013/02/turkish-judiciary-akp-us-relations.html.

Danforth, Nick. "How the West Lost Turkey." *ForeignPolicy.com*, November 25, 2009. http://foreignpolicy.com/2009/11/25/how-the-west-lost-turkey.

Davis, Julie Hirschfeld. "John Kerry Says U.S. Will Give Tunisia More Financial Aid." *New York Times*, November 13, 2015. http://www.nytimes.com/2015/11/14/world/africa/john-kerry-says-us-will-give-tunisia-more-financial-aid.html.

Day, Allan J., reviewed by Richard German and Elizabeth Taylor. "Libya: Economy." In *The Middle East and North Africa 2004*, edited by Lucy Dean, 794–808. 50th ed. London: Europa Publications, 2004.

de Bellaigue, Christopher. "Turkey at the Turning Point?" *New York Review of Books*, October 25, 2007. www.nybooks.com/articles/2007/10/25/turkey-at-the-turning-point.

Democracy International. *Observing Egypt's Roadmap Elections: Democracy International's Statements and Reports, 2013–2015*. Bethesda, MD: Democracy International, March 2016. http://democracyinternational.com/media/Observing%20Egypt%E2%80%99s%20Roadmap%20Elections%20Democracy%20International%E2%80%99s%20Statements%20and%20Reports,%202013-2015.pdf.

Democracy International. "Preliminary Statement: Egypt's House of Representative Elections." Egypt International Election Observation Mission, December 9, 2015. http://democracyinternational.com/publications/preliminary-statement-egypts-2015-house-representatives-elections.

Dillman, Bradford. "Transition to Democracy in Algeria." In *State and Society in Algeria*, edited by John P. Entelis and Philip C. Naylor, 31–52. Boulder, CO: Westview Press, 1992.

Doğan, Pınar, and Dani Rodrik. "'Back to the Future' Documents in the Sledgehammer Case." *Balyoz Davası ve Gerçekler* (blog), November 2010. https://cdogangercekler.files.wordpress.com/2010/11/back_to_the_future_documents_in_the_sledgehammer_case.pdf.

Doğan, Pınar, and Dani Rodrik. "The Sledgehammer Coup Allegations in Turkey: Fake Documents, Fraudulent Claims." *Balyoz Davası ve Gerçekler* (blog), April 19, 2010. https://cdogangercekler.files.wordpress.com/2010/04/sledgehammer_presentation.pdf.

Doğan, Pınar, and Dani Rodrik. "The Sledgehammer Coup Plan and the Case of Çetin Doğan—An Update." *Balyoz Davası ve Gerçekler* (blog), March 9, 2010. https://cdogangercekler.files.wordpress.com/2010/03/the-case-of-cetin-dogan-2.pdf.

Dombey, Daniel, and Lina Saigol. "Turkish Unions to Join Anti-Government Protests." *Financial Times*, June 4, 2013. http://www.ft.com/intl/cms/s/0/2401af76-cc31-11e2-9cf7-00144feab7de.html.

Dunne, Michele. "Crisis in Egypt." Testimony before the Senate Committee on Foreign Relations, 13th Congress, 1st Session, July 25, 2013. Washington, DC: Atlantic Council. http://www.foreign.senate.gov/imo/media/doc/Dunne_Testimony.pdf.

Dwyer, Kevin. *Arab Voices: The Human Rights Debate*. Berkeley, CA: University of California Press, 1991.

The Economist. "The Awakening." *Economist* 398 (February 19, 2011): 11–12. http://www.economist.com/node/18180416.

The Economist. "A Golden Opportunity?" *Economist* 399 (April 2, 2011). http://www.economist.com/node/18486089.

The Economist. "The Lesson from Turkey." *Economist* 384 (July 26, 2007): 15. http://www.economist.com/node/9549614.

Egypt Independent. "FJP Drafts Amendment to Israel Peace Treaty for Morsy, Parliament to Review." November 11, 2012. http://www.egyptindependent. com/news/fjp-drafts-amendment-israel-peace-treaty-morsy-parliament-review.

Egyptian Ministry of Economic Development. "Major Economic Indicators 1967–1980." Cairo: Arab Republic of Egypt.

Election Network in the Arab Region. "Presidential Elections in Egypt: Hopeful Steps" [Arabic]. Amman: Election Network in the Arab Region, July 25, 2012. http://www.arabew.org/images/stories/news/pdf/Egypt_pr_2012.pdf.

Electoral Institute for Sustainable Democracy in Africa (EISA). *EISA Election Witnessing Mission Report: Egypt.* Report no. 45. Johannesburg: Electoral Institute for Sustainable Democracy in Africa, 2013. https://eisa.org.za/pdf/ egy2012eom24.pdf.

El-Haddad, Gehad. "Anti-coup Alliance Response to Secretary John Kerry's Statements Supporting Military Coup in Egypt." *IkhwanWeb*, August 2, 2013. http://www.ikhwanweb.com/article.php?id=31205.

El-Hamalawy, Hossam. "#Jan25 The Workers, Middle Class, Military Junta, and the Permanent Revolution." *3arabawy* (blog), February 12, 2011. http:// arabawy.org/24959/permanent-revolution.

El Laithy, Heba, Michael Lokshin, and Arup Benerji. "Poverty and Economic Growth in Egypt, 1995–2000." Policy Research Working Paper no. 3068. Washington, DC: World Bank, June 2003. http://elibrary.worldbank.org/doi/ pdf/10.1596/1813-9450-3068.

Erdle, Steffen. *Ben Ali's "New Tunisia" (1987–2009): A Case Study of Authoritarian Modernization in the Arab World.* Berlin: Klaus Schwarz Verlag, 2010.

Erdoğan, Recep Tayyip. "President Erdoğan Responds to Kiliçdaroglu's 'Bellyaching'" [Turkish]. *HaberTürk*, January 24, 2016. http://www.haberturk.com/gundem/haber/ 1185822-cumhurbaskani-erdogandan-kilicdarogluda-karinagrisi-yaniti.

Erdoğan, Recep Tayyip. "Remarks on the Occasion of the Ambassadors Conference" [Turkish]. Ankara: Republic of Turkey, January 12, 2016. http:// www.tccb.gov.tr/konusmalar/353/37541/8-buyukelciler-konferansi-vesilesiyle- duzenlenen-yemekte-yaptiklari-konusma.html.

Escribà-Folch, Abel, and Joseph Wright. "Dealing with Tyranny: International Sanctions and the Survival of Authoritarian Rulers." *International Studies Quarterly* 54, no. 2 (June 2010): 335–59.

Esposito, John L., and James Piscatori. "Democratization and Islam." *Middle East Journal* 45, no. 3 (Summer 1991): 427–40.

Essebsi, Beji Caid. "My Three Goals as Tunisia's President." *Washington Post*, December 26, 2014. https://www.washingtonpost.com/opinions/beji-caid- essebsi-my-three-goals-as-tunisias-president/2014/12/26/46a4dad6-8b8d-11e4- a085-34e9b9f09a58_story.html.

European Commission. "Commission Recommends to Start Negotiations with Turkey under Certain Conditions." Press Release. Brussels: European

Commission, October 6, 2004. http://europa.eu/rapid/press-release_IP-04-1180_en.pdf.

European Commission. "Conditions for Membership." Brussels: European Commission, October 12, 2015. http://ec.europa.eu/enlargement/policy/conditions-membership/index_en.htm.

European Commission. "EU/Tunisia: €300 Million Macro-Financial Assistance Package Signed." Memo. Brussels: European Commission, September 4, 2014. http://europa.eu/rapid/press-release_MEMO-14-515_en.htm.

European Commission. "EU-Tunisia: Commission Proposes Further EUR 500 Million in Macro-Financial Assistance." Press Release. Brussels: European Commission, February 12, 2016. http://europa.eu/rapid/press-release_IP-16-289_en.htm.

Evans, Gareth, and Mohamed Sahnoun, et al. *The Responsibility to Protect.* International Commission on Intervention and State Sovereignty. Ottawa: International Development Research Centre, December 2001. http://responsibilitytoprotect.org/ICISS%20Report.pdf.

Exum, Andrew, and J. Dana Stuster. "Policing Reform & Reforming Police." *Sada* (blog), February 16, 2012. http://carnegieendowment.org/sada/?fa=47200.

Falk, Richard. "Imperial Vibrations, 9/11, and the Ordeal of the Middle East." *Journal of Palestine Studies* 34, no. 3 (Spring 2005): 65–76.

Federation of American Scientists (FAS). *Turkey–Guide to Ergenekon.* Open Source Center Report. Washington, DC: Federation of American Scientists, March 19, 2010. http://fas.org/irp/world/turkey/ergenekon.pdf.

Feldman, Noah. "Islamists' Victory in Tunisia a Win for Democracy." *Bloomberg*, October 30, 2011. https://www.bloomberg.com/view/articles/2011-10-30/islamists-victory-in-tunisia-a-win-for-democracy-noah-feldman.

Finkel, Isobel. "Why Investors Are Calling This the Most Important Turkish Election in Forever." *Bloomberg*, June 5, 2015. http://www.bloomberg.com/news/articles/2015-06-05/why-investors-are-calling-this-the-most-important-turkish-election-ever.

Fraser, Suzan, and Elena Becatoros. "Turkey's Erdogan Blasts Foreign Countries over Coup Reaction." *Associated Press* via *Washington Post*, August 2, 2016. https://www.washingtonpost.com/world/middle_east/turkey-sends-2nd-document-to-us-seeking-clerics-arrest/2016/08/02/06eee052-5892-11e6-8b48-0cb344221131_story.html.

Freedman, Robert O. *Soviet Policy toward the Middle East Since 1970.* 3rd ed. New York: Praeger, 1982.

Fry, Maxwell J. *Finance and Development Planning in Turkey.* Vol. 5. Leiden: Brill Archive, 1972.

Gal, Carlotta. "Tunisian President Looks for Help in Sustaining Arab Spring Progress." *New York Times*, May 18, 2015. http://www.nytimes.com/2015/05/19/world/africa/tunisian-president-looks-for-help-in-sustaining-progress.html.

Gartenstein-Ross, Daveed. "How Many Fighters Does the Islamic State Really Have?" *War on the Rocks*, February 9, 2015. http://warontherocks.com/2015/02/how-many-fighters-does-the-islamic-state-really-have.

Gasiorowski, Mark J. "Economic Crisis and Political Regime Change: An Event in History Analysis." *American Political Science Review* 89, no. 4 (December 1995): 882–97.

Gause, F. Gregory, III. "The Middle East Academic Community and the 'Winter of Arab Discontent': Why Did We Miss It?" In *Seismic Shift: Understanding Change in the Middle East*, edited by Ellen Laipson, 11–26. Washington, DC: Henry L. Stimson Center, May 2011. http://www.stimson.org/sites/default/files/Full_Pub-Seismic_Shift.pdf.

Gause, F. Gregory, III. "The Persistence of Monarchy in the Arabian Peninsula: A Comparative Analysis." In *Middle East Monarchies: The Challenge of Modernity*, edited by Joseph Kostiner, 167–86. Boulder, CO: Lynne Rienner, 2000.

Gause, F. Gregory, III. "Why Middle East Studies Missed the Arab Spring." *Foreign Affairs* 90, no. 4 (July/August 2011): 81–90.

Geddes, Barbara. "What Do We Know about Democratization after Twenty Years?" *Annual Review of Political Science* 2 (1999): 115–44.

Gellner, Ernest. *Culture, Identity and Politics*. Cambridge: Cambridge University Press, 1987.

Gerecht, Reuel Marc. "The Islamist Road to Democracy." *Wall Street Journal*, April 23, 2012. http://www.wsj.com/articles/SB10001424052702304299304577350200925769444.

Gharib, Ali. "The Case for Cutting Aid to Egypt." *Daily Beast*, July 11, 2013. http://www.thedailybeast.com/articles/2013/07/11/the-case-for-cutting-off-aid-to-egypt.html.

Ghazal, Amal, and Larbi Sadiki. "ISIS: The 'Islamic State' between Orientalism and the Interiority of MENA's Intellectuals." *Jadaliyya.com*, January 19, 2016. http://www.jadaliyya.com/pages/index/23616/isis_the-islamic-state-between-orientalism-and-the.

Ghedira, Mahmoud. "Will Ennahda Apologize for the Attacks of 1987?" *TunisiaLive*, September 5, 2011. http://www.tunisia-live.net/2011/09/05/will-ennahda-apologize-for-the-attacks-of-1987.

Giddens, Anthony. "My Chat with the Colonel." *Guardian*, March 8, 2007. https://www.theguardian.com/commentisfree/2007/mar/09/comment.libya.

Giddens, Anthony. "The Colonel and His Third Way." *New Statesman*, August 26, 2006. http://www.newstatesman.com/politics/politics/2014/04/colonel-and-his-third-way.

Ginsburg, Tom, and Tamir Moustafa. *Rule by Law: The Politics of Courts in Authoritarian Regimes*. Cambridge: Cambridge University Press, 2008.

Girit, Selin. "Turkey Election: The Least Predictable for over a Decade." *BBC News*, June 5, 2015. http://www.bbc.com/news/world-europe-32993721.

Gleditsch, Kristian. *All International Politics Is Local: The Diffusion of Conflict, Integration, and Democratization.* Ann Arbor: University of Michigan Press, 2002.

Glicksberg, Joseph. "The Islamist Movement and the Subversion of Secularism in Egypt." PhD diss., University of Pennsylvania, 2003.

Goldberg, Jeffrey. "The Obama Doctrine." *Atlantic Monthly* 317, no. 3 (April 2016): 70–90.

Goldstone, Jack A. "Understanding the Revolutions of 2011." *Foreign Affairs* (May/June 2011): 8–16.

Goldstone, Jack. *Revolution and Rebellion in the Early Modern World.* Berkeley: University of California Press, 1991.

Gordon, Joel. *Nasser's Blessed Movement: Egypt's Free Officers and the July Revolution.* Cairo: American University in Cairo Press, 1996.

Graefe, Laurel. "Oil Shock of 1978–79." *FederalReserveHistory.org*, November 22, 2013. http://www.federalreservehistory.org/Events/DetailView/40.

Gray, Kevin. "Tripoli: Once a Pariah, Now a Hot Spot." *New York Times*, August 27, 2006. http://www.nytimes.com/2006/08/27/travel/27journeys.html.

Great Socialist People's Libyan Arab Jamahiriyya. "The Great Green Charter of Human Rights of the Jamahiriyan Era [Libya]." Reproduced on *RefWorld.org*, June 12, 1988. http://www.refworld.org/docid/3dda540f4. html.

Griswold, Eliza. "The Heir." *New Republic*, July 20, 2010. https://newrepublic. com/article/75949/the-heir.

Grove, Lloyd. "The Man Who Freed the Bomber." *Daily Beast*, August 24, 2009. http://www.thedailybeast.com/articles/2009/08/24/the-man-who-freed-the-bomber.html.

Gül, Abdullah. "The U.S.-Turkish Relationship: Prospects and Perils." Policy Watch no. 776. Washington, DC: Washington Institute for Near East Policy, July 25, 2003. http://www.washingtoninstitute.org/policy-analysis/view/ the-u.s.-turkish-relationship-prospects-and-perils.

Gurfinkiel, Michel. "Is Turkey Lost?" *Commentary*, March 1, 2007. https://www. commentarymagazine.com/articles/is-turkey-lost.

Gurr, Ted. *Why Men Rebel.* Princeton, NJ: Princeton University Press, 1970.

Haass, Richard N. *War of Necessity, War of Choice: A Memoir of Two Iraq Wars.* New York: Simon & Schuster, 2009.

Hale, William, and Ergun Özbudun. *Islamism, Democracy and Liberalism in Turkey: The Case of the AKP.* New York: Routledge, 2010.

Hamdan, Gamal. *The Character of Egypt: A Study in the Genius of the Place* [Arabic]. Vols. 1–4. Cairo: Alam al-Kutub, 1980.

Hamid, Shadi. "Beyond Guns and Butter: A U.S.-Egyptian Relationship for a Democratic Era." Saban Center for Middle East Policy Memo no. 22. Washington, DC: Brookings Institution Press, April 2012. https://www. brookings.edu/wp-content/uploads/2016/06/04_guns_butter_hamid1.pdf.

Hamid, Shadi. "The Real Reason the U.S. Should Consider Cutting Military Aid to Egypt." *Atlantic Monthly*, July 2, 2012. http://www.theatlantic.com/international/archive/2012/07/the-real-reason-the-us-should-consider-cutting-military-aid-to-egypt/259302.

Hanna, Sami Ayad, and George H. Gardner, eds. *Arab Socialism: A Documentary Survey*. Leiden: Brill Archive, 1969.

Hasan, Mehdi. "In Turkey the Right to Free Speech Is Being Lost." *Guardian*, June 10, 2012. http://www.theguardian.com/commentisfree/2012/jun/10/turkey-free-speech-erdogan-crackdown.

Hashemite Kingdom of Jordan. "Jordanian National Charter." December 1990 (adopted June 1991). http://www.kinghussein.gov.jo/charter-national.html.

Hassen, Bilal. "Fate of the Egyptian-Israeli Peace Treaty." *Asharq Alawsat*. Reproduced on the website of the American Task Force on Palestine, August 31, 2011. http://www.americantaskforce.org/daily_news_article/2011/09/01/1314849600_10.

Hawthorne, Amy. "What's Happening with Suspended Military Aid for Egypt?—Part I: The Apaches et al., One Year One." *Atlantic Council*, October 17, 2014. http://www.atlanticcouncil.org/images/publications/Whats_Happening_with_Military_Aid_to_Egypt_Part_I.pdf.

Hawthorne, Amy. "What's Happening with U.S. Military Aid to Egypt? Part II: Everything You Ever Wanted to Know about Foreign Military Financing (FMF) for Egypt." *AtlanticCouncil.org*, November 19, 2014. http://www.atlanticcouncil.org/images/Hawthorne_Whats_Happening_with_FMF_for_Egypt_Nov19.pdf.

Helfont, Samuel, and Michael Brill. "Saddam's ISIS?" *ForeignAffairs.com*, January 12, 2016. https://www.foreignaffairs.com/articles/iraq/2016-01-12/saddams-isis.

Heper, Metin, and Aylin Güney. "The Military and Democracy in the Third Turkish Republic." *Armed Forces and Society* 22, no. 4 (Summer 1996): 619–42.

Herb, Michael. "Princes and Parliaments in the Arab World." *Middle East Journal* 58, no. 3 (Summer 2004): 367–84.

Heydemann, Steven. "Social Pacts and the Persistence of Authoritarianism in the Middle East." In *Debating Arab Authoritarianism*, edited by Oliver Schlumberger, 21–38. Stanford, CA: Stanford University Press, 2007.

Heydemann, Steven. "Upgrading Authoritarianism in the Arab World." *Saban Center for Middle East Policy*, Analysis Paper no. 13. Washington, DC: Brookings Institution Press, October 2007. https://www.brookings.edu/wp-content/uploads/2016/06/10arabworld.pdf.

Hinnesbusch, Raymond A., Jr. *Egyptian Politics under Sadat: The Post-Populist Development of an Authoritarian-Modernizing State*. Boulder, CO: Lynne Rienner, 1988.

Hirschman, Albert O. "The Political Economy of Import-Substituting Industrialization in Latin America." *Quarterly Journal of Economics* 82, no. 1 (February 1968): 1–32.

Hitchens, Christopher. "The Iraq Effect." *Fighting Words* (blog), March 28, 2011. http://www.slate.com/articles/news_and_politics/fighting_words/2011/03/the_iraq_effect.html.

Holmes, Kim. "Egypt: Fruits of the Obama Administration's Neglect." *Daily Signal*, July 8, 2013. http://dailysignal.com//2013/07/08/egypt-fruits-of-the-obama-administrations-neglect.

Holmes, Oliver. "Fighters Clash Again Near Tripoli, Several Dead." *Reuters*, November 12, 2011. http://www.reuters.com/article/us-libya-clashes-idUSTRE7AB0HU20111112#tfpEKyKHFMB07Mpt.97.

Hopwood, Derek. *Habib Bourguiba of Tunisia*. New York: St. Martin's Press, 1992.

Hounshell, Blake. "You're So Vain, You Probably Think These Protests Are About You," *ForeignPolicy.com*, January 26, 2011. http://foreignpolicy.com/2011/01/26/youre-so-vain-you-probably-think-these-protests-are-about-you.

Hourani, Albert. *Arabic Thought in the Liberal Age, 1798–1939*. New York: Cambridge University Press, 1983.

Hudson, Michael C. "After the Gulf War: Prospects for Democratization in the Arab World." *Middle East Journal* 45, no. 3 (Summer 1991): 414.

Hudson, Michael C. "Presidential Address 1987: Democratization and the Problem of Legitimacy in Middle East Politics." *Middle East Studies Association Bulletin* 22, no. 2 (December 1988): 158–59.

Human Rights Watch. "Tunisia: Counterterror Law Endangers Rights." July 31, 2015. https://www.hrw.org/news/2015/07/31/tunisia-counterterror-law-endangers-rights.

Huntington, Samuel P. "The Clash of Civilizations?" *Foreign Affairs* 72, no. 3 (Summer 1993): 22–49.

Huntington, Samuel P. *Political Order in Changing Societies*. New Haven, CT: Yale University Press, 1968.

Huntington, Samuel P. *The Third Wave: Democratization in the Late Twentieth Century*. Norman: University of Oklahoma Press, 1991.

Hürriyet, "Breaking News. . .The President Explained: This Is One of the Places Where All the Scum Is! We Will Close It Down" [Turkish]. August 2, 2016. http://www.hurriyet.com.tr/erdogandan-flas-aciklamalar-40178919.

Hürriyet Daily News. " 'Who Are the Two Drunks' Turkish Politicians Ask after PM's Remarks." May 29, 2013. http://www.hurriyetdailynews.com/who-are-the-two-drunks-turkish-politicians-ask-after-pms-remarks.aspx?pageID=238&nID=47817&NewsCatID=338.

Husni, Abdul Moneim, ed. "Law No. 43 of 1974" [Arabic]. In *A Compendium of Egyptian Law and Statutes*, 229–261. Vol. 5. Giza: Merkaz Husni l-il-Dirasat al-Qanuniyyah, 1987.

Hussein, Mahmoud. "Muslim Brotherhood Secretary-General Criticizes John Kerry Remarks." *IkhwanWeb.com*, November 23, 2013. http://www.ikhwanweb.com/article.php?id=31430&ref=search.php.

Hussein, Taha. *The Future of Culture in Egypt*. Cairo: American University in Cairo Press, 1998.

Ignatius, David. "Hillary Clinton Was Right on Egypt." *Washington Post*, January 28, 2016. https://www.washingtonpost.com/opinions/hillary-clinton-was-right-on-egypt/2016/01/28/fe7fe922-c609-11e5-8965-0607e0e265ce_story.html.

Ignatius, David. "U.S. and Turkey Find a Relationship That Works." *Washington Post*, December 7, 2011. https://www.washingtonpost.com/opinions/us-and-turkey-find-a-relationship-that-works/2011/12/06/gIQAh5UcdO_story.html.

Ignatius, David. "Why Turkey Voted against Authoritarianism." *Washington Post*, June 9, 2015. https://www.washingtonpost.com/opinions/turkeys-resilient-democracy/2015/06/09/28fec564-0edc-11e5-a0dc-2b6f404ff5cf_story.html.

IkhwanWeb. "Muslim Brotherhood Statement on Unfolding Conspiracy against January 25 Revolution." August 8, 2012. http://www.ikhwanweb.com/article.php?id=30236.

Industries Chimiques. *Chemical Industries in Tunisia, 2014* [French]. Annual Report. Tunis: Agency for the Promotion of Industry and Innovation, 2014. http://www.tunisieindustrie.nat.tn/fr/download/CEPI/mono_ich.pdf.

International Crisis Group. "Making Sense of Libya." Media Release. Brussels: International Crisis Group, June 6, 2011. http://www.crisisgroup.org/en/publication-type/media-releases/2011/making-sense-of-Libya.aspx.

International Monetary Fund (IMF). "IMF Survey: Tunisia Gets $2.9 Billion IMF Loan to Strengthen Job Creation and Economic Growth." IMF Survey. Washington, DC: International Monetary Fund, June 2, 2016. https://www.imf.org/en/News/Articles/2015/09/28/04/53/sonew060216a.

International Monetary Fund (IMF). "Press Release: IMF Executive Board Completes Fifth Review under Stand-By Arrangement for Tunisia; Approves US$104.8 Million Disbursement." Press Release. Washington, DC: International Monetary Fund, December 12, 2014. https://www.imf.org/external/np/sec/pr/2014/pr14573.htm.

International Republican Institute. "IRI Iraq Index: October 2010 Survey of Iraqi Public Opinion." February 2, 2011. http://www.iri.org/sites/default/files/2011%20February%202%20IRI%20Index,%20October%2023-30,%202010.pdf.

International Stabilisation Response Team (ISRT). *Libya, 20 May—30 June 2011*. International Stabilisation Response Team report. London: Department for International Development, 2011. https://www.gov.uk/government/uploads/system/uploads/attachment_data/file/67470/libya-isrt-June2011.pdf.

Issacharoff, Avi. "Morsi Mulling Amendments to Egypt's Peace Accord with Israel, Says Advisor." *Haaretz.com*, August 14, 2012. http://www.haaretz.com/israel-news/morsi-mulling-amendments-to-egypt-s-peace-accord-with-israel-says-adviser-1.458204.

Istanbulian. "The Songs of Gezi: Top 15." Blog, June 2013. http://istanbulian.blogspot.com/2013/06/the-songs-of-occupy-gezi-top-10.html.

Jamieson, Alastair, and Colin Freeman. "Profile: Colonel Gaddafi's Son Saif al-Islam." *Telegraph*, August 22, 2009. http://www.telegraph.co.uk/news/worldnews/africaandindianocean/libya/6073809/Profile-Colonel-Gaddafis-son-Saif-al-Islam.html.

Jankowski, James P. *Nasser's Egypt: Arab Nationalism and the United Arab Republic*. Boulder, CO: Lynne Rienner, 2002.

Jenkins, Jack. "What *The Atlantic* Left Out about ISIS According to Their Own Expert." *ThinkProgress* (blog), February 20, 2015. http://thinkprogress.org/world/2015/02/20/3625446/atlantic-left-isis-conversation-bernard-haykel.

Johnson, Chalmers. *Revolutionary Change*. Stanford, CA: Stanford University Press, 1966.

Johnson, Charles Michael, Jr. "Egypt: U.S. Government Should Examine Options for Using Unobligated Funds and Evaluating Security Assistance Programs." GAO-15-259. Washington, DC: Government Accountability Office, February 2015. http://www.gao.gov/assets/670/668448.pdf.

Johnson, Keith, and Marc Champion. "Egypt's Islamist Riddle." *Wall Street Journal*, February 2, 2011. http://www.wsj.com/articles/SB10001424052748703445904576118493401195136.

Jones, Bruce. "The West, the Rest, and the New Middle East: Obama in London." *UpFront* (blog), May 27, 2011. http://www.brookings.edu/blogs/up-front/posts/2011/05/27-global-order-jones.

Joscelyn, Thomas. "Ansar al Sharia Libya Fights on under a New Leader." *Long War Journal*, June 30, 2015. http://www.longwarjournal.org/archives/2015/06/ansar-al-sharia-libya-fights-on-under-new-leader.php.

Kagan, Robert. "The U.S. Is Complicit in Egyptian Military Actions." *Washington Post*, August 1, 2013. https://www.washingtonpost.com/opinions/the-us-is-complicit-in-egyptian-militarys-actions/2013/08/01/f0d5235c-fac6-11e2-9bde-7ddaa186b751_story.html.

Kagan, Robert, and Michele Dunne. "Why Egypt Has to Be the U.S. Priority in the Middle East." *Washington Post*, March 7, 2011. http://www.washingtonpost.com/wp-dyn/content/article/2011/03/06/AR2011030602928.html.

Kalaycıoğlu, Ersin. "Elections and Governance." In *Politics, Parties, and Elections in Turkey*, edited by Sabri Sayari and Yılmaz Esmer, 55–72. Boulder, CO: Lynne Rienner, 2001.

Kalın, İbrahim. "Turkey and the Arab Spring." *Al Jazeera English*, May 25, 2011. http://www.aljazeera.com/indepth/opinion/2011/05/201152592939180898.html.

Kaplan, Fred. "Stop Paying the Generals." *Slate*, August 6, 2013. http://www.slate.com/articles/news_and_politics/war_stories/2013/08/president_obama_should_end_aid_to_egypt_the_country_s_generals_act_on_their.single.html.

Karadsheh, Jomana. "Libyan War Over, but Fighting Continues among Regional Militias." *CNN*, November 2, 2011. http://www.cnn.com/2011/11/02/world/africa/libya-infighting.

Kassem, Maye. *Egyptian Politics: The Dynamics of Authoritarian Rule*. Boulder, CO: Lynne Rienner, 2004.

Katulis, Brian. "Maintaining the Delicate Balancing Act in the Israel Egypt Security Relationship." Washington, DC: Center for American Progress, March 11, 2013. https://www.americanprogress.org/issues/security/news/ 2013/03/11/56192/maintaining-the-delicate-balancing-act-in-the-israel-egypt- security-relationship.

Kayserilioğlu, Alp, Güney Işıkara, and Max Zirngast. "The Social and Economic Project of the AKP and Its Discontents." In *Another Brick in the Barricade: The Gezi Resistance and Its Aftermath*, edited by Güneş Koç and Harun Aksu, 226–48. Bremen, Germany: Wiener Verlag für Sozialforschung, 2015.

Kenawy, Ezzat Molouk. "The Economic Development in Egypt during the 1952–2007 Period." *Australian Journal of Basic and Applied Sciences* 3, no. 2 (2009): 588–603.

Keohane, Robert O., and Joseph S. Nye Jr. *Power and Interdependence*. 4th ed. Boston: Longman, 2012.

Khalidi, Rashid. "The Arab Spring." *The Nation*, March 21, 2011. https://www. thenation.com/article/arab-spring.

Khanfar, Wadah. "Those Who Support Democracy Must Welcome the Rise of Political Islam." *Guardian*, November 27, 2011. https://www.theguardian. com/commentisfree/2011/nov/27/islamist-arab-spring-west-fears.

Kienle, Eberhard. *A Grand Delusion: Democracy and Economic Reform in Egypt*. London: I. B. Tauris, 2001.

King, Stephen J. *The New Authoritarianism in the Middle East and North Africa*. Bloomington: Indiana University Press, 2009.

Kirkpatrick, David D. "Authorities Bar 3 Leading Candidates in Egypt Race." *New York Times*, April 14, 2012. http://www.nytimes.com/2012/04/15/world/ middleeast/ten-candidates-barred-from-egyptian-election.html.

Kirkpatrick, David D. "Egypt Army Sets 6-Month Blueprint, but Future Role Is Unclear." *New York Times*, February 14, 2011. http://www.nytimes.com/2011/ 02/15/world/middleeast/15egypt.html.

Kirkpatrick, David D., and Mayy El Sheikh. "With Gaza Attacks, Egypt's President Balances Hamas against Israeli Peace." *New York Times*, November 15, 2011. http://www.nytimes.com/2012/11/16/world/middleeast/israels-gaza- strikes-test-egyptian-leader.html.

Koran, Bahgat, Rex Brynen, and Paul Noble. *Political Liberalization and Democratization in the Arab World*. Vol. 2, *Comparative Experiences*. Boulder, CO: Lynne Rienner, 1998.

Krämer, Gudrun. "Liberalization and Democracy in the Arab World." *Middle East Report*, no. 174 (January–February 1992): 22–25, 35.

Kramer, Martin. "A U.S. Visa for an Islamist Extremist?" Policy Watch no. 121. Washington, DC: Washington Institute for Near East Policy, June 29, 1994. Reproduced on the website of Martin Kramer. http://martinkramer.org/ sandbox/reader/archives/a-u-s-visa-for-rachid-ghannouchi.

Kramer, Martin. "Karen Hughes: Avoid the Man." *Sandbox: Martin Kramer on the Middle East* (blog), February 17, 2006. http://martinkramer.org/sandbox/2006/02/karen-hughes-avoid-this-man.

Kramer, Martin. "Review of *Rachid Ghannoushi: A Democrat within Islamism*, by Azzam Tammimi." *Middle East Quarterly* (Fall 2002): 77–78.

Krauss, Clifford. "Militias and Army Jostle for Influence in Libya." *New York Times*, November 18, 2011. http://www.nytimes.com/2011/11/19/world/africa/militias-and-army-compete-for-influence-in-libya.html.

Krauthammer, Charles. "From Baghdad to Benghazi." *Washington Post*, March 4, 2011. http://www.washingtonpost.com/wp-dyn/content/article/2011/03/03/AR2011030304239.html.

Kristof, Nicholas D. "We Are All Egyptians." *New York Times*, February 3, 2011. http://www.nytimes.com/2011/02/04/opinion/04kristof.html.

Kuran, Timur. "Now Out of Never: The Element of Surprise in the East European Revolution of 1989." *World Politics* 44, no. 1 (October 1991): 7–48.

Kurzman, Charles. *The Unthinkable Revolution in Iran*. Cambridge, MA: Harvard University Press, 2004.

Laitin, David D. *Identity in Formation: The Russian Speaking Populations in the Near Abroad*. Ithaca, NY: Cornell University Press, 1998.

Lake, Eli. "U.S. 'Paid a Price' on Egypt." *Daily Beast*, October 4, 2011. http://www.thedailybeast.com/articles/2011/10/04/james-jones-ex-obama-adviser-u-s-paid-a-price-on-egypt.html.

Lally, Kathy, and Mary Beth Sheridan. "U.S. Offers Aid for Egyptian Democracy, but Quietly." *Washington Post*, March 5, 2011. http://www.washingtonpost.com/wp-dyn/content/article/2011/03/04/AR2011030402248.html.

Langohr, Vickie. "Too Much Civil Society, Too Little Politics? Egypt and Other Liberalizing Arab Regimes." In *Authoritarianism in the Middle East: Regimes and Resistance*, edited by Marsha Pripstein Posusney and Michele Penner Angrist, 193–218. Boulder, CO: Lynne Rienner, 2005.

Lawrence, Bruce, ed. *Messages to the World: The Statements of Osama Bin Laden*. Translated by James Howarth. London: Verso, 2005.

Lawson, Fred H. "Intraregime Dynamics, Uncertainty, and the Persistence of Authoritarianism in the Contemporary Arab World." In *Debating Arab Authoritarianism*, edited by Oliver Schlumberger, 109–28. Stanford, CA: Stanford University Press, 2007.

Le Monde. "The Main Tunisian Union Calls for a General Strike on Friday" [French]. February 7, 2013. http://www.lemonde.fr/tunisie/article/2013/02/07/les-islamists-d-ennahda-refusent-la-dissolution-du-gouvernement_1828487_1466522.html.

Leitz, Christian. *Nazi Germany and Neutral Europe during the Second World War*. Manchester: University of Manchester Press, 2000.

Lerner, Barbara. "Losing Turkey to Islamists." *National Review*, August 2, 2010. http://www.nationalreview.com/article/243584/losing-turkey-islamists-barbara-lerner.

Lesch, Ann M. "Democracy in Doses: Mubarak Launches His Second Term as President." *Arab Studies Quarterly* 11, no. 4 (1989): 87–107.

Letsch, Constanze, and Ian Traynor. "Erdoğan Concedes No Party Has Mandate in Shock Turkish Vote." *Guardian*, June 8, 2015. http://www.theguardian.com/world/2015/jun/08/turkey-may-face-fresh-poll-as-recep-tayyip-erdogan-is-snubbed-by-voters.

Levitsky, Steven, and Lucan Way. "International Linkage and Democratization." *Journal of Democracy* 16, no. 3 (July 2005): 20–34.

Lewis, Bernard. "The Roots of Muslim Rage." *Atlantic Monthly* 266, no. 3 (September 1990): 47–60.

Linz, Juan J. *Totalitarian and Authoritarian Regimes*. Boulder, CO: Lynne Rienner, 2000.

Linz, Juan J. "Transitions to Democracy." *Washington Quarterly* 13, no. 3 (Summer 1990): 143–64.

Lipset, Seymour Martin. "Some Social Requisites of Democracy: Economic Development and Political Legitimacy." *American Political Science Review* 53, no. 1 (March 1959): 69–105.

Little, Tom. *Egypt*. New York: Frederick A. Praeger, 1958.

Looney, Robert E. "The Economics of Middle East Military Expenditures: Implications for Arms Reduction in the Region." *Security Dialogue* 22, no. 4 (1991): 407–17.

Lustick, Ian S. "Hegemony and the Riddle of Nationalism: The Dialectics of Political Identity in the Middle East." In *Ethnic Conflict and International Politics in the Middle East*, edited by Leonard Binder, 332–59. Gainesville: University Press of Florida, 1999.

Lust-Okar, Ellen. "Divided They Rule: The Management and Manipulation of Political Opposition." *Comparative Politics* 36, no. 2 (January 2004): 159–79.

Lynch, Marc. "Obama and the Middle East." *Foreign Affairs* (September/October 2015): 18–27.

Lynch, Marc, ed. "Transnational Diffusion and Cooperation in the Middle East." POMPES Studies 21. Washington, DC: Project on Middle East Political Science, August 24, 2016. http://pomeps.org/wp-content/uploads/2016/08/POMEPS_Studies_21_Transnational_Web.pdf.

Mabro, Robert. *The Egyptian Economy: 1952–1972*. Oxford: Oxford University Press, 1974.

Maddy-Weitzman, Bruce. *Middle East Contemporary Survey*. Vol. 23. Tel Aviv: Moshe Dayan Center for Middle Eastern and African Studies, 2002.

Magaloni, Beatriz, and Ruth Kricheli. "Political Order and One-Party Rule." *Annual Review of Political Science* 13 (June 2010): 123–43.

Maher, Ahmed. "Frustration Grows in Tunisian Revolution Birthplace." *BBC News*, August 3, 2013. http://www.bbc.com/news/world-africa-23563203.

Mahfoudh, Mohammed. "Calm and Hope" [French]. *La Presse de Tunisie*, November 8, 1987.

Mahfoudh, Mohammed. "The Dawn of a New Day" [French]. *La Presse de Tunisie*, November 8, 1987.

Mahfoudh, Mohammed. "An Operation of Purification" [French]. *La Presse de Tunisie*, November 8, 1987.

Mahfoudh, Mohammed. "In the Street: Serenity, Confidence, and Optimism" [French]. *La Presse de Tunisie*, November 8, 1987.

Malinowski, Tom. "Jefferson in Benghazi. *New Republic,* June 9, 2011. https://newrepublic.com/article/89645/benghazi-libya-rebels.

March, James G., and Johan P. Olsen. *Rediscovering Institutions: The Organizational Basis of Politics*. New York: Free Press, 1989.

Marcus, Aliza. *Blood and Belief: The PKK and the Kurdish Fight for Independence*. New York: New York University Press, 2007.

Mardin, Şerif. "Religion and Secularism in Turkey." In *The Modern Middle East*, edited by Albert Hourani, Philip Khoury, and Mary C. Wilson, 347–74. Berkeley: University of California Press, 1993.

Marks, Monica. "Tunisia Opts for an Inclusive New Government." *Monkey Cage* (blog), *Washington Post*, February 3, 2015. https://www.washingtonpost.com/blogs/monkey-cage/wp/2015/02/03/tunisia-opts-for-an-inclusive-new-government.

Marks, Monica. "Tunisia's Ennahda: Rethinking Islamism in the Context of ISIS and the Egyptian Coup." Rethinking Political Islam Working Paper. Washington, DC: Brookings Institution Press, August 2015. https://www.brookings.edu/wp-content/uploads/2016/07/Tunisia_Marks-FINALE-5.pdf.

Marks, Monica. "Turmoil in Tunisia." *ForeignPolicy.com*, July 26, 2013. http://foreignpolicy.com/2013/07/26/tunisia-in-turmoil.

Massoud, Ali A., and Thomas D. Willett. "Egypt's Exchange Rate Regime Policy after the Float." *International Journal of Social Science Studies* 2, no. 4 (October 2014): 1–16.

McCants, William. *The ISIS Apocalypse: The History, Strategy, and Doomsday Vision of the Islamic State*. New York: St. Martin's Press, 2015.

McInerney, Stephen. "Islamist Victory in Tunisia Presents Opportunity for U.S. Engagement." *Fikra Forum*, November 8, 2011. http://fikraforum.org/?p=1685#.VqkLx_krK7o.

McInerney, Stephen, and Cole Bockenfeld. *The Federal Budget and Appropriations for Fiscal Year 2017: Democracy, Governance, and Human Rights in the Middle East & North Africa*. Washington, DC: Project on Middle East Democracy, April 2016. http://pomed.org/wp-content/uploads/2016/07/POMED_BudgetReport_FY17_Final-Web.pdf.

Mead, Walter Russell. "Erdogan's Big Fat Turkish Idea." *American Interest*, August 17, 2011. http://www.the-american-interest.com/2011/08/17/erdogans-big-fat-turkish-idea.

Mersch, Sarah. "Tunisia: Sweeping History under the Rug Rather than Confronting the Past?" *Deutsche Welle*, September 9, 2015. http://www.

dw.com/en/tunisia-sweeping-history-under-the-rug-rather-than-confronting-the-past/a-18703824.

Mersch, Sarah. "Tunisia's Ineffective Counterterrorism Law." *Sada* (blog), August 6, 2015. http://carnegieendowment.org/sada/?fa=60958.

Meyersson, Erik. "How Turkey's Social Conservatives Won the Day for HDP." *Erik Meyersson* (blog), June 8, 2015. http://erikmeyersson.com/2015/06/08/how-turkeys-social-conservatives-won-the-day-for-hdp.

Mezran, Karim. "Can Libya's Liberals and Islamists Get Along?" *Atlantic Monthly*, July 12, 2012. http://www.theatlantic.com/international/archive/2012/07/can-libyas-liberals-and-islamists-get-along/260129.

Mitchell, Richard P. *The Society of the Muslim Brothers*. New York: Oxford University Press, 1993.

Morsi, Mohammed. "President Mohammed Morsi's Speech" [Arabic]. *Aswat Masriyya*, June 27, 2013. http://www.aswatmasriya.com/news/view.aspx?id=6bc27c5a-6109-46d1-92e3-408ecd92d0b3.

Mortimer, Robert. "Islam and Multiparty Politics in Algeria." *Middle East Journal* 45, no. 4 (Autumn 1991): 575–93.

Moshiri, Nazinine. "Interview with Rachid Ghannouchi." *Al Jazeera English*, February 7, 2011. http://www.aljazeera.com/news/africa/2011/02/2011233464273624.html.

Muasher, Marwan, and Katherine Wilkens. "Awakening to a New Arab World." *Global Ten* (blog), November 29, 2012. http://carnegieendowment.org/globalten/?fa=50146.

Müftüler-Baç, Meltem. "Turkey's Political Reforms and the Impact of the European Union." *South European Society & Politics* 10, no. 1 (March 2005): 16–30.

Murata, Akira. "Designing Youth Employment Policies in Egypt." *Global Economy and Development* Working Paper no. 68. Washington, DC: Brookings Institution Press, 2014.

Murkhaji, Aroop. "Egypt's Regime Will Change." *New Republic*, September 4, 2010. https://newrepublic.com/article/77424/egypts-regime-will-change-mubarak-obama-middle-east.

Murphy, Emma C. *Economic and Political Change in Tunisia from Bourguiba to Ben Ali*. New York: Columbia University Press, 1999.

Muslih, Mohammed, and Augustus Richard Norton. "The Need for Arab Democracy." *Foreign Policy* 83 (Summer 1991): 3–19.

Muslim Brotherhood. "Section 4: Regional Leadership." In *Electoral Program of the Muslim Brotherhood, 2010 People's Assembly Elections* [Arabic]. Cairo, November 2010.

Muslim Brotherhood. *Program of the Party of the Muslim Brotherhood*, first draft [Arabic]. Cairo, August 25, 2007.

Nader, Emir. "Education Organisation Shuttered, Citing NGOs Law." *Daily News Egypt*, August 12, 2015. http://www.dailynewsegypt.com/2015/08/12/educational-organisation-shutters-citing-restrictive-ngos-law.

Naffsinger, Peter A. "Face among the Arabs." *Studies in Intelligence* 8, no. 3 (Summer 1964): 49.

Najar, Ridha. "A New Era" [French]. *La Presse de Tunisie*, November 8, 1987.

Najar, Ridha. "Dignity! . . ." [French]. *La Presse de Tunisie*, November 12, 1987.

Najar, Ridha. "Tunisia, the Promise" [French]. *La Presse de Tunisie*, November 9, 1987.

Najar, Ridha. "The Young Face the Event: The Advantage of Liberty, Less Unemployment" [French]. *Le Temps*, November 11, 1987.

Nasser, Gamal Abdel. "Public Address of President Gamal Abdel Nasser on the 4th Anniversary of the Revolution" [Arabic]. *Nasser.org*, July 26, 1952. http://www.nasser.org/Speeches/browser.aspx?SID=495&lang=ar.

National Counter Terrorism Center (NCTC). "Ansar al-Sharia." *Counter Terrorism Guide*. Washington, DC: National Counter Terrorism Center. http://www.nctc.gov/site/groups/ansar_al_sharia.html#.

National Public Radio (NPR). "Turkish Democracy: A Model for Other Countries?" *All Things Considered*, April 14, 2011. http://www.npr.org/2011/04/14/135407687/turkish-democracy-a-model-for-other-countries.

National Transitional Council (NTC). "A Vision of a Democratic Libya." Benghazi: NTC, March 29, 2011. Reproduced on the website of Al Jazeera. http://www.aljazeera.com/mritems/Documents/2011/3/29/2011329113923943811The%20Interim%20Transitional%20National%20Council%20Statement.pdf.

National Transitional Council (NTC). "Constitutional Declaration." Benghazi: NTC, August 3, 2011. Reproduced on Al-Bab.com. http://www.al-bab.com/arab/docs/libya/Libya-Draft-Constitutional-Charter-for-the-transitional-stage.pdf.

Neuman, Scott. "Joyful Egyptians Await Assurances about Future." *NPR*, February 12, 2011. http://www.npr.org/2011/02/12/133708981/egyptians-continue-celebration-await-assurances.

New York Times. "Democracy in Turkey." Editorial. September 1, 2007. http://www.nytimes.com/2007/09/01/opinion/01sat4.html.

New York Times. "Democracy Wins in Turkey." Editorial. June 8, 2015. http://www.nytimes.com/2015/06/09/opinion/democracy-wins-in-turkey.html.

Niblock, Tim. *Pariah States and Sanctions in the Middle East: Iraq, Libya, Sudan*. Boulder, CO: Lynne Rienner, 2002.

Nobel Peace Prize for 2015. "The Nobel Peace Prize for 2015." Press Release. Oslo: Nobel Media AB, October 10, 2015. http://www.nobelprize.org/nobel_prizes/peace/laureates/2015/press.html.

Norton, Augustus Richard. "The Future of Civil Society in the Middle East." *Middle East Journal* 47, no. 2 (Spring 1993): 205–16.

Nouira, Asma. "Obstacles on the Path of Tunisia's Democratic Transformation." *Sada* (blog), March 30, 2011. http://carnegieendowment.org/sada/?fa=43347.

Nuland, Victoria. "The United States' Reaction to Egypt's November 22 Decisions." Press Release. Washington, DC: US Department of State, November 23, 2012. http://www.state.gov/r/pa/prs/ps/2012/11/200983.htm.

Nye, Joseph S., Jr. "Tripoli Diarist." *New Republic*, December 10, 2007. https://newrepublic.com/article/65686/tripoli-diarist.

Obama, Barack. "Readout of President Obama's Call with Prime Minister Erdogan of Turkey." Washington, DC: The White House, Office of the Press Secretary, June 24, 2013. https://www.whitehouse.gov/the-press-office/2013/06/24/readout-president-obamas-call-prime-minister-erdogan-turkey.

Obama, Barack. "Readout of President Obama's Call with Prime Minister Erdogan of Turkey." Washington, DC: The White House, Office of the Press Secretary, February 19, 2014. https://www.whitehouse.gov/the-press-office/2014/02/19/readout-president-obama-s-call-prime-minister-erdogan.

Obama, Barack. "Remarks by President Obama to the Turkish Parliament." Washington, DC: The White House, Office of the Press Secretary, April 6, 2009. https://www.whitehouse.gov/the-press-office/remarks-president-obama-turkish-parliament.

Obama, Barack. "Remarks by the President on Egypt." Washington, DC: The White House, Office of the Press Secretary, February 11, 2011. https://www.whitehouse.gov/the-press-office/2011/02/11/remarks-president-egypt.

Obama, Barack. "Remarks by the President on the Middle East and North Africa." Washington, DC: The White House, Office of the Press Secretary, May 19, 2011. https://www.whitehouse.gov/the-press-office/2011/05/19/remarks-president-middle-east-and-north-africa.

Obama, Barack. "State of the Union Address." Washington, DC: The White House, Office of the Press Secretary, January 13, 2016. https://www.whitehouse.gov/the-press-office/2016/01/12/remarks-president-barack-obama-%E2%80%93-prepared-delivery-state-union-address.

Obama, Barack. "On a New Beginning: Remarks by the President at Cairo University." Washington, DC: The White House, Office of the Press Secretary, June 4, 2009. http://www.whitehouse.gov/the_press_office/Remarks-by-the-President-at-Cairo-University-6-04-09.

Obama, Barack, and Beji Caid Essebsi. "Helping Tunisia Realize Its Democratic Promise." *Washington Post*, May 20, 2015. https://www.washingtonpost.com/opinions/us-helping-tunisia-to-make-sure-democracy-delivers/2015/05/20/05b029e4-fe75-11e4-833c-a2de05b6b2a4_story.html.

Obama, Barack, and Narendra Modi. "A Renewal of the U.S.-India Partnership for the 21st Century." *Washington Post*, September 30, 2014. https://www.washingtonpost.com/opinions/narendra-modi-and-barack-obama-a-us-india-partnership-for-the-21st-century/2014/09/29/dac66812-4824-11e4-891d-713f052086a0_story.html.

Office of Inspector General. "Audit of USAID/Egypt's Democracy and Governance Activities." Audit Report no. 6-263-10-001-P. Cairo: US Agency for International Development, October 27, 2009. http://pdf.usaid.gov/pdf_docs/PDACS076.pdf.

Öktem, Kerem. "Harbingers of Turkey's Second Republic." *Middle East Research and Information Project*, August 1, 2007. http://www.merip.org/mero/mero080107.

Olson, Mancur, Jr. "Rapid Growth as a Destabilizing Force." *Journal of Economic History* 23, no. 4 (December 1963): 529–52.

Öniş, Ziya. "Turgut Özal and His Economic Legacy: Turkish Neo-Liberalism in Critical Perspective." *Middle Eastern Studies* 40, no. 4 (2004): 113–34.

Oppenheimer, Daniel. *Exit Right: The People Who Left the Left and Reshaped the American Century.* New York: Simon & Schuster, 2016.

Ornarlı, Barış. "Davutoğlu: Turkey Poised to Lead in Syria and New Middle East." *Middle East Voices*, April 27, 2012. http://middleeastvoices.voanews.com/2012/04/davutoglu-turkey-poised-to-lead-in-syria-and-new-middle-east-79775/#ixzz3xTwnGtx1.

Orton, Kyle W. "How Saddam Gave Us ISIS." *New York Times*, December 23, 2015. http://www.nytimes.com/2015/12/23/opinion/how-saddam-hussein-gave-us-isis.html.

Oskarsoon, Katerina. "Economic Sanctions on Authoritarian States: Lessons Learned." *Middle East Policy* 19, no. 4 (Winter 2012): 88–102.

Özbudun, Ergun. "Turkey, Crises, Interruptions, and Reequilibrations." In *Politics in Developing Countries: Comparing Experiences with Democracy*, edited by Larry Diamond, Juan Linz, and Seymour Martin Lipset, 175–217. 2nd ed. Boulder, CO: Lynne Rienner, 1995.

Özbudun, Ergun. "Turkey: How Far from Consolidation?" *Journal of Democracy* 7, no. 3 (July 1996): 123–38.

Özbudun, Ergun, and Ömer Faruk Gençkaya. *Democratization and the Politics of Constitution-Making in Turkey.* Budapest: Central European University Press, 2009.

Özkan, Behlül. "Turkey, Davutoglu and the Idea of Pan-Islamism." *Survival* 56, no. 4 (August–September 2014): 119–40.

Pack, Jason. "Two Deals, No Solution." *Libya-Analysis.com*, December 15, 2015. http://www.libya-analysis.com/two-deals-no-solution.

Pargeter, Alison. "Why Elections Won't Save Libya." *Al Jazeera*, July 2014. http://america.aljazeera.com/opinions/2014/7/libya-council-ofdeputieselectionsislamistssecuritybenghazi.html.

Perkins, Kenneth. *A History of Modern Tunisia.* 2nd ed. New York: Cambridge University Press, 2014.

Pérouse, Jean-François. "The State without the Public: Some Conjectures about the Administration for Collective Housing (TOKİ)." In *Order and Compromise: Government Practices in Turkey from the Late Ottoman Empire to the Early 21st Century*, edited by Marc Aymes, Benjamin Gourisse, and Élise Massicard, 169–91. Leiden: Brill, 2015.

Perry, Tom. "Brotherhood Sees Egypt "Coup" Fueling Hatred of West." *Reuters*, July 6, 2013. http://www.reuters.com/article/us-egypt-protests-west-hatred-idUSBRE9650HY20130706.

Petré, Christine. "Nidaa Tunis Tensions Come at a Crucial Period for Tunisia." *Al-Monitor*, November 9, 2015. http://www.al-monitor.com/pulse/originals/2015/11/tunisia-nidaa-tounes-tensions-crucial-period.html.

Pew Research Center. "A Year after Iraq War." March 16, 2004. http://www.pewglobal.org/2004/03/16/a-year-after-iraq-war.

Phillips, James. "Time to Freeze U.S. Aid to Egypt." *Heritage Foundation*, June 12, 2013. http://www.heritage.org/research/reports/2013/06/time-to-freeze-us-aid-to-egypt.

Pollack, Kenneth M. *A Path Out of the Desert: A Grand Strategy for America in the Middle East.* New York: Random House, 2008.

Pollack, Kenneth M. *Arabs at War: Military Effectiveness, 1948–1991.* Lincoln: University of Nebraska Press, 2002.

Pollack, Kenneth M. *The Threatening Storm: The Case for Invading Iraq.* New York: Random House, 2002.

Pollack, Kenneth M., ed. *The Arab Awakening: America and the Transformation of the Middle East.* Washington, DC: Brookings Institution Press, 2011.

Powell, Colin. "Powell Cites Opportunities for U.S.-Turkish Cooperation in Iraq." *IIP Digital*, April 2, 2003. http://iipdigital.usembassy.gov/st/english/texttrans/2003/04/20030405135351ynneddo.1897852.html#axzz41BZJzzjk.

Power, Samantha. *A Problem from Hell.* New York: Basic Books, 2002.

Presidential Daily Brief. "Bin Ladin Determined to Strike in US." August 6, 2001 (declassified April 10, 2004). http://nsarchive.gwu.edu/NSAEBB/NSAEBB116/pdb8-6-2001.pdf.

Pripstein Posusney, Marsha. "Multiparty Elections in the Arab World: Election Rules and Opposition Responses." In *Authoritarianism in the Middle East: Regimes and Resistance*, edited by Marsha Pripstein Posusney and Michele Penner Angrist, 91–118. Boulder, CO: Lynne Rienner, 2005.

Pryce-Jones, David. "Hamas's New Strength." *National Review*, November 28, 2012. https://www.nationalreview.com/nrd/articles/334382/hamass-new-strength.

Quandt, William B. *Between Ballots and Bullets: Algeria's Transition from Authoritarianism.* Washington, DC: Brookings Institution Press, 1998.

Rabobank. "The Turkish 2000–01 Banking Crisis." Economic Report. *Rabobank Economic Research*, September 4, 2013. https://economics.rabobank.com/publications/2013/september/the-turkish-2000-01-banking-crisis.

Rath, Katherine. "The Process of Democratization in Jordan." *Middle Eastern Studies* 30, no. 3 (July 1994): 530–57.

Republic of Tunisia. "Constitution of Tunisia, 2014." Translated by the United Nations Development Programme (UNDP) and reviewed by International Institute for Democracy and Electoral Assistance (IDEA). Content provided by International IDEA. Tunis: Republic of Tunisia, January 2014. https://www.constituteproject.org/constitution/Tunisia_2014.pdf.

Republic of Tunisia. Law No. 53/2013. "Organic Law on Establishing and Organizing Justice Transitional Justice." Unofficial translation by the International Center for Traditional Justice. Content provided by the Office of the United Nations High Commissioner for Human Rights (OHCHR). Tunis: Ministry of Human Rights and Transitional Justice, December 24, 2013. http://www.ohchr.org/Documents/Countries/TN/TransitionalJusticeTunisia.pdf.

Republic of Tunisia. Law No. 88/32/33. "Organizing Political Parties." Tunis, May 3, 1988. http://aceproject.org/ero-en/regions/africa/TN/tunisie-loi-88-32-33-du-3-mai-organisant-les/view.

Republic of Tunisia. Law No. 22/2015. "Relating to the Battle against Terrorism and the Suppression of Money Laundering" [French]. Tunis, July 24, 2015. http://majles.marsad.tn/2014/fr/lois/55157b1e12bdaa55e64cde6f/texte.

Republic of Turkey. Law No. 2709. "Constitution of the Republic of Turkey." Tunis, November 7, 1982. http://www.refworld.org/cgi-bin/texis/vtx/rwmain?docid=3ae6b5be0.

Republic of Turkey. "Letter of Intent and Memorandum of Economic Policies to International Monetary Fund, May 3, 2001." *International Monetary Fund*, May 3, 2001. http://www.imf.org/external/np/loi/2001/tur/02.

Republic of Turkey. "Regular Progress Reports for Turkey." *Ministry for European Union Affairs*, 1998–2015. http://www.ab.gov.tr/?p=123&l=2.

Reuters. "U.S. Urges Restraint in Egypt, Says Government Stable." January 25, 2011. http://www.reuters.com/article/2011/01/25/ozatp-egypt-protest-clinton-idAFJOE70O0KF20110125.

Reynolds, Michael A. "The Key to the Future Lies in the Past: The Worldview of Erdoğan and Davutoğlu." *Current Trends in Islamist Ideology* 19 (September 2015): 5–38.

Rice, Condoleezza. "Remarks at the American University in Cairo." Washington, DC: US Department of State, June 20, 2005. http://2001-2009.state.gov/secretary/rm/2005/48328.htm.

Richards, Alan, and John Waterbury. *A Political Economy of the Middle East: State, Class, and Economic Development.* Boulder, CO: Westview Press, 1990.

Rijkers, Bob, Caroline Freund, and Antonio Nucifora. "All in the Family: State Capture in Tunisia." Policy Research Working Paper no. 6810. Washington, DC: World Bank, March 2014. http://elibrary.worldbank.org/doi/pdf/10.1596/1813-9450-6810.

Roy, Olivier. "Islam: The Democracy Dilemma." In *The Islamists Are Coming: Who They Really Are*, edited by Robin Wright, 13–19. Washington, DC: Woodrow Wilson Center Press and US Institute of Peace Press, 2012.

Roy, Olivier. "Muslim Brotherhood, Other Islamists Have Changed Their Worldview." *Washington Post*, January 20, 2012. https://www.washingtonpost.com/opinions/muslim-brotherhood-other-islamists-have-changed-their-worldview/2012/01/10/gIQAZgjoEQ_story.html.

Rubin, Michael. "Mr. Erdogan's Turkey." *Wall Street Journal*, October 19, 2006. http://www.wsj.com/articles/SB116121690776497100.

Rubin, Michael. "Turkey, from Ally to Enemy." *Commentary* 130, no. 1 (July/August 2010): 81–86.

Ryan, Yasmine. "Anonymous and the Arab Uprisings." *Al Jazeera*, May 19, 2011. http://www.aljazeera.com/news/middleeast/2011/05/201151917634659824.html.

Sadiki, Larbi. "Political Liberalization in Ben Ali's Tunisia: Façade Democracy." *Democratization* 9, no. 4 (Winter 2002): 122–41.

Salah, Omar Belhadj. "Nidaa Tounes Drifting Apart?" *Sada* (blog), July 14, 2015. http://carnegieendowment.org/sada/?fa=60699.

Salamé, Ghassan. "Where Are the Democrats?" In *Democracy without Democrats? The Renewal of Politics in the Muslim World*, edited by Ghassan Salamé, 1–20. New York: I. B. Taurus, 1994.

Saletan, William. "Springtime for Twitter: Is the Internet Driving the Revolutions of the Arab Spring?" *Slate*, July 18, 2011. http://www.slate.com/articles/technology/future_tense/2011/07/springtime_for_twitter.html.

Samti, Farah. "In Tunisia, a New Reconciliation Law Stokes Protest and Conflict Instead." *ForeignPolicy.com*, September 15, 2015. http://foreignpolicy.com/2015/09/15/in-tunisia-a-new-reconciliation-law-stokes-protest-and-conflict-instead.

Satloff, Robert. "Ideas for U.S. Middle East Policy in the Wake of the Egypt Crisis." Policy Watch no. 1756. Washington, DC: Washington Institute for Near East Policy, February 9, 2011. http://www.washingtoninstitute.org/policy-analysis/view/ideas-for-u.s.-middle-east-policy-in-the-wake-of-the-egypt-crisis.

Satloff, Robert. "Morsi's Victory in Egypt: Early Implications for America and the Broader Middle East." *Policy Watch* no. 1958. Washington, DC: Washington Institute for Near East Policy, June 25, 2012. http://www.washingtoninstitute.org/policy-analysis/view/morsis-victory-in-egypt-early-implications-for-america-and-the-broader-midd.

Schenker, David. "Egypt's Enduring Challenges: Shaping the Post-Mubarak Environment." Policy Focus no. 110. Washington, DC: Washington Institute for Near East Policy, April 2011. http://www.washingtoninstitute.org/policy-analysis/view/egypts-enduring-challenges-shaping-the-post-mubarak-environment.

Secretariat-General for European Union Affairs. "Political Reforms in Turkey." Ankara: Ministry of Foreign Affairs, Republic of Turkey, 2007. http://www.ab.gov.tr/files/pub/prt.pdf.

Şen, Mustafa. "Transformation of Turkish Islamism and the Rise of the Justice and Development Party." *Turkish Studies* 11, no. 1 (March 2010): 59–84.

Serwer, Daniel P. "Post-Qaddafi Instability in Libya." Contingency Planning Memorandum no. 12. New York: Council on Foreign Relations, 2011.

Sewell, William H., Jr. "Ideologies and Social Revolutions: Reflections on the French Case." *Journal of Modern History* 57, no. 1 (March 1985): 57–85.

Sfeir, George. "The Tunisian Code of Personal Status." *Middle East Journal* 11, no. 3 (Summer 1957): 309–18.

Shaikh, Salman, Mohamad Arafat, Steven A. Cook, and Ahmed Maher. "A Generation Revolts: Egyptian Youth and the New Middle East." Washington, DC: Brookings Institution Press, April 4, 2011. Write-up of event available at https://www.brookings.edu/events/a-generation-revolts-egyptian-youth-and-the-new-middle-east.

Shapiro, Samantha M. "Revolution, Facebook-Style." *New York Times Magazine*, January 22, 2009. http://www.nytimes.com/2009/01/25/magazine/25bloggers-t.html.

Sharabi, Hisham. *Neopatriarchy: A Theory of Distorted Change in Arab Society.* New York: Oxford University Press, 1992.

Sharp, Jeremy M. "Egypt: Background and U.S. Relations." CRS Report no. RL33003. Washington, DC: Congressional Research Service, February 2016. https://www.fas.org/sgp/crs/mideast/RL33003.pdf.

Simes, Dmitri K. "Throwing an Ally Off a Cliff." *National Interest*, February 14, 2011. http://nationalinterest.org/commentary/throwing-ally-cliff-4880.

Skocpol, Theda. "Cultural Idioms and Political Ideologies in the Revolutionary Reconstruction of State Power: A Rejoinder to Sewell." *Journal of Modern History* 57, no. 1 (March 1985): 63–96.

Skocpol, Theda. *States and Social Revolutions: A Comparative Analysis of France, Russia, and China.* New York: Cambridge University Press, 1979.

Smith, Anthony. *National Identity.* Las Vegas: University of Nevada Press, 1991.

Snyder, Jack L. *From Voting to Violence: Democratization and Nationalist Conflict.* New York: W. W. Norton, 2000.

Solomon, Andrew. "Circle of Fire." *New Yorker*, May 8, 2010. http://www.newyorker.com/magazine/2006/05/08/circle-of-fire.

Solt, Frederick. "The Standardized World Income Inequality Database." Working Paper. SWIID Version 5.0, October 2014. http://myweb.uiowa.edu/fsolt/swiid/swiid.html.

Sönmez, Mustafa. "Turkey's Second Privatization Agency: TOKI." *ReflectionsTurkey.com*, May 2012. http://www.reflectionsturkey.com/?p=489.

Spencer, Richard, and Praveen Swami. "Egypt Sets Six-Month Target for Elections." *Telegraph*, February 13, 2011. http://www.telegraph.co.uk/news/worldnews/africaandindianocean/egypt/8321838/Egypt-sets-six-month-target-for-elections.html.

Springborg, Robert. "Sisi's Islamist Agenda for Egypt." *ForeignAffairs.com*, July 25, 2013. https://www.foreignaffairs.com/articles/middle-east/2013-07-25/sisis-islamist-agenda-egypt.

Springborg, Robert. "Sisi's Secret Islamism," *ForeignAffairs.com*, May 26, 2014. https://www.foreignaffairs.com/articles/middle-east/2014-05-26/sisis-secret-islamism.

St. John, Ronald Bruce. *Historical Dictionary of Libya.* Lanham, MD: Rowman & Littlefield, 2014.

Stacher, Joshua. *Adaptable Autocrats: Regime Power in Egypt and Syria.* Stanford, CA: Stanford University Press, 2012.

Starr, Harvey. "Democratic Dominoes: Diffusion Approaches to the Spread of Democracy in the International System." *Journal of Conflict Resolution* 35, no. 2 (June 1991): 356–81.

Stenner, Karen. *The Authoritarian Dynamic.* New York: Cambridge University Press, 2005.

Stephen, Chris, "Libya: Tripoli Airport Closed after Rogue Militia Attacks Garrison." *Guardian*, December 11, 2011. https://www.theguardian.com/world/2011/dec/11/libya-tripoli-airport-militia.

Stephen, Chris, Kareem Shaheen, and Mark Tran. "Tunis Museum Attack: 20 People Killed after Hostage Drama." *Guardian*, March 18, 2015. http://www.theguardian.com/world/2015/mar/18/eight-people-killed-in-attack-on-tunisia-bardo-museum.

Stern, Jessica, and J. M. Berger. *ISIS: The State of Terror.* New York: Ecco, 2015.

Stock, Raymond. "It's Obama, McCain, Graham Who Made 'Huge Mistake' in Egypt." *FOX News Opinion*, August 9, 2013. http://www.foxnews.com/opinion/2013/08/08/obama-mccain-and-graham-make-huge-mistake-in-egypt.html.

Strand, Håvard, Håvard Hegre, Scott Gates, and Marianne Dahl. "Why Waves? Global Patterns of Democratization, 1820–2008." *Polarization and Conflict Project* working paper. College Park, MD: Center for International Development and Conflict Management, June 29, 2012. http://www.cidcm.umd.edu/workshop/papers/dahl_cidcm2013.pdf.

Sulaiman, Samee. "Spectacle and Soundscape: Narrative Authority and Ethical Formations in the Arab Spring." MA thesis, University of Chicago, June 2014.

Supreme Electoral Council of the Republic of Turkey. "Results of Turkish General Election including Votes Cast at Customs" [Turkish]. June 22, 2011. http://www.ysk.gov.tr/ysk/docs/2011MilletvekiliSecimi/gumrukdahil/gumrukdahil.pdf.

Tahi, Mohand Salah. "Algeria's Democratisation Process: A Frustrated Hope." *Third World Quarterly* 16, no. 2 (June 1995): 197–220.

Tajine, Synda. "A Jihadist Comes Home and Tunisia Cracks Down." Translated by Rani Geha. *Al-Monitor*, September 20, 2012. http://www.al-monitor.com/pulse/politics/2012/09/has-tunisias-government-turned-against-the-salafists.html.

Takeyh, Ray. "The Rogue Who Came in from the Cold." *Foreign Affairs* 80, no. 3 (May 2001): 63–66.

Tamimi, Azzam S. *Rachid Ghannouchi: A Democrat within Islamism.* New York: Oxford University Press, 2001.

Tapscott, Don. "Social Media Can Build Arab Governments Too." *Guardian*, May 20, 2011. http://www.theguardian.com/commentisfree/2011/may/20/arab-spring-digital-brainstorm-internet.

Tarek, Sherif. "SCAF Hails Security, Warns of Foreign Plots." *Ahram Online*, December 19, 2011. http://english.ahram.org.eg/NewsContent/1/64/29727/Egypt/Politics-/SCAF-hails-security-forces,-warns-of-foreign-plots.aspx.

Taşpınar, Ömer. "Turkey's General Dilemma." *ForeignAffairs.com*, August 8, 2011. https://www.foreignaffairs.com/articles/turkey/2011-08-08/turkeys-general-dilemma.

Tharoor, Ishaan. "Turkey's Election Is a Blow to Erdogan and a Victory for the Kurds." *Washington Post*, June 8, 2015. https://www.washingtonpost.com/world/turkeys-erdogan-may-see-ambitions-checked-by-parliamentary-election/2015/06/07/d76db05a-0cf3-11e5-9726-49d6fa26a8c6_story.html.

Thomas, Landon, Jr. "In Turkey's Example, Some See Map for Egypt." *New York Times*, February 5, 2011. http://www.nytimes.com/2011/02/06/world/middleeast/06turkey.html.

Thomas, Landon, Jr. "Unknotting Father's Reins in Hope of 'Reinventing' Libya." *New York Times*, February 28, 2010. http://www.nytimes.com/2010/03/01/world/middleeast/01libya.html.

Tibi, Bassam. "Islamists Approach Europe: Turkey's Islamist Danger." *Middle East Quarterly* 16, no. 1 (Winter 2009): 47–54.

Tillman, Erik. "Sultanism or Not? Debating Turkish Politics." *From the Potomac to the Euphrates* (blog), February 23, 2015. http://blogs.cfr.org/cook/2015/02/23/sultanism-or-not-debating-turkish-politics.

Tilly, Charles. *From Mobilization to Revolution*. Reading, MA: Addison-Wesley, 1978.

Tilly, Charles. "Citizenship, Identity, and Social History." In *Citizenship, Identity, and Social History*, edited by Charles Tilly, 1–17. Cambridge: Press Syndicate of the University of Cambridge, 1995.

Toksabay, Ece, and Nick Tattersall. "Erdogan Says Turkey's Coup Script Was 'Written Abroad.'" *Reuters*, August 2, 2016. http://www.reuters.com/article/us-turkey-security-idUSKCN10D1NN.

Toprak, Binnaz. "The Religious Right." In *Turkey in Transition: New Perspectives*, edited by Irvin C. Schick and Ertuğrul Ahmet Tonak, 218–35. Oxford: Oxford University Press, 1987.

Totten, Michael J. "Tunisia on the Brink." *World Affairs*, July 29, 2013. http://www.worldaffairsjournal.org/blog/michael-j-totten/tunisia-brink.

Trager, Eric. *Arab Fall: How the Muslim Brotherhood Won and Lost Egypt in 891 Days*. Washington, DC: Georgetown University Press, 2016.

Trager, Eric. "Obama's Big Egypt Test: Sinai." *Atlantic Monthly*, January 7, 2013. http://www.theatlantic.com/international/archive/2013/01/obamas-big-egypt-test-sinai/266878.

Turkish Statistical Institute. "Seasonally and Calendar Adjusted Gross Domestic Product in Constant Prices—By Kind of Economic Activity (at 1998 prices)" [Turkish and English]. Spreadsheet. http://www.turkstat.gov.tr/PreIstatistikTablo.do?istab_id=2273.

Ulfelder, Jay. "The Arab Spring and the Limits of Understanding." *Dart-Throwing Chimp* (blog), February 2, 1014. https://dartthrowingchimp.wordpress.com/2014/02/04/the-arab-spring-and-the-limits-of-understanding.

Ülgen, Sinan. "Turkey at a Democratic Crossroad." *New York Times*, June 17, 2015. http://www.nytimes.com/2015/06/18/opinion/turkey-at-a-democratic-crossroad.html.

Ülgen, Sinan, Nathan J. Brown, Marina Ottaway, and Paul Salem. "The Emerging Order in the Middle East." Policy Outlook. Washington, DC: Carnegie Endowment for International Peace, May 24, 2012. http://carnegieendowment.org/files/middle_east_order1.pdf.

United Nations. UN Security Council Resolution 748 (1992). March 31, 1992. http://www.un.org/en/ga/search/view_doc.asp?symbol=S/RES/748(1992).

United Nations. UN Security Council Resolution 883 (1993). November 11, 1993. http://www.un.org/en/ga/search/view_doc.asp?symbol=S/RES/883(1993).

University of Maryland and Zogby International. *2009 Annual Arab Public Opinion Survey*. April–May 2009. https://www.brookings.edu/wp-content/uploads/2012/04/2009_arab_public_opinion_poll.pdf.

US Department of State. "Daily Press Briefing." Washington, DC, June 17, 2013. http://www.state.gov/r/pa/prs/dpb/2013/06/210746.htm.

US Department of State. "Daily Press Briefing." Washington, DC, May 31, 2013. http://www.state.gov/r/pa/prs/dpb/2013/05/210149.htm.

US Department of State. "Accountability Review Board Report for Benghazi." Unclassified. Washington, DC: Government Printing Office, December 19, 2012. http://www.state.gov/documents/organization/202446.pdf.

US Department of State. "Egypt: Economic, Technical, and Related Assistance." In *1978–79*, 4609–621. Vol. 30, part 4 of *United States Treaties and Other International Agreements*. Washington, DC: Government Printing Office, 1980.

US Department of State. "Human Rights Report 2011: Tunisia." Country Reports on Human Rights Practices for 2011. Washington, DC: Bureau of Democracy, Human Rights, and Labor, 2011. http://www.state.gov/documents/organization/186663.pdf.

US Department of State. "The Middle East Partnership Initiative Story." Washington, DC: Government Printing Office, 2005. http://2002-2009-mepi.state.gov/outreach.

US Embassy Ankara. "Despite Allegations, Media Takeover Probably Not Political." Cable, April 5, 2007. Wikileaks, US Embassy of Public Diplomacy. https://wikileaks.org/plusd/cables/07ANKARA778_a.html.

US Energy Information Administration (EIA). "Country Analysis Brief: Libya." Washington, DC: US Energy Information Administration, November 19, 2015. http://www.eia.gov/beta/international/analysis.cfm?iso=LBY.

US Senate. "FY2016 State, Foreign Operations, and Related Programs Appropriations Bill Omnibus Agreement Summary." 114th Congress. Washington, DC: Government Printing Office, 2015. http://www.appropriations.senate.gov/imo/media/doc/SFOPS-OMNI-SUMMARY.pdf.

Vandewalle, Dirk J. *A History of Modern Libya*. 2nd ed. Cambridge: Cambridge University Press, 2012.

Vandewalle, Dirk J. "Ben Ali's New Tunisia." Field Staff Report no. 8 (1989–1990). Indianapolis: Universities Field Staff International, 1989.

van Langendonck, Gert. "Libya Militias Taking Law into Own Hands." *Christian Science Monitor*, November 4, 2011. http://www.csmonitor.com/World/Middle-East/2011/1104/Libya-militias-taking-law-into-own-hands.

Villelabeitia, Ibon. "Can Arabs Learn from Turkish Model of Islam and Democracy." *Faithworld* (blog), February 3, 2011. http://blogs.reuters.com/faithworld/2011/02/03/can-arabs-learn-from-turkish-model-of-islam-and-democracy.

Walker, Joshua. "Will Turkey Remain an American Ally?" *Huffington Post*, December 14, 2010. http://www.huffingtonpost.com/joshua-w-walker/will-turkey-remain-an-ame_b_796710.html.

Walt, Stephen M. "A Requiem for the 'Arab Spring?' " *ForeignPolicy.com*, November 28, 2011. http://foreignpolicy.com/2011/11/28/requiem-for-the-arab-spring/November 28, 2011.

Waltz, Susan. "Islamist Appeal in Tunisia." *Middle East Journal* 40, no. 4 (Autumn 1986): 652–670.

Washington Post. "More Bucks for Mr. Mubarak." Editorial. May 21, 2006. http://www.washingtonpost.com/wp-dyn/content/article/2006/05/20/AR2006052000935.html.

Waterbury, John. *The Egypt of Nasser and Sadat: The Political Economy of Two Regimes*. Princeton, NJ: Princeton University Press, 1983.

Waterbury, John. *Exposed to Innumerable Delusions: Public Enterprise and State Power in Egypt, India, Mexico, and Turkey*. New York: Cambridge University Press, 1993.

Weaver, Mary Anne. "Pharaohs in Waiting." *Atlantic Monthly* 292, no. 3 (October 2003): 79–92.

Weaver, Mary Anne. "Inventing al-Zarqawi." *Atlantic Monthly* 298, no. 1 (July/August 2006): 87–88, 90–96, 98, 100.

Wehner, Peter. "The Slap Heard Round the World." *Commentary*, January 31, 2011. https://www.commentarymagazine.com/foreign-policy/middle-east/the-slap-heard-round-the-world.

Wehr, Hans. *The Hans Wehr Dictionary of Modern Written Arabic*, edited by J. M. Cowan. Ithaca, NY: Spoken Language Services, 1994.

Wehrey, Frederic. "Libya Doesn't Need More Militias." *New York Times*, June 10, 2013. http://www.nytimes.com/2013/06/11/opinion/libya-doesnt-need-more-militias.html.

Wehrey, Frederic, and Wolfram Lacher. "Libya's Legitimacy Crisis." *ForeignAffairs.com*, October 6, 2014. https://www.foreignaffairs.com/articles/middle-east/2014-10-06/libyas-legitimacy-crisis.

Weiss, Michael, and Hassan Hassan. *ISIS: Inside the Army of Terror*. New York: Regan Arts, 2015.

White, Jenny. *Muslim Nationalism and the New Turks*. Princeton, NJ: Princeton University Press, 2013.

Wiktorowicz, Quintan. "Civil Society as Social Control: State Power in Jordan." *Comparative Politics* 33, no. 1 (October 2000): 43–61.

Wilkinson, Peter. "First Taste of a Once Forbidden Fruit." *New York Times*, December 5, 2004. http://www.nytimes.com/2004/12/05/travel/first-taste-of-a-onceforbidden-fruit.html.

Wittes, Tamara Cofman, and Shadi Hamid. "Camp David Peace Treaty Collapse." Memorandum to the President, January 17. Washington, DC: Brookings Institution Press, 2013. http://www.brookings.edu/research/papers/2013/01/camp-david-peace-treaty-collapse.

World Bank. "IBRD Statement of Loans—Latest Available Snapshot." Washington, DC: World Bank. https://finances.worldbank.org/Loan-and-Credit-Administration/IBRD-Statement-of-Loans-Latest-Available-Snapshot.

World Bank. *The Unfinished Revolution: Bringing Opportunity, Good Jobs and Greater Wealth to All Tunisians.* Washington, DC: World Bank Group, May 2014. http://documents.worldbank.org/curated/en/658461468312323813/pdf/861790DPR0P12800Box385314B00PUBLIC0.pdf.

World Bank. "World Development Indicators." Online Database. http://data.worldbank.org.

Yalpat, Altan. "Turkey's Economy under the Generals." *MERIP Report,* no. 122 (March–April 1984): 16–24.

Yeşilada, Birol A., and Barry Rubin, eds. *Islamization of Turkey under AKP Rule.* New York: Routledge, 2011.

Youssef, Abdelrahman. "Blame for Sinai Tension Also Lies in Cairo." *Al-Monitor,* May 31, 2013. http://www.al-monitor.com/pulse/originals/2013/05/sinai-tension-cairo-israel-camp-david.html.

Zacharia, Janine. "Mubarak Ally Watches Egypt from Uncertain Exile." *Washington Post,* March 3, 2011. http://www.washingtonpost.com/wp-dyn/content/article/2011/03/02/AR2011030206744.html.

Zelin, Aaron Y. "The War between ISIS and al-Qaeda for Supremacy of the Global Jihadist Movement." Research Notes no. 20. Washington, DC: Washington Institute for Near East Policy, June 2014. http://www.washingtoninstitute.org/uploads/Documents/pubs/ResearchNote_20_Zelin.pdf.

Zelin, Aaron Y. "Tunis Designates Ansar al-Sharia in Tunis." *Al-Wasat,* August 28, 2013. https://thewasat.wordpress.com/2013/08/28/tunis-designates-ansar-al-sharia-in-tunisia.

Zogby, James, Elizabeth Zogby, and Sarah Hope Zogby. "Today's Middle East: Pressure and Challenges." Washington, DC: Zogby Research Services, 2014. http://static1.squarespace.com/static/52750dd3e4b08c252c723404/t/54933ce3e4b0c552e2b854f9/1418935523821/Sir+Bani+Yas+2014+11-01.pdf.

INDEX